THE ABCs OF RBCs

George McCandless

THE ABCs OF RBCs

AN INTRODUCTION TO Dynamic Macroeconomic Models

HARVARD UNIVERSITY PRESS   Cambridge, Massachusetts, and London, England

2008

Library of Congress Cataloging-in-Publication Data

McCandless, George T.

  The ABCs of RBCs : an introduction to dynamic macroeconomic models / George McCandless.

    p. cm.

  Includes bibliographical references and index.

  ISBN 978-0-674-02814-2 (cloth : alk. paper)

    1. Business cycles—Econometric models.   2. Macroeconomics—Econometric models. I. Title.

HB141.M395 2008   2007061809

For
Thomas Patrick
and
Isabel Lucia

Contents

3   Infinitely Lived Agents   33

4   Recursive Deterministic Models   50

5   Recursive Stochastic Models   69

6   Hansen's RBC Model   89

Preface

The literature on Real Business Cycle or New Keynesian models is large and quite well developed. Serious work has been going on in this area since the publication of Kydland and Prescott's [52] paper that described how to build a numerical stochastic general equilibrium model of the U.S. economy, a paper that helped them win the 2004 Nobel Prize in Economics[1]. The methods that they used were quite complicated, as is often the case with pathbreaking work. Over the years, many techniques have been developed to make writing and solving these models a lot simpler and quicker.

There already are a number of very good books on macroeconomics and macroeconomic policy that use the methods presented in this book (Ljungqvist and Sargent [54], Stokey, Lucas and Prescott [83], Walsh [89], and Woodford [90] are examples), and one can honestly ask why this book is necessary. Two of the difficulties of the books listed above is that they assume that the reader already has substantial familiarity with the topics and, in most cases, a good command of the mathematics involved.

Some years back, I set out to build a RBC model for Argentina as part of my work with the Argentine Central Bank. While I had never built these models before, I had used and taught many of the techniques involved. As I read though the literature, I found that, except for the excellent notes by Uhlig [86], most everything was written for the those already initiated. Working though a sequence of models, I gradually discovered for myself many of the

---

1. Strictly speaking, the prize they won is The Sveriges Riksbank Prize in Economic Sciences in Memory of Alfred Nobel.

tricks of the trade and I started to write out each model as a way of assuring myself that I really could use the techniques involved.

At some point, I realized that my set of notes was a chronicle of learning what is required to be able to use RBC and New Keynesian models, and that these notes could serve as a guide for others. It was then that this book was born.

The first set of notes evolved into a second set that I used in an advanced macroeconomic course I teach in the masters program at the Universidad de CEMA in Buenos Aires. Additional material on financial markets and open economies came a bit later and filled out what would be required to be able to construct a fairly interesting model for a small open economy. Suggestions from a referee caused me to add the section on Friedman and Taylor rules in Chapter 12.

This book is not meant to be all inclusive; it is an introduction. There are large areas of RBC models that are not covered here. Home production, agency costs, search theory, and higher order Taylor solution techniques are just a few of these. In the appropriate places, I have tried to point the interested reader to some leading articles in these areas, but the coverage is not comprehensive. At the rate this area of macroeconomics is growing, covering everything would be extraordinarily difficult.

I have received useful comments on the manuscript from my students at UCEMA and in the workshop I taught for colleagues at the Banco Central de la República Argentina. Francisco Lepone and Claudio Irigoyen provided many helpful discussions and it is to Claudio I owe the title of this book. Some of what Andrew Blake, Fabio Conova, Guillermo Escudé, and Emilio Fernandez-Corugedo taught me has ended up in this book. Two anonymous referees provided a number of very useful suggestions. Special thanks are due to Juan Martin Sotes Paladino who read and commented on the entire manuscript and checked the mathematics. Michael Aronson has been a gracious and supportive editor.

A number of other people have given important and long term support. Tom Sargent taught me that if I really wanted to understand some technology, I needed to write about it. Without that, this book wouldn't exist. Neil Wallace, as advisor, coauthor and friend, has been my standard for intellectual clarity and honesty. The kindnesses of Lars Hansen, Robert Lucas, Gary Krueger, Warren Weber, Art Rolnick, and Andrew Powell are especially remembered.

Not everyone who helped make this book possible are economists. I thank Roberto Freytes, Juan Manual Furmento, Nestor Perez Alisedo and their families, Alejandro Puente, Jorge Torres Zabaleta, Ignacio Zalduendo, Juan Antonio Ketterer, Robert Shakotko, and Patricio Gatti for their continuing friendship and support. My eldest daughter, Micaela, has been my loudest cheerleader. I especially thank my wife, Maria Rosa Furmento, who has kindly and gently sustained this project during its long evolution.

THE ABCs OF RBCs

Introduction

In his critique on econometric policy evaluation, Lucas [55] makes the case that the then current macroeconomic models were essentially useless in predicting the outcomes of economic policy that was not yet in use. His solution was to build macroeconomic models with clear and specific microeconomic foundations in which expectations of future government policies were included. Kydland and Prescott [51] went somewhat further and recommended including economic policy in models in the form of policy rules.

Building models with the required microeconomic foundations has not been easy, but, following on Kydland and Prescott [52], a body of techniques has been developed that now allows one to build quite complicated microeconomic-based macroeconomic models in which consumers and producers are optimizing, have rational expectations, can have market power over wages or prices, and can utilize domestic and foreign financial markets, and where government policies operate under budget constraints and rules. These techniques have developed around a Solow [80] growth model that is usually solved for a stationary state and then approximated (either linearly or, more recently, with higher-order Taylor approximations) around that stationary state to observe the dynamic responses of the model to the stochastic shocks imposed. These models are called variously Real Business Cycle (RBC) or New Keynesian models, depending on the mix of techniques included and the choice in the sources of stochastic shocks.

Real Business Cycle and New Keynesian models are particularly useful for evaluating policy changes, since the changes can be put directly into the government policy equations and the resulting changes in both the long run (stationary states) and the short run dynamics can be observed. They are also being developed for forecasting (for example, Smets and Wouters [79]) and are beginning to compete reasonably well with vector autoregressions (VARs) in their forecasting power.

This book is intended as an introduction to these RBC and New Keynesian models. It is designed to take professional economists or graduate-level students to a point where they can build relatively complex linear stochastic dynamic general equilibrium models and solve them numerically. Except for the solution techniques given in Chapters 4 and 5, where techniques are presented for finding approximations to nonlinear value functions (Bellman equations) and their associated nonlinear policy functions, the dynamic models are all log-linear approximations of more general models.[1] First-order Taylor expansions are used to produce the log-linear approximations.[2] This book does not deal very much with issues of calibration nor with techniques of estimation of these models. The solution techniques presented are numerical, and many of the Matlab programs that were used to find these solutions are included at the end of chapters.

A bit more needs to be said about calibration. In this book, the parameters of the models are mostly borrowed from other papers: from Hansen [48] for most of the underlying (sometimes called "deep") parameters of the model, from Cooley and Hansen [36] for those associated with nominal variables, and from Uribe [87] for some of the open economy parameters. Some are determined by requirements of internal consistency (the stationary state inflation and borrowing interest rate in Chapter 12, for example). It is not the objective of this book to model any particular real economy, but rather to show techniques that can be used to build a model of most any economy. The methods for finding parameters that are commonly used in RBC models include using coefficients that come from microeconomic studies for parameters like the time discount factor, rental income over total income for the parameters of a Cobb-Douglas production function, and adjusting parameters so that stationary state values approximate those of the great ratios such as consumption over income and capital over income. In addition, once some of these parameters have been chosen, it is frequently possible to use Bayesian methods on historical data of the economy of interest to get estimates of the remaining ones. A good book for the econometric techniques involved is by Canova [21].

---

1. Chapter 7 shows how to solve models with quadratic objective functions subject to linear constraints. The resulting policy functions are linear and are normally very close to those found using the log linearization technique.

2. This book does not deal with how to build and solve higher-order Taylor approximations of a model.

The first seven chapters of this book introduce simple models and present a number of solution techniques. Chapter 1 presents a basic Solow model (the basis for all the other models) and introduces some of the techniques and issues of the book. Chapter 2 covers overlapping generations models. While these models are not directly a part of the Real Business Cycle literature, variations on these models are included in a range of RBC models. This chapter can be skipped on the first reading. Chapter 3 introduces models with infinitely lived agents. These are the models that serve as the basis for generic, recursive RBC models. This chapter illustrates how to use variational methods for finding stationary states.

Chapters 4 through 7 show various methods of solving Real Business Cycle models. Chapter 4 deals with how to solve a simple deterministic model when the economy is recursive. Beginning with Chapter 5, the models become stochastic. Chapter 5 deals with stochastic recursive models when the stochastic variable has only a finite number of realizations. Chapter 6 shows how to solve a log-linear approximation of the model when the probability space is large. Chapter 7 presents another form of approximating the model, in this case by taking a quadratic approximation of the objective function and using linear budget constraints. The simple model of Hansen, with both divisible and indivisible labor, is used throughout.

The second part of the book begins with Chapter 8 and covers a variety of extensions to the basic model. In each chapter, I present a general equilibrium model that contains the new elements, find a stationary state, log-linearize the model and solve the linear version numerically for policy functions, and present the second-order properties of the model. Throughout, we find the impulse response functions for each new model. The benefits and problems of each new model can be seen by comparing its impulse response function to the earlier ones and to the basic Hansen model. The orderly presentation of these impulse response functions is an important contribution of this book. The presentation technique might sometimes seem repetitive, but the object is to let the reader see every step in the production of the model, including many of the (sometimes confusing) details that are frequently left out of journal articles, and to facilitate in learning the process of constructing these models.

Money is added to the models using either a cash-in-advance constraint (as in Chapter 8) or a money-in-the-utility-function technique (as in Chapter 9). Chapters 10 and 11 show how to add sticky prices and wages to the model using a method introduced by Calvo. Models with sticky prices and wages are often referred to as New Keynesian models. We find that these models help increase the persistence of monetary shocks. Chapter 12 introduces a simple form of a financial system into the model. We impose a type of cash-in-advance constraint on the firms: they need to have cash in the form of working capital to be able to pay wages before they are able to sell their good. Our working capital models demonstrate some interesting characteristics of monetary models and how sensitive they can be to where the modeler chooses to inject money. Chapter 12 also introduces some rules for monetary policy and compares a Taylor rule to a Friedman rule. A reader very interested in monetary policy can jump directly from Chapter 8 to Chapter 12. Chapter 13 allows for a foreign asset in a small open economy. The problem here is that there are too many assets that give the same rate of return, and one needs to use some method to "close" this open economy. While a number of these methods exist, we illustrate the problem with one of the more simple ways of getting a determined stationary state. A monetary version of an open economy is also given, allowing one to deal with exchange rates.

PART ONE

BASIC MODELS AND SOLUTION METHODS

The Basic Solow Model

Solow [80, 82] introduced a model of economic growth that has served as the basis for most growth theory, for Real Business Cycle models and for New Keynesian modeling. This model is quite simple, but elegant, and generates a number of very specific and testable results about growth. Not all of these results are confirmed by the data, however, and, after the initial enthusiasm for the Solow model, this fact first had the result of causing the model to fall into disuse. Later revisions of the model by Paul Romer [69] and by Robert Lucas [56] have made the model more consistent with the growth data, and it has once again become popular. Kydland and Prescott [52] used a stochastic version of this model to study business cycles and thus started the branch of macroeconomics now known as Real Business Cycle theory (including New Keynesian).

Solow's model is quite simple: there is a constant returns-to-scale production function, a law for the evolution of capital, and a savings rate. Equilibrium conditions are simply that investment equals savings. From this basis, a first-order difference equation for the evolution of capital per worker is found, and the time path of the economy springs from this equation.

1.1 THE BASIC MODEL

The production function is

$$Y_t = A_t F(K_t, H_t),$$

where Y_t is output of the single good in the economy at date t, A_t is the level of technology, K_t is the capital stock, and H_t is the quantity of labor used in production. The production function is homogeneous of degree one with the usual properties. Technology is equal to $A_t = (1 + \alpha)^t A_0$, where A_0 is the time 0 level of technology and α is the net rate of growth of technology. Writing this in terms of output per worker, $y_t = Y_t/H_t$, and using the constant returns-to-scale properties of the function $F(K_t, H_t)$,[1] we get

$$y_t = \frac{Y_t}{H_t} = A_t F(\frac{K_t}{H_t}, \frac{H_t}{H_t}) = A_t F(k_t, 1) \equiv A_t f(k_t),$$

where $k_t \equiv K_t/H_t$ is the capital per worker.

Assume that the labor force grows at a constant net rate n, so that $H_{t+1} = (1 + n)H_t$, and that capital grows by

$$K_{t+1} = (1 - \delta)K_t + I_t,$$

where δ is the rate of depreciation and I_t is investment at time t. With these assumptions, capital per worker grows according to the rule

$$k_{t+1} = \frac{(1 - \delta)k_t + i_t}{1 + n},$$

where $i_t = I_t/H_t$ is the inversion per worker in time t. Savings is defined as a fixed fraction of output,

$$s_t = \sigma y_t,$$

where σ is the fraction of output per worker that is saved. This assumption about savings is probably the most important simplification of the Solow model. In equilibrium in a closed economy, $i_t = s_t$. First substituting savings for investment in the capital growth rule, replacing savings by the constant times output, and finally replacing output by the production function per worker, one gets the difference equation,

$$(1 + n)k_{t+1} = (1 - \delta)k_t + \sigma(1 + \alpha)^t A_0 f(k_t).$$

In the simplest case, where technology growth is zero, $\alpha = 0$, this results in the equation

$$(1 + n)k_{t+1} = (1 - \delta)k_t + \sigma A_0 f(k_t).$$

---

1. The usual assumptions about the shape of the production function are that $F_i(K_t, H_t) > 0$, $F_{ii}(K_t, H_t) < 0$, $F_{ij}(K_t, H_t) > 0$, for $i = K, H$ and $i \neq j$. $F_i(K_t, H_t) \to \infty$ as the quantity of factor i goes to 0, and $F_i(K_t, H_t) \to 0$ as the quantity of factor i goes to ∞. Also, $F(K_t, 0) = F(0, H_t) = 0$.

A stationary state can be found from this equation for the case where $k_{t+1} = k_t = \bar{k}$. This stationary state occurs when

$$(1+n)\bar{k} = (1-\delta)\bar{k} + \sigma A_0 f(\bar{k}),$$

or when

$$(\delta + n)\bar{k} = \sigma A_0 f(\bar{k}).$$

Given the conditions of the function $f(\cdot)$, there is a stationary state at $\bar{k} = 0$, and one for a positive $\bar{k}$. All economies with $k_0 \neq 0$ converge to the positive stationary state.

The stability conditions of the positive stationary state can be seen from the equation

$$k_{t+1} = g(k_t) = \frac{(1-\delta)k_t + \sigma A_0 f(k_t)}{(1+n)} \tag{1.1}$$

shown in Figure 1.1. Notice that between 0 and the positive $\bar{k}$, the function, $g(k_t)$, is above the 45 degree line, so that k_{t+1} is greater that k_t. In this range, capital per worker is growing and converges to the positive $\bar{k}$. Above the positive $\bar{k}$, the value of the function, $g(k_t)$, is less than k_t, so the capital stock declines, converging to the positive $\bar{k}$.

One of the important results of the Solow growth model is that, if all economies have access to the same technology, poorer ones (those with less initial

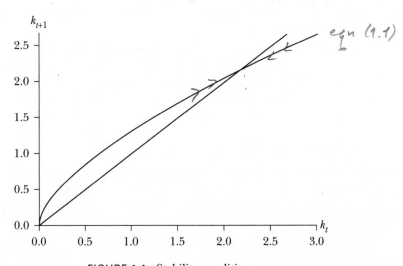

FIGURE 1.1 Stability conditions

capital) will grow faster than richer ones (those with more initial capital). Let $\gamma_t = k_{t+1}/k_t$ be the gross growth of the capital stock from time t to time $t + 1$. Using equation 1.1, we can write the growth rate as

$$\gamma_t = \frac{k_{t+1}}{k_t} = \frac{(1 - \delta)k_t + \sigma A_0 f(k_t)}{(1 + n)k_t}.$$

To see how the growth rate depends on the initial capital stock, we take the derivative of γ_t with respect to k_t. This results in

$$\frac{d\gamma_t}{dk_t} = \frac{\sigma A_0}{(1 + n)k_t^2} \left[f'(k_t)k_t - f(k_t) \right],$$

which is negative when $k_t > 0$. The growth rate of capital declines as the capital stock increases. Since output per worker is increasing in per worker capital stock, the growth rate of output per worker also declines.

The main results of the simplest version of the Solow model are, when all countries have access to the same technology and all have the same savings rate, that all countries converge to the same levels of capital and output per worker and that poorer countries grow faster than richer ones.

> **EXERCISE 1.1** Suppose that in every period an economy needs to pay 4 percent of its output to the rest of the world as interest payments on past government debt. The government collects the funds for the transfer using lump sum taxes. How is the growth rate of this country different from one that does not need to make the payments?

> **EXERCISE 1.2** What happens to the rental rate on capital (the marginal product of capital) as an economy grows from some initial per worker capital stock below the positive stationary state?

1.2 TECHNOLOGICAL GROWTH

With a constant rate of technological growth, all economies converge toward what is called a *balanced growth path*. This is a growth path where the growth rate of capital and output are constant. For an economy with a Cobb-Douglas production function, $f(k_t) = k_t^\theta$, where θ is the fraction of the economy's income that goes to capital, this constant growth path is easy to find. We look for an equilibrium where capital grows at some unknown constant rate, $\gamma = k_{t+1}/k_t$. Using the difference equation with technological growth and normalizing initial capital, $A_0 = 1$, we get

$$\gamma = \frac{k_{t+1}}{k_t} = \frac{(1-\delta)k_t + \sigma(1+\alpha)^t k_t^\theta}{(1+n)k_t} = \frac{(1-\delta)}{(1+n)} + \frac{\sigma(1+\alpha)^t}{(1+n)k_t^{1-\theta}}.$$

Rewriting this, we get

$$k_t = \left[\frac{\sigma(1+\alpha)^t}{(1+n)\gamma - (1-\delta)} \right]^{\frac{1}{1-\theta}} = (1+\alpha)^{\frac{t}{1-\theta}} \left[\frac{\sigma}{(1+n)\gamma - (1-\delta)} \right]^{\frac{1}{1-\theta}}.$$

This implies that along a balanced growth path, the constant growth rate of capital per worker, γ, must be equal to

$$\lambda = \frac{k_{t+1}}{k_t} = \frac{(1+\alpha)^{\frac{t+1}{1-\theta}} \left[\frac{\sigma}{(1+n)\gamma - (1-\delta)} \right]^{\frac{1}{1-\theta}}}{(1+\alpha)^{\frac{t}{1-\theta}} \left[\frac{\sigma}{(1+n)\gamma - (1-\delta)} \right]^{\frac{1}{1-\theta}}} = (1+\alpha)^{\frac{1}{1-\theta}}.$$

As it turns out, along this path output per worker grows by

$$\frac{y_{t+1}}{y_t} = \frac{(1+\alpha)^{t+1} k_{t+1}^\theta}{(1+\alpha)^t k_t^\theta} = (1+\alpha) \left(\frac{k_{t+1}}{k_t} \right)^\theta$$

$$= (1+\alpha) \left((1+\alpha)^{\frac{1}{1-\theta}} \right)^\theta = (1+\alpha)^{\frac{1}{1-\theta}},$$

which is the same rate as the growth rate of capital per worker.

1.3   THE GOLDEN RULE

To maximize welfare in a stationary state, given that welfare is a function of only consumption, one wants to maximize the steady state level of consumption. We consider welfare only in an economy without technological growth. What is a variable in this case is the savings rate. The savings rate that maximizes consumption is known as the *golden rule* savings rate. The golden rule was first developed by Phelps [68]. Since production can be either saved (invested) or consumed, the per worker consumption in each period is equal to

$$c_t = (1-\sigma)y_t = (1-\sigma)A_0 f(\bar{k}),$$

where the use of $\bar{k}$ indicates that we are looking at stationary states. For the model without technical growth, the condition for a stationary state is

$$(\delta + n)\bar{k} = \sigma A_0 f(\bar{k}).$$

Substituting the condition for the stationary state into the equation for consumption yields

$$\bar{c} = A_0 f(\bar{k}) - (\delta + n)\bar{k}.$$

First-order conditions for maximizing consumption give

$$A_0 f'(\bar{k}) = \delta + n.$$

Put the value of $\bar{k}^*$ that solves the above equation in

$$(\delta + n)\bar{k}^* = \sigma A_0 f(\bar{k}^*)$$

and solve for the savings rate, σ. The golden rule value of σ is

$$\sigma = \frac{(\delta + n)\bar{k}^*}{A_0 f(\bar{k}^*)}.$$

1.4   A STOCHASTIC SOLOW MODEL

Adding a stochastic shock to the standard Solow model is relatively simple, although there are a number of ways that it could be done. Among the variables that could be made to follow some simple stochastic process are the technology level, the discount factor, the savings rate, or the growth rate of population. In our version of the model, a technology shock and a shock to the savings rate are essentially identical in the way they affect the evolution of output. We develop a version where technology is stochastic. The effects of stochastic technology growth are the basis for Real Business Cycle theory. Changes in technology that come from trying to match the Solow model to the data are often referred to as the Solow residual (see Solow [81]).

There are several common ways of defining the stochastic process for technology. One is a first-order moving average of the form

$$A_t = \psi \bar{A} + (1 - \psi)A_{t-1} + \varepsilon_t,$$

where $0 < \psi < 1$ and $\bar{A}$ is a non-negative constant. In this case, the probability distribution of ε_t needs to be bounded from below by $-\psi\bar{A}$ or, with some positive probability, technology will become negative. A lower bound is not normally a problem if one is simulating an economy, but it does make the analytics more complicated. An alternative that does not have the lower bound problem is to define

$$A_t = \bar{A}e^{\varepsilon_t},$$

where ε_t has a normal distribution with mean 0. In this case, A_t has a log normal distribution of the form

$$\ln A_t = \ln \bar{A} + \varepsilon_t.$$

We will use the second formulation and suppose that technology follows the stochastic process

doesn't have a lower bound problem as

$$A_t = \bar{A}e^{\varepsilon_t},$$

where $\bar{A}$ is positive and the random term ε_t has a normal distribution with mean zero. The first-order difference equation that describes the time path of the economy in the model is mechanical,[2] in the sense that the savings rate is a constant, and equation 1.1 is written simply as

$$k_{t+1} = \frac{(1-\delta)k_t + \sigma\bar{A}e^{\varepsilon_t}f(k_t)}{(1+n)}. \qquad (1.2) \;\;*$$

where $f(k_t) = k_t^{\theta}, \;\; \theta \in [0,1]$

Divide both sides of this equation by k_t to get the growth rate, $\gamma_t = k_{t+1}/k_t$, on the left-hand side, rearrange, and then take logarithms. One ends up with

$$\ln\left[\gamma_t - \frac{1-\delta}{1+n}\right] = \ln\frac{\sigma\bar{A}}{(1+n)} + \ln\frac{f(k_t)}{k_t} + \varepsilon_t. \qquad (1.3)$$

As before, we assume a Cobb-Douglas production function, the per worker production function is $f(k_t) = k_t^{\theta}$, and equation 1.3 becomes

$$\ln\left[\gamma_t - \frac{1-\delta}{1+n}\right] = \varphi - (1-\theta)\ln k_t + \varepsilon_t,$$

$= \ln[\sigma\bar{A}/(1+n)] - (1-\theta)\ln k_t + \varepsilon_t$

where the constant $\varphi \equiv \ln\left[\sigma\bar{A}/(1+n)\right]$. The gross growth rate of per worker capital is a nonlinear function of the current per worker capital stock and of the shocks. Variance of the growth rate of per worker capital depends on the initial level of per worker capital as well as the variance of the shocks.

Figure 1.2 shows three runs of simulations of the exact stochastic version of the Solow model given in equation 1.2.* The parameters used are $\bar{A} = 1$, $n = .02$, $\delta = .1$, $\theta = .36$, $\sigma = .2$, and the standard error of the shock is .2.

2. The process is mechanical in the sense that there is no feedback from the technology shock to the decision about savings. A model with habit formation would imply that the savings rate would decline in response to a negative shock to output. Here the savings rate is always σ.

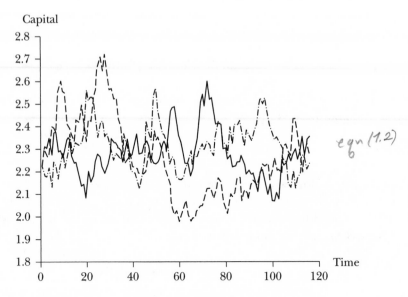

FIGURE 1.2   Three simulations of the exact Solow model

1.5   LOG-LINEAR VERSION OF THE SOLOW MODEL

Given that the model is nonlinear, a simple expression for the variance of per worker capital in terms of the shocks is not easy to find or even to define in general. However, it is possible to find a linear approximation of the model around a stationary state and to use this version to study some of the second-order characteristics of the model. In particular, one is interested in the size of the technology shock that is required so that the variance of output is similar to that of real economies around their long-term trend.[3] We will be using log-linear versions of a number of our future models, so this section is very important for understanding the process of producing a log-linear version of a model.

Define the log differences[4] of a variable, $\tilde{X}_t$, as

$$\tilde{X}_t = \ln X_t - \ln \bar{X},$$

where X_t is the time t value of the variable and $\bar{X}$ is its value in the stationary state. This definition of the log differences lets us write the variable as

---

3. We speak of variance around the trend since the version we are using here excludes technological growth or any other trend. Various filters (one of the most popular is the Hodrick-Prescott) are used to detrend the series.

4. More extended material on this topic can be found in Uhlig [86] and in Section 6.2.2.

$$X_t = \bar{X}e^{\tilde{X}_t}.$$

To find a log-linear version of a model, it is frequently possible simply to replace the variable by the version in log differences. The following rules for first-order approximations are useful for small values of $\tilde{X}_t$ and $\tilde{Y}_t$:

$$e^{\tilde{X}_t} \approx 1 + \tilde{X}_t,$$

$$e^{\tilde{X}_t + a\tilde{Y}_t} \approx 1 + \tilde{X}_t + a\tilde{Y}_t,$$

$$\tilde{X}_t \tilde{Y}_t \approx 0,$$

$$E_t\left[ae^{\tilde{X}_{t+1}}\right] \approx E_t\left[a\tilde{X}_{t+1}\right] + \text{ a constant.}$$

1.5.1 Capital

For the Solow model, we begin with a stochastic, Cobb-Douglas, zero technological growth version of the first-order difference equation,

$$(1+n)\,k_{t+1} = (1-\delta)k_t + \sigma\bar{A}e^{\varepsilon_t}k_t^{\theta}, \qquad \widehat{k_j} = \ln\left(\frac{k}{\bar{k}}\right)$$

and replace k_j by $\bar{k}e^{\tilde{k}_j}$, where $\tilde{k}_j = \ln k_j - \ln \bar{k}$. This yields

$$(1+n)\,\bar{k}e^{\tilde{k}_{t+1}} = (1-\delta)\bar{k}e^{\tilde{k}_t} + \sigma\bar{A}e^{\varepsilon_t}\bar{k}^{\theta}e^{\theta\tilde{k}_t},$$

which becomes, using the first rule of approximation given above,

$$(1+n)\,\bar{k}\left(1+\tilde{k}_{t+1}\right) = (1-\delta)\bar{k}\left(1+\tilde{k}_t\right) + \sigma\bar{A}\left(1+\varepsilon_t\right)\bar{k}^{\theta}\left(1+\theta\tilde{k}_t\right).$$

In the nonstochastic stationary state

$$(1+n)\,\bar{k} = (1-\delta)\bar{k} + \sigma\bar{A}\bar{k}^{\theta}.$$

Removing the nonstochastic stationary state terms from the approximation above gives

$$(1+n)\,\bar{k}\tilde{k}_{t+1} = (1-\delta)\bar{k}\tilde{k}_t + \sigma\bar{A}\varepsilon_t\bar{k}^{\theta} + \sigma\bar{A}\bar{k}^{\theta}\theta\tilde{k}_t + \sigma\bar{A}\bar{k}^{\theta}\theta\varepsilon_t\tilde{k}_t.$$

Since $\varepsilon_t\tilde{k}_t \approx 0$, this becomes

$$(1+n)\,\bar{k}\tilde{k}_{t+1} = (1-\delta)\bar{k}\tilde{k}_t + \sigma\bar{A}\varepsilon_t\bar{k}^{\theta} + \sigma\bar{A}\bar{k}^{\theta}\theta\tilde{k}_t.$$

Combining terms, we arrive at the first-order difference equation,

$$\tilde{k}_{t+1} = B\tilde{k}_t + C\varepsilon_t, \tag{1.4}$$

where

$$B = \frac{1-\delta}{1+n} + \frac{\theta\sigma\bar{A}\bar{k}^{\theta-1}}{1+n} = \frac{1-\delta}{1+n} + \frac{\theta(\delta+n)}{1+n} = \frac{1+\theta n - \delta(1-\theta)}{1+n} < 1,$$

and

$$C = \frac{\sigma\bar{A}\bar{k}^{\theta-1}}{1+n} = \frac{\delta+n}{1+n}.$$

Recursively substituting $\tilde{k}_{t-j}$, for $j = 0, \ldots, \infty$ in equation 1.4 results in the approximation

$$\tilde{k}_{t+1} = C\sum_{i=0}^{\infty} B^i \varepsilon_{t-i}. \tag{1.5}$$

We can use expression 1.5 to calculate the variance of capital around its stationary state, $\tilde{k}_{t+1}$, as

$$\text{var}\left(\tilde{k}_{t+1}\right) = E\left[\tilde{k}_{t+1}\tilde{k}_{t+1}\right] = E\left[\left(C\sum_{i=0}^{\infty} B^i \varepsilon_{t-i}\right)\left(C\sum_{i=0}^{\infty} B^i \varepsilon_{t-i}\right)\right].$$

If the technology shocks are independent, in the sense that $E\left[\varepsilon_t\varepsilon_s\right] = 0$ if $t \neq s$, the above expression becomes

$$\text{var}\left(\tilde{k}\right) = C^2\sum_{i=0}^{\infty} B^{2i}\text{var}(\varepsilon) = \frac{C^2}{1-B^2}\text{var}(\varepsilon),$$

where

$$\frac{C^2}{1-B^2} = \frac{[\delta+n]^2}{[1+n]^2 - [1+\theta n - \delta(1-\theta)]^2}.$$

Assuming that $\delta = 0.1$, $\sigma = .2$, $n = 0.02$, and $\theta = 0.36$, we find that the variance of capital around its stationary state is 0.0955 times the variance of the shock to technology. Figure 1.3 shows a simulation for the log-linear version of the Solow model along with one of the exact model using the same error process.

1.5.2 Output

To determine the variance of the technology shock relative to that of output, we first find a log-linear version of the production function. This is found from

$$y_t = \bar{A}e^{\varepsilon_t}k_t^{\theta}$$

Savings in an OLG Model

savings → cost savings/ minimize cost

One major weakness of the standard Solow model of growth is that the savings rate is given exogenously, that is to say, it is not determined as part of an optimization problem of the agents of the economy. Models with overlapping generations of individuals, each of whom lives a finite number of years, offer a relatively simple way of including the savings decision in a growth model.

Peter Diamond [38] produced a version of the overlapping generations models introduced by Samuelson [70] in which the savings rate is endogenous and can change with other parameters of the economy. The model is comprised of individuals who live two periods and who must make decisions in the first period of their lives about their consumption in both periods of life. Individuals who have substantial income in the first period of life save some of this in the form of capital or lending and are able to consume more than they otherwise might in the second period of life. People live two periods in these economies because this is the smallest number of periods that permits a savings decision and is therefore likely to be the simplest.

The basics of the model are quite simple. In each period, a new group of individuals (called a generation) is born. Members of this group live, work, and consume in the period of their birth and in the next. After this they die and disappear from the economy. The utility they receive comes only from their consumption during the two periods of their life. In the second period of their life, another generation is born and lives during that period and the next. This process continues indefinitely, and in each period there is a generation that has just been born, the young, and another in the second and last period of life, the old. While the model goes on infinitely, each person makes decisions

only about what they will do in two periods, so the savings problem, which is
the problem of interest, is relatively simple.

2.1 THE BASIC OLG MODEL

First we need to define the physical environment of the economy. There is an
infinite sequence of discrete periods denominated by the integers. In general
we are interested in periods $t = 0, 1, 2, \ldots \infty$. For the generation born in
period t, know as *generation* t, what occurred in periods $t - 1$ or earlier is
the past and is taken as given. There are $N(t)$ members of generation t. As
mentioned above, people live for two periods and the members of generation
t are young in period t and old in period $t + 1$. In period $t + 2$, members of
generation t no longer exist and no longer participate in the economy.

There is only one aggregate good in the economy, and an individual's utility
comes from his/her consumption of that good in the two periods of life. A
member h of generation t has the utility function.

$$u_t^h(c_t^h(t), c_t^h(t + 1)),$$

where $c_t^h(s)$ is the consumption of the one aggregate good by individual h of
generation t in period s.

Production takes place in competitive firms that use a homogeneous-of-
degree-one production technology. Total production in period t is

$$Y(t) = F(K(t), H(t)),$$

where $H(t)$ is the total labor used in production and $K(t)$ is the total capital,
and the production function, $F(K(t), H(t))$, has the same properties we
assumed in Chapter 1.

Individuals are endowed with a lifetime endowment of labor given by the
ordered pair

$$h_t^h = \left[h_t^h(t), h_t^h(t + 1) \right],$$

where $h_t^h(s)$ is the labor endowment of individual h of generation t in period s.
Individuals are assumed to supply all of their labor endowment to firms at the
competitive wage. The total labor that is used in period t is the sum of the
labor supply of the young and the old who are alive in that period. Therefore,

$$H(t) = \sum_{h=1}^{N(t)} h_t^h(t) + \sum_{h=1}^{N(t-1)} h_{t-1}^h(t).$$

It will be useful to define the aggregate labor endowment of the young at time t as

$$H_t(t) = \sum_{h=1}^{N(t)} h_t^h(t),$$

and the aggregate labor endowment of the old at time t as

$$H_{t-1}(t) = \sum_{h=1}^{N(t-1)} h_{t-1}^h(t).$$

In period t, the economy has an amount of capital $K(t)$ that it inherits from period $t - 1$ and that cannot be changed in period t. This capital depreciates completely during its use in period t. This assumption removes the complication of a capital market between members of different generations.

Feasibility constraints for period t imply that

$$Y(t) = F(K(t), H(t)) \geq \sum_{h=1}^{N(t)} c_t^h(t) + \sum_{h=1}^{N(t-1)} c_{t-1}^h(t) + K(t+1).$$

The production of period t goes either to consumption of the young or the old or to capital for use in period $t + 1$.

The economic organization that we assume for this economy is one of perfectly competitive markets where individuals are owners of their own labor. Members of generation t earn income in period t by offering all their labor endowment to firms at the market wage and use that income for consumption in period t, for private lending to other members of generation t, and for the accumulation of private capital. Their budget constraint when young is

$$w_t h_t^h(t) = c_t^h(t) + l^h(t) + k^h(t+1), \tag{2.1}$$

where w_t is the market wage at time t and $l^h(t)$ is the amount of loans that they make to other members of generation t ($l^h(t) < 0$ if individual h is borrowing). Because of the overlapping nature of the generations, borrowing and lending can occur only among members of the same generation.

Suppose that a young person of generation t lends some goods to an old member of generation $t - 1$ in period t with the expectation of being paid back in period $t + 1$. In period $t + 1$, this rather naive young person hunts for the member of generation $t - 1$ so that he/she can be paid back. Unfortunately, members of generation $t - 1$ are now all dead and the dead cannot be forced to pay back their debts. Individuals know this and will not make loans to members of other generations. Members of the same generation are alive in the same two periods, so a young person can make a loan to a member of his/her own generation with expectation of collecting on that loan in the next period when both lender and borrower are old. Since members of one generation lend only to other members of that same generation, we have the condition that

$$0 = \sum_{h=1}^{N(t)} l_h(t).$$

Net lending of any generation t is equal to zero.

In period $t + 1$, a member of generation t has income from the labor supplied in period $t + 1$, from interest earned on any loans that were made in period t, and from the rent on capital that they accumulated in period t. Since this is the last period of life, all income will be consumed. Therefore, the budget constraint for individual h of generation t in period $t + 1$ is

$$c_t^h(t + 1) = w_{t+1} h_t^h(t + 1) + r_t l^h(t) + \text{rental}_{t+1} k^h(t + 1), \qquad (2.2)$$

where r_t is the interest paid on loans between period t and $t + 1$ and rental_{t+1} is the competitive rent paid on capital during period $t + 1$.

Individuals are assumed to have perfect foresight in the sense that they know, when young, what wages and rentals will be when they are old. In addition, no fraud is permitted so that all loans are paid back with the agreed-upon interest.

The assumption of perfect competition means that market wages in period t will be equal to the marginal product of labor in that period and that the rentals in period t will be equal to that period's marginal product of capital. So

$$w_t = F_H(K(t), H(t)),$$

and

$$\text{rental}_t = F_K(K(t), H(t)),$$

where $F_i(\cdot, \cdot)$ is the partial derivative of the production function with respect to its ith component.

One can combine the budget constraint when young (equation 2.1) and the budget constraint when old (equation 2.2), by substituting loans, to get a lifetime budget constraint,

$$c_t^h(t) + \frac{c_t^h(t + 1)}{r_t} = w_t h^h(t) + \frac{w_{t+1} h_t^h(t + 1)}{r_t} - k^h(t + 1) \left[1 - \frac{\text{rental}_{t+1}}{r_t} \right].$$

A no-arbitrage condition implies that, in a perfect foresight equilibrium,

$$\text{rental}_{t+1} = r_t.$$

To see why this is an arbitrage condition, suppose that it does not hold and that instead

$$\text{rental}_{t+1} > r_t.$$

Since this is perfectly known (in a perfect foresight equilibrium), every member of generation t will want to borrow an infinite amount at time t and hold it as capital into period $t + 1$. For each unit of borrowing that gets converted to capital, a profit of $\text{rental}_{t+1} - r_t$ will be made. Since infinite borrowing by all members of a generation is impossible, this inequality cannot hold in equilibrium. Suppose that the opposite condition holds,

$$\text{rental}_{t+1} < r_t.$$

Then everyone will want to lend and no one will hold capital. Since the conditions of the production function are such that the marginal product of capital goes to infinity as the quantity of capital goes to zero, the rental on capital in period $t + 1$ will be infinite and production in period $t + 1$ will be zero. Since we are prohibiting fraud (again, by our assumption of perfect foresight), this cannot be an equilibrium since the loans plus interest cannot be paid back.

Since, in equilibrium, rental_{t+1} can be neither smaller nor greater than r_t, it must be equal to it.

With this no-arbitrage condition, the lifetime budget constraint can be written as

$$c_t^h(t) + \frac{c_t^h(t + 1)}{r_t} = w_t h_t^h(t) + \frac{w_{t+1} h_t^h(t + 1)}{r_t},$$

or that the present value of lifetime consumption must equal the present value of lifetime wage income.

DEFINITION 2.1 *A competitive equilibrium for this economy is defined as a sequence of prices,*

$$\left\{ w_t, \text{rental}_t, r_t \right\}_{t=0}^{\infty},$$

and quantities,

$$\left\{ \left\{ c_t^h(t) \right\}_{h=1}^{N(t)}, \left\{ c_{t-1}^h(t) \right\}_{h=1}^{N(t-1)}, K(t + 1) \right\}_{t=0}^{\infty},$$

such that each member h of each generation $t > 0$ maximizes the utility function

$$u_t^h(c_t^h(t), c_t^h(t+1)),$$

subject to the lifetime budget constraint,

$$c_t^h(t) + \frac{c_t^h(t+1)}{r_t} = w_t h_t^h(t) + \frac{w_{t+1} h_t^h(t+1)}{r_t},$$

and the equilibrium conditions,

$$\text{rental}_{t+1} = r_t$$

$$w_t = F_H(K(t), H(t))),$$

$$\text{rental}_t = F_K(K(t), H(t)),$$

$$H(t) = \sum_{h=1}^{N(t)} h_t^h(t) + \sum_{h=1}^{N(t-1)} h_{t-1}^h(t),$$

hold in every period.

Notice that in the above definition we did not define the individual holdings of either lending or of capital. This is because they offer exactly the same return and there are an infinite number of distributions of lending and capital holdings among members of a generation that would meet the equilibrium conditions. Two example distributions for an economy where all members of a generation are identical are 1) person $h = 1$ borrows from everyone else and holds all the capital and 2) no one borrows and each person holds $K(t+1)/N(t)$ units of capital. These two distributions would result in the same total capital stock and the same equilibrium by the above definition.

Substituting the lifetime budget constraint into the utility function, the utility maximization problem for person h of generation t can be written as

$$\max_{c_t^h(t)} u(c_t^h(t), r_t w_t h_t^h(t) + w_{t+1} h_t^h(t+1) - r_t c_t^h(t)),$$

where, for individual h, the assumption of perfect foresight means that the values of all the other parameters are known. The first-order condition is

$$u_1(c_t^h(t), r_t w_t h_t^h(t) + w_{t+1} h_t^h(t+1) - r_t c_t^h(t)) \qquad (2.3)$$

$$= r_t u_2(c_t^h(t), r_t w_t h_t^h(t) + w_{t+1} h_t^h(t+1) - r_t c_t^h(t)),$$

where $u_i(,)$ is the partial derivative of the utility function with respect to its ith element. Using the budget constraint when young (equation 2.1), we can find a savings function for individual h of generation t, $s_t^h(\cdot)$, where

$$s_t^h(w_t, w_{t+1}, r_t) = l^h(t) + k^h(t+1).$$

Summing the savings of all members of generation t, we define an aggregate savings function $S_t(\cdot)$, as equal to

$$S_t(\cdot) = \sum_{h=1}^{N(t)} s_t^h(\cdot) = \sum_{h=1}^{N(t)} l^h(t) + \sum_{h=1}^{N(t)} k^h(t+1).$$

Given that, in equilibrium,

$$\sum_{h=1}^{N(t)} l^h(t) = 0$$

and

$$K(t+1) = \sum_{h=1}^{N(t)} k^h(t+1),$$

the aggregate savings equation can be written as

$$S_t(w_t, w_{t+1}, r_t) = K(t+1).$$

Substituting rental$_{t+1}$ for r_t and using the equilibrium conditions for the factor markets in periods t and $t+1$, we can write the aggregate savings equation as

$$S_t(F_H(K(t), H(t)), F_H(K(t+1), H(t+1)),$$

$$F_K(K(t+1), H(t+1))) = K(t+1).$$

The above expression gives $K(t+1)$ as an implicit function of the labor supplies in each period, $H_t(t)$, $H_{t-1}(t)$, $H_t(t+1)$, $H_{t+1}(t+1)$, the parameters of the utility functions and the production function, and $K(t)$. Since, as the model is constructed, all of these except $K(t)$ are constants through time, one can find the capital stock in time $t+1$ as a function of the capital stock in time t,

$$K(t+1) = G(K(t)). \tag{2.4}$$

This is a first-order difference equation that describes the growth path of the economy.

2.1.1   An Example Economy

For an example economy where the utility function is of the form

$$u_t^h = u(c_t^h(t), c_t^h(t+1)) = c_t^h(t)c_t^h(t+1)^\beta,$$

and the production function is a simple Cobb-Douglas

$$Y_t = F(K(t), H(t)) = K(t)^\theta H(t)^{1-\theta},$$

with $0 < \beta$ and $0 < \theta < 1$, the function $G()$ in equation 2.4 can be written explicitly as[1]

$$K(t+1) = G(K(t)) = \frac{\theta\beta \frac{H_t(t)}{H(t)^\theta}}{\left[\frac{H_t(t+1)}{H(t+1)}\right] + \frac{\theta(1+\beta)}{(1-\theta)}} K(t)^\theta = \kappa K(t)^\theta, \qquad (2.5)$$

where all of the elements that make up κ are constants so that κ is a positive constant. This first-order difference equation has stationary states at $\overline{K} = 0$ and at $\overline{K} = \kappa^{\frac{1}{1-\theta}}$. The constant κ is a function of the exponent on consumption in the second period of life, β, and can be rewritten as

$$\kappa = \frac{\beta\psi}{(1+\beta)+\rho},$$

where $\psi = (1-\theta)\left[\frac{1}{H(t)}\right]^\theta H_t(t)$ and $\rho = \frac{1-\theta}{\theta}\left[\frac{H_t(t+1)}{H(t+1)}\right]$ are positive constants. Recall that the larger is β, the more weight is given to second-period consumption in determining utility. Taking the derivative of κ with respect to β yields

$$\frac{d\kappa}{d\beta} = \frac{\psi(1+\rho)}{(1+\beta+\rho)^2} > 0.$$

As one would expect, savings and capital (which are equal when we have complete depreciation of capital) in the positive stationary state, $\kappa^{\frac{1}{1-\theta}}$, are an increasing function of the weight put on second-period consumption in the utility function, β.

> **EXERCISE 2.1**   Work out the example economy and find equation 2.5.

1. See McCandless and Wallace [61], Chapter 9, for a detailed development of this model.

2.2 DYNAMICS

The behavior of this model out of a stationary state is similar to that of the Solow model. If the initial capital stock is between the two stationary states, $0 < K(0) < \kappa^{\frac{1}{1-\theta}}$, the capital stock will grow, converging on the positive stationary state. This can be seen by simply looking for the range of initial capital stocks for which $K(t+1) > K(t)$, or where

$$K(t+1) - K(t) = \kappa K(t)^\theta - K(t) > 0.$$

Simple manipulation of this equation leads to the result that this condition holds for positive $K(t)$ when $K(t) < \kappa^{\frac{1}{1-\theta}}$. In addition, the rate of growth of the capital stock declines as it grows. Define the gross rate of growth of capital as $\Delta K(t) = K(t+1)/K(t)$. This can be written as

$$\Delta K(t) = \frac{\kappa K(t)^\theta}{K(t)}.$$

Taking the derivative of the growth rate with respect to the capital stock yields

$$\frac{d\Delta K(t)}{dK(t)} = (\theta - 1)\kappa K(t)^{\theta-2} < 0.$$

As in the earlier version of the Solow model, the larger the initial capital stock, the slower the growth rate of capital. In addition, since output is defined as $Y(t) = K(t)^\theta H(t)^{1-\theta}$, the gross growth rate of output, $\Delta Y(t) = Y(t+1)/Y(t)$, is equal to

$$\Delta Y(t) = \frac{K(t+1)^\theta H(t+1)^{1-\theta}}{K(t)^\theta H(t)^{1-\theta}} = \frac{K(t+1)^\theta}{K(t)^\theta} = \Delta K(t)^\theta,$$

where the second part of the expression comes about because labor supply is constant. The derivative of the gross growth rate of output with respect to the capital stock is

$$\frac{d\Delta Y(t)}{dK(t)} = \frac{d\left[\frac{\kappa K(t)^\theta}{K(t)}\right]^\theta}{dK(t)} = \theta\left[\frac{\kappa K(t)^\theta}{K(t)}\right]^{\theta-1}(\theta-1)\kappa K(t)^{\theta-2} < 0,$$

so output growth slows as the capital stock increases.

The dynamics of the model can also be seen from a graph of equation 2.5. Using values of $\kappa = 4$ and $\theta = .36$, the equation is shown in Figure 2.1 as the function labeled $G(K(t))$. In addition, a 45 degree line (the line of stationary states) is drawn in. The graph indicates that for initial values of $K(t)$ below the stationary state (where $G(K(t))$ crosses the 45 degree line),

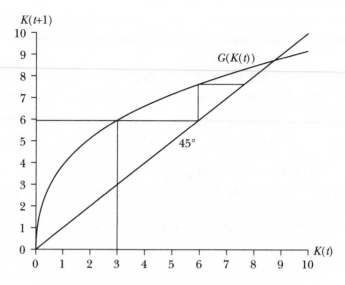

FIGURE 2.1   Graph of dynamics of OLG model

the value of $K(t+1) = G(K(t))$ is greater than $K(t)$ so the capital stock is increasing. As can be seen from the graph, the relative increase of $K(t+1)$ is smaller the greater is $K(t)$. This graphical example confirms the dynamics obtained analytically above.

> **EXERCISE 2.2**   Show how this model would change if capital depreciation in each period were $0 < \delta < 1$ and secondary markets for capital existed.

> **EXERCISE 2.3**   Consider a version of the model with full capital depreciation but where the production function is $Y(t) = (1 + g)K(t)^\theta H(t)^{1-\theta}$, where $g > 0$ is net technology growth. Show how you would find a balanced growth path for this economy.

2.3   A STOCHASTIC VERSION

Suppose that production follows a stochastic process given by

$$Y_t = \lambda_t K(t)^\theta H(t)^{1-\theta},$$

where

$$\lambda_t = (1 - \gamma) + \gamma \lambda_{t-1} + \varepsilon_t,$$

with $0 < \gamma < 1$ and ε_t has $E_t \varepsilon_{t+1} = 0$, is bounded below by $-(1-\gamma)$ and is bounded above. Notice that these assumptions mean that technology will always be positive and will have a stationary state or nonstochastic value (which is when all $\varepsilon_t = 0$) of one.

It is easier to work with the same utility function as above but now expressed in terms of logs. Therefore, we assume that a member of generation t maximizes an expected utility of

$$u_t^h = E_t u(c_t^h(t), c_t^h(t+1))$$

$$= E_t \left[\ln c_t^h(t) + \beta \ln c_t^h(t+1) \right]$$

$$= \ln c_t^h(t) + \beta E_t \ln c_t^h(t+1)$$

Using logs makes the utility function additive and this simplifies computation. Since the time t, technology shock is known at time t, output at time t is known and so is time t consumption. Time $t+1$ output and consumption are not known at time t, but their expected values can be calculated.

Individual budget constrains are

$$c_t^h(t) = w_t h_t^h(t) - k_t^h(t+1),$$

when young, and

$$c_t^h(t+1) = w_{t+1} h_t^h(t+1) + \text{rental}_{t+1} k_t^h(t+1).$$

The individual's optimization problem is to max

$$\ln c_t^h(t) + \beta E_t \ln c_t^h(t+1)$$

subject to the two budget constraints. We can solve this as a Lagrangian (being careful with the expectations operators in the utility function) and get the first-order condition of the individual maximization problem as

$$\frac{1}{c_t^h(t)} = \beta E_t \frac{\text{rental}_{t+1}}{c_t^h(t+1)}.$$

Competitive factor markets imply that wages and rentals equal their marginal products, so

$$w_t = (1-\theta) \lambda_t K(t)^\theta H(t)^{-\theta},$$

and

$$\text{rental}_{t+1} = \theta \lambda_{t+1} K(t+1)^{\theta-1} H(t+1)^{1-\theta}.$$

The capital that will be carried into period $t + 1$ is observed in period t as the solution to the optimization problem. The amount of labor that the young and old provide is fixed in this model, so it is also known at date t. The only time $t + 1$ variable that is not known at date t is the value of the technology shock in period $t + 1$. Interestingly, knowing this exactly is not important for solving the optimization problem of the time t young.

Taking the first-order condition for the time t young, we substitute the budget constraints, writing everything in aggregate terms since the young at time t are identical, and get

$$\frac{1}{w_t H_t(t) - K(t+1)} = \beta E_t \frac{\text{rental}_{t+1}}{w_{t+1} H_t(t+1) + \text{rental}_{t+1} K(t+1)}.$$

Recall that $H_t(s)$ is the labor provided by generation t in period $s = t, t + 1$. We divide through by rental_{t+1} on the right-hand side of this equation and get

$$\frac{1}{w_t H_t(t) - K(t+1)} = \beta E_t \frac{1}{\frac{w_{t+1}}{\text{rental}_{t+1}} H_t(t+1) + K(t+1)}.$$

Replacing wages and rentals by their marginal products, we get

$$\frac{1}{(1-\theta)\lambda_t K(t)^\theta H(t)^{-\theta} H_t(t) - K(t+1)}$$

$$= \beta E_t \frac{1}{\frac{(1-\theta)\lambda_{t+1} K(t+1)^\theta H(t+1)^{-\theta}}{\theta \lambda_{t+1} K(t+1)^{\theta-1} H(t+1)^{1-\theta}} H_t(t+1) + K(t+1)}.$$

Simplifying the right-hand side yields

$$\frac{1}{(1-\theta)\lambda_t K(t)^\theta H(t)^{-\theta} H_t(t) - K(t+1)} = \beta \frac{1}{\left[\frac{(1-\theta)}{\theta}\frac{H_t(t+1)}{H(t+1)} + 1\right] K(t+1)}.$$

The expectation operator drops out because, in this last step, we canceled λ_{t+1} from the right-hand side. There is no longer a need to take expectations to find the stochastic growth path. With a bit of algebra, the model can be written as

$$K(t+1) = \kappa \lambda_t K(t)^\theta,$$

where

$$\kappa = \frac{\theta \beta \frac{H_t(t)}{H(t)^\theta}}{\frac{H_t(t+1)}{H(t+1)} + \frac{\theta(1+\beta)}{(1-\theta)}}.$$

does not change through time. Note that κ is the same as that in the non-stochastic version of the model. Given some initial $K(0)$, the time path for a stochastic version of this economy can be found by simulating the stochastic shocks for λ_t.

For an example economy where $\beta = .99$, $\theta = .36$, $H(t) = 65$, $H_t(t) = 60.2$, and $H_t(t + 1) = 4.8$, we get $\kappa = 4.00$. Assuming that $\gamma = .6$ and a uniform distribution for ε_t over $[-.02, .02]$, and starting from the three values of $K(0) = \{6.9792, 8.7241, 10.4689\}$, we get the time paths for capital and output shown in Figure 2.2. Output was found using the production function and the labor supply of $H(t) = 65$. Notice that with $\theta = .36$, the differences in the initial capital stock disappear relatively quickly. Since the technology shock enters directly into the production function, we observe more movement of the output than we do of the capital stock. In our overlapping generations model with complete depreciation, the return on capital needs to be high to make one want to hold it. The marginal product of capital is high enough only when the amount of capital (equal to around 9 units of goods) is much smaller than output (around 32 units of goods in the example economy). These results might not seem very consistent with capital-output ratios found

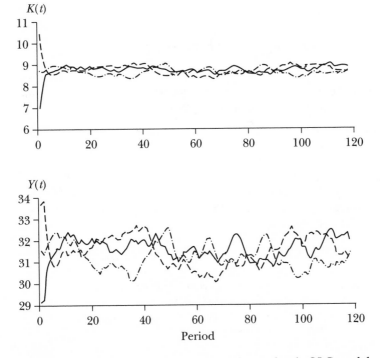

FIGURE 2.2 Simulations of three runs of the stochastic OLG model

in the literature that normally fall between 2 and 3. Here, however, there are only two periods of life, so each one is approximately 30 years. Thirty years of output measured against the stock of capital might not be very different from the approximately 1/3 that we find for this model. Capital is a stock, and it matters a lot the length of the output flow we are using for a capital-output ratio.

2.4   REPRISE

An overlapping generations model allows us to make the savings decision endogenous to the model in a relatively simple way. Since agents live only two periods, their optimization problem involves only those two periods. The overlapping nature of the economy and the fact that the old are holding all the capital that they saved from the previous period gives the model some persistence. In the version shown here, we did not make the labor supply decision endogenous, but this can be done relatively easily, since it adds only two more variables to the decision problem of each agent: the labor to supply when young and that when old.

For more information on overlapping generations models, one can refer to, in increasing level of difficulty, McCandless and Wallace [61], Sargent [72], and Azariadis [4]. A nice introduction to the use of OLG models for studying monetary economics can be found in Champ and Freeman [25].

2.5   MATLAB CODE USED TO PRODUCE FIGURE 2.2

The following program was used to generate the simulated time series for capital and output using the OLG model. This program is quite simple, but might be instructive to those learning Matlab.

```
kappa=4;
theta=.36;
roe=.9;
K0=[.8*kappa^(1/(1-theta))
      kappa^(1/(1-theta))
      1.2*kappa^(1/(1-theta))];
lambda(1:3,1)=[1 1 1]';
K(1:3,1)=K0;
Y(:,1)=lambda(:,1).*K(:,1).^theta.*65.^(1-theta);
for k=2:118
    lambda(:,k)=(1-roe)+roe.*lambda(:,k-1)+.02.*(rand(3,1)-.5);
    K(:,k)=kappa.*lambda(:,k).*K(:,k-1).^theta;
    Y(:,k)=lambda(:,k).*K(:,k-1).^theta.*65.^(1-theta);
end
subplot(2,1,1),plot(K')
subplot(2,1,2),plot(Y')
```

3

Infinitely Lived Agents

A frequently used method of handling endogenous savings is to allow the agents to live forever and to make plans taking into account their future consumption stream. One can think of the agents as family dynasties, where those members of the dynasty who are alive today take into account the welfare of all members of the family, including those of generations not yet born. One of the main reasons for choosing this structure of infinitely lived agents is technical. Under conditions where certain structures of the economy (such as utility functions) don't change through time, we can use standard variational or recursive methods to solve for stationary states.

While it is obvious that people do not live forever, models with infinitely lived agents may be good approximations for the kinds of decisions that are made by young people. When the expected time of death is far enough into the future and future consumption is discounted ($\beta < 1$), the weight given to consumption after the expected date of death in utility can be small enough so that it has no effect on current economic decisions. If there is a bequest motive, then taking into account the consumption of one's spawn and that of their spawn soon gives an infinite horizon utility function. In addition, in models where agents live lots of periods, it is easier to think of the model as having potential for representing business cycles. Business cycles are normally thought to be less than ten years, and lives in a two-period-lived overlapping generations model are much too long to imagine that these models give a good representation of business cycles. The only obvious problem with infinitely lived agents is that there is little room for discussing retirement decisions, but overlapping generations models like those of Chapter 2 are often used for modeling retirement.

In this chapter, we find stationary states for a deterministic economy where individuals have perfect foresight using variational methods. In the next chapter we will use recursive methods to solve the same problem. Here, we first consider the case of a Robinson Crusoe type of economy where there is only one individual (or a social planner) who makes the savings decisions. Later in this chapter, we look for the stationary state of an economy comprised of many individuals who receive income from their work and from the earnings on their savings.

3.1 A ROBINSON CRUSOE ECONOMY WITH FIXED LABOR

Consider an economy with only one individual.[1] At time t, an infinitely lived individual wants to maximize a lifetime utility function of the form

$$\sum_{i=0}^{\infty} \beta^i u(c_{t+i}),$$

where $u()$ is a subutility function that does not change with time, $0 < \beta < 1$ is the factor by which future utility is discounted, and c_t is the consumption of the individual in period t. The function $u()$ is assumed to be increasing, continuous, concave, and with as many derivatives as are required.

The individual begins period t with a given amount of capital stock carried over from the previous period, k_t, will provide one unit of labor in every period, and decides how much to consume subject to the sequence of single-period budget constraints of the form

$$k_{t+1} = (1 - \delta)k_t + i_t$$

and

$$y_t = f(k_t) \geq c_t + i_t.$$

Here, the capital stock, k_t, is per worker capital by definition in a one-person economy and by the assumption that Robinson Crusoe provides one unit of labor in each period. Investment, i_t, is the only other use for production that is not consumed. As in the initial Solow model, δ is the depreciation rate.

3.1.1 Variational Methods

Variational methods are useful for finding the stationary state of a dynamic problem. They can also be used to find first-order conditions for dynamic

---

1. I have been using the convention of writing individual variables in the lowercase and aggregate in the uppercase. In the Robinson Crusoe economy, the individual is the aggregate, so there is room for ambiguity. I choose to use lowercase for a single-person economy.

models, as we will see later. The basic technique is to assume that the values for the endogenous variables for periods $s - 1$ and $s + 1$ are given and then maximize the objective equation for the values in period s. The resulting first-order conditions must hold in a stationary state along with the condition that the value for each of the variables is the same at times $s - 1, s$, and $s + 1$. These conditions are sufficient to find a stationary state.

The most direct technique for a simple model like the one we are using here is to replace consumption in the lifetime utility function using the budget constraints and then maximize by choosing the sequence of optimizing capital stocks. Using the two budget constraints at equality, one can write consumption at time t as

$$c_t = f(k_t) - k_{t+1} + (1 - \delta)k_t.$$

The lifetime utility function can be written as

$$\sum_{i=0}^{\infty} \beta^i u(f(k_{t+i}) - k_{t+i+1} + (1 - \delta)k_{t+i}). \tag{3.1}$$

Assuming that the capital stocks k_{s-1} and k_{s+1} are given, the first-order condition for some time $s \geq t$ capital stock is

$$0 = \beta^{s-t}u'(f(k_s) - k_{s+1} + (1 - \delta)k_s)\left(f'(k_s) + (1 - \delta)\right)$$

$$- \beta^{s-t-1}u'(f(k_{s-1}) - k_s + (1 - \delta)k_{s-1}).$$

or that

$$f'(k_s) + (1 - \delta) = \frac{u'(f(k_{s-1}) - k_s + (1 - \delta)k_{s-1})}{\beta u'(f(k_s) - k_{s+1} + (1 - \delta)k_s)}.$$

From this Euler equation (as the first-order condition is sometimes known), one can find the stationary state values for the capital stock. Assuming that $k_{s+1} = k_s = k_{s-1} = \overline{k}$, as they must in a stationary state, the first-order condition yields

$$f'(\overline{k}) = \frac{1}{\beta} - 1 + \delta.$$

Since the parameters β and δ are known, as is the function $f(\cdot)$, this equation can be solved for $\overline{k}$. The equation states that in a stationary state, the marginal product of capital is equal to the net real interest rate implicit in the discount factor plus depreciation. Once the stationary state capital stock is determined, the budget constraints can be used to determine the stationary state values of output and consumption.

Of course, the above maximization problem could just as easily have been handled using Lagrangian multipliers. In that case, the maximization problem for some period s would have been written as

$$\max_{k_s, c_s, i_s} \sum_{i=0}^{\infty} \beta^i \left[u(c_{t+i}) - \lambda^1_{t+i} \left(k_{t+1+i} - (1 - \delta)k_{t+i} - i_{t+i} \right) \right.$$

$$\left. -\lambda^2_{t+i} \left(f(k_{t+i}) - c_{t+i} - i_{t+i} \right) \right].$$

The stationary state that results from solving the first-order conditions is exactly the same as that found by substitution.

The conditions given above are necessary conditions for an optimum. However, an extra condition is required: a boundary or limit condition called the *transversality condition*. This condition can best be seen in a general version. Later it is shown for the Robinson Crusoe model.

One can write the problem for Robinson Crusoe as the general problem

$$\max_{\{x_x\}_{s=t}^{\infty}} \sum_{i=0}^{\infty} \beta^i F \left(x_{t+i}, x_{t+1+i} \right).$$

The necessary Euler condition that was given above can be written as

$$0 = F_2 \left(x_{s-1}, x_s \right) + \beta F_1 \left(x_s, x_{s+1} \right),$$

where $F_j (,)$ is the partial derivative with respect to the jth component of $F (,)$. The transversality condition for this general problem is the limit condition

$$\lim_{s \to \infty} \beta^s F_1 \left(x_s, x_{s+1} \right) x_s = 0.$$

This condition says that in an optimal path, the values of x_s for s far enough into the future have zero weight in the maximization problem.

For the problem given in equation 3.1, the transversality condition is

$$\lim_{i \to \infty} \beta^i u' \left(f(k_{t+i}) - k_{t+i+1} + (1 - \delta)k_{t+i} \right) \left(f'(k_{t+i}) + (1 - \delta) \right) k_{t+i} = 0.$$

This equation can be interpreted as saying that the utility gains from accumulating capital eventually grow slower than $1/\beta$. If this were not the case, it might be optimal to postpone consumption indefinitely and no stationary state equilibrium would exist.

Here is an example where the transversality condition does not hold. Consider an economy where $f(k_t) = .2k_t$ and $u(c_t) = c_t$. Both production and the utility function are linear. Let $\delta = .1$ and $\beta = .98$. Imagine, first, that an individual in this economy will die in period T and wants to maximize

$$\sum_{i=0}^{T} \beta^i u \left(f \left(k_{t+i} \right) - k_{t+1+i} + (1 - \delta) k_{t+i} \right),$$

or, after putting in the specific equations,

$$\sum_{i=0}^{T} (.98)^i \left((1.1)k_{t+i} - k_{t+1+i} \right).$$

The maximum utility that can be achieved, given an initial capital of k_0, is the corner solution:

$$(.98 \cdot 1.1)^T k_0.$$

This utility is achieved by consuming nothing until period T, when all accumulated capital is consumed. This is optimal because the next period's utility rises more from any marginal savings than it is reduced because of the discount factor.

Now take an infinitely lived person. Total discounted utility is found by letting $T \to \infty$. Utility is maximized by infinitely delaying consumption and having the discounted utility value of the capital stock go to infinity. The transversality condition is

$$\lim_{t \to \infty} \left(.98^t \cdot 1.1 \right) (1.1)^{t-1} k_0$$

and this does not go to zero.

Stationary state allocations exist for this example economy: let $c_t = .1k_t$, for any value of k_t is one. However, no stationary state allocation is a utility-maximizing path.

The transversality condition removes the kinds of problems that the above example illustrates. Even when we do not explicitly do so in this book, one must check that the transversality conditions hold. They usually do in standard economies where the utility functions and production functions are concave and continuously differentiable and where the set of possible allocations in each period are convex and nonempty. (See Stokey, Lucas, and Prescott [83], section 4.5, for details and a theorem on the sufficiency of the Euler and transversality conditions.)

The main weakness of variational methods is that they do not provide an easy way of describing the dynamics of the model. To do that correctly, the values at both time $s - 1$ and time $s + 1$ are needed to find the solution. Therefore, the entire infinite sequence of capital needs to be solved simultaneously, a problem that is normally not one that we can handle in a tractable manner. Solving a stationary state dramatically reduces the dimensionality of the problem. Stationary states are tractable because the past and future values are going to be the same as the one we solve for. We reduce an infinite dimensional problem to one of just a single period.

3.2 A ROBINSON CRUSOE ECONOMY WITH VARIABLE LABOR

The first step in making the R.C. model a bit more realistic is to allow him to decide how to split his time between enjoying leisure and working.

3.2.1 The General Model

One can make the amount of labor that Robinson Crusoe supplies an individual choice as well. Assume that the utility function of the form

$$\sum_{i=0}^{\infty} \beta^i \overline{u}(c_{t+i}, l_{t+i}),$$

where $0 < l_{t+i} < 1$, is the amount of leisure that Robinson Crusoe chooses to consume in period $t + i$. Since there is a unit of time available each period, consuming l_{t+i} units of leisure in period $t + i$ means that one is using $h_{t+i} = 1 - l_{t+i}$ units of labor to produce goods. One can substitute this constraint into the utility function so that we think of utility as depending on consumption of goods and labor supplied,

$$\sum_{i=0}^{\infty} \beta^i u(c_{t+i}, h_{t+i}) \equiv \sum_{i=0}^{\infty} \beta^i \overline{u}(c_{t+i}, 1 - h_{t+i}) = \sum_{i=0}^{\infty} \beta^i \overline{u}(c_{t+i}, l_{t+i}),$$

where the partial derivatives are $u_c(c_{t+i}, h_{t+i}) > 0$ and $u_h(c_{t+i}, h_{t+i}) < 0$. The other budget constraints are the same capital accumulation equation as before,

$$k_{t+1} = (1 - \delta)k_t + i_t,$$

and a new feasibility constraint where the production function includes the labor supply,

$$y_t = f(k_t, h_t) \geq c_t + i_t.$$

The Lagrangian is written as

$$\mathcal{L} = \sum_{i=0}^{\infty} \beta^i \left[u(c_{t+i}, h_{t+i}) - \lambda_{t+i}^1 \left(k_{t+1+i} - (1-\delta)k_{t+i} - i_{t+i} \right) \right.$$

$$\left. - \lambda_{t+i}^2 \left(f(k_{t+i}, h_{t+i}) - c_{t+i} - i_{t+i} \right) \right].$$

The four first-order conditions (maximizing with respect to time s consumption, labor supply, capital, and investment, for some period $s \geq t$) are

$$\frac{\partial \mathcal{L}}{\partial c_s} = 0 = u_c(c_s, h_s) + \lambda_s^2,$$

$$\frac{\partial \mathcal{L}}{\partial h_s} = 0 = u_h(c_s, h_s) - \lambda_s^2 f_h(k_s, h_s),$$

$$\frac{\partial \mathcal{L}}{\partial k_{s+1}} = 0 = -\lambda_s^1 + \beta \lambda_{s+1}^1 (1-\delta) - \beta \lambda_{s+1}^2 f_k(k_{s+1}, h_{s+1}),$$

$$\frac{\partial \mathcal{L}}{\partial i_s} = 0 = \lambda_s^1 + \lambda_s^2.$$

We close the system by adding the two budget constraints,

$$k_{s+1} = (1-\delta)k_s + i_s$$

and

$$f(k_s, h_s) = c_s + i_s.$$

These simplify to the conditions that

$$u_c(c_s, h_s) = \lambda_s^1 = -\lambda_s^2,$$

$$\frac{u_h(c_s, h_s)}{u_c(c_s, h_s)} = -f_h(k_s, h_s),$$

$$\frac{u_c(c_s, h_s)}{u_c(c_{s+1}, h_{s+1})} = \beta \left[f_k(k_{s+1}, h_{s+1}) + (1-\delta) \right],$$

and the budget constraint

$$k_{s+1} = (1-\delta)k_s + f(k_s, h_s) - c_s.$$

In a stationary state, the third condition reduces to

$$\frac{1}{\beta} - (1-\delta) = f_k(k, h),$$

and the fourth to

$$\delta k = f(k, h) - c.$$

In a stationary state, the second condition is

$$\frac{u_h(c, h)}{u_c(c, h)} = -f_h(k, h).$$

We have three independent equations in three unknowns: c, h, and k, so a solution to the stationary state is normally available.

3.2.2   Solution for a Sample Economy

Consider a sample economy where the production function is Cobb-Douglas,

$$y_t = f(k_t, h_t) = k_t^\theta h_t^{1-\theta}.$$

In the literature, there are two subutility functions that are commonly used. One uses the log of consumption,

$$u(c_t, h_t) = \ln(c_t) + v(h_t),$$

and the other is the constant elasticity of substitution form,

$$u(c_t, h_t) = \frac{c_t^{1-\phi}}{1-\phi} v(h_t),$$

with $\phi > 0$ but $\phi \neq 1$, and where $v(h_t)$ is a concave function such that $v(h_t) \to -\infty$ as $h_t \to 1$. A function that is frequently used for the utility of labor is

$$v(h_t) = B \ln(1 - h_t),$$

for some positive constant B. For our example economy here, we use

$$u(c_t, h_t) = \ln(c_t) + B \ln(1 - h_t).$$

With these assumptions, the conditions for the stationary state are

$$\frac{1}{\beta} - (1 - \delta) = \theta \overline{k}^{\theta-1} \overline{h}^{1-\theta},$$

$$\delta \overline{k} = \overline{k}^{\theta} \overline{h}^{1-\theta} - c.$$

and

$$B\frac{c}{1-\overline{h}} = (1-\theta)\,\overline{k}^{\theta}\overline{h}^{-\theta}.$$

From the first of these three conditions, we get stationary state labor supply as a function of the stationary state capital,

$$\overline{h} = \left[\frac{1}{\beta\theta} - \frac{(1-\delta)}{\theta}\right]^{\frac{1}{1-\theta}}\overline{k} = G\overline{k},$$

where $G = \left[1/\beta\theta - (1-\delta)/\theta\right]^{\frac{1}{1-\theta}}$ is a constant. The first and second give the stationary state consumption as a function of the stationary state capital,

$$\overline{c} = \left[\frac{1}{\beta\theta} - \frac{(1-\delta)}{\theta} - \delta\right]\overline{k} = J\overline{k},$$

and J is the constant defined by this equation. The second and third give

$$B\frac{\overline{c}}{1-\overline{h}} = (1-\theta)\frac{\delta\overline{k} + \overline{c}}{\overline{h}}.$$

Combining these three gives the stationary state value of capital,

$$\overline{k} = \frac{(1-\theta)\,(\delta + J)}{G\,(BJ + (1-\theta)\,(\delta + J))}.$$

Given the stationary state value of capital, the stationary state values for the labor supply and consumption are immediate.

> **EXERCISE 3.1** Find the stationary state conditions for an example economy where the subutility function has the constant elasticity of substitution form given above.

3.3 A COMPETITIVE ECONOMY

In the Robinson Crusoe economy, one person made consumption and production decisions for the whole economy. In a competitive economy, there are consumers who provide labor to the market and firms who hire this labor at the competitive wage, w_t. In this section, we assume that there is a continuum of identical agents of a unit mass and that all agents can provide up to one unit of labor to the market. All individuals are the same so that we can take the behavior of one agent as that of the whole economy since we simply integrate from 0 to 1 over identical agents.

As above, individual i gets utility out of consumption and disutility out of work, h_t^i, which is the amount of labor provided to the market by individual i. Each individual is endowed with one unit of time in each period, so the leisure of individual i in period t is equal to $l_t^i = 1 - h_t^i$. Subutility functions are of the form

$$u(c_t^i, h_t^i) = \overline{u}(c_t^i, 1 - h_t^i) = \overline{u}(c_t^i, l_t^i).$$

Firms produce goods each period according to a production function, $f(K_t, H_t)$, with the usual properties, where the uppercase letters K_t and H_t denote the society's aggregate amount of capital and labor applied to production. The firms pay a competitive wage, w_t, to workers and pay a competitive rent, r_t, for the use of capital, so the marginal product of labor is equal to the real wage and the marginal product of capital is equal to the rent paid for capital.

The general problem for an individual, i, at time 0 is to maximize

$$\sum_{t=0}^{\infty} \beta^t u(c_t^i, h_t^i),$$

subject to the constraints from a competitive economy of

$$c_t^i = w_t h_t^i + r_t k_t^i - I_t^i,$$

$$w_t = f_h(K_t, H_t),$$

$$r_t = f_k(K_t, H_t),$$

$$k_{t+1}^i = (1 - \delta)k_t^i + I_t^i,$$

where all variables are defined as above except I_t^i is the investment of individual i in period t. The individual's maximization problem can be written as the Lagrangian

$$\mathcal{L}^i = \sum_{t=0}^{\infty} \beta^t \left[u(c_t^i, h_t^i) - \lambda_t^1 \left(k_{t+1}^i - (1 - \delta)k_t^i - I_t^i \right) \right.$$

$$\left. - \lambda_t^2 \left(f_h(K_t, H_t)h_t^i + f_k(K_t, H_t)k_t^i - c_t^i - I_t^i \right) \right],$$

subject to the aggregation rules that

$$H_t = \int_0^1 h_t^i di \quad \text{and} \quad K_t = \int_0^1 k_t^i di.$$

The use of capital letters for capital and labor in the production function reminds us that these are society-wide variables and are viewed as constants in the individual choice problem.

First-order conditions from the maximization problem of individual i in period s are

$$\frac{\partial \mathcal{L}^i}{\partial c_s^i} = 0 = u_c(c_s^i, h_s^i) + \lambda_s^2,$$

$$\frac{\partial \mathcal{L}^i}{\partial h_s^i} = 0 = u_h(c_s^i, h_s^i) - \lambda_s^2 f_h(K_s, H_s),$$

$$\frac{\partial \mathcal{L}^i}{\partial k_{s+1}^i} = 0 = -\lambda_s^1 + \beta \lambda_{s+1}^1 (1 - \delta) - \beta \lambda_{s+1}^2 f_k(K_{s+1}, H_{s+1}),$$

$$\frac{\partial \mathcal{L}^i}{\partial I_s^i} = 0 = \lambda_s^1 + \lambda_s^2.$$

These can be simplified to get

$$u_c(c_s^i, h_s^i) = \lambda_s^1 = -\lambda_s^2,$$

$$\frac{u_h(c_s^i, h_s^i)}{u_c(c_s^i, h_s^i)} = -f_h(K_s, H_s), \tag{3.2}$$

$$\frac{u_c(c_s^i, h_s^i)}{u_c(c_{s+1}^i, h_{s+1}^i)} = \beta \left[f_k(K_{s+1}, H_{s+1}) + (1 - \delta) \right]. \tag{3.3}$$

To complete the system, we add the budget constraint

$$k_{t+1}^i = (1 - \delta)k_t^i + f_h(K_t, H_t)h_t^i + f_k(K_t, H_t)k_t^i - c_t^i,$$

and the aggregation rules

$$H_t = \int_0^1 h_t^i di \quad \text{and} \quad K_t = \int_0^1 k_t^i di.$$

When all of the unit mass of individuals are identical, the aggregation rules simplify to $H_t = h_t^i$ and $K_t = k_t^i$.

The production function is homogeneous of degree one (constant returns to scale) and under conditions of perfect competition with free entry, firms do not make any profits. Given the aggregation rule, this implies that

$$f_h(K_t, H_t)H_t + f_k(K_t, H_t)K_t = f(K_t, H_t)$$

and that the budget constraint given above can be written as

$$K_{t+1} = (1 - \delta)K_t + f(K_t, H_t) - C_t,$$

where aggregate consumption is

$$C_t = \int_0^1 c_t^i di.$$

When all the households are identical, the first-order conditions can be written as the aggregate conditions

$$\frac{u_h(C_s, H_s)}{u_c(C_s, H_s)} = -f_h(K_s, H_s),$$

$$\frac{u_c(C_s, H_s)}{u_c(C_{s+1}, H_{s+1})} = \beta \left[f_k(K_{s+1}, H_{s+1}) + (1 - \delta) \right].$$

The result here is interesting. The conditions for the equilibrium in the competitive economy turn out to be an aggregate version of the same conditions of the Robinson Crusoe (R.C.) economy. When we find the stationary state equilibrium for this economy, it is the same stationary state that we found for the R.C. economy. Here, each individual supplies the same labor as the single individual did in the R.C. economy and each individual owns exactly the same amount of capital. Therefore, each individual has exactly the same income and faces the same marginal conditions as in the R.C. economy.

3.4   THE SECOND WELFARE THEOREM

The result that the equilibrium of a representative agent economy and that of a perfectly competitive one that is otherwise identical is not surprising. Mas-Colell, Whinston, and Green [59] write the second fundamental theorem of welfare economics as follows:

> The Second Fundamental Welfare Theorem. If household preferences and firm production sets are convex, there is a complete set of markets with publicly known prices, and every agent acts as a price taker, then *any Pareto optimal outcome can be achieved as a competitive equilibrium if appropriate lump-sum transfers of wealth are arranged.* (p. 308)

This statement of the second fundamental welfare theorem holds for finite dimensional economies. Our economies have an infinite number of periods and, therefore, an infinite number of goods. The conditions for existence of a competitive equilibrium in infinite horizon economies are somewhat more complex than those for finite dimensional ones and some extra assumptions are required. See Stokey, Lucas, and Prescott [83], Chapter 16, for details. Here, we simply assume that a competitive equilibrium exists and are interested in its relationship to the social planner (Robinson Crusoe) economy.

The equilibrium that was found in the R. C. economy is Pareto optimal. It is the result of the "social planner" Robinson Crusoe finding production and consumption points that maximize the utility of the single individual in the economy, given his technological constraints.

The first fundamental welfare theorem tells us that any competitive equilibrium is necessarily Pareto optimal, so that the equilibrium found using a decentralized economy with factor and goods markets is also Pareto optimal. The second welfare theorem tells us that, since the production technologies and preferences are the same in the two economies, then with the right initial wealth conditions, the competitive economy can achieve an equilibrium that is identical to the social planner economy. It might achieve a different one if the initial wealth distribution were not correct. In our case, all individuals have an initial wealth that is identical to that of Robinson Crusoe, have identical preferences, and face the same technologies. Therefore, this initial distribution of wealth is sufficient to result in the same equilibrium as in the R. C. economy.

It is the second fundamental welfare theorem that permits us to use a representative agent economy to mimic a competitive economy. Since the second fundamental theorem is carefully worded, it should be clear that using a representative agent economy will not always give the appropriate results. If the economy is not perfectly competitive, if part of the economy has some monopoly power or if there are some external or internal restrictions that prevent some agents from behaving perfectly competitive, then the equilibrium found by the decentralized economy will not necessarily be achievable with a representative agent economy.

However, when the conditions are right, solving a representative agent economy is often technically much simpler than solving a decentralized economy. In this case, the second fundamental welfare theorem states that, with appropriate initial conditions, the solution of the representative agent economy is one for the decentralized economy.

3.4.1 An Example Where the Representative Agent Economy and the Decentralized Economy Are Not Equal

It is not difficult to find an example where distortions in the competitive economy cause the equilibrium to be different from that found in a representative agent economy. In the economy given here, the government applies a proportional tax on wage income and rebates the revenues to the households using

a lump sum transfer. The tax on wage income changes the equilibrium so that
it is no longer the same as that of the Robinson Crusoe economy.

Suppose that, in a simple decentralized economy, there exists a government
that does nothing more than impose a wage tax and rebate the tax revenue
by giving identical lump sum transfers to each family. Let the wage tax rate be
t_w and the lump sum transfers in period t be T_t. The government makes no
other use of this income, so its budget constraint is

$$t_w w_t H_t = T_t.$$

The general problem for an individual, i, at time 0 is to maximize

$$\sum_{t=0}^{\infty} \beta^t u(c_t^i, h_t^i),$$

subject to the constraints from a competitive economy of

$$c_t^i = \left(1 - t_w\right) w_t h_t^i + r_t k_t^i + T_t - I_t^i,$$

$$w_t = f_h(K_t, H_t),$$

$$r_t = f_k(K_t, H_t),$$

$$k_{t+1}^i = (1 - \delta)k_t^i + I_t^i.$$

The individual's maximization problem can be written as the Lagrangian

$$\mathcal{L}^i = \sum_{t=0}^{\infty} \beta^t \left[u(c_t^i, h_t^i) - \lambda_t^1 \left(k_{t+1}^i - (1 - \delta)k_t^i - I_t^i \right) \right.$$

$$\left. - \lambda_t^2 \left((1 - t_w) f_h(K_t, H_t)h_t^i + f_k(K_t, H_t)k_t^i + T_t - c_t^i - I_t^i \right) \right],$$

subject to the aggregation rules that

$$H_t = \int_0^1 h_t^i di \quad \text{and} \quad H_t = \int_0^1 k_t^i di.$$

The government's budget constraint is an equilibrium condition and needs
to be applied to the economy after the individual optimization.

The first-order conditions are

$$\frac{\partial \mathcal{L}^i}{\partial c_s^i} = 0 = u_c(c_s^i, h_s^i) + \lambda_s^2,$$

$$\frac{\partial \mathcal{L}^i}{\partial h_s^i} = 0 = u_h(c_s^i, h_s^i) - \lambda_s^2 \left(1 - t_w\right) f_h(K_s, H_s),$$

$$\frac{\partial \mathcal{L}^i}{\partial k_{s+1}^i} = 0 = -\lambda_s^1 + \beta \lambda_{s+1}^1 (1 - \delta) - \beta \lambda_{s+1}^2 f_k(K_{s+1}, H_{s+1}),$$

$$\frac{\partial \mathcal{L}^i}{\partial I_s^i} = 0 = \lambda_s^1 + \lambda_s^2.$$

These simplify to

$$u_c(c_s^i, h_s) = \lambda_s^1 = -\lambda_s^2,$$

$$\frac{u_h(c_s^i, h_s^i)}{u_c(c_s^i, h_s)} = -\left(1 - t_w\right) f_h(K_s, H_s),$$

$$\frac{u_c(c_s^i, h_s^i)}{u_c(c_{s+1}^i, h_{s+1}^i)} = \beta \left[f_k(K_{s+1}, H_{s+1}) + (1 - \delta) \right].$$

Now that the first-order conditions are determined, we add the aggregation (equilibrium) conditions. Production is homogeneous of degree 1, so

$$f(K_t, H_t) = f_h(K_t, H_t)H_t + f_k(K_t, H_t)K_t$$

$$= \left(1 - t_w\right) f_h(K_s, H_s)H_t + f_k(K_t, H_t)K_t + t_w f_h(K_s, H_s)H_t$$

$$= \left(1 - t_w\right) f_h(K_s, H_s)H_t + f_k(K_t, H_t)K_t + T_t.$$

The aggregate version of the individual budget constraint can be written as

$$K_{t+1} = (1 - \delta)K_t + f(K_t, H_t) - C_t$$

and is the same as in the economy without the wage tax. When all the households are identical, the first-order conditions can be written as the aggregate conditions

$$\frac{u_h(C_s, H_s)}{u_c(C_s, H_s)} = -\left(1 - t_w\right) f_h(K_s, H_s),$$

$$\frac{u_c(C_s, H_s)}{u_c(C_{s+1}, H_{s+1})} = \beta \left[f_k(K_{s+1}, H_{s+1}) + (1 - \delta) \right].$$

In a stationary state for the economy with a wage tax, the equations of the model are

$$\delta \overline{K} = f(\overline{K}, \overline{H}) - \overline{C},$$

$$1 = \beta \left[f_k(\overline{K}, \overline{H}) + (1 - \delta) \right],$$

$$\frac{u_h(\overline{C}, \overline{H})}{u_c(\overline{C}, \overline{H})} = - \left(1 - t_w \right) f_h(\overline{K}, \overline{H}).$$

The second equation uses the fact that in a stationary state, $u_c(C_s, H_s) = u_c(C_{s+1}, H_{s+1}) = u_c(\overline{C}, \overline{H})$.

Compare the set of equations above to the equations for the stationary state of the same economy without the wage tax, when $t_w = 0$. The first two equations are the same, but the last one is simply

$$\frac{u_h(\overline{C}, \overline{H})}{u_c(\overline{C}, \overline{H})} = -f_h(\overline{K}, \overline{H}).$$

The stationary states will be different for different values of t_w. In the economy with a wage tax, the individuals pay a tax to the government through a percentage tax on wages and receive a lump sum transfer from the government for exactly the same amount as the tax they paid. These two amounts cancel out in the budget constraint. However, one of the first-order conditions is different, so the stationary states will, in general, be different.

Consider an example economy with a Cobb-Douglas production function,

$$f(K_t, H_t) = K_t^\theta H_t^{1-\theta},$$

and a subutility function,

$$u(c_t^i, h_t^i) = \ln \left(c_t^i \right) + A \ln \left(1 - h_t^i \right).$$

The parameters are $\beta = .98$, $\delta = .1$, $\theta = .36$, and $A = .5$. The stationary states for this economy with tax rates of $t_w = \{0, .1, .2\}$ are found by using a simple Matlab program and are shown in Table 3.1. In the table, $\overline{u}$ is the value of the subutility function in every period.

Table 3.1 shows how utility changes as the (distorting) wage tax rate increases. Stationary state economies where $t_w > 0$ are clearly not Pareto optimal, since they are dominated in every period by the economy where $t_w = 0$. The subutility value, $-.6953$, for $t_w = 0$ is greater than the subutility values for the higher values of t_w.

In the economy shown here, the distorting wage tax makes the competitive equilibrium different from the equilibrium found for a similar representative

Table 3.1 Stationary state values for example economies

t_w	0	.1	.2
$\overline{C}$	0.8387	0.8070	0.7705
$\overline{K}$	3.5770	3.4417	3.2862
$\overline{H}$	0.6461	0.6217	0.5936
$\overline{u}$	−.6953	−.7005	−.7109

agent economy. One needs to be careful when using representative agent economies and extremely careful when trying to use them for economies with distortions.

> **EXERCISE 3.2** Find the stationary state equilibria for an economy with a government that finances lump sum transfers to the public with a 10% tax on the income from capital. Compare this equilibrium to that of the same economy with no taxes. Compare the utility in this economy with that of an economy with a wage tax that raises the same amount of revenue for the government.

3.5 REPRISE

It is relatively easy to find stationary states for economies with single agents that live a long time and have utility that is comprised of additive discounted subutilities. These single agent economies can be thought of as representative agent economies for market economies where the individuals are identical. Variational methods are frequently good enough for finding stationary states, but they do not usually permit us to study the dynamic properties of the economy. If one is simply interested in comparing stationary states or finding the stationary state characteristics of an economy, variational methods are sufficient. As is often the case in economics, problems can arise when one wants to consider economies with many different types of agents. However, simple economies, such as the growth model given above, with groups of agents with different utility functions can frequently be solved using variational methods. One has to be careful during the aggregation procedures.

A classic text on variational methods is Hadley and Kemp [46].

4

Recursive Deterministic Models

In some infinite horizon economies, the *nature* of the optimization problem that individuals face does not depend on the period in which they are making their decisions. For example, in a Solow-type model where the subutility functions are the same in each period, where the discount factor is constant though time, and where the production functions are the same in every period, the problem that individuals face is the same, independent of the period in which they have to solve this problem. The problems that we solved in the previous chapter using variational methods required these characteristics because we were solving for stationary states. Yet, for those economies, even on a path that is not a stationary state, the nature of the problem does not change with time. What changes from period to period are the initial conditions, the values of the variables that have been determined by the past or by nature.

These kinds of problems can also be solved with *recursive methods*. One of the advantages of recursive methods is that we can solve directly for time paths that are not stationary states. As we will see later, recursive methods also permit the inclusion, in a very natural way, of stochastic shocks. With recursive methods, one looks for a *policy function*, a mapping from the initial conditions, given by the past or the present, to a set of decisions about what to do with the variables we can choose during this period. Because these are normally infinite horizon problems, how we will want to behave in the future matters in determining what we want to do today. Since what one will want to do in the future matters and the whole future time path can be determined, the recursive methods we describe are also known as *dynamic programing*.

4.1 STATES AND CONTROLS

It is helpful to separate the set of variables that we are using into state variables and control variables. In some period t, the *state variables* are those whose values are already determined, either by our actions in the past or by some other process (such as nature). Normally, for a growth model of the type we have been working with, the capital stock that we inherit from the past must be considered a state variable. One might also think that the technology level (recall our earlier model where technology was stochastic) in each period is determined by nature and therefore, in any period, the agents living in that economy must take it as a given.

The past values of other variables might be important as well. In models with habit formation,[1] past consumption matters in determining utility, so a subutility function for period t might be written as

$$u(c_t - \xi c_{t-1}).$$

In that case, an individual's utility depends on consumption today relative to past consumption. This is why it is called habit formation: since the consumer formed the "habit" of consuming a given amount in the previous period, welfare improves or declines relative to this habitual consumption. Since period $t - 1$ consumption has already been determined, it must be considered a state variable for decisions that are to be made in period t.

The *control variables* in period t are those variables whose values individuals explicitly choose in that period with the goal of maximizing some objective function. Frequently, a modeler has a choice about which variables will be states and which will be control variables.

Consider the simple version of our Robinson Crusoe model. In that model, the objective function our Robinson Crusoe wants to maximize is the discounted lifetime utility of consumption,

$$\max \sum_{i=0}^{\infty} \beta^i u(c_{t+i}),$$

subject to the budget restrictions

$$k_{t+1} = (1 - \delta)k_t + i_t$$

and

$$y_t = f(k_t) = c_t + i_t.$$

---

1. For an example of models with habit formation, see Amato and Laubach [1].

In this model, the capital stock inherited from period $t - 1$, k_t, is clearly a state variable; it is predetermined and known. However, there are a number of ways of choosing a control variable.

Robinson Crusoe could directly choose consumption, c_t. Consumption appears directly in the objective function. Once consumption in period t is determined, the second budget constraint determines investment, i_t, and the first budget constraint then determines the capital stock that will be available in period $t + 1$, k_{t+1}. In this case, consumption is the control variable.

An alternative would be for Robinson Crusoe to choose the amount of capital that will be available in period $t + 1$, k_{t+1}. In that case, a combined budget constraint could be written as

$$c_t = f(k_t) + (1 - \delta)k_t - k_{t+1},$$

and after substitution, the objective function is

$$\max \sum_{i=0}^{\infty} \beta^i u(f(k_{t+i}) + (1 - \delta)k_{t+i} - k_{t+i+1}).$$

In this case, k_{t+1} is the control variable in period t.

Whatever our choice of a control variable, there must be enough budget constraints or market conditions so that the values of the rest of the relevant variables in period t are determined. What may be surprising is that the choice of control variables can matter in how easily we can solve our models. Some choices will simply be more convenient than others. This claim will be demonstrated explicitly further on.

4.2 THE VALUE FUNCTION

Assume that it is possible to calculate the value of the discounted value of utility that an agent receives when that agent is maximizing the infinite horizon objective function subject to the budget constraints. For our case of the Robinson Crusoe economy with fixed labor supply, this value is clearly a function of the initial per worker capital stock, k_t. As shown above, we can write out a version of this problem where the R.C. economy is using the capital stock to be carried over to the next period, k_{t+1}, as the control variable. For that example, the value of utility is equal to

$$V(k_t) = \max_{\{k_s\}_{s=t+1}^{\infty}} \sum_{i=0}^{\infty} \beta^i u(f(k_{t+i}) - k_{t+1+i} + (1 - \delta)k_{t+i}), \qquad (4.1)$$

where we denote the value of the discounted utility by $V(k_t)$, to stress that it is a function of the value of the initial capital stock, k_t. For any value of k_t, limited to the appropriate domain, the value of the *value function*, $V(k_t)$, is the discounted value of utility when the maximization problem has been solved and when k_t was the initial capital stock.

Since $V(k_t)$ is a function, its value can be found for any permitted value of k_t. In particular, the value of the function can be found for the value of k_{t+1} that was chosen in period t. This is possible because the economy is recursive as mentioned above. In period $t + 1$, the value of k_{t+1} is given (it is a state variable) and the problem to be solved is simply the maximization of utility beginning in period $t + 1$. The maximization problem can be written as

$$V(k_{t+1}) = \max_{\{k_s\}_{s=t+2}^{\infty}} \sum_{i=0}^{\infty} \beta^i u(f(k_{t+1+i}) - k_{t+2+i} + (1-\delta)k_{t+1+i}), \quad (4.2)$$

and its value, $V(k_{t+1})$, is a function of the stock of capital per worker at time $t + 1$.

By separating the period t problem from that of future periods, we can rewrite the value function of equation 4.1 as

$$V(k_t) = \max_{k_{t+1}} \left[u\left(f(k_t) - k_{t+1} + (1-\delta)k_t\right) \right.$$

$$\left. + \max_{\{k_s\}_{s=t+2}^{\infty}} \sum_{i=1}^{\infty} \beta^i u(f(k_{t+i}) - k_{t+1+i} + (1-\delta)k_{t+i}) \right].$$

Adjusting the indices of the second part gives

$$V(k_t) = \max_{k_{t+1}} \left[u\left(f(k_t) - k_{t+1} + (1-\delta)k_t\right) \right.$$

$$\left. +\beta \max_{\{k_s\}_{s=t+2}^{\infty}} \sum_{i=0}^{\infty} \beta^i u(f(k_{t+1+i}) - k_{t+2+i} + (1-\delta)k_{t+1+i}) \right].$$

The summation in the last part of this equation is simply the value function $V(k_{t+1})$ that we wrote out in equation 4.2. Making the substitution, the value function in equation 4.1 can be written recursively as

$$V(k_t) = \max_{k_{t+1}} \left[u(f(k_t) - k_{t+1} + (1-\delta)k_t) + \beta V(k_{t+1}) \right]. \quad (4.3)$$

An equation of the form of equation 4.3 is known as a Bellman equation (Bellman [7]). It presents exactly the same problem as that shown in equation 4.1, but written in a recursive form. Writing out the problem recursively makes it conceptually simpler. The value of the choice variable, k_{t+1}, is being chosen to maximize an objective function of only a single period. The problem is reduced from one of infinite dimensions to one of only one dimension. However, the simplification comes at a cost. The problem is now one where both the time t one-period problem, $u(f(k_t) - k_{t+1} + (1 - \delta)k_t)$, and the discounted value function evaluated at k_{t+1}, $\beta V(k_{t+1})$, are included. The complication is that the value of the function $V(k_{t+1})$ evaluated at k_{t+1} is not yet known. If it were known, then the value of the function $V(k_t)$ would also be known—it is the same function—and solving the maximization problem at time t would be trivial.

To proceed, we assume that the value function $V(\cdot)$ exists and has a first derivative. We can then proceed with the one-period maximization problem of equation 4.3 by taking the derivative of that equation with respect to k_{t+1}. The resulting first-order condition is

$$0 = -u'(f(k_t) - k_{t+1} + (1 - \delta)k_t) + \beta V'(k_{t+1}). \tag{4.4}$$

Unfortunately, we seem not to have progressed very far. The first-order condition contains $V'(k_{t+1})$, the derivative of value function $V()$, evaluated at k_{t+1}. This is inconvenient since we need to know the derivative of $V()$ to be able to determine the same function $V()$. We do not know that derivative.

Under certain conditions, and this model has been written so that the conditions hold, one can find the derivative of $V()$ simply by taking the partial derivative of the value function as written in equation 4.3 with respect to k_t. Theorems that provide the sufficient conditions for getting a derivative and that tell us how to find it are called *envelope theorems*.[2] This partial derivative is

$$V'(k_t) = u'(f(k_t) - k_{t+1} + (1 - \delta)k_t) \left(f'(k_t) + (1 - \delta) \right).$$

We can substitute this definition of the derivative (evaluated at k_{t+1}) into the first-order condition shown in equation 4.4 to get an Euler equation of

$$\frac{u'(c_t)}{u'(c_{t+1})} = \beta \left(f'(k_{t+1}) + (1 - \delta) \right).$$

In a stationary state, where $c_t = c_{t+1}$, this Euler equation is

$$\frac{1}{\beta} - (1 - \delta) = f'(\bar{k}).$$

Using recursive methods, we find that for a stationary state, the rental on capital is equal to the net interest rate implicit in the discount factor plus the depreciation rate. This is the same condition that we found when we solved for the stationary state using variational methods.

---

2. The envelope theorems we need for fairly standard economies are given in Benveniste and Scheinkman [8] and for more general economies in Milgrom and Segal [65].

4.3   A GENERAL VERSION

Let x_t be a vector of the period t state variables and let y_t be a vector of the control variables. In the example above, $x_t = [k_t]$ and $y_t = [k_{t+1}]$.[3] Let $F(x_t, y_t)$ be the time t value of the objective function that is to be maximized. In the example economy, the objective function is the utility function. Given initial values of the state variables, x_t, the problem to be solved at time t is the value function

$$V(x_t) = \max_{\{y_s\}_{s=t}^{\infty}} \sum_{s=t}^{\infty} \beta^{s-t} F(x_s, y_s),$$

subject to the set of budget constraints given by

$$x_{s+1} = G(x_s, y_s)$$

for $s \geq t$. The objective function, $F(\cdot, \cdot)$, and the budget constraints, $G(\cdot, \cdot)$, are the same for all periods $s \geq t$. Notice that, in general, we permit both time t state variables and control variables to be in the objective function and the budget constraints at time t. Using the same recursive argument that we used above, we can write the value function as a Bellman equation,

$$V(x_t) = \max_{y_t} \left[F(x_s, y_s) + \beta V(x_{t+1}) \right],$$

subject to the budget constraints

$$x_{s+1} = G(x_s, y_s),$$

or, by replacing the future value of the state variables by the budget constraints, as the single problem

$$V(x_t) = \max_{y_t} \left[F(x_t, y_t) + \beta V(G(x_t, y_t)) \right]. \tag{4.5}$$

The solution to this problem gives the values of the control variables as a function of the time t state variables,

$$y_t = H(x_t).$$

We call the function $H(x_t)$ a *policy function*, since it describes how the controls behave as a function of the current state variables, x_t. Equation 4.5 is really a *functional equation*, since it must hold for every value of x_t within the permitted

---

3. Notice that in this particular case, it turns out that $y_t = x_{t+1}$, that the control at time t becomes the state at time $t + 1$. This is one of the aspects of the specific example that makes it simple to solve and should not be considered the normal relationship between controls and states.

domain. Solutions to functional equations are functions, which is why we call the solution to the Bellman equation a policy *function*. Since the policy function optimizes the choice of the controls for every permitted value of x_t, it must fulfill the condition that

$$V(x_t) = F(x_t, H(x_t)) + \beta V(G(x_t, H(x_t))), \qquad (4.6)$$

where maximization is no longer required because it is implicit in the policy function, $H(x_t)$.

To find the policy function, $H(x_t)$, we find the first-order conditions for the problem in equation 4.5 with respect to the control variables. The first-order conditions are

$$0 = F_y(x_t, y_t) + \beta V'(G(x_t, y_t))G_y(x_t, y_t), \qquad (4.7)$$

where $F_y(x_t, y_t)$ is the vector of derivatives of the objective function with respect to the control variables, $V'(G(x_t, y_t))$ is the vector of derivatives of the value function with respect to the time $t+1$ state variables, and $G_y(x_t, y_t)$ is the vector of derivatives of the budget constraints with respect to the control variables. We encounter the same problem that we had in the specific example, that we need to know the derivatives of the value function to be able to solve for the policy function, and the value function is unknown.

However, it may be possible to use the envelope theorem from Benveniste-Scheinkman [8] to find an expression for the derivative for the value function. Taking the derivative of the value function, equation 4.5, with respect to the time t state variables, x_t, one gets the Benveniste-Scheinkman envelope theorem,[4]

---

4. The envelope theorem of Benveniste and Scheinkman [8] gives a set of sufficient assumptions under which one can write the derivative of the value function. We are using a somewhat different notation of the form

$$V(x_t) = \max \left[F\left(x_t, y_t\right) + \beta V(x_{t+1}) \right]$$

subject to the budget constraint

$$x_{t+1} = G\left(x_t, y_t\right)$$

that gives the Benveniste-Scheinkman derivative as

$$V'(x_t) = F_x\left(x_t, y_t\right) + \beta V'\left(G\left(x_t, y_t\right)\right) G_x\left(x_t, y_t\right).$$

The following four assumptions are sufficient so that the requirements of Benveniste-Scheinkman are met:

1. $x_t \in X$, where X is a convex set with a nonempty interior
2. $F(\cdot, \cdot)$ is concave and differentiable
3. $G(\cdot, \cdot)$ is concave and differentiable and invertible in y_t
4. $y_t \in Y$, where Y is a convex set with a nonempty interior

$$V'(x_t) = F_x(x_t, y_t) + \beta V'(G(x_t, y_t))G_x(x_t, y_t).$$

If, as can frequently be done, the controls have been chosen so that $G_x(x_t, y_t) = 0$, then it is possible to simplify this expression to

$$V'(x_t) = F_x(x_t, y_t).$$

The first-order conditions of equation 4.7 can be written as

$$0 = F_y(x_t, y_t) + \beta F_x(G(x_t, y_t), y_{t+1})G_y(x_t, y_t).$$

If the function $F_x(G(x_t, y_t), y_{t+1})$ is independent of y_{t+1}, then this equation can be solved for the implicit function, $y_t = H(x_t)$, which is the required policy function. One can substitute this policy function into equation 4.6 and solve for the implicit value function $V(\cdot)$. If the function $F_x(G(x_t, y_t), y_{t+1})$ is not independent of y_{t+1}, then one can solve for the stationary state as we did in the example economy above, using the condition that $y_{t+1} = y_t$ in a stationary state.

If it is not the case that $G_x(x_t, y_t) = 0$, then an alternative solution method is to find an approximation to the value function numerically.[5] Consider some initial guess for the value function, $V_0(x_t)$. It doesn't matter very much what this initial guess, is and a convenient one is to assume that it has a constant value of zero. One can then calculate an updated value function, $V_1(x_t)$, using the formula

$$V_1(x_t) = \max_{y_t} \left[F(x_t, y_t) + \beta V_0(G(x_t, y_t)) \right],$$

and doing the maximization numerically (using a computer maximization algorithm) over a sufficiently dense set of values from the domain of x_t. This maximization defines, approximately, the function $V_1(x_t)$. Using this new function (and interpolating when necessary), one can update again and get a new approximate value function $V_2(x_t)$, using

$$V_2(x_t) = \max_{y_t} \left[F(x_t, y_t) + \beta V_1(G(x_t, y_t)) \right]$$

over a dense set of values from the domain of x_t. Repeated application of this process results in a sequence of approximate value functions $\{V_i(x_t)\}_{i=0}^{\infty}$. Bellman showed that, under a set of conditions that are often met in economic problems, this sequence converges to the value function, $V(x_t)$.

---

5. The approximation can be done in any case, but if $G_x(x_t, y_t) = 0$, then one can find exact representations of the value function, and approximation is not necessary.

To get some intuition as to why this convergence might occur, consider what happens to the initial guess of the function $V_0(\cdot)$. In the calculation of $V_1(\cdot)$, one is maximizing the real objective function, $F(x_t, y_t)$, and discounting the initial guess, $V_0(\cdot)$, by β, where $0 < \beta < 1$. In the calculation of $V_2(\cdot)$, the real objective function is once again used in the maximization, and the initial guess, now hidden inside $V_1(\cdot)$, has been discounted by $\beta^2 < \beta$. As the process is repeated, the importance of the initial guess, $V_0(\cdot)$, goes to zero and what remains are the effects of the repeated maximizations of the objective function.

It turns out that in the repeated calculations of the value function, one is also calculating repeated approximations to the policy function. The limit of the sequence of y_t's that are found in the maximization process for each x_t are precisely the values that solve $y_t = H(x_t)$ for that value of x_t. The numerical method of successive approximations described above gives both the desired value function and the required policy functions.

4.4   RETURNING TO OUR EXAMPLE ECONOMY

It is useful to write out the example economy showing how each component matches with the general version.

In the example economy that we used in the first section of this chapter, we chose the capital stock at time t to be the state variable at time t, so $x_t = k_t$, and the capital stock at time $t + 1$ to be the control variable, so $y_t = k_{t+1}$. In this particular example, the control variable at time t was chosen so that it becomes the state variable at time $t + 1$. One should not expect this to be the normal case.

The objective function for the example economy is

$$F(x_t, y_t) = u(f(k_t) - k_{t+1} + (1 - \delta)k_t),$$

and the budget constraint is written so that the time $t + 1$ state variable is

$$k_{t+1} = x_{t+1} = G(x_t, y_t) = y_t = k_{t+1}.$$

This statement says simply that the time $t + 1$ state variable (the part: $k_{t+1} = x_{t+1}$) is equal to the time t budget constraint, which in this case is equal to the time t control variable (that $y_t = G(x_t, y_t) = k_{t+1}$). The first-order condition for this economy is

$$0 = F_y(x_t, y_t) + \beta V'(G(x_t, y_t))G_y(x_t, y_t)$$

$$= -u'(f(k_t) - k_{t+1} + (1 - \delta)k_t) + \beta V'(G(x_t, y_t)) \cdot 1. \qquad (4.8)$$

This choice for the budget constraint is very useful for solving the model. Recall that the Benveniste-Scheinkman envelope theorem gives

$$V'(x_t) = F_x(x_t, y_t) + \beta V'(G(x_t, y_t))G_x(x_t, y_t).$$

For our example, the derivative of the budget constraint with respect to the time t state variable is simply

$$G_x(x_t, y_t) = \frac{\partial x_{t+1}}{\partial x_t} = 0,$$

so that the envelope theorem condition can be simplified to

$$V'(x_t) = F_x(x_t, y_t) = u'(f(k_t) - k_{t+1} + (1-\delta)k_t)\left(f'(k_t) + (1-\delta)\right),$$

and the derivative of the value function is defined in terms of functions that we know. We substitute this into equation 4.8 and get the result that

$$0 = -u'(f(k_t) - k_{t+1} + (1-\delta)k_t)$$
$$+ \beta\left[u'(f(k_{t+1}) - k_{t+2} + (1-\delta)k_{t+1})\left(f'(k_{t+1}) + (1-\delta)\right)\right].$$

This second-order difference equation can be solved for the stationary state, where $\bar{k} = k_t = k_{t+1} = k_{t+2}$, to give

$$f'(\bar{k}) = \frac{1}{\beta} - (1-\delta). \tag{4.9}$$

4.4.1 Another Version of the Same Economy

The example economy can be written with different choices for the control variables. The state variable in this version is still time t capital, $x_t = k_t$, but one can choose time t consumption to be the time t control variable, $y_t = c_t$. In that case, we need to redefine the objective function and the budget constraints. With this definition of controls, the objective function is

$$F(x_t, y_t) = u(c_t),$$

and the budget constraint is

$$k_{t+1} = x_{t+1} = G(x_t, y_t) = f(k_t) + (1-\delta)k_t - c_t.$$

Writing out the model, we have the Bellman equation,

$$V(k_t) = \max_{c_t}\left[u(c_t) + \beta V\left(f(k_t) + (1-\delta)k_t - c_t\right)\right],$$

where we have replaced the time $t+1$ state variable, $x_{t+1} = k_{t+1}$, by the budget constraint in the $V(x_{t+1})$ part of the Bellman equation. It should be clear that the problem given above is the exact same economic problem that we solved in the first version of the example economy.

This version is somewhat less convenient than the earlier version when we try to write out the condition from the Benveniste-Scheinkman envelope theorem. When we take the derivative of the budget constraint with respect to the time t state variable, we get

$$\frac{\partial G(x_t, y_t)}{\partial x_t} = f'(k_t) + (1 - \delta),$$

and this is generally not equal to zero. If we then write out the envelope theorem condition, we get

$$V'(x_t) = F_x(x_t, y_t) + \beta V'(G(x_t, y_t))G_x(x_t, y_t)$$
$$= \beta V'(f(k_t) + (1 - \delta)k_t - c_t)\left(f'(k_t) + (1 - \delta)\right),$$

and we have the derivative of the value function in terms of the derivative of the value function and some other terms, which is no improvement.

One of the important tricks (simplifications) of working with the Bellman equation is to write out the objective function and the budget constraints so that one gets a convenient version of the envelope theorem, that is, so that $G_x(x_t, y_t) = 0$. Doing this usually means putting as much of the model as possible into the objective function and requires keeping the time t state variable out of the budget constraint.

4.5　AN APPROXIMATION OF THE VALUE FUNCTION

As claimed above, we can use numerical methods to find an approximation of the value function (and the policy function) for specific economies. Consider the specific functions of the example economy that we used in Chapter 3 but with fixed labor supply at $h_t = 1$, where the production function is

$$f(k_t) = k_t^\theta,$$

for $0 < \theta < 1$, and the utility function is

$$u(c_t) = \ln(c_t).$$

We can write the Bellman equation as

$$V(k_t) = \max_{k_{t+1}} \left[\ln(k_t^\theta - k_{t+1} + (1 - \delta)k_t) + \beta V(k_{t+1})\right].$$

To use the recursive method of calculating the approximate $V(\cdot)$, we need to choose values for δ, θ, β, and a functional form for $V_0(\cdot)$. Let $\delta = 0.1$ and $\theta = 0.36$ as in the example economy of Chapter 1. Let $\beta = .98$, which is consistent with estimations of the discount factor for models with annual data. The simplest form to choose for the initial guess of the value function is the constant function, $V_0(k_{t+1}) \equiv 0$, for all values of k_{t+1}. Using the equation for the stationary state that we found above (equation 4.9), we find that stationary state values for this model are at $k = 0$, and where

$$.36 \cdot \bar{k}^{-.64} = \frac{1}{.98} - (1 - .1),$$

or where $\bar{k} = 5.537$.

After three iterations of the recursive approximation procedure, the calculated value function has moved from a constant at zero (the line labeled $V_0(k_t)$) to the line labeled "third iteration" in Figure 4.1. The discount parameter, β, is close to one so the iterations of the value function converge relatively slowly to the true value function. Figure 4.2 shows how the value function is converging after 240 iterations. Each of the lines shown in the figure represents the results of 48 iterations, so there are a total of 6 lines shown (the initial line at zero and the 5 lines that come from the calculations). The highest line is the last calculated and is marked 240. The number associated with each line is the number of iterations. It should be clear from the graph that the steps are gradually getting smaller as the number of iterations increases and the line moves upward.

The policy function for this economy, which finds the optimizing value of k_{t+1} for each value of k_t, is generated at the same time as the value functions. The one for our example economy, after 240 iterations, is shown in Figure 4.3

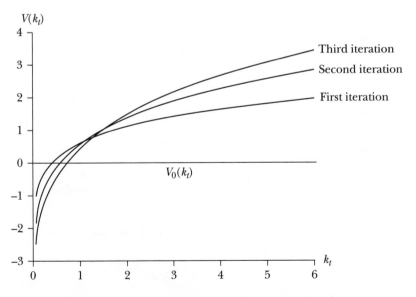

FIGURE 4.1 Value function, first three approximations

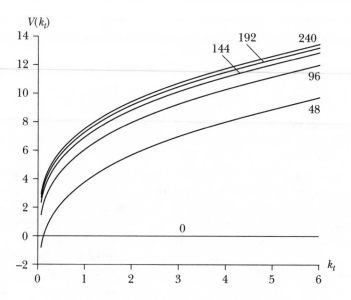

FIGURE 4.2   Approximating the value function

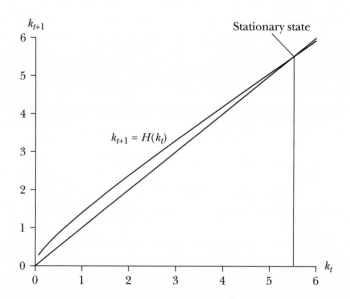

FIGURE 4.3   The policy function after 240 iterations

as the function $k_{t+1} = H(k_t)$. Notice that this function crosses the 45 degree line at the stationary state value of 5.537.

4.6 AN EXAMPLE WITH VARIABLE LABOR

It might be useful to show that recursive methods can be applied to the Robinson Crusoe economy from Chapter 3 where labor was a variable input. Recall that the utility function used there was

$$\sum_{i=0}^{\infty} \beta^i u(c_{t+i}, h_{t+i}),$$

which was maximized subject to the constraints

$$k_{t+1} = (1 - \delta)k_t + i_t,$$

$$y_t = f(k_t, h_t) \geq c_t + i_t,$$

$$h_t \leq 1.$$

This problem can be written quite naturally as the Bellman equation,

$$V(k_t) = \max_{h_t, k_{t+1}} \left[u(f(k_t, h_t) + (1 - \delta)k_t - k_{t+1}, h_t) + \beta V(k_{t+1}) \right].$$

Here the budget constraint is

$$k_{t+1} = G(k_{t+1}) = k_{t+1},$$

which implies that the condition $G_x(x_t, y_t) = 0$ is met, so Benveniste-Scheinkman's envelope theorem condition has a simple representation.

There are now two first-order conditions since there are two controls, h_t and k_{t+1}. These conditions are

$$\frac{\partial V(k_t)}{\partial h_t} = 0 = u_c(f(k_t, h_t) + (1 - \delta)k_t - k_{t+1}, h_t) f_h(k_t, h_t)$$

$$+ u_h(f(k_t, h_t) + (1 - \delta)k_t - k_{t+1}, h_t)$$

and

$$\frac{\partial V(k_t)}{\partial k_{t+1}} = 0 = -u_c(f(k_t, h_t) + (1 - \delta)k_t - k_{t+1}, h_t) + \beta V'(k_{t+1}).$$

The envelope theorem condition is

$$V'(k_t) = u_c(f(k_t, h_t) + (1 - \delta)k_t - k_{t+1}, h_t) \left(f_k(k_t, h_t) + (1 - \delta) \right).$$

These conditions result in the equations

$$\frac{u_h(f(k_t, h_t) + (1 - \delta)k_t - k_{t+1}, h_t)}{u_c(f(k_t, h_t) + (1 - \delta)k_t - k_{t+1}, h_t)} = -f_h(k_t, h_t)$$

and

$$\frac{u_c(f(k_t, h_t) + (1 - \delta)k_t - k_{t+1}, h_t)}{u_c(f(k_{t+1}, h_{t+1}) + (1 - \delta)k_{t+1} - k_{t+2}, h_{t+1})} = \beta\left[f_k(k_{t+1}, h_{t+1}) + (1 - \delta)\right],$$

which are the same conditions we found for this model in Chapter 3 (equations 3.2 and 3.3) and lead to the same results for a stationary state as we found there.

This model can also be calculated numerically to find approximations for the value function, $V(\cdot)$, and for the *two* policy functions, $k_{t+1} = H^k(k_t)$ and $h_t = H^h(k_t)$. One chooses an initial guess for the value function ($V_0(\cdot) = 0$ is frequently convenient) and repeatedly calculates

$$V_{j+1}(k_t) = \max_{h_t, k_{t+1}} \left[u(f(k_t, h_t) + (1 - \delta)k_t - k_{t+1}, h_t) + \beta V_j(k_{t+1})\right],$$

for $j = 0, \ldots$ over a sufficiently dense set of k_t. The sequence of functions, $V_{j+1}(k_t)$, converge to the value function, $V(k_t)$, as $j \to \infty$. As in the case above where labor was fixed, each iteration of this procedure will find the optimizing values for k_{t+1} and h_t for each member of the k_t set that was used. This sequence of functions gives approximations for the policy functions that converge to the policy functions $H^k(\cdot)$ and $H^h(\cdot)$ as $j \to \infty$.

We find the value function for an example economy similar to the one that we used earlier in this chapter: the parameters are $\delta = .1, \theta = .36, \beta = .98,$ and $A = .5$, the utility function used is

$$u(c_t, h_t) = \ln(c_t) + A \ln(1 - h_t),$$

and the production function used is

$$f(k_t, h_t) = k_t^{\theta} h_t^{1-\theta}.$$

Figure 4.4 shows the approximate value functions converging upward. The lines shown are $V_m(k_t)$, for iterations numbered $m = 30, 60, 90, \ldots, 240$. Figure 4.5 shows the final policy functions (after 240 iterations) for time $t + 1$ capital, $k_{t+1} = H^k(k_t)$, and for time t labor input, $h_t = H^h(k_t)$, along with the 45 degree line so that the value of k_t in the stationary state can be seen. As one might suspect, the amount of labor supplied along an equilibrium path declines as the capital stock increases.

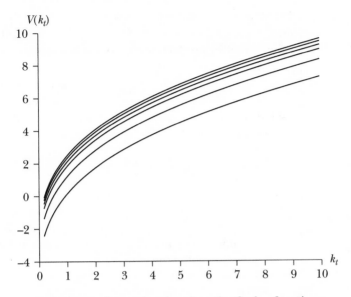

FIGURE 4.4 Approximating the pair of value functions

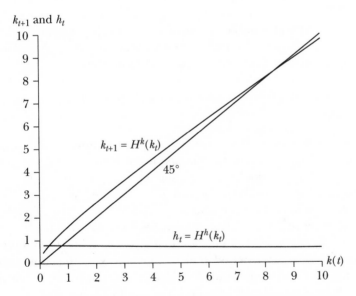

FIGURE 4.5 The two policy functions after 240 iterations

EXERCISE 4.1 A Robinson Crusoe economy has the production function $y_t = k_t^\theta h_t^\psi n_t^{1-\theta-\psi}$, where n_t is human capital used in production and $0 < \psi < 1$. Human capital grows according to the technology, $n_{t+1} = N(n_t, s_t) = (1 - \gamma) n_t + \kappa s_t$, where $0 < \gamma < 1$ is the rate of depreciation of human capital, $\kappa > 0$, and $s_t > 0$ is the time spent studying. An individual has an endowment of one unit of labor each period and spends it according to the budget constraint

$$1 = l_t + h_t + s_t.$$

The utility function is a discounted infinite horizon one with the subutility function $u(c_t, l_t) = \ln(c_t) + A \ln(l_t)$. Write out the recursive optimization problem and find the first-order conditions. (As an additional task, modify the Matlab program at the end of this chapter to find the approximate value and policy functions.)

EXERCISE 4.2 Write out the value function for a Robinson Crusoe economy with habit persistence with a utility function of the form $u(c_t, c_{t-1}) = \ln c_t - \xi \ln c_{t-1}$ with $0 < \xi < 1$ and with the rest of the economy the same as the one in section 4.1. Define the state and control variables. Find the approximate value function using Matlab.

4.7 REPRISE

Recursive models have a particular and useful structure. In every period, an agent is solving the same optimization problem: in our case, maximizing the same additive infinite horizon discounted utility function subject to the same budget constraints. What can be different in every period are the state variables, the results of the previous period's decisions and initial conditions that determine the values of some variables today. This structure permits surmising that there exists a function that gives the value of the optimized discounted utility in each period. If such a function exists, the infinite horizon problem can be rewritten as a single-period problem, the Bellman equation.

Unfortunately, the value function is not usually known, but Bellman has shown that, for problems where the functions are given, an iterative process allows us to approximate it with whatever degree of accuracy our computer and patience permits. As we find the value function, we also find the policy functions: the functions that tell us the values we should choose for the choice variables given the state variables.

Since Bellman proved his result, the literature on dynamic programming has grown to be very large. Of particular interest to economists are the books of Ljungqvist and Sargent [54] and of Stokey, Lucas, and Prescott [83]. The first of these books is more accessible and demonstrates a wide range of economic problems that can be treated with these techniques. The second book is technically more difficult and provides the mathematical foundations for the techniques. Only a small part of these books deals with the deterministic problem, so they are also references for future chapters.

4.8   MATLAB CODE FOR FIGURES 4.2 AND 4.3

MAIN PROGRAM

```
global vlast beta delta theta k0 kt
hold off
hold all
%set initial conditions
vlast=zeros(1,100);
k0=0.06:0.06:6;
beta=.98;
delta=.1;
theta=.36;
numits=240;
%begin the recursive calculations
for k=1:numits
    for j=1:100
        kt=j*.06;
        %find the maximum of the value function
        ktp1=fminbnd(@valfun,0.01,6.2);
        v(j)=-valfun(ktp1);
        kt1(j)=ktp1;
    end
    if k/48==round(k/48)
        %plot the steps in finding the value function
        plot(k0,v)
        drawnow
    end
    vlast=v;
end
hold off
% plot the final policy function
plot(k0,kt1)
```

SUBROUTINE (VALFUN.M) TO CALCULATE VALUE FUNCTION

```
function val=valfun(k)
    global vlast beta delta theta k0 kt
```

```
%smooth out the previous value function
g=interp1(k0,vlast,k,'linear');
%Calculate consumption with given parameters
kk=kt^theta-k+(1-delta)*kt;
if kk <= 0
    %trick to keep values from going negative
    val=-888-800*abs(kk);
else
    %calculate the value of the value function at k
    val=log(kk)+beta*g;
end
%change value to negative since "fminbnd" finds minimum
val=-val;
```

5

Recursive Stochastic Models

Up to this point, except for short sections of Chapters 1 and 2, our models have been deterministic. The values of all of the parameters of the models and the form of the functions are known with certainty. Given some initial condition, these economies follow a prescribed path.

Models are approximations of reality and being approximations are at least (or, at best, only) partially false. The predictions that a model makes, even a very good and very complete model, will not coincide with what occurs. This failure of models to predict perfectly comes from two potential sources.

One source of this failure to predict perfectly is that these are variables that are not included in the model but that impact on the values of the variables included. Our (admittedly very simple) model of a deterministic Robinson Crusoe economy tells us how the decisions about how much to save and how much to work affect the amount of output in the economy but does not account for how the economy responds to the weather, to the physical and mental health of Robinson, or to the chance arrival of a book on tropical horticulture that gets washed up on a beach. Under this logic, if a model were sufficiently rich, it would be able to predict future outcomes with very great accuracy. However, our capacity to collect information and to construct, to test, and to solve models is limited, not the least by the capacity of our minds. Since we know we can't include everything in a model, one way to handle that which we cannot include is to allow the model to be stochastic. We simply let some part of the model, the value of some parameters in each period, for example, be determined by "nature," where nature embodies everything that is not in our model.

A second source may be that the universe is simply naturally stochastic and there are things that we cannot predict with absolute certainty even if we have full information about the current state of the universe. This idea is fairly well accepted in quantum physics, but is much more open to debate when more macro processes are studied. Many people are uncomfortable with the idea that their world could be inherently random. In fact, the whole area of mathematics know as "chaos theory" is based on adding extra dimensions to problems so that what looks like chaotic or random behavior in low dimensions is explained by a perfectly deterministic model in higher dimensions. The goal of chaos theory is to eliminate randomness.

Whatever its source, for an economist it is convenient to assume that the world is stochastic and that the way this randomness intrudes in our models can be described by probabilities. Adding a little randomness goes a long way in helping the predictions of our models better match the data that we observe.

5.1 PROBABILITY

Before discussing models with stochastic shocks, it is worth taking some time to briefly define exactly what is meant by probability and by a probability space. A probability space $(\Omega, \mathcal{F}, P)$ is comprised of three elements: 1) Ω, a set that contains all the states of nature that might occur, 2) $\mathcal{F}$, a collection of subsets of Ω, where each subset is called an event,[1] and 3) P, a probability measure over $\mathcal{F}$.

First consider what this means when Ω is a finite set of possible states of nature. For example, it might contain just two possible values for technology, A_1 and A_2. Then a natural way to define $\mathcal{F}$ is with four elements: the empty set, [ ], A_1, A_2, and the set $[A_1, A_2]$. A probability measure for these four sets is 0 for the empty set, some value $0 \le p_1 \le 1$ for A_1, $p_2 = 1 - p_1$ for A_2, and 1 for the set $[A_1, A_2]$. This says that either A_1 or A_2 will occur and, for a large enough sample, A_1 will occur with frequency p_1. For larger finite sets of possible states of nature, the structure is the same, but there are simply more elements to $\mathcal{F}$. If Ω were comprised of three elements, $A_1 = .9$, $A_2 = 1.05$, $A_3 = 1.10$, then, in addition to the sets given above, $\mathcal{F}$ would include A_3, $[A_1, A_3]$, $[A_2, A_3]$, and $[A_1, A_2, A_3]$. The event $[A_2, A_3]$ contains all possible technology levels greater than 1 and occurs with probability $p_2 + p_3$ (when the underlying events are independent and A_1 occurs with probability p_1, A_2 with p_2, A_3 with p_3 and $p_1 + p_2 + p_3 = 1$).

---

1. Strictly speaking, the set $\mathcal{F}$ of subsets of Ω needs to be a σ-field. A σ-field has the following properties: if subset A is a member of $\mathcal{F}$, then so is the complement of A (all elements of Ω excluding those in A). If subsets A and B are members of $\mathcal{F}$, so are the intersection, $A \cap B$, and union, $A \cup B$. In addition, a countably infinite union of sets in $\mathcal{F}$ is in $\mathcal{F}$.

It may seem like one goes to too much trouble with defining $\mathcal{F}$, the set of subsets of Ω, and then probabilities over this subset. In the finite case, with independent underlying events, one can frequently simply define the probability measure over the elements of Ω. Each underlying event has its probability, and the probability of any subset of these events is found by summing the probabilities of the events that make up the subset.

When the set of possible states of nature is continuous, then the definition is more useful. Consider a growth model where technology, A_t, can take on any value in the set [.9, 1.2], the closed continuous set of values between .9 and 1.2, that includes the end points. Suppose that the probability distribution is uniform, so that, in some sense, any value is equally as likely as any other inside the set. In this case, the probability that in some given period t, $A_t =$ 1.15565, for example, is zero. With a uniform distribution, or any continuous distribution, for that matter, the probability that technology has any specific value in any specific period is always zero.

It is in this case that defining subsets of [.9, 1.2] becomes useful. Imagine that we want to know the probability that technology will have a value in period t between .97 and 1.03. Since this is a uniform distribution, this probability can be calculated as $.06/.3 = .2$, or 20%. Although the probability of any one value occurring for A_t is always zero in this example, for any positive range of values, one can usually find a positive probability. Therefore, by defining probabilities over subsets of the states of nature, the definition encompasses situations with a continuous range of possible states of nature.

Note that it is not always the case that in situations with a continuous range of states of nature, the probability of a single value is zero. Consider the range of states of nature for the exact daily rainfall in Buenos Aires. Over the last 100 years, the range has been from zero to slightly over 300 millimeters. However, there have been a great many days in which the rainfall was zero so that the probability of zero rainfall has a positive value. The probability of any other specific number is zero. The probability distribution is not continuous at zero, and the point zero contains a positive mass of probability.

5.2 A SIMPLE STOCHASTIC GROWTH MODEL

Imagine that the economy is much like that in the infinite horizon Robinson Crusoe model except that the production function in period t is

$$y_t = A^t f(k_t),$$

where the production function, $f(k_t)$, is an increasing, concave function of the capital stock (assuming that a constant 1 unit of labor is supplied) and A^t can take on two values (two states of nature, as they are called) where the level of technology given by

$$A^t = \begin{cases} A_1 \text{ with probability } p_1 \\ A_2 \text{ with probability } p_2 \end{cases}.$$

We assume that A_1 and A_2 are the only values that technology can take, so $p_1 + p_2 = 1$. The realization of A_i in any period is independent of the realizations that occurred in the past and those that will occur in the future. The probabilities p_1 and p_2 should be interpreted to mean that as the sample size increases, the fraction of periods in which we observe A_1 goes to p_1 and the fraction of periods in which we observe A_2 goes to p_2. To put some order on things, we assume that $A_1 > A_2$, or that the technology is more productive in state 1 than it is in state 2. As this model is written, there is no technological growth. There are two kinds of periods, one where, with the same capital, output is greater than in the other. One can think of a farming economy where state 1, in which the technology has the value A_1, is when good weather occurs and state 2, with the technology of value A_2, is when bad weather occurs. This is an appropriate example because we often speak of the states 1 and 2 as states of nature in which nature, with probabilities p_1 and p_2, chooses the state that occurs in any period t.

The rest of the model is similar, but not identical, to earlier growth models. The capital stock grows by the equation

$$k_{t+1} = A^t f(k_t) + (1 - \delta)k_t - c_t.$$

At time 0, Robinson Crusoe wants to maximize an *expected* discounted utility function of the form

$$E_0 \sum_{t=0}^{\infty} \beta^t u(c_t).$$

The choice of consumption in each period will depend on both the capital stock of that period and the realization of technology in that period. Since future realizations of technology are not known, it is not possible to choose a complete consumption path. In fact, future consumption plans are represented by a kind of tree. Given some initial capital k_0, in period 0 there are two possible technology levels that could occur and two different amounts of production, represented by the ordered pair $[A_1 f(k_0), A_2 f(k_0)]$, with probabilities $[p_1, p_2]$. Depending on which state occurs in period 0, R.C. will choose some time 1 capital stocks of $[k_1^1, k_1^2]$. In period 1, production will be one of these four possibilities, $[A_1 f(k_1^1), A_2 f(k_1^1), A_1 f(k_1^2), A_2 f(k_1^2)]$, with probabilities $[p_1 p_1, p_1 p_2, p_2 p_1, p_2 p_2]$. These probabilities occur because there was a probability of p_1 that the capital would be k_1^1, and once that capital stock was chosen there was a probability p_1 that nature would choose the technology level A_1 in period 1. Notice that the four probabilities sum to one, $p_1 p_1 + p_1 p_2 = p_1$ and $p_2 p_1 + p_2 p_2 = p_2$, and $p_1 + p_2 = 1$. In period 1 there are four possible k_2^i that can be chosen that result in eight possible levels of output in period 2. In this way, the number of possible consumptions doubles in each period. One doesn't know which path will occur, but one can find the probability of each path.

Suppose that one can write the value of the maximum expected discounted utility given an initial capital stock of k_0, when the time 0 realization of technology is A_1, as

$$V(k_0, A_1) = \max_{\{c_t\}_{t=0}^{\infty}} E_0 \sum_{t=0}^{\infty} \beta^t u(c_t),$$

subject to the budget constraint for $t = 0$,

$$k_1 = A_1 f(k_0) + (1 - \delta)k_0 - c_0,$$

and those for $t \geq 1$,

$$k_{t+1} = A^t f(k_t) + (1 - \delta)k_t - c_t,$$

and the independent realizations of $A^t = [A_1, A_2]$ with probabilities $[p_1, p_2]$. One can write an almost identical expression for $V(k_0, A_2)$, the maximum expected discounted utility for the same initial capital stock when the time 0 realization of technology is A_2, by simply replacing A_1 with A_2 in the first budget constraint.

Notice that the value of expected utility is a function of two state variables, the amount of capital that is available in the period and the realization of the technology shock in that period. As shown in the previous chapter, this expression can be written recursively as

$$V(k_0, A^0) = \max_{c_0} \left[u(c_0) + \beta E_0 V \left(k_1, A^1 \right) \right]$$

subject to the budget constraint

$$k_1 = A^0 f(k_0) + (1 - \delta)k_0 - c_0.$$

There is a subtle change in how the value function is written; it is now written as a *function* of the time 0 realization of the technology shock. As this function is written, k_0 and A^0 are the state variables and c_0 is the control variable. The second part of the value function is written with the expectations term because given a choice for c_0 (and through the budget constraint of k_1), it will have a value of $V(k_1, A_1)$ with probability p_1, and a value of $V(k_1, A_2)$ with probability p_2. For any particular choice $\widehat{k}_1$ of the time 1 capital stock, the expectations expression is equal to

$$E_0 V \left(\widehat{k}_1, A^1 \right) = p_1 V \left(\widehat{k}_1, A_1 \right) + p_2 V \left(\widehat{k}_1, A_2 \right).$$

For any initial time period t, the problem can be written as

$$V(k_t, A^t) = \max_{c_t} \left[u(c_t) + \beta E_t V \left(k_{t+1}, A^{t+1} \right) \right],$$

subject to the budget constraint

$$k_{t+1} = A^t f(k_t) + (1 - \delta)k_t - c_t.$$

Of course, as we have seen earlier, there are other ways to define the object function and budget constraints so that we have different choices for state variables and control variables. When we rewrite the problem with k_{t+1} as the control variable, it becomes

$$V(k_t, A^t) = \max_{k_{t+1}} \left[u(A^t f(k_t) + (1 - \delta)k_t - k_{t+1}) + \beta E_t V \left(k_{t+1}, A^{t+1} \right) \right], \quad (5.1)$$

and the budget constraint (using the notation of Chapter 4) is

$$k_{t+1} = G(x_t, y_t) = k_{t+1}.$$

The solution to a stochastic recursive problem like that in equation 5.1 finds a function that gives the values of the control variables that maximizes the value function over the domain of the state variables. Since the state variables include both the results of previous choices of control variables and the results of nature's choices of the value for the stochastic state variables, we call the solution function a *plan* and write it (for the problem in equation 5.1) as

$$k_{t+1} = H(k_t, A^t).$$

The plan gives the optimizing choice of the control variables in every period as a function of the regular state variables and of the states of nature. A plan fulfills the condition that

$$V(k_t, A^t) = u(A^t f(k_t) + (1 - \delta)k_t - H(k_t, A^t)) + \beta E_t V \left(H(k_t, A^t), A^{t+1} \right),$$

where no maximization is required because the plan chooses the maximizing values for the control variables.

5.3   A GENERAL VERSION

Using the notation of section 4.3, we can write the value function as

$$V(x_t, z_t) = \max_{\{y_s\}_{s=t}^{\infty}} E_t \sum_{s=t}^{\infty} \beta^{s-t} F(x_s, y_s, z_s),$$

subject to the set of budget constraints given by

$$x_{s+1} = G(x_s, y_s, z_s),$$

for $s \geq t$, where x_t is the set of "regular" state variables and z_t is the set of state variables determined by nature, the stochastic state variables. The y_t are the control variables. Both the objective function, $F(x_s, y_s, z_s)$, and the budget constraints, $G(x_s, y_s, z_s)$, can be functions of the stochastic state variables.

This problem can be written recursively as a Bellman equation of the form

$$V(x_t, z_t) = \max_{y_t} \left[F(x_t, y_t, z_t) + \beta E_t V(x_{t+1}, z_{t+1}) \right], \qquad (5.2)$$

subject to the budget constraint

$$x_{t+1} = G(x_t, y_t, z_t).$$

The solution (what was previously called a policy function) is a *plan* (a function) of the form

$$y_t = H(x_t, z_t),$$

where

$$V(x_t, z_t) = F(x_t, H(x_t, z_t), z_t) + \beta E_t V(G(x_t, H(x_t, z_t), z_t), z_{t+1})$$

holds for all values of the state variables (including the stochastic state variables).

The first-order conditions for the problem in equation 5.2, and its budget constraints, are

$$0 = F_y(x_t, y_t, z_t) + \beta E_t \left[V_x(G(x_t, y_t, z_t), z_{t+1}) G_y(x_t, y_t, z_t) \right],$$

where $X_q()$ is the partial derivative of function $X()$ with respect to variable q, where q can be a vector.

In addition, for interior solutions, we have the Benveniste-Scheinkman envelope theorem result,

$$V_x(x_t, z_t) = F_x(x_t, y_t, z_t) + \beta E_t \left[V_x(G(x_t, y_t, z_t), z_{t+1}) G_x(x_t, y_t, z_t) \right].$$

When one is able to choose the controls so that $G_x(x_t, y_t, z_t) = 0$, the above equation is

$$V_x(x_t, z_t) = F_x(x_t, y_t, z_t),$$

and the first-order conditions give the Euler equation (a stochastic Euler equation),

$$0 = F_y(x_t, y_t, z_t) + \beta E_t \left[F_x(G(x_t, y_t, z_t), y_{t+1}, z_{t+1}) G_y(x_t, y_t, z_t) \right].$$

Up to this point, the discussion of the general version has said nothing about the dimension of the stochastic variable z_t. In the example economy in the beginning of this chapter, the stochastic variable had only two possible realizations in any period. That the stochastic shock could take on so few values makes the exposition simple. In theory, there is no necessity that the dimension be small, and it is quite possible to describe a model in which the realization of the stochastic variable comes from a continuous distribution (one with an uncountable infinite set of possible realizations). In practice, the dimension of the state space and the variables in it do matter.

5.3.1   The Problem of Dimensionality

Logically, it should be possible to follow the same technique that we used in the deterministic case and begin with an initial guess for the value function, a function $V_0(x_t, z_t)$, and iterate on the equation

$$V_{j+1}(x_t, z_t) = \max_{y_t} \left[F(x_t, y_t, z_t) + \beta E_t V_j(G(x_t, y_t, z_t), z_{t+1}) \right]$$

to find approximations of the value function and the policy functions (the plans) that converge on the actual value function and plans. Indeed, it is possible to find the approximations numerically if the dimensions of x_t and z_t are not too big. For the calculations in the deterministic case, we used a reasonable dense discrete subset of the continuous domain of x_t and, when needed, found values between these points using a linear interpolation. If the dimension of the discrete domain of x_t (call it $dim\left(x_t\right)$) is not too large and the $V(x_t)$ function does not have too much curvature, this process gives useful results.

Once we add the stochastic state variables, the dimension of the optimization problem increases by the product of the dimension of these stochastic variables. If we add only one stochastic variable, the dimension of that variable is the discrete sampling that we do of its domain (call it $dim(z_t)$). The dimension of the calculations for the stochastic case is then $dim\left(x_t\right) dim(z_t)$, the product of the dimension of the discrete domain of the original state variable times the discrete domain of the stochastic variable. If one is using numerical techniques to calculate iterations of the value function, the number of points to be found in each iteration can become quite burdensome.

5.4 THE VALUE FUNCTION FOR THE SIMPLE ECONOMY

Using the model we built in the first section of this chapter, we describe how to find the value functions and the plans. The stochastic variable, A^t, has only two possible realizations, given by the ordered pair $[A_1, A_2]$ with constant probabilities $[p_1, p_2]$. We can write equation 5.1 as a pair of Bellman equations, one for each of the two possible time t realizations of A^t, as

$$V(k_t, A_1) = \max_{k_{t+1}} \left[u(A_1 f(k_t) + (1 - \delta)k_t - k_{t+1}) \right.$$

$$\left. + \beta \left[p_1 V\left(k_{t+1}, A_1\right) + p_2 V\left(k_{t+1}, A_2\right)\right]\right]$$

and

$$V(k_t, A_2) = \max_{k_{t+1}} \left[u(A_2 f(k_t) + (1 - \delta)k_t - k_{t+1}) \right.$$

$$\left. + \beta \left[p_1 V\left(k_{t+1}, A_1\right) + p_2 V\left(k_{t+1}, A_2\right)\right]\right]$$

where the expectations part of the value function, $E_t V\left(k_{t+1}, A^{t+1}\right)$, is replaced by its explicit representation, $p_1 V\left(k_{t+1}, A_1\right) + p_2 V\left(k_{t+1}, A_2\right)$. In this economy, for each choice of k_{t+1}, the expected value, $E_t V\left(k_{t+1}, A^{t+1}\right)$, is equal to the time $t + 1$ value of discounted utility when nature chooses A_1 as the technology shock times the probability of this shock being chosen plus the value of discounted utility when nature chooses A_2 times the probability of nature choosing A_2.

The iteration process requires choosing starting functions for both $V_0(k_t, A_1)$ and $V_0(k_t, A_2)$. Given these initial functions, the functions from the first iteration, $V_1(k_t, A_1)$ and $V_1(k_t, A_2)$, are found by simultaneously calculating

$$V_1(k_t, A_1) = \max_{k_{t+1}} \left[u(A_1 f(k_t) + (1 - \delta)k_t - k_{t+1}) \right.$$

$$\left. + \beta \left[p_1 V_0\left(k_{t+1}, A_1\right) + p_2 V_0\left(k_{t+1}, A_2\right)\right]\right]$$

and

$$V_1(k_t, A_2) = \max_{k_{t+1}} \left[u(A_2 f(k_t) + (1 - \delta)k_t - k_{t+1}) \right.$$

$$\left. + \beta \left[p_1 V_0\left(k_{t+1}, A_1\right) + p_2 V_0\left(k_{t+1}, A_2\right)\right]\right]$$

over the discrete subset of values of k_t. To find the results of the next iterations, $V_2(k_t, A_1)$ and $V_2(k_t, A_2)$, we calculate

$$V_2(k_t, A_1) = \max_{k_{t+1}} \left[u(A_1 f(k_t) + (1 - \delta)k_t - k_{t+1}) \right.$$

$$\left. + \beta \left[p_1 V_1 \left(k_{t+1}, A_1 \right) + p_2 V_1 \left(k_{t+1}, A_2 \right) \right] \right]$$

and

$$V_2(k_t, A_2) = \max_{k_{t+1}} \left[u(A_2 f(k_t) + (1 - \delta)k_t - k_{t+1}) \right.$$

$$\left. + \beta \left[p_1 V_1 \left(k_{t+1}, A_1 \right) + p_2 V_1 \left(k_{t+1}, A_2 \right) \right] \right],$$

using the two $V_1(k_t, A^t)$ functions we found in the previous iteration. Repeated iterations result in a sequence of pairs of functions $\left\{ V_j(k_t, A_1), V_j(k_t, A_2) \right\}_{j=0}^{\infty}$ that converge to the desired pair of value functions, $\left[V(k_t, A_1), V(k_t, A_2) \right]$.

5.4.1 Calculating the Value Functions

Using the parameters from our standard example economy, $\delta = .1$, $\beta = .98$, $\theta = .36$, the production function, $f(k_t) = k_t^\theta$, and the subutility function, $\ln(c_t)$, we add the values of the stochastic state variable, $A_1 = 1.75$, $p_1 = .8$, $A_2 = .75$, and $p_2 = .2$. We choose constant initial value functions, $V_0(k_t, A_1) = 20$ and $V_0(k_t, A_2) = 20$. The first round of iterations results in calculations for $V_1(k_t, A^t)$ of

$$V_1(k_t, A_1 = 1.75) = \max_{k_{t+1}} \ln(1.75k_t^{.36} + .9k_t - k_{t+1}) + 19.6$$

and

$$V_1(k_t, A_2 = .75) = \max_{k_{t+1}} \ln(.75k_t^{.36} + .9k_t - k_{t+1}) + 19.6,$$

where the number 19.6 is simply 20 discounted by .98. The values of the two discounted next period value functions are the same in these two equations because we chose the same value for the initial guesses. In the next round, $V_1(k_t, A^t)$ will have different values for $A^t = A_1 = 1.75$ and $A^t = A_2 = .75$. The $V_2(k_t, A^t)$ functions are found maximizing

$$V_2(k_t, 1.75) = \max_{k_{t+1}} \left\{ \ln(1.75k_t^{.36} + .9k_t - k_{t+1}) \right.$$

$$\left. + \beta \left[.8V_1 \left(k_{t+1}, 1.75 \right) + .2V_1 \left(k_{t+1}, .75 \right) \right] \right\}$$

and

$$V_2(k_t, .75) = \max_{k_{t+1}} \left\{ \ln(.75k_t^{.36} + .9k_t - k_{t+1}) \right.$$

$$\left. + \beta \left[.8V_1 \left(k_{t+1}, 1.75 \right) + .2V_1 \left(k_{t+1}, .75 \right) \right] \right\}.$$

Continued iterations result in the value functions shown in Figure 5.1. In this figure, the two curves are shown every 50 iterations (the last is at iteration 250). The pair of policy functions that we have after 250 iterations is shown in Figure 5.2, where the lower one is for $A^t = .75$.

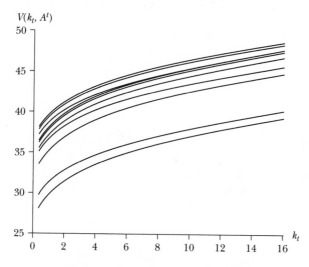

FIGURE 5.1   Iterations on the value function

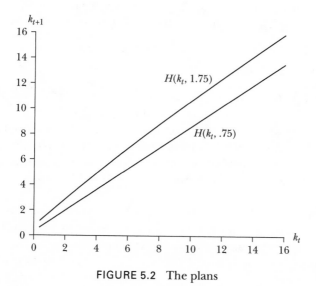

FIGURE 5.2   The plans

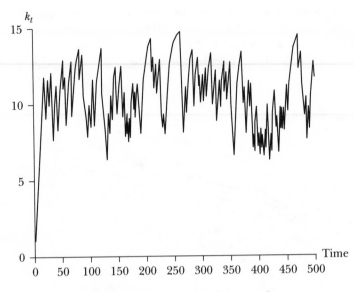

FIGURE 5.3   A simulated time path

One can generate simulations of the time paths of this economy using the plan and a uniform random number generation. Figure 5.3 shows a simulation of the time path of this economy beginning with $k_0 = 1$ and where, in each period, a uniform random number generation that produced numbers between 0 and 1 is used to determine whether nature has chosen state one or state two. State A_1 occurred in each period where the random number generator produced a value less than or equal to .8. Otherwise, state A_2 occurred.

5.5   MARKOV CHAINS

A somewhat richer random process can be obtained by the use of Markov chains. In a Markov chain, the probabilities for the realizations of the states of nature in period t are a function of the realization that occurred in period $t - 1$ and only in period $t - 1$. To be able to use our recursive methods, we want a Markov chain that is invariant with time; the probabilities depend on the realization that occurred in the previous period but not on which time period we are in.

There are three elements to a Markov chain stochastic process. The first is the set of realizations for the state of nature; in the example we have been using, it is the set of values that our A^t variable can take on. This set has a fixed, finite dimension, n, and $\{A^t\} = \{A_1, A_2, \ldots, A_n\}$. The dimension n and the values A_i are the same in every period. In the example economy above, $n = 2$ and $\{A^t\} = \{A_1 = 1.75, A_2 = .75\}$.

The second element of a Markov chain stochastic process is a matrix of transition probabilities, P, where element $p_{i,j}$ is the probability that state j will occur when the state of nature in the previous period was state i (which is the same as saying that A^{t-1} had value A_i). For, example, assume that A^t is the set from the earlier example, $A^t = \{1.75, .75\}$, and the probability matrix is

$$P = \begin{bmatrix} p_{11} & p_{12} \\ p_{21} & p_{22} \end{bmatrix} = \begin{bmatrix} .90 & .10 \\ .40 & .60 \end{bmatrix}.$$

In this case, if the previous realization of the state of nature, A^{t-1}, had been $A_1 = 1.75$, then there is a 90% probability that the realization in period t will have the same value and a 10% probability that it will have the value .75. If the realization of A^{t-1} had been $A_2 = .75$, then in period t, there is a 60% probability that this same value will occur and a 40% probability that the realization will have the value 1.75. A Markov chain allows the stochastic process to, among other things, show more persistence than in the first example economy. The values in the example are chosen so that there is a higher probability that the economy will stay in the current state of nature than that the economy will move to the other state.

The third element of a Markov chain stochastic process is the initial state of nature, from period $t - 1$, that determines the row of the P matrix where we begin (or the probability distribution of the initial period's stochastic variable if this is different from a row of P). With the initial distribution given, the probability of any future outcome can be calculated.

The probabilities given by the matrix P are conditional probabilities in the sense that once the economy is in the state of nature A_1, the top row of the P matrix describes the probabilities for the state of nature in the next period. Once the economy is in the state of nature A_2, the second row of the P matrix describes the probabilities of ending up in the state of nature A_1 or A_2 in the next period. These are conditional probabilities since they tell how the economy will proceed once it is in a particular state. We may also be interested in the *unconditional probabilities* of the occurrence of the states of nature in this economy. These are the probabilities that the economy will be in state of nature A_1 or in state of nature A_2 when we know nothing about previous states. If we run the economy long enough, the unconditional probabilities will tell us how often we observe state of nature A_1,[2] independent of the initial conditions. Unique invariant unconditional probability distributions exist if

---

2. The frequency with which we observe state of nature A_2 is simply equal to one minus the frequency with which we observe state of nature A_1.

every element of the P matrix is positive, if every $p_{i,j} > 0.$[3] When every element of P is positive, there is a positive probability of moving from any state of nature to any other state of nature.

We can use an example to show how the convergence works. Suppose that p_0 is the initial probability distribution (the one for period 1). The unconditional probability distribution for period 2 is $p_0 P$, given the initial distribution. Multiplying p_0 by the transition probabilities gives the probability distribution for period 2. In period 3, the distribution is $p_0 P^2 = p_0 P P$. In any period $n + 1$, the probability distribution for the states of nature is $p_0 P^n$. The claim is that as $n \to \infty$, $p_0 P^n \to P^\infty$ independently of the initial probability p_0.

Using the 2×2 matrix P above, we calculate a sequence of P^n's, for $n = 1, 2, \ldots.$ The first elements of this sequence are

$$P = \begin{bmatrix} .90 & .10 \\ .40 & .60 \end{bmatrix},$$

$$P^2 = \begin{bmatrix} .85 & .15 \\ .60 & .40 \end{bmatrix},$$

$$P^3 = \begin{bmatrix} .825 & .175 \\ .70 & .30 \end{bmatrix},$$

and in the limit,

$$P^\infty = \begin{bmatrix} .80 & .20 \\ .80 & .20 \end{bmatrix}.$$

Notice a special characteristic of the P^∞ matrix: all the rows of the matrix are identical. Every row gives the unique invariant unconditional probability distribution. This is because, independent of the initial state, the economy goes to this distribution. Therefore, if the economy starts in state 1 (the first row), it goes to the distribution [.80   .20], and if it starts in state 2 (the second row), it also goes to the distribution [.80   .20]. Suppose that there is an initial probability distribution p_0. Let us choose $p_0 = [.36   .64]$, for example, but it could be any distribution. If we multiply this vector by the matrix P^∞, the result is

---

3. There are weaker conditions for having a unique invariant unconditional distribution. A discussion of these can be found in Ljungqvist and Sargent [54] or Breiman [16].

$$p_0 P^\infty = [\, .36 \quad .64 \,] \begin{bmatrix} .80 & .20 \\ .80 & .20 \end{bmatrix}$$

$$= [\, .36 \times .80 + .64 \times .80 \quad .36 \times .20 + .64 \times .20 \,]$$

$$= [\, .80 \quad .20 \,].$$

For an economy that begins with initial probabilities for the two states given by p_0 and follows transition probabilities P long enough, the resulting limit probabilities for the two states are the unique invariant unconditional probability distribution.

We can write the value function for an economy with a Markov chain stochastic process as

$$V_{j+1}(x_t, z_t) = \max_{y_t} \left[F(x_t, y_t, z_t) + \beta E_t V_j(G(x_t, y_t, z_t), z_{t+1}) \mid z_t \right],$$

where the addition of the expression, "$\mid z_t$," means that the expectations are taken *conditional on* the realization of z_t. For the growth economy, modified by using the Markov chain process described above, the value functions are

$$V(k_t, A_1) = \max_{k_{t+1}} \left[u(A_1 f(k_t) + (1 - \delta)k_t - k_{t+1}) \right.$$

$$\left. + \beta \left[p_{11} V \left(k_{t+1}, A_1 \right) + p_{12} V \left(k_{t+1}, A_2 \right) \right] \right]$$

and

$$V(k_t, A_2) = \max_{k_{t+1}} \left[u(A_2 f(k_t) + (1 - \delta)k_t - k_{t+1}) \right.$$

$$\left. + \beta \left[p_{21} V \left(k_{t+1}, A_1 \right) + p_{22} V \left(k_{t+1}, A_2 \right) \right] \right],$$

where the probabilities in each equation are those that are appropriate for the given realization of A^t.

As before, for specific economies, the value function is found by iterating, given some initial choice of the function: $V_0(k_t, A^t)$. For the example economy we have been using, but with the matrix P used in place of the constant probabilities, the $j + 1$th iteration of the value function is

$$V_{j+1}(k_t, 1.75) = \max_{k_{t+1}} \left\{ \ln(1.75 k_t^{.36} + .9k_t - k_{t+1}) \right.$$

$$\left. + \beta \left[.9 V_j \left(k_{t+1}, 1.75 \right) + .1 V_j \left(k_{t+1}, .75 \right) \right] \right\}$$

and

$$V_{j+1}(k_t, .75) = \max_{k_{t+1}} \left\{ \ln(.75k_t^{.36} + .9k_t - k_{t+1}) \right.$$

$$\left. + \beta \left[.4V_j \left(k_{t+1}, 1.75 \right) + .6V_j \left(k_{t+1}, .75 \right) \right] \right\}.$$

As before, these value functions converge to a $V(k_t, A^t)$ and the contingent plans that result are shown in Figure 5.4. A_1 is the state where technology is 1.75 and A_2 is the state where it is .75. These policy functions are similar to those shown in Figure 5.2. This should not be surprising since the unconditional distributions on the state variables are the same. However, they are not exactly the same because the conditional distributions are different. When we run some simulations of this economy, we notice that there is substantially more persistence in states than there was in the first stochastic version of the model. Compare the time path in Figure 5.5 to that of the simple stochastic model in Figure 5.3. Both of these time series were generated using the same realizations of a uniform random variable. The additional persistence is seen in both the continuation of the high technology state and the extended periods of convergence toward the higher stationary state and the longer periods in the low state.

One weakness of putting much of the persistence of the model into the Markov chain is that it rather avoids the *economic* problem of what generates

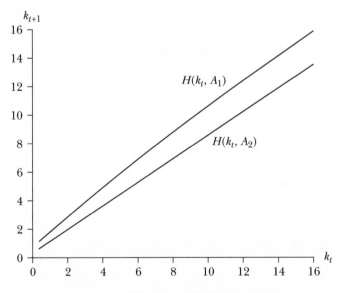

FIGURE 5.4   The plans with Markov chains

that persistence. The time series that result from these kinds of models can be made to display persistence, but this persistence is not explained in economic terms. If one is simply trying to replicate some time series, using larger-dimension Markov chains may do a good job of capturing the variation and the persistence. However, if one is using these models to try to understand what is causing the persistence, Markov chains do not really help.

> **EXERCISE 5.1** Not all conditional probabilities described by Markov chains result in unique invariant unconditional probability distributions. Consider a Markov chain with transition probabilities described by
>
> $$P = \begin{bmatrix} 0 & 1 & 0 \\ 0 & 0 & 1 \\ 1 & 0 & 0 \end{bmatrix}.$$
>
> Find P^3, P^6, P^7, P^8, and P^9. What does this suggest about the nature of this process?

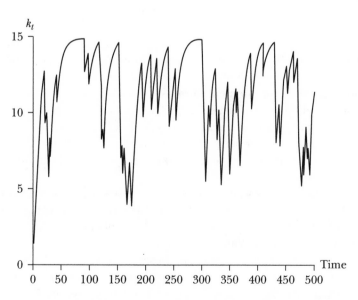

FIGURE 5.5 A simulation with Markov chains

EXERCISE 5.2   Find the unique invariant unconditional probability distribution for the Markov chain with transition probabilities described by

$$P = \begin{bmatrix} .7 & .2 & .1 \\ .3 & .4 & .3 \\ .1 & .1 & .8 \end{bmatrix}.$$

A doubling technique might be helpful. Define $Q = PP$. Then define $Q = QQ$ and repeatedly solve for Q. This process produces the sequence P^2, P^4, P^8, P^{16}, etc., and normally converges quite rapidly.

5.6   REPRISE

Adding finite dimensioned stochastic shocks to a recursive model is fairly simple. Logically little changes, the calculations are just a bit more complicated. The realization in each period of the stochastic shock is treated as a new state variable; the state of nature and its value helps determine the policy that the optimizing agent will follow. To emphasize the fact that the policy function needs to respond to the state of nature as well as the other state variables, and the realizations of future states of nature are yet unknown, we refer to the policy function as a plan.

In the Bellman equation with stochastic states of nature, the distribution (probabilities) of these states of nature show up as weights for determining the expectation of the next period's value of the value function. We use the same technique as before for finding an approximation of the value function, only this time we find a value function for each of the values that the stochastic variable can have. Once the value functions (and the plans) are known, we can start with some initial values for the state variables and, using a random number generator from our computer package, we can simulate time paths for the economy.

More persistence (as well as other characteristics) can be added to the model by using Markov chains for the stochastic processes. In a Markov chain, the probabilities of transition to the next state of nature depend on the current state of nature. While this permits us to find time paths for our economy that can better approximate those of the real world, the method is heavy on probability theory and light on economic theory. The persistence comes through the Markov chains and not through our ability to produce an economic model that captures why the persistence occurs.

The bibliographic references of Chapter 4 are also relevant for this chapter, especially Ljungqvist and Sargent [54], which deals extensively with Markov chains.

5.7 MATLAB CODE

The following program gives the Matlab code for finding the value functions and plans of the Markov chain example in the text.

THE MAIN PROGRAM

The main program first sets the parameters and then does a loop that iterates on the two value functions. The value function is found for values for capital beginning at .4 and going to 16 in steps of .4. It draws the current pair of value functions every 50 iterations. At the end is the plot command that draws the final plans.

```
global vlast1 vlast2 beta delta theta k0 kt At p1 p2
hold off
hold all
vlast1=20*ones(1,40);
vlast2=vlast1;
k0=0.4:0.4:16;
kt11=k0;
kt12=k0;
beta=.98;
delta=.1;
theta=.36;
A1=1.75;
p11=.9;
p12=1-p11;
p21=.4;
p22=1-p21;
A2=.75;
numits=250;
for k=1:numits
    for j=1:40
        kt=k0(j);
        At=A1;
        p1=p11;
        p2=p12;
        %we are using a bounded function minimization routine here
        z=fminbnd(@valfunsto,.41,15.99);
        v1(j)=-valfunsto(z);
        kt11(j)=z;
        At=A2;
```

```
      p1=p21;
      p2=p22;
      z=fminbnd(@valfunsto,.41,15.99);
      v2(j)=-valfunsto(z);
      kt12(j)=z;
   end
   if k/50==round(k/50)
      plot(k0,v1,k0,v2)
      drawnow
   end
   vlast1=v1;
   vlast2=v2;
end
hold off
%optional plotting program for the plans
%plot(k0,kt11,k0,kt12)
```

SUBROUTINE valfunsto

Note that interpolation of the previous value function is linear.

```
function val=valfunsto(x)
global vlast1 vlast2 beta delta theta k0 kt At p1 p2
k=x;
g1=interp1(k0,vlast1,k,'linear');
g2=interp1(k0,vlast2,k,'linear');
kk=At*kt^theta-k+(1-delta)*kt;
val=log(kk)+beta*(p1*g1+p2*g2);
val=-val;
```

Hansen's RBC Model

While Kydland and Prescott [52] published what was the first Real Business Cycle (RBC) model, this model contained quite a number of complications designed to increase the persistence and amplification of the stochastic shocks to technology. The model included time to build for converting investment into capital, so that the new capital that comes available in time t was built using investment from a number of periods anterior to period t. In addition, leisure was included in the utility function as a function of current and past time spent not working. Inventories were necessary so that previous investment commitments could be met in a period of a very large negative technology shock. Finally, technology shocks were designed to contain both a temporary and a permanent component. The model produced the required persistence and amplification, but is difficult to interpret in terms of determining which elements of the model are responsible for its success.

Gary Hansen [48] produced a pair of models that have become the reference for RBC studies. The first is a stochastic, variable labor model much like that of section 4.6, and the second is an almost identical model where a type of indivisibility in labor was introduced. Hansen's objective was to show how the addition of indivisible labor could improve the ability of the model to match the second moments of the time series data from the United States.

In this chapter, we present the basic model and find the first-order conditions and the stationary state for capital and labor. The second section introduces the techniques of log linearization, which we then apply to the basic model to get a linear version that permits us to study the dynamics of the system. The solution method we use for the linear version of the models requires finding the roots to a matrix quadratic equation. Since the model cannot be solved analytically, we need to specify a version of the model with the parameters given. Calibration is the name used to describe the method of choosing the values of the parameters. One takes values from other studies and then uses some results of simulations (or calculations) of the model to determine the rest. We calibrate the basic model, find the laws of motion (a linear contingent plan), calculate the variances that the model generates for the endogenous set of variables, and compare these to the variances that Hansen found for the United States. We then do the same for Hansen's model with indivisible labor and compare the results to those of the first model. At this stage, the success of an RBC model is determined by how well it can match the variance and covariance structure that comes from the time series of macroeconomic variables of the particular economy being studied.

6.1 HANSEN'S BASIC MODEL

In a Robinson Crusoe type economy, the one agent maximizes the discounted utility function

$$\max \sum_{t=0}^{\infty} \beta^t u(c_t, l_t),$$

where c_t is time t consumption and l_t is time t leisure, where $l_t = 1 - h_t$, and h_t is time t labor. The specific utility function that we use is

$$u(c_t, 1 - h_t) = \ln c_t + A \ln(1 - h_t),$$

with $A > 0$. The production function is Cobb-Douglas with a stochastic technology,

$$f(\lambda_t, k_t, h_t) = \lambda_t k_t^\theta h_t^{1-\theta},$$

where λ_t is a random technology variable that follows the process

$$\lambda_{t+1} = \gamma \lambda_t + \varepsilon_{t+1},$$

for $0 < \gamma < 1$. The ε_t shocks are identically and independently distributed, are positive, bounded above, and have a mean of $1 - \gamma$. These assumptions imply that the mean of λ_t is 1 and that output cannot go negative. Capital accumulation follows the process

$$k_{t+1} = (1 - \delta)k_t + i_t,$$

and the feasibility constraint is

$$f(\lambda_t, k_t, h_t) \geq c_t + i_t$$

for every period t.

The model can be written as a Bellman equation of the form

$$V(k_t, \lambda_t) = \max_{c_t, h_t} \left[\ln c_t + A \ln(1 - h_t) + \beta E_t \left[V(k_{t+1}, \lambda_{t+1}) \mid \lambda_t \right] \right],$$

subject to

$$\lambda_t k_t^\theta h_t^{1-\theta} \geq c_t + i_t,$$

$$\lambda_{t+1} = \gamma \lambda_t + \varepsilon_{t+1}, \text{ and}$$

$$k_{t+1} = (1 - \delta)k_t + i_t.$$

The expectations operator in the value function, $E_t \left[V(k_{t+1}, \lambda_{t+1}) \mid \lambda_t \right]$, indicates that expectations are conditional on the realization of λ_t, a fact that comes from the stochastic process for technology. With substitution, the Bellman equation becomes

$$V(k_t, \lambda_t) = \max_{k_{t+1}, h_t} \left[\ln \left(\lambda_t k_t^\theta h_t^{1-\theta} + (1 - \delta)k_t - k_{t+1} \right) + A \ln(1 - h_t) \right.$$

$$\left. + \beta E_t \left[V(k_{t+1}, \lambda_{t+1}) \mid \lambda_t \right] \right],$$

with k_{t+1} and h_t as the control variables.

The first-order conditions are

$$\frac{\partial V(k_t, \lambda_t)}{\partial k_{t+1}} = 0 = -\frac{1}{\lambda_t k_t^\theta h_t^{1-\theta} + (1 - \delta)k_t - k_{t+1}} + \beta E_t \left[V_k(k_{t+1}, \lambda_{t+1}) \mid \lambda_t \right],$$

and

$$\frac{\partial V(k_t, \lambda_t)}{\partial h_t} = 0 = (1 - \theta) \frac{1}{\lambda_t k_t^\theta h_t^{1-\theta} + (1 - \delta)k_t - k_{t+1}} \left(\lambda_t k_t^\theta h_t^{-\theta} \right) - A \frac{1}{1 - h_t}.$$

The Benveniste-Scheinkman envelope theorem condition is

$$\frac{\partial V(k_t, \lambda_t)}{\partial k_t} = \frac{1}{\lambda_t k_t^\theta h_t^{1-\theta} + (1 - \delta)k_t - k_{t+1}} \left(\theta \lambda_t k_t^{\theta-1} h_t^{1-\theta} + (1 - \delta) \right).$$

These first-order conditions can be written as

$$\frac{1}{\lambda_t k_t^\theta h_t^{1-\theta} + (1 - \delta)k_t - k_{t+1}} \tag{6.1}$$

$$= \beta E_t \left[\frac{\theta \lambda_{t+1} k_{t+1}^{\theta-1} h_{t+1}^{1-\theta} + (1 - \delta)}{\lambda_{t+1} k_{t+1}^\theta h_{t+1}^{1-\theta} + (1 - \delta)k_{t+1} - k_{t+2}} \mid \lambda_t \right],$$

and

$$(1 - \theta)\left(1 - h_t\right)\left(\lambda_t k_t^\theta h_t^{-\theta}\right) = A\left(\lambda_t k_t^\theta h_t^{1-\theta} + (1 - \delta)k_t - k_{t+1}\right). \quad (6.2)$$

Since, at equality,

$$c_t = \lambda_t k_t^\theta h_t^{1-\theta} + (1 - \delta)k_t - k_{t+1},$$

and with perfect factor markets so that factor rentals equal their marginal products,

$$r_t = \theta \lambda_t k_t^{\theta-1} h_t^{1-\theta}$$

and

$$w_t = (1 - \theta)\,\lambda_t k_t^\theta h_t^{-\theta},$$

these conditions simplify to

$$\frac{1}{c_t} = \beta E_t\left[\frac{r_{t+1} + (1 - \delta)}{c_{t+1}} \mid \lambda_t\right]$$

and

$$\left(1 - h_t\right) w_t = A c_t.$$

One can solve these two equations for the stationary state case by imposing the conditions that $\bar{k} = k_t = k_{t+1} = k_{t+2}$ and $\bar{h} = h_t = h_{t+1}$. With these restrictions, the expectations operator disappears since expectations equal the realized values in a stationary state. The stationary state problem here is the same as for the deterministic economy. The rest is just algebra and the stationary state value of $\bar{h}$ is found to be

$$\bar{h} = \frac{1}{1 + \frac{A}{(1-\theta)}\left[1 - \frac{\beta\delta\theta}{1-\beta(1-\delta)}\right]},$$

and the stationary state value of $\bar{k}$ is determined by

$$\bar{k} = \bar{h}\left[\frac{\theta\bar{\lambda}}{\frac{1}{\beta} - (1 - \delta)}\right]^{\frac{1}{1-\theta}}.$$

To determine the behavior of the economy outside of the stationary state, a number of approaches are possible, all of which give approximate solutions.

If the set of possible states of nature for the technology variable were small, one could use the techniques of the previous chapter and calculate an approximate version of the value function and of the plans. Then one could run simulations, using an appropriate random number generator, and find the second moments, the variances and covariances, of the variables of interest in the economy. This method would have two advantages. It would preserve the curvature of the model, and in cases where the curvature is important, it would generate good approximate second moments. It would also allow study of the model in equilibria that are far from the stationary state. Once the value function is calculated, one can begin the economy at any level of capital stock within the domain used to calculate the value functions.

Unfortunately, given the definition of the stochastic process for technology, $\lambda_{t+1} = \gamma \lambda_t + \varepsilon_{t+1}$, even a very small dimension for ε_{t+1} results in a very large dimension for λ_t. The smallest dimension that ε_{t+1} can have and still be a random variable is two. Suppose that the values that are possible for ε_{t+1} are $1 - \gamma + \Delta$ and $1 - \gamma - \Delta$, where Δ is a very small positive number, and suppose that it can have each of these values with probability .5. Suppose that at time t, $\lambda_t = 1$. At time $t + 1$, λ_{t+1} can have values $1 + \Delta$, and $1 - \Delta$. At time $t + 2$, λ_{t+2} can have values $1 + (1 + \gamma)\Delta$, $1 - (1 - \gamma)\Delta$, $1 + (1 - \gamma)\Delta$ and $1 - (1 + \gamma)\Delta$. At time $t + n$, λ_{t+n} can take on 2^n values. As n goes to infinity so does the number of possible values for λ_{t+n}.

It is still possible to find approximations for the value function as a function of the two variables, k_t and λ_t. One needs to choose domains for both of these variables so that in simulations it is very unlikely that λ_t will go outside of this domain. Take sufficiently dense discrete samplings of these domains, choose an initial guess for $V_0(k_t, \lambda_t)$, and iterate on the value function and the contingent plans. The calculations will need to do two-dimensional interpolations of the previous iteration's value function during the calculations but these calculations, are quite feasible. Modern computing power makes this solution method possible if one is patient with the calculations.

However, even modern computing power begins to lose its usefulness for direct approximations if the model becomes more complicated and the dimension of the state variables increases. In those cases, two forms of linear approximations[1] are available: 1) log-linear approximations of the first-order conditions and the budget constraints and 2) quadratic approximation of the objective function and linearization of the budget constraints to allow the use of linear quadratic dynamic programming. In this chapter we will continue

---

1. Quadratic approximation techniques are being developed but are outside the scope of this book. See, for example, Kim, Kim, Schaumburg, and Sims [50] and Schmitt-Grohé and Uribe [75]. Quadratic apaproximation techniques may do a better job of approximating the underlying system when one is a bit further from the stationary state.

with log-linear approximations of the first-order conditions. Linear quadratic dynamic programming will come in Chapter 7.

Before we go on with the log linearization, it helps to simplify the Hansen model by making a couple of substitutions of variables. We will add definitions and additional budget constraints to carry along, but these additions will make the linearization of the model easier. In addition, we consider the problem to be that of a social planner and will write the model in aggregate terms, where variables in capital letters are the aggregate values.[2] Write the first-order conditions[3] (equations 6.1 and 6.2) as

$$1 = \beta E_t \left[\frac{C_t}{C_{t+1}} \left(r_{t+1} + (1 - \delta) \right) \right]$$

and

$$\left(1 - H_t \right) (1 - \theta) \frac{Y_t}{H_t} = A C_t,$$

where the budget constraints give

$$C_t = Y_t + (1 - \delta) K_t - K_{t+1}$$

and

$$Y_t = \lambda_t K_t^{\theta} H_t^{1-\theta},$$

and the rental on capital, r_t, is

$$r_t = \theta \frac{Y_t}{K_t}.$$

Here, r_t is equal to the marginal product of a unit of capital. If one owns a unit of capital at the beginning of period t and rents that capital out in a competitive market, r_t is the rental that one receives for the use of the capital during that period. These five equations contain the same information as the two first-order conditions and budget constraints in a more simplified format.

6.2   LOG LINEARIZATION TECHNIQUES

Handling and solving models with substantial nonlinearity is often difficult. As we showed earlier, when the model is relatively simple, one can find an

---

2. Applying the second welfare theorem.

3. We are no longer going to write out exactly what information is included in forming the expectation E_t; that is why the term "| λ_t" is no longer included.

approximation to the policy function by recursively solving for the value function. This method works if a model is relatively small and can be written as the solution to a single optimization problem.[4]

Linear models are often much easier to solve, and there exist well-developed methods for solving linear models. The problem is to convert a nonlinear model into a sufficiently good linear approximation so that the solutions to the linear approximation are helpful in understanding the behavior of the underlying nonlinear system. A now standard method for a linear approximation is to log-linearize a model around its stationary state. The assumption is that, if the model is not too far from the stationary state, the linear version that results closely approximates the original model.

6.2.1 The Basics of Log Linearization

Consider a nonlinear model that can be represented by a set of equations of the general form

$$F(x_t) = \frac{G(x_t)}{H(x_t)},$$

where x_t is a vector of the variables of the model that can include expectational variables and lagged variables in addition to contemporaneous variables. The process of log linearization is to first take the logarithms of the functions $F()$, $G()$, and $H()$, and then take a first-order Taylor series approximation. Taking the logarithms gives

$$\ln(F(x_t)) = \ln(G(x_t)) - \ln(H(x_t)),$$

and taking the first-order Taylor series expansion around the stationary state values, $\bar{x}$, gives

$$\ln(F(\bar{x})) + \frac{F'(\bar{x})}{F(\bar{x})}(x_t - \bar{x}) \approx \ln(G(\bar{x})) + \frac{G'(\bar{x})}{G(\bar{x})}(x_t - \bar{x})$$

$$- \ln(H(\bar{x})) - \frac{H'(\bar{x})}{H(\bar{x})}(x_t - \bar{x}),$$

where the notation $X'(\bar{x})$ is used to indicate the gradient at the stationary state. Notice that the model is now linear in x_t, since $F'(\bar{x})/F(\bar{x})$, $G'(\bar{x})/G(\bar{x})$, $H'(\bar{x})/H(\bar{x})$, $\ln(F(\bar{x}))$, $\ln(G(\bar{x}))$, and $\ln(H(\bar{x}))$ are constants. Given that the

---

4. However, somewhat more complicated models can be included if simple solutions to secondary optimization problems are included as constraints.

log version of the model holds at the stationary state,

$$\ln(F(\bar{x})) = \ln(G(\bar{x})) - \ln(H(\bar{x})),$$

we can eliminate the three $\ln(\cdot)$ components, and the equation simplifies to

$$\frac{F'(\bar{x})}{F(\bar{x})}(x_t - \bar{x}) \approx \frac{G'(\bar{x})}{G(\bar{x})}(x_t - \bar{x}) - \frac{H'(\bar{x})}{H(\bar{x})}(x_t - \bar{x}).$$

The implicit assumption is that one is staying close enough to the stationary state, $\bar{x}$, so that the second-order or higher terms of the Taylor expansion are small enough to be irrelevant and can safely be left out.

What follows shows how to do this log linearization in two cases that are commonly encountered in economic problems.

EXAMPLE 6.1   *Consider the Cobb-Douglas production function*

$$Y_t = \lambda_t K_t^\theta H_t^{1-\theta}.$$

First one takes the logarithms of both sides of the production function to get

$$\ln Y_t = \ln \lambda_t + \theta \ln K_t + (1-\theta) \ln H_t,$$

and then the first-order Taylor expansion gives

$$\ln \bar{Y} + \frac{1}{\bar{Y}}\left(Y_t - \bar{Y}\right) \approx \ln \bar{\lambda} + \frac{1}{\bar{\lambda}}\left(\lambda_t - \bar{\lambda}\right) + \theta \ln \bar{K} + \frac{\theta}{\bar{K}}\left(K_t - \bar{K}\right)$$

$$+ (1-\theta) \ln \bar{H} + \frac{(1-\theta)}{\bar{H}}\left(H_t - \bar{H}\right).$$

Since in a stationary state

$$\ln \bar{Y} = \ln \bar{\lambda} + \theta \ln \bar{K} + (1-\theta) \ln \bar{H},$$

the zero-order terms can be removed to get

$$\frac{1}{\bar{Y}}\left(Y_t - \bar{Y}\right) \approx \frac{1}{\bar{\lambda}}\left(\lambda_t - \bar{\lambda}\right) + \frac{\theta}{\bar{K}}\left(K_t - \bar{K}\right) + \frac{(1-\theta)}{\bar{H}}\left(H_t - \bar{H}\right).$$

Further simplification gives

$$\frac{Y_t}{\bar{Y}} + 1 \approx \frac{\lambda_t}{\bar{\lambda}} + \frac{\theta K_t}{\bar{K}} + \frac{(1-\theta) H_t}{\bar{H}}.$$

The production function is now expressed as a linear equation.

EXAMPLE 6.2 *Consider the infinite horizon CES utility function of the form*

$$\sum_{t=0}^{\infty} \beta^t \left[\frac{C_t^{1-\eta}}{1-\eta} - \frac{H_t^{1-\phi}}{1-\phi} \right],$$

subject to the budget constraint

$$C_t = \lambda_t K_t^{\theta} H_t^{1-\theta} + (1-\delta) K_t - K_{t+1}.$$

The first-order conditions (found by substitution and variational methods) are

$$\beta \left[\theta \lambda_{t+1} K_{t+1}^{\theta-1} H_{t+1}^{1-\theta} + (1-\delta) \right] C_{t+1}^{-\eta} = C_t^{-\eta}$$

and

$$C_t^{-\eta} \left[(1-\theta) \lambda_t K_t^{\theta} H_t^{-\theta} \right] = H_t^{-\phi}.$$

The log versions of the budget constraint and the first-order conditions are

$$\ln C_t = \ln \left[\lambda_t K_t^{\theta} H_t^{1-\theta} + (1-\delta) K_t - K_{t+1} \right],$$

$$-\eta \ln C_t = \ln \beta + \ln \left[\theta \lambda_{t+1} K_{t+1}^{\theta-1} H_{t+1}^{1-\theta} + (1-\delta) \right] - \eta \ln C_{t+1},$$

$$-\phi \ln H_t = -\eta \ln C_t + \ln (1-\theta) + \ln \lambda_t + \theta \ln K_t - \theta \ln H_t.$$

Taking the first-order Taylor expansion and removing the equalities from the stationary state gives

$$\frac{C_t}{\bar{C}} + \frac{\bar{\lambda} \bar{K}^{\theta} \bar{H}^{1-\theta}}{\left[\bar{\lambda} \bar{K}^{\theta} \bar{H}^{1-\theta} - \delta \bar{K} \right]} = \frac{\left(\bar{K}^{\theta} \bar{H}^{1-\theta} \right)}{\left[\bar{\lambda} \bar{K}^{\theta} \bar{H}^{1-\theta} - \delta \bar{K} \right]} \lambda_t + \frac{\theta \bar{\lambda} \bar{K}^{\theta-1} \bar{H}^{1-\theta} + (1-\delta)}{\left[\bar{\lambda} \bar{K}^{\theta} \bar{H}^{1-\theta} - \delta \bar{K} \right]} K_t$$

$$+ \frac{\left((1-\theta) \bar{\lambda} \bar{K}^{\theta} \bar{H}^{-\theta} \right)}{\left[\bar{\lambda} \bar{K}^{\theta} \bar{H}^{1-\theta} - \delta \bar{K} \right]} H_t - \frac{1}{\left[\bar{\lambda} \bar{K}^{\theta} \bar{H}^{1-\theta} - \delta \bar{K} \right]} K_{t+1},$$

$$-\eta \frac{C_t}{\bar{C}} = -\frac{2\theta \bar{\lambda} \bar{K}^{\theta-1} \bar{H}^{1-\theta}}{\theta \bar{\lambda} \bar{K}^{\theta-1} \bar{H}^{1-\theta} + (1-\delta)} + \frac{\theta \bar{K}^{\theta-1} \bar{H}^{1-\theta}}{\theta \bar{\lambda} \bar{K}^{\theta-1} \bar{H}^{1-\theta} + (1-\delta)} \lambda_{t+1}$$

$$+ \frac{(\theta-1) \theta \bar{\lambda} \bar{K}^{\theta-2} \bar{H}^{1-\theta}}{\theta \bar{\lambda} \bar{K}^{\theta-1} \bar{H}^{1-\theta} + (1-\delta)} K_{t+1} + \frac{(1-\theta) \theta \bar{\lambda} \bar{K}^{\theta-1} \bar{H}^{-\theta}}{\theta \bar{\lambda} \bar{K}^{\theta-1} \bar{H}^{1-\theta} + (1-\delta)} H_{t+1} - \eta \frac{C_{t+1}}{\bar{C}},$$

and

$$1 - \phi \frac{H_t}{\bar{H}} = -\eta \frac{C_t}{\bar{C}} + \frac{\lambda_t}{\bar{\lambda}} + \theta \frac{K_t}{\bar{K}} - \theta \frac{H_t}{\bar{H}} + (\eta - \phi).$$

The constant terms of some of these equations are messy, but they are constants, and the three equations are all linear.

6.2.2 Uhlig's Method of Log Linearization

Harald Uhlig [86] recommends using a simpler method for finding log-linear approximations of functions. His method does not require taking derivatives and gives the same result as the above method, except that the linear model is expressed in terms of log differences of the variables.

Consider an equation of a set of variables X_t. Define $\tilde{X}_t = \ln X_t - \ln \bar{X}$. The tilde variables are the log difference of the original variables from the value $\bar{X}$. One can write the original variable as

$$X_t = \bar{X} e^{\tilde{X}_t},$$

since

$$\bar{X} e^{\tilde{X}_t} = \bar{X} e^{\ln X_t - \ln \bar{X}} = \bar{X} e^{\ln X_t / \bar{X}} = \bar{X} \cdot X_t / \bar{X} = X_t.$$

Uhlig's method is to first multiply out all the variables, getting rid of as many variables in the denominator as possible. Then each variable X_t is replaced by the equivalent $\bar{X} e^{\tilde{X}_t}$. Up to this point, one has only done a slight change of variable and all equalities still hold exactly. Now, bring together all the exponential terms that you can. For example,

$$\frac{A_t B_t^\alpha}{C_t^\delta} = \frac{\bar{A} e^{\tilde{A}_t} \bar{B}^\alpha e^{\alpha \tilde{B}_t}}{\bar{C}^\delta e^{\delta \tilde{C}_t}}$$

becomes

$$\frac{\bar{A} \bar{B}^\alpha}{\bar{C}^\delta} e^{\tilde{A}_t + \alpha \tilde{B}_t - \delta \tilde{C}_t}. \tag{6.3}$$

At this point, one applies the linear approximation of the tilde variables. Taking the Taylor expansion of the exponential term around its stationary value gives

$$e^{\tilde{A}_t + \alpha \tilde{B}_t - \delta \tilde{C}_t} \approx e^{\tilde{A} + \alpha \tilde{B} - \delta \tilde{C}} + e^{\tilde{A} + \alpha \tilde{B} - \delta \tilde{C}} \left(\tilde{A}_t - \tilde{A} \right)$$

$$+ \alpha e^{\tilde{A} + \alpha \tilde{B} - \delta \tilde{C}} \left(\tilde{B}_t - \tilde{B} \right) - \delta e^{\tilde{A} + \alpha \tilde{B} - \delta \tilde{C}} \left(\tilde{C}_t - \tilde{C} \right)$$

$$= 1 + \tilde{A}_t + \alpha \tilde{B}_t - \delta \tilde{C}_t,$$

where terms without date subscripts are the stationary state values of the tilde variables (the log differences). Naturally, we assume that the stationary state value of the differences is zero. The approximation of expression 6.3 above is

$$\frac{\bar{A}\bar{B}^\alpha}{\bar{C}^\delta}\left(1+\tilde{A}_t+\alpha\tilde{B}_t-\delta\tilde{C}_t\right).$$

The example below uses Uhlig's method to find a log-linear approximation for the same Cobb-Douglas production function we did above.

EXAMPLE 6.3   *Consider the Cobb-Douglas production function*

$$Y_t = \lambda_t K_t^\theta H_t^{1-\theta}.$$

Substitute $X_t = \bar{X}e^{\tilde{X}_t}$ for each variable and get

$$\bar{Y}e^{\tilde{Y}_t} = \bar{\lambda}\bar{K}^\theta\bar{H}^{1-\theta}e^{\tilde{\lambda}_t+\theta\tilde{K}_t+(1-\theta)\tilde{H}_t}.$$

This is approximated by the Taylor expansion (or Uhlig's rules, if one prefers) to get

$$\bar{Y}\left(1+\tilde{Y}_t\right) = \bar{\lambda}\bar{K}^\theta\bar{H}^{1-\theta}\left(1+\tilde{\lambda}_t+\theta\tilde{K}_t+(1-\theta)\tilde{H}_t\right).$$

Given that in the stationary state $\bar{Y}=\bar{\lambda}\bar{K}^\theta\bar{H}^{1-\theta}$, this simplifies to

$$\tilde{Y}_t = \tilde{\lambda}_t + \theta\tilde{K}_t + (1-\theta)\tilde{H}_t.$$

This result may not seem the same as the one in the example using direct log linearization. However, the result of the first method is

$$\frac{Y_t}{\bar{Y}}+1\approx\frac{\lambda_t}{\bar{\lambda}}+\frac{\theta K_t}{\bar{K}}+\frac{(1-\theta)H_t}{\bar{H}},$$

which is given in levels and not changes. Replacing each variable X_t by the term written as differences, $X_t \approx \bar{X}(1+\tilde{X}_t)$, gives

$$\frac{\bar{Y}\left(1+\tilde{Y}_t\right)}{\bar{Y}}+1\approx\frac{\bar{\lambda}\left(1+\tilde{\lambda}_t\right)}{\bar{\lambda}}+\frac{\theta\bar{K}\left(1+\tilde{K}_t\right)}{\bar{K}}+.\frac{(1-\theta)\bar{H}\left(1+\tilde{H}_t\right)}{\bar{H}},$$

and this simplifies to

$$\tilde{Y}_t \approx \tilde{\lambda}_t + \theta\tilde{K}_t + (1-\theta)\tilde{H}_t.$$

The advantage of Uhlig's method is that one does not need to take explicit derivatives. The substitutions are direct and mostly mechanical. There are a number of rules that are useful for using this technique. These rules help keep the process simple. However, when comparing the results of log linearization using Uhlig's rules, one needs to remember that the results are given in log differences from the stationary state.

Uhlig's definitions are

$$\tilde{X}_t = \ln X_t - \ln \bar{X}$$

and

$$X_t = \bar{X} e^{\tilde{X}_t}.$$

His rules are

$$e^{\tilde{X}_t + a\tilde{Y}_t} \approx 1 + \tilde{X}_t + a\tilde{Y}_t,$$

$$\tilde{X}_t \tilde{Y}_t \approx 0,$$

$$E_t \left[a e^{\tilde{X}_{t+1}} \right] \approx a + a E_t \left[\tilde{X}_{t+1} \right].$$

The first rule is the most direct; it is best to try to write as many of the equations in this form as possible. If this is done adequately, the second rule, which says that second-order terms are approximately zero, is not usually necessary. A useful version of the expectations rule is that

$$E_t \left[X_{t+1} \right] = \bar{X} \left(1 + E_t \left[\tilde{X}_{t+1} \right] \right).$$

> **EXERCISE 6.1** Use Uhlig's method to find the log-linear approximation of the budget constraint and first-order conditions of example 6.2 above.

6.3 LOG-LINEAR VERSION OF HANSEN'S MODEL

The five equations of the Hansen model are

$$1 = \beta E_t \left[\frac{C_t}{C_{t+1}} \left(r_{t+1} + (1 - \delta) \right) \right],$$

$$AC_t = (1 - \theta) \left(1 - H_t \right) \frac{Y_t}{H_t},$$

$$C_t = Y_t + (1 - \delta) K_t - K_{t+1},$$

$$Y_t = \lambda_t K_t^\theta H_t^{1-\theta},$$

$$r_t = \theta \frac{Y_t}{K_t}.$$

Beginning with the first, we substitute each variable for its log difference around a set of stationary state values, designated by a bar above the variable, and, after taking the linear approximation, get

$$1 = \beta E_t \left[\frac{\bar{C} e^{\tilde{C}_t}}{\bar{C} e^{\tilde{C}_{t+1}}} \bar{r} e^{\tilde{r}_{t+1}} + (1 - \delta) \frac{\bar{C} e^{\tilde{C}_t}}{\bar{C} e^{\tilde{C}_{t+1}}} \right]$$

$$= \beta E_t \left[\bar{r} e^{\tilde{C}_t - \tilde{C}_{t+1} + \tilde{r}_{t+1}} + (1 - \delta) e^{\tilde{C}_t - \tilde{C}_{t+1}} \right]$$

$$\approx \beta \left(\bar{r} E_t \left[1 + \tilde{C}_t - \tilde{C}_{t+1} + \tilde{r}_{t+1} \right] + (1 - \delta) E_t \left[1 + \tilde{C}_t - \tilde{C}_{t+1} \right] \right)$$

$$= E_t \left[1 + \tilde{C}_t - \tilde{C}_{t+1} + \beta \bar{r} \tilde{r}_{t+1} \right],$$

or

$$0 \approx \tilde{C}_t - E_t \tilde{C}_{t+1} + \beta \bar{r} E_t \tilde{r}_{t+1},$$

where $\tilde{C}_t = \ln C_t - \ln \bar{C}$. In this simplification, we used the fact that $1/\beta = \bar{r} + (1 - \delta)$ in a stationary state equilibrium.

Applying the log linearization techniques to the second equation gives

$$0 \approx \tilde{Y}_t - \frac{\tilde{H}_t}{1 - \bar{H}} - \tilde{C}_t.$$

The next three equations are

$$0 \approx \bar{Y} \tilde{Y}_t - \bar{C} \tilde{C}_t + \bar{K} \left[(1 - \delta) \tilde{K}_t - \tilde{K}_{t+1} \right],$$

$$0 \approx \tilde{\lambda}_t + \theta \tilde{K}_t + (1 - \theta) \tilde{H}_t - \tilde{Y}_t,$$

and

$$0 \approx \tilde{Y}_t - \tilde{K}_t - \tilde{r}_t,$$

where $\bar{r} = \theta \bar{Y} / \bar{K}$.

The stochastic process,

$$\lambda_{t+1} = \gamma \lambda_t + \varepsilon_{t+1},$$

can be written as

$$\bar{\lambda} e^{\tilde{\lambda}_{t+1}} = \gamma \bar{\lambda} e^{\tilde{\lambda}_t} + \varepsilon_{t+1},$$

which can be approximated by

$$\bar{\lambda}\left(1 + \tilde{\lambda}_{t+1}\right) = \gamma\bar{\lambda}\left(1 + \tilde{\lambda}_t\right) + \varepsilon_{t+1},$$

or

$$\tilde{\lambda}_{t+1} = \gamma\tilde{\lambda}_t + \mu_{t+1},$$

where $\bar{\lambda} = 1$ and $\mu_{t+1} = \varepsilon_{t+1} - (1 - \gamma)$. Notice that the change of variable gives $E_t\left(\mu_{t+1}\right) = 0$.

Define the vector of endogenous variables at time t as

$$x_t = [\ \tilde{K}_{t+1} \quad \tilde{Y}_t \quad \tilde{C}_t \quad \tilde{H}_t \quad \tilde{r}_t\ ]',$$

and the exogenous stochastic variable as

$$z_t = \tilde{\lambda}_t.$$

The model given above can be written in matrix form as

$$0 = E_t\left[Fx_{t+1} + Gx_t + Hx_{t-1} + Lz_{t+1} + Mz_t\right],$$

where

$$F = \begin{bmatrix} 0 & 0 & -1 & 0 & \beta\bar{r} \\ 0 & 0 & 0 & 0 & 0 \\ 0 & 0 & 0 & 0 & 0 \\ 0 & 0 & 0 & 0 & 0 \\ 0 & 0 & 0 & 0 & 0 \end{bmatrix},$$

$$G = \begin{bmatrix} 0 & 0 & 1 & 0 & 0 \\ 0 & 1 & -1 & -\frac{1}{1-\bar{H}} & 0 \\ -\bar{K} & \bar{Y} & -\bar{C} & 0 & 0 \\ 0 & -1 & 0 & 1-\theta & 0 \\ 0 & 1 & 0 & 0 & -1 \end{bmatrix},$$

$$H = \begin{bmatrix} 0 & 0 & 0 & 0 & 0 \\ 0 & 0 & 0 & 0 & 0 \\ \bar{K}(1-\delta) & 0 & 0 & 0 & 0 \\ \theta & 0 & 0 & 0 & 0 \\ -1 & 0 & 0 & 0 & 0 \end{bmatrix},$$

$$L = [0 \quad 0 \quad 0 \quad 0 \quad 0]',$$

$$M = [0 \quad 0 \quad 0 \quad 1 \quad 0]'.$$

Write the stochastic process as

$$z_{t+1} = Nz_t + \mu_{t+1},$$

with $E_t\left(\mu_{t+1}\right) = 0$, and, in this case, N is simply the one-element matrix $N = [\gamma]$.

We look for a solution to the problem, matrices P and Q, that gives the equilibrium laws of motion,

$$x_t = Px_{t-1} + Qz_t,$$

where the equilibrium described by this process is stable.

Theorem 1 from Uhlig [86] shows that, if a solution exists, the matrix P can be found by solving the matrix quadratic equation

$$0 = FP^2 + GP + H,$$

and the matrix Q comes from

$$V\mathrm{vec}\,(Q) = -\mathrm{vec}(LN + M),$$

where $\mathrm{vec}(\cdot)$ is columnwise vectorization and

$$V = N' \otimes F + I_k \otimes (FP + G),$$

with I_k a k-dimensional identity matrix, k the number of stochastic variables (the dimension of z_t), and $\otimes$ the Kronecker product.[5] This result can be found by substituting the solution,

$$x_t = Px_{t-1} + Qz_t,$$

and the stochastic process, as expectations,

$$E_t z_{t+1} = Nz_t,$$

---

5. Given a $k \times l$ matrix A and an $m \times n$ matrix B, the $km \times ln$ Kronecker product $A \otimes B$ is found by multiplying each element of the matrix B by the entire matrix A. For example,

$$A = \begin{bmatrix} 1 & 2 \\ 3 & 4 \end{bmatrix}, B = \begin{bmatrix} 5 & 6 \\ 7 & 8 \end{bmatrix}, \text{ then } A \otimes B = \begin{bmatrix} 5 & 6 & 10 & 12 \\ 7 & 8 & 14 & 16 \\ 15 & 18 & 20 & 24 \\ 21 & 24 & 28 & 32 \end{bmatrix}.$$

into the equation

$$0 = E_t \left[F x_{t+1} + G x_t + H x_{t-1} + L z_{t+1} + M z_t \right],$$

to get

$$0 = \left[F P^2 + G P + H \right] x_{t-1} + [FPQ + FQN + GQ + LN + M] z_t.$$

For this equation to hold for all permitted values of x_{t-1} and z_t, each expression in square brackets must be equal to zero. The vec and Kronecker notations are necessary to solve for Q. (See Appendix 1 of this chapter for further explanation.) This problem can sometimes be difficult to solve because finding the roots of the matrix quadratic equation in P can be complex and computationally demanding, especially if the model is large.

6.3.1   Solution Using Jump Variables

Solution of the linear version of the economy is usually easier if one defines a vector of endogenous state variables, x_t, and a vector of other endogenous variables, y_t, which depend on the values of the state variables. The other endogenous variables are often called the jump variables. The name *jump variables* comes from the saddle point dynamics of continuous time systems. The system is stable (and converges) along the ridge of the saddle path. Normally, the control variables naturally follow the ridge, but the values of other variables need to jump (instantaneously) to get the system on the stable ridge. We are somewhat misusing the name *jump variable* here since, as we saw in the previous section, all variables can be included in what we are calling the "controls" vector.

In the example economy, we could choose

$$x_t = \left[\tilde{K}_{t+1} \right]$$

as the one element vector of endogenous state variables and

$$y_t = \left[\tilde{Y}_t, \tilde{C}_t, \tilde{H}_t, \tilde{r}_t \right]'$$

as the vector of other endogenous variables. Separating equations that include expectations from those that do not, the linear version of the model can be written as

$$0 = A x_t + B x_{t-1} + C y_t + D z_t,$$

$$0 = E_t \left[F x_{t+1} + G x_t + H x_{t-1} + J y_{t+1} + K y_t + L z_{t+1} + M z_t \right],$$

$$z_{t+1} = N z_t + \varepsilon_{t+1} \quad E_t(\varepsilon_{t+1}) = 0.$$

For our model,

$$A = [\, 0 \quad -\bar{K} \quad 0 \quad 0\,]',$$

$$B = [\, 0 \quad (1-\delta)\bar{K} \quad \theta \quad -1\,]',$$

$$C = \begin{bmatrix} 1 & -1 & -\frac{1}{1-\bar{H}} & 0 \\ \bar{Y} & -\bar{C} & 0 & 0 \\ -1 & 0 & 1-\theta & 0 \\ 1 & 0 & 0 & -1 \end{bmatrix},$$

$$D = [\, 0 \quad 0 \quad 1 \quad 0\,]',$$

$$F = [0], \quad G = [0], \quad H = [0],$$

$$J = [\, 0 \quad -1 \quad 0 \quad \beta\bar{r}\,],$$

$$K = [\, 0 \quad 1 \quad 0 \quad 0\,],$$

$$L = [0], \quad M = [0], \quad N = [\gamma].$$

The solution for this economy is a set of matrices, P, Q, R, and S, that describe the equilibrium laws of motion,

$$x_t = Px_{t-1} + Qz_t,$$

and

$$y_t = Rx_{t-1} + Sz_t.$$

Note that, for our model, the matrix C is of full rank[6] and has a well-defined inverse, C^{-1}.[7] From Corollary 1 of Uhlig [86], if equilibrium laws of motion exist, they must fulfill

$$0 = (F - JC^{-1}A)P^2 - (JC^{-1}B - G + KC^{-1}A)P - KC^{-1}B + H,$$

$$R = -C^{-1}(AP + B).$$

Q satisfies the equation

$$\left(N' \otimes (F - JC^{-1}A) + I_k \otimes (JR + FP + G - KC^{-1}A)\right) \mathrm{vec}(Q)$$

$$= \mathrm{vec}\left(\left(JC^{-1}D - L\right)N + KC^{-1}D - M\right),$$

---

6. Almost always. There is a set of measure zero of parameter values that could make it of less than full rank.

7. The problem can usually be solved even if C is not of full rank, but it is somewhat more complicated. Uhlig [86] considers this case as well.

and

$$S = -C^{-1}(AQ + D).$$

The identity matrix I_k has dimension $k \times k$, where k is the number of columns in the matrix Q.

Here, the matrix quadratic equation is quite simple. The matrix, P, has one element, so we are finding the solution to a standard quadratic equation. The rest is matrix algebra.

6.3.2   Calibration of the Log-Linear Model

To find the laws of motion using our numerical technique, we need to fix the values of the parameters of the model and determine the stationary state values of the variables (since many of these show up in the matrices that we are using in the linear version of the model). The source for these values is varied. For some parameters, for example, θ, the economic interpretation of the variable is quite clear; with a Cobb-Douglas production function, θ is the fraction of national income that goes to capital, and the value can be found easily from aggregate data. Others, such as β or δ, have been the objects of a large number of microeconomic-based studies, and there is a set of values that are more or less generally accepted. Still others, such as A, γ, and the probability distribution of u_{t+1}, are open questions, and we need some rules to help us choose them. These parameters we *calibrate*. Since we cannot see the variables directly, we choose values for these variables so that other relationships in the model have values similar to the ones we see in the data. For example, we choose A so that, given the parameters already chosen, the time spent working is near one-third of total time (approximately 8 hours per day). We choose γ and the distribution of u_{t+1} so that the variance and covariance of y_t that comes from multiple simulations of the model are similar to those observed in the data.

Hansen's model is calibrated for quarterly observations of the data. Therefore, we use values for the parameters that are different from those used in earlier chapters. Here $\beta = .99$, $\delta = .025$, $\theta = .36$. The equations for the stationary state values of $\bar{H}$ and $\bar{K}$ we found above, and are

$$\bar{H} = \frac{1}{1 + \frac{A}{(1-\theta)}\left[1 - \frac{\beta\delta\theta}{1-\beta(1-\delta)}\right]} \tag{6.4}$$

and

$$\bar{K} = \bar{H}\left[\frac{\theta\bar{\lambda}}{\frac{1}{\beta} - (1-\delta)}\right]^{\frac{1}{1-\theta}}. \tag{6.5}$$

The stochastic process for technology was chosen so that $\bar{\lambda} = 1$. What remains to be determined are the values for A and γ. Hansen chose a value of $A = 2$, which, for his choice of parameters, resulted in $\bar{H} = 1/3$, or that, in equilibrium, people spent a third of their time working. For the parameters we are using here, Figure 6.1 shows the relationship between A and the resulting $\bar{H}$ that come from equation 6.4. In this equation, all the other parameters are already determined, so there is a simple relationship between the value of A and that of $\bar{H}$, that shown in the figure. For our choice of parameters, a value of $A = 1.72$ results in about one-third of the available time spent working. We will use this value in our calculations.

The value for γ comes from estimations of a log version of the production function,

$$\ln \lambda_t = \ln Y_t - \theta \ln K_t - (1 - \theta)H_t,$$

using data from the United States. In this series, the first lag autocorrelations coefficient on the series $\{\lambda_t\}$ is about .95. We use this value so $\gamma = .95$.

Choosing a distribution for μ_{t+1} is more complicated. Typically, the variance is chosen so that simulations of the model result in a variance output, Y_t, that is similar to the ones observed in the data from the United States. This, however, is done after the laws of motion have been calculated, so we will determine this value later.

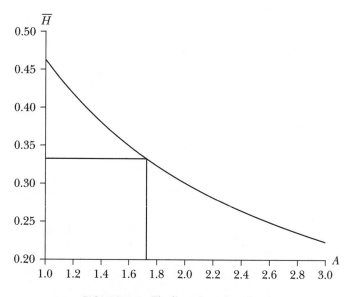

FIGURE 6.1 Finding the value for A

With $A = 1.72$, $\bar{H} = .3335$. Using this value in equation 6.5, one finds that $\bar{K} = 12.6695$. The stationary state value of output, $\bar{Y}$, is found from the production function evaluated at the stationary state values of capital and labor,

$$\bar{Y} = \bar{K}^\theta \bar{H}^{(1-\theta)} = (12.6695)^{.36}(.3335)^{.64} = 1.2353.$$

Stationary state consumption, $\bar{C}$, is found from the stationary state version of the budget constraint

$$\bar{Y} + (1 - \delta)\bar{K} = \bar{C} + \bar{K},$$

or

$$\bar{C} = \bar{Y} - \delta\bar{K} = 1.2353 - .025 \times 12.6695 = 0.9186.$$

Using the values for $\bar{Y}$ and $\bar{K}$, the $\bar{Y}/\bar{K}$ that we need for the matrices is equal to 0.0975. The last stationary state value that we need is that of $\bar{r}$, and we have from above that

$$\frac{1}{\beta} = \bar{r} + (1 - \delta) = \theta\frac{\bar{Y}}{\bar{K}} + (1 - \delta),$$

so the two calculations of $\bar{r}$ can serve as a check to see that we have done our other calculations correctly:

$$\bar{r} = \frac{1}{\beta} - (1 - \delta) = \frac{1}{.99} - 1 + .025 = 0.0351,$$

and

$$\bar{r} = \theta\frac{\bar{Y}}{\bar{K}} = .36 \times \frac{1.2353}{12.6695} = 0.0351.$$

Putting all these values into the matrices A to N, we get

$$A = [\, 0 \quad -12.6698 \quad 0 \quad 0\,]',$$

$$B = [\, 0 \quad 12.3530 \quad .36 \quad -1\,]',$$

$$C = \begin{bmatrix} 1 & -1 & -1.5004 & 0 \\ 1.2353 & -0.9186 & 0 & 0 \\ -1 & 0 & .64 & 0 \\ 1 & 0 & 0 & -1 \end{bmatrix},$$

$$D = [\,0 \quad 0 \quad 1 \quad 0\,]',$$

$$F = [0]\,, \quad G = [0]\,, \quad H = [0]\,,$$

$$J = [\,0 \quad -1 \quad 0 \quad .0348\,]\,,$$

$$K = [\,0 \quad 1 \quad 0 \quad 0\,]\,,$$

$$L = [0]\,, \quad M = [0]\,, \quad N = [.95]\,.$$

Using these matrices to find the quadratic equation, we look for the P that solves

$$0 = 7.0734 \cdot P^2 - 14.2376 \cdot P + 7.1448.$$

These are $P = 1.0592$ and $P = 0.9537$. The second value of P results in a stable equilibrium (it has an absolute value less than one), so that is what we use. Continuing with the calculations, we get $Q = 0.1132$,

$$R = [\,0.2045 \quad 0.5691 \quad -0.2430 \quad -0.7955\,]'\,,$$

and

$$S = [\,1.4523 \quad 0.3920 \quad 0.7067 \quad 1.4523\,]'\,.$$

The five equations of the laws of motion around the stationary state can be written out as

$$\tilde{K}_{t+1} = 0.9537\tilde{K}_t + 0.1132\tilde{\lambda}_t,$$

$$\tilde{Y}_t = 0.2045\tilde{K}_t + 1.4523\tilde{\lambda}_t,$$

$$\tilde{C}_t = 0.5691\tilde{K}_t + 0.3920\tilde{\lambda}_t,$$

$$\tilde{H}_t = -0.2430\tilde{K}_t + 0.7067\tilde{\lambda}_t,$$

$$\tilde{r}_t = -0.7955\tilde{K}_t + 1.4523\tilde{\lambda}_t.$$

Matlab code for finding these laws of motion is given at the end of this chapter.

6.3.3 Variances of the Variables in the Model

One needs to determine a variance for the stock to the technology process that is consistent with the data. Hansen reports that for the data set he was using (quarterly U.S. data from 1955.3 to 1984.1), output had a standard deviation of 1.76 percent. The variables we solve for in our model are log differences around a stationary state, $\tilde{Y}_t = \ln Y_t - \ln \bar{Y}$, so a standard error of 1.76 percent in the log of output is simply a standard error of .0176 for $\tilde{Y}_t$.

We use two of the laws of motion,

$$\tilde{K}_{t+1} = a\tilde{K}_t + b\tilde{\lambda}_t,$$

$$\tilde{Y}_t = c\tilde{K}_t + d\tilde{\lambda}_t,$$

and the process for technology,

$$\tilde{\lambda}_t = \gamma\tilde{\lambda}_{t-1} + \varepsilon_t,$$

to find an expression for determining the standard error of $\tilde{Y}_t$ as a function of the standard error of ε_t. We want to find the standard error for ε_t, σ_ε, that will result in a standard error of $\tilde{Y}_t$ equal to .0176 when we use the values for $a, b, c, d,$ and γ that we found for the laws of motion.

First take the law of motion for capital and substitute the process for technology to get the expression

$$\tilde{K}_{t+1} = a\tilde{K}_t + b\gamma\tilde{\lambda}_{t-1} + b\varepsilon_t.$$

One then recursively substitutes lagged versions of this equation and the process for technology to get an expression for capital in terms of the history of shocks to technology,

$$\tilde{K}_{t+1} = b\sum_{i=0}^{\infty}\sum_{j=0}^{i} a^j \gamma^{i-j}\varepsilon_{t-i}.$$

Note that the current technology level at time t, $\tilde{\lambda}_t$, can be written recursively as

$$\tilde{\lambda}_t = \sum_{i=0}^{\infty} \gamma^i \varepsilon_{t-i}.$$

These two expressions (capital lagged one period) can be substituted into the law of motion for output to give

$$\tilde{Y}_t = d\varepsilon_t + \sum_{i=0}^{\infty}\left[cb\sum_{j=0}^{i} a^j\gamma^{i-j} + d\gamma^{i+1}\right]\varepsilon_{t-1-i}.$$

Since the shocks to technology are independent, the variance for output is equal to

$$\mathrm{var}\,\tilde{Y}_t = \left(d^2 + \sum_{i=0}^{\infty}\left[cb\sum_{j=0}^{i} a^j\gamma^{i-j} + d\gamma^{i+1}\right]^2\right)\mathrm{var}\,\varepsilon_t. \tag{6.6}$$

Table 6.1 Standard errors from model

	$\tilde{Y}_t$	$\tilde{C}_t$	$\tilde{H}_t$	$\tilde{r}_t$	$\tilde{I}_t$
Standard error	$5.484\sigma_\varepsilon$	$4.065\sigma_\varepsilon$	$1.640\sigma_\varepsilon$	$3.492\sigma_\varepsilon$	$11.742\sigma_\varepsilon$
As % of output	100%	74.12%	29.90%	63.67%	214.1%

The term in the parenthesis is difficult to solve but, since the sequence converges, can be approximated to any desired degree of precision. A Matlab program that does this can be found at the end of this chapter. Using the values from the laws of motion above and $\gamma = .95$, the expression in parenthesis equals 30.0757.

The standard error of .0176 for output gives $\text{var}\,\tilde{Y}_t = .00030976$, and that implies $\text{var}\varepsilon_t = .000010299$, or a standard error for the shock to technology of .0032.

Equation 6.6 can be used, with different values for c and d, to find the variances of consumption, hours worked, and the rental on capital. For example, to find the variance of consumption, simply use $c = .5691$ and $d = .3920$ along with the original values for a, b, and γ and the value for the variance of the shock that we have just found. The resulting standard errors are reported in Table 6.1. The standard error for investment is found using the budget constraint,

$$\bar{I}\tilde{I}_t = \bar{Y}\tilde{Y}_t - \bar{C}\tilde{C}_t,$$

and gives a law of motion equal to

$$\tilde{I}_t = \hat{c}\tilde{K}_t + \hat{d}\tilde{\lambda}_t,$$

where $\hat{c} = .2045\bar{Y}/\bar{I} - .5691\bar{C}/\bar{I} = -.8530$ and $\hat{d} = 1.4523\bar{Y}/\bar{I} - 0.3920\bar{C}/\bar{I} = 4.5277$. We use these values in equation 6.6 to find the variance for investment.

Hansen calculated the variance of logged, detrended series from the United States from 1955.3 to 1984.1, using quarterly data. As mentioned earlier, he found that the variance of output was 1.76 percent. He claimed that the standard error for the shock to technology should belong to the interval $[.007, .01]$. Clearly, the number we found, .0032, is much smaller than that. Hansen's data gave standard errors for consumption, hours worked, and investment as a fraction of the standard errors of output that are shown in Table 6.2.[8] The basic Hansen model does reasonably well with consumption but fails rather badly with investment and hours worked.

---

8. Data for this table comes from Hansen [48], page 321.

Table 6.2   Standard errors from Hansen's data

	$\tilde{Y}_t$	$\tilde{C}_t$	$\tilde{H}_t$	$\tilde{I}_t$
As % of output	100%	73.30%	94.32%	488.64%

6.4   HANSEN'S MODEL WITH INDIVISIBLE LABOR

The structure of manufacturing production in the real world implies that a group of workers need to be present simultaneously to be able to run production lines. This need has led to the organization of labor through contracts for workweeks with a fixed number of hours. Workweeks tend to be 40 hours long, and there are relatively few workers who have the ability of smoothly adjusting the number of hours that they work. Many (if not most) are employed for a full workweek or they are unemployed. Hansen [48] adds this characteristic to a simple dynamic model.

Households sign contracts with firms to provide h_0 units of labor in period t with probability α_t. A random process determines if the household is one of those that works in period t. In each period, α_t of the households work h_0 hours and $1 - \alpha_t$ of the households do not work at all. All households get paid the same wages whether they work or not, so the contract is like perfect unemployment insurance. Since $\alpha_t h_0$ hours of work are being provided to the market, the labor demanded by the firms is $h_t = \alpha_t h_0$, and the firms pay a wage w_t, determined by the marginal product of h_t units of labor.

There is a good technical reason for introducing these unemployment insurance type contracts into the model. Without them, a family would have to decide to work or not. At a wage low enough, it would choose not to work and live off of the income from its capital holdings. Each family would have some wage, w^*, below which it would not provide work to the labor force and would have no labor income. The family's goods consumption would take a sharp jump at wage w^*, and its consumption of leisure would fall sharply at the same time. This jump upward in goods consumption and fall in consumption of leisure makes the consumption set nonconvex. A set is convex if a line joining any two points inside the set is also inside the set. The shaded part in Figure 6.2 is the set of goods consumption. The jump in consumption occurs at point w^*. Notice that the line from point A to point B has a section that is outside the set. Therefore, the goods consumption set is not convex. Utility could be continuous at point w^*, since the increase in utility from additional consumption is compensated for by the decline in utility from the loss of leisure.

Introducing the labor contracts in which wages are paid to all families but only a fraction of the families end up working (a fraction α_t chosen randomly from the set of all families) smooths out the goods consumption set and makes it convex over goods consumption and expected hours worked. Optimization problems have well-defined solutions when the objective functions are concave and the optimization takes place over convex sets. Adding unemployment insurance contracts makes our optimization problem well defined.

The budget constraint for each family is

$$c_t + i_t = w_t h_t + r_t k_t.$$

The expected utility in period t is equal to

$$u(c_t, \alpha_t) = \ln c_t + h_t \frac{A \ln(1 - h_0)}{h_0} + A(1 - \frac{h_t}{h_0}) \ln(1),$$

where $\frac{h_t}{h_0} = \alpha_t$, the probability that a particular household will be chosen to provide labor. Since $\ln(1) = 0$, the expected utility in period t reduces to

$$u(c_t, \alpha_t) = \ln c_t + h_t \frac{A \ln(1 - h_0)}{h_0}.$$

To simplify notation, define the constant

$$B = \frac{A \ln(1 - h_0)}{h_0}.$$

Given initial values for k_0 and λ_0, an infinitely lived household maximizes

$$\max \sum_{t=0}^{\infty} \beta^t \left[\ln c_t + B h_t \right],$$

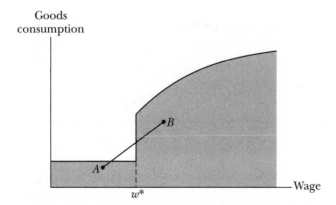

FIGURE 6.2 Nonconvex set

subject to the budget constraints

$$c_t + i_t = w_t h_t + r_t k_t$$

and

$$k_{t+1} = (1 - \delta)k_t + i_t.$$

In this economy, the production function is the same as before, except that $h_t = \alpha_t h_0$. Technology follows the same stochastic process, $\ln \lambda_{t+1} = \gamma \ln \lambda_t + \varepsilon_{t+1}$.

The social planner's problem (which gives the same solution as the competitive equilibrium) is

$$\max \sum_{t=0}^{\infty} \beta^t \left[\ln c_t + B h_t \right],$$

subject to

$$\lambda_t k_t^{\theta} h_t^{1-\theta} = c_t + k_{t+1} - (1 - \delta)k_t,$$

and

$$\ln \lambda_{t+1} = \gamma \ln \lambda_t + \varepsilon_{t+1}.$$

Recall that because production is perfectly competitive, the firms make no profits, and all income to the firms is paid out as wages and rentals; that is,

$$\lambda_t k_t^{\theta} h_t^{1-\theta} = w_t h_t + r_t k_t.$$

This problem can be written as a Bellman equation as

$$V(k_t, \lambda_t) = \max_{c_t, h_t} \left[\ln \left[c_t \right] + B h_t + \beta E_t V(k_{t+1}, \lambda_{t+1}) \right],$$

subject to

$$\lambda_t k_t^{\theta} h_t^{1-\theta} = c_t + k_{t+1} - (1 - \delta)k_t,$$

and

$$\ln \lambda_{t+1} = \gamma \ln \lambda_t + \varepsilon_{t+1}.$$

A version of the Bellman equation that is easier to work with is

$$V(k_t, \lambda_t) = \max_{k_{t+1}, h_t} \left\{ \ln \left[\lambda_t k_t^{\theta} h_t^{1-\theta} - k_{t+1} + (1 - \delta)k_t \right] + B h_t + \beta E_t V(k_{t+1}, \lambda_{t+1}) \right\}.$$

The first-order conditions from this problem, after replacing $\lambda_t k_t^\theta h_t^{1-\theta} - k_{t+1} + (1 - \delta)k_t$ with c_t, are

$$0 = \frac{1}{c_t} \left((1 - \theta) \, \lambda_t k_t^\theta h_t^{-\theta} \right) + B,$$

$$0 = -\frac{1}{c_t} + E_t \left[\frac{1}{c_{t+1}} \theta \lambda_{t+1} k_t^{\theta-1} h_t^{1-\theta} + (1 - \delta) \right].$$

We use the factor market conditions that wages equal the marginal product of labor and rentals equal the marginal product of capital. In addition, since families are identical and there is a unit mass of them, we replace individual family variables, in lowercase, with the aggregate values, in uppercase. The first-order conditions simplify to

$$1 = \beta E_t \left[\frac{C_t}{C_{t+1}} \left(r_{t+1} + (1 - \delta) \right) \right],$$

$$C_t = -\frac{(1 - \theta) \, Y_t}{B H_t}.$$

To complete the model, we add the flow budget constraint, in aggregate terms, the production function, and the two factor market conditions,

$$C_t + K_{t+1} = Y_t + (1 - \delta)K_t,$$

$$r_t = \theta \lambda_t K_t^{\theta-1} H_t^{1-\theta},$$

$$Y_t = \lambda_t K_t^\theta H_t^{1-\theta}.$$

In the first budget constraint, the zero profit condition allowed $w_t H_t + r_t K_t$ to be replaced by Y_t. This system is in the same form as the one for the model with divisible labor. The only difference is in the second first-order condition.

6.4.1   Stationary State

The stationary state occurs when $\bar{X} = X_t = X_{t+1}$, for all t, for every variable $\bar{X}$, given that all variables in this model are measured in real terms (this will change in future chapters once we introduce money to the models). The stationary state value of technology is $\bar{\lambda} = 1$. The stationary state versions of the first-order condition are

$$\frac{1}{\beta} = \bar{r} + (1 - \delta)$$

and

$$\bar{C} = -\frac{(1-\theta)\,\bar{Y}}{B\bar{H}}.$$ (6.7)

The capital market condition and the production function are

$$\bar{r} = \theta \bar{K}^{\theta-1}\bar{H}^{1-\theta},$$

$$\bar{Y} = \bar{K}^{\theta}\bar{H}^{1-\theta}.$$

The stationary state version of the flow budget constraint is

$$\bar{C} = \bar{Y} - \delta\bar{K}.$$

These can be solved to give

$$\bar{H} = -\frac{(1-\theta)}{B\left(1 - \frac{\delta\theta\beta}{1-\beta(1-\delta)}\right)}.$$ (6.8)

Since the rental on capital is known from the first equation, the stationary state capital stock is found from

$$\bar{K} = \left[\frac{\theta\beta}{1-\beta(1-\delta)}\right]^{\frac{1}{1-\theta}}\bar{H}.$$

The rest of the stationary state values follow directly.

Before we proceed with the laws of motion, it is helpful to recall that B is a function of the number of hours that a household works when it is its turn to work. The stationary state quantity of labor $\bar{H}$ is equal to $\bar{\alpha}h_0$. We want to choose values of $\bar{\alpha}$ and h_0, so that $\bar{\alpha}h_0 = \bar{H}$, where $\bar{H}$ has the value it had in the first Hansen model. With this value of labor, the second equation says that the stationary state capital stock, $\bar{K}$, will be the same as well. With capital and labor the same as in the earlier stationary state, the production function and the budget constraint imply that output, $\bar{Y}$, and consumption, $\bar{C}$, will be the same as in the first model. We want to find the values of $\bar{\alpha}$ and h_0. Equation 6.4 gives

$$\bar{H} = \frac{1}{1 + \frac{A}{(1-\theta)}\left[1 - \frac{\beta\delta\theta}{1-\beta(1-\delta)}\right]},$$

and we want our equation 6.8 to have the same value for $\bar{H}$; the definition of B implies that

$$\bar{H} = -\frac{(1-\theta)}{B\left(1 - \frac{\delta\theta\beta}{1-\beta(1-\delta)}\right)} = -\frac{(1-\theta)}{\frac{A\ln(1-h_0)}{h_0}\left(1 - \frac{\delta\theta\beta}{1-\beta(1-\delta)}\right)}.$$

Combining these two equations for $\bar{H}$ gives

$$\frac{1}{1 + \frac{A}{(1-\theta)}\left[1 - \frac{\beta\delta\theta}{1-\beta(1-\delta)}\right]} = -\frac{(1-\theta)}{\frac{A\ln(1-h_0)}{h_0}\left(1 - \frac{\delta\theta\beta}{1-\beta(1-\delta)}\right)},$$

which simplifies to

$$\frac{h_0}{\ln(1-h_0)} = -\frac{\frac{A}{(1-\theta)}\left[1 - \frac{\beta\delta\theta}{1-\beta(1-\delta)}\right]}{1 + \frac{A}{(1-\theta)}\left[1 - \frac{\beta\delta\theta}{1-\beta(1-\delta)}\right]} = G, \qquad (6.9)$$

where the constant G is comprised of parameters of the model and, with the parameter values we have been using for the first Hansen model, $G = -.6665$. In Figure 6.3, the two lines are the right- and left-hand sides of equation 6.9. The lines cross where $h_0 = .583$, and that is the value we will use in our exercises. With $\bar{H} = .3335$ in the first Hansen model, $\bar{\alpha} = \bar{H}/h_0 = .3335/.583 = .572$. For those who work in period t, $h_t = .583$, and there is a 57.2 percent chance that a given household will be supplying labor in period t. For the model with these values for h_0 and $\bar{\alpha}$, Table 6.3 gives the stationary state values for this economy.

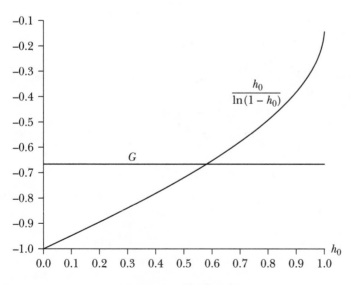

FIGURE 6.3 Finding h_0

Table 6.3   Value of variables in stationary state

Variable	$\bar{H}$	$\bar{K}$	$\bar{Y}$	$\bar{C}$	$\bar{w}$	$\bar{r}$
Value	.3335	12.6698	1.2353	.9186	2.3706	.0351

6.4.2   Log-Linear Version of the Indivisible Labor Model

The log-linear version of Hansen's model with indivisible labor is

$$0 \approx \tilde{C}_t - E_t\tilde{C}_{t+1} + \beta\bar{r}E_t\tilde{r}_{t+1},$$

$$0 \approx \tilde{C}_t + \tilde{H}_t - \tilde{Y}_t,$$

$$0 \approx \bar{Y}\tilde{Y}_t - \bar{C}\tilde{C}_t + (1-\delta)\bar{K}\tilde{K}_t - \bar{K}\tilde{K}_{t+1},$$

$$0 \approx \tilde{Y}_t - \tilde{\lambda}_t - \theta\tilde{K}_t - (1-\theta)\tilde{H}_t,$$

and

$$0 \approx \tilde{Y}_t - \tilde{K}_t - \tilde{r}_t.$$

Since there is only one condition (the first) in expectations, we can write the log-linear version of the model as

$$0 = Ax_t + Bx_{t-1} + Cy_t + Dz_t,$$

$$0 = E_t \left[Fx_{t+1} + Gx_t + Hx_{t-1} + Jy_{t+1} + Ky_t + Lz_{t+1} + Mz_t \right],$$

$$z_{t+1} = Nz_t + \varepsilon_{t+1} \quad E_t(\varepsilon_{t+1}) = 0,$$

where $x_t = \left[\tilde{K}_{t+1}\right]$, $y_t = \left[\tilde{Y}_t, \tilde{C}_t, \tilde{H}_t, \tilde{r}_t\right]$, and $z_t = \left[\tilde{\lambda}_t\right]$. For our model,

$$A = [\, 0 \quad -\bar{K} \quad 0 \quad 0\,]',$$

$$B = [\, 0 \quad \bar{K}(1-\delta) \quad \theta \quad -1\,]',$$

$$C = \begin{bmatrix} 1 & -1 & -1 & 0 \\ \bar{Y} & -\bar{C} & 0 & 0 \\ -1 & 0 & (1-\theta) & 0 \\ 1 & 0 & 0 & -1 \end{bmatrix},$$

$$D = [\, 0 \quad 0 \quad 1 \quad 0\,]',$$

$$F = [0], \quad G = [0], \quad H = [0],$$

$$J = [\, 0 \quad -1 \quad 0 \quad \beta \bar{r}\,],$$

$$K = [\, 0 \quad 1 \quad 0 \quad 0\,],$$

$$L = [0], \quad M = [0], N = [\gamma].$$

As before, the solution for this economy is a set of matrices, P, Q, R, and S, that describe the equilibrium laws of motion,

$$x_t = P x_{t-1} + Q z_t$$

and

$$y_t = R x_{t-1} + S z_t.$$

Given these values of h_0 and $\bar{\alpha}$, the only change in the matrices is in the third element of the first row of matrix C. The rest of the model is unchanged. Solving the model in exactly the same way we did before gives

$$\tilde{K}_{t+1} = .9418 \tilde{K}_t + .1552 \lambda_t$$

and

$$y_t = R \tilde{K}_t + S \lambda_t,$$

where

$$R = \left[0.0550, 0.5316, -0.4766, -0.9450 \right]'$$

and

$$S = \left[1.9418, 0.4703, 1.4715, 1.9417 \right]'.$$

Using these values for the laws of motion, one can calculate, as we did above, the standard errors of the variables in the vector y_t. Table 6.4 shows these standard errors.

The table shows that the relative standard (relative to output) of labor supply has increased when compared to the basic version of the model. Compared

Table 6.4 Standard errors of indivisible labor model

	$\tilde{Y}_t$	$\tilde{C}_t$	$\tilde{H}_t$	$\tilde{r}_t$	$\tilde{I}_t$
Standard errors	$6.431\sigma_\varepsilon$	$4.081\sigma_\varepsilon$	$3.444\sigma_\varepsilon$	$4.514\sigma_\varepsilon$	$15.722\sigma_\varepsilon$
As % of output	100%	63.46%	53.55%	70.19%	244.5%

to the data, the relative standard error of consumption, investment, and even labor supply are still too low, although investment is better in this model than in the basic one. Consumption standard error is worse than in the basic version. The standard error of the shock to technology, σ_ε, is smaller than in the basic version. Since the standard error of output is $6.431\sigma_\varepsilon = .0176$, σ_ε is now only .0027. This version of the model contains substantially more amplification[9] than the basic version, so the shock to technology that is required to account for the standard error in output is only about 85 percent of what it was in the version of this model with divisible labor.

6.5 IMPULSE RESPONSE FUNCTIONS

Comparing standard errors and correlations of the model with those from the data is one way of evaluating the performance of the model. At one level, we can say the model is doing a good job of representing the economy if these statistical characteristics, found either analytically as in this chapter or from simulations (as will be done in Chapter 7), are close to those of the economy. In fact, a model is frequently deemed better than others if it does a better job of mimicking the statistics of the economy.

Another way of looking at the dynamic properties of an economy, either a real one or a model, is by studying its impulse response functions. The name tells all. We are interested in observing how a model or an economy responds to an impulse applied to one of its error terms. The economy begins in a stationary state, with all shocks to stochastic processes set to zero (or their mean value if it is not zero) and, since this is a model in log differences from the stationary state, with all variables set to zero. One then applies a small, positive, one-period change to the shock of interest and calculates how the economy responds to this shock. In the log-linear version of Hansen's model, the only stochastic shock is to technology,

$$\tilde{\lambda}_t = \gamma \tilde{\lambda}_{t-1} + \varepsilon_t, \tag{6.10}$$

where the shock is ε_t. The time path the economy follows is defined by the laws of motion (the linear policy functions)

$$\tilde{K}_{t+1} = P\tilde{K}_t + Q\tilde{\lambda}_t \tag{6.11}$$

and

$$y_t = R\tilde{K}_t + S\tilde{\lambda}_t, \tag{6.12}$$

9. Amplification can be thought of as the ratio of the variance of important variables of the model, output or prices, for example, to the variance of the shocks.

where $y_t = [\tilde{Y}_t, \tilde{C}_t, \tilde{H}_t, \tilde{r}_t]'$. With $\gamma = .95$, a one-time shock to technology of $\varepsilon_t = .01$ applied to equation 6.10 will generate the time path for technology that is shown in Figure 6.4. This time path for technology will generate the time paths for $\tilde{K}_t$ and for the variables in y_t that are shown in Figure 6.5. One first finds the time path for capital by recursively applying equation 6.11. Using these time paths for technology and capital, one repeatedly applies equation 6.12 to find the time paths for the variables in y_t. These time paths are the responses of the model to the one-time impulse in the technology shock, ε_t.

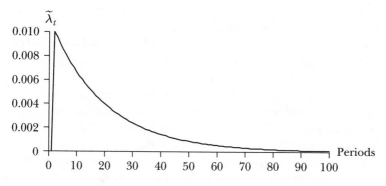

FIGURE 6.4 Response of technology to a .01 impulse

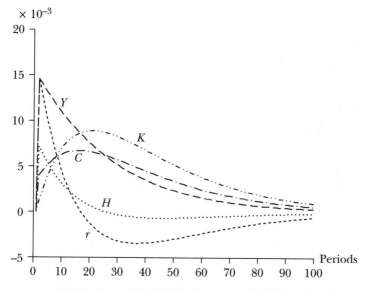

FIGURE 6.5 Responses of Hansen's basic model

Figure 6.6 shows the responses for the same variables to the same shock in Hansen's model with indivisible labor. It should be fairly clear that the model with indivisible labor produces a bigger response than does the basic model.

A useful, but as yet not very common, way to compare the responses of two models to the same impulse is to plot the responses of each variable in one model against the same variable in the second model. Imagine taking Figure 6.5 and Figure 6.6 and plotting them in the same three-dimensional graph where they share the time axis. Figure 6.7 shows this three-dimensional graph. Time goes to the back and to the left. The horizontal axis to the right measures the responses of the basic model. The vertical axis measures the responses of the model with indivisible labor. We now rotate the three-dimensional graph so that the time axis goes directly away from us and we only see a two-dimensional graph with the responses of each variable of the basic model measured on the horizontal axis and those of the model with indivisible labor on the vertical axis. This is shown in Figure 6.8. The relative response can be compared by looking at the line for each variable relative to the 45 degree line (that is drawn in). A response line above the 45 degree line means that the response of the model with indivisible labor for this variable is greater than the model with divisible labor. If a line were in the upper left or the lower right quadrants, then the responses of the corresponding variable would be in the opposite direction in the two models. In this case, all variables respond in the same direction, but

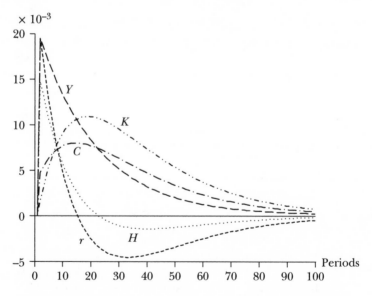

FIGURE 6.6   Responses for Hansen's model with indivisible labor

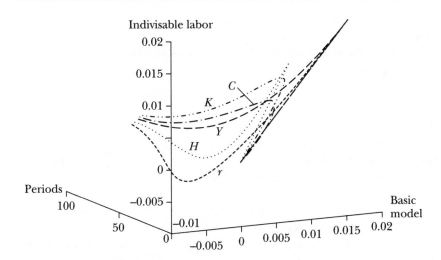

FIGURE 6.7   Responses for both Hansen models

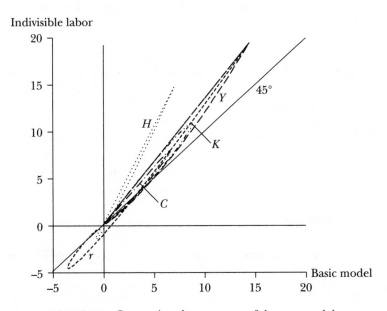

FIGURE 6.8   Comparing the response of the two models

the responses of the variables in the model with indivisible labor are larger. Figure 6.8 illustrates our observation that the economy with indivisible labor has bigger responses to a technology shock and that the biggest differences in the response are in labor, H in the figure.

6.6 REPRISE

Adding indivisible labor to Hansen's simple growth model produces simulations where the variance in labor is much closer to that observed for the United States. Adding the idea of indivisible labor to the economy has a number of advantages, one of the most interesting of which is that it allows one to think about unemployment and how changes in policies can end up changing unemployment. The way that indivisible labor is added results in only one technical change in the model (labor becomes linear in the utility function) and only one change in the log-linear version of the model (the coefficient on labor in the second first-order condition goes from $1/(1 - \bar{H})$ to 1). This change in the coefficient increases the rate at which labor responds to shocks to the economy and increases the relative variance of labor compared to that of output.

Using first-order (linear) approximations of the model for dynamic simulations as we have done in this chapter is fine if one believes that the economy is quite near the stationary state and the shocks are small enough so that the economy never goes very far from that stationary state. The techniques of log linearization that are shown in this chapter are quite simple, although some care needs to be taken with the algebra. Once the log-linear version of the model was found, the fact that there was only one equation with expectational variables meant that the solution to the quadratic equation (for finding the P matrix) could be found without matrix methods. In a later chapter we will show how to use matrix methods when there is more than one equation with expectational variables.

The basic theory for solving linear difference equations in a world with rational expectations was developed by Blanchard and Kahn [14]; see Appendix 2 for an explanation of their solution method. Further extensions of what was developed in this chapter and additional detail can be found in Uhlig [86] and Christiano [28].

6.7 APPENDIX 1: SOLVING THE LOG-LINEAR MODEL

In this appendix we show how we find the conditions for solving the log-linear version of the model once it has been divided into a set of equations without expectations and a set of equations in expectations.

The model is divided into the sets of matrix equations

$$0 = Ax_t + Bx_{t-1} + Cy_t + Dz_t,$$

$$0 = E_t \left[Fx_{t+1} + Gx_t + Hx_{t-1} + Jy_{t+1} + Ky_t + Lz_{t+1} + Mz_t \right],$$

and a stochastic process

$$z_{t+1} = Nz_t + \varepsilon_{t+1} \quad E_t(\varepsilon_{t+1}) = 0.$$

The division of the model is important in the sense that we try to keep the dimension of the second (the expectational) equation small and, if possible, to have the matrix C of full rank and, therefore, invertible.

We look for a solution for linear laws of motion of the model of the form

$$x_t = Px_{t-1} + Qz_t,$$

$$y_t = Rx_{t-1} + Sz_t.$$

The problem we have is to find the values for the matrices P, Q, R, and S. We begin by substituting the laws of motion into the two equations above (in some cases twice) and reduce each equation to one in which there are only two variables: x_{t-1} and z_t. One needs to use the stochastic process in the expectational equation to replace z_{t+1} by $Nz_t + \varepsilon_{t+1}$. When one takes expectations, the $\varepsilon_{t+1} = 0$ and disappear. After the substitutions, the two equations are

$$0 = [AP + B + CR]x_{t-1} + [AQ + CS + D]z_t$$

and

$$0 = [FPP + GP + H + JRP + KR]x_{t-1}$$
$$+ [FPQ + FQN + GQ + JRQ + JSN + KS + LN + M]z_t.$$

Both equations must equal zero for any initial condition x_{t-1} and for any stochastic shock z_t. Since the period t shocks are independent of the period $t - 1$ values of the endogenous variables, the only way that the equations can equal zero is if the parts in square brackets are equal to zero. Given that the parts in square brackets are all equal to zero, we have four equations to find the four matrices we are looking for:

$$0 = AP + B + CR$$

and

$$0 = AQ + CS + D$$

from the first equation, and

$$0 = FP^2 + GP + H + JRP + KR$$

and

$$0 = FPQ + FQN + GQ + JRQ + JSN + KS + LN + M$$

from the second.

We use the first equation to solve for R,

$$R = -C^{-1}[AP + B],$$

and the second to find S,

$$S = -C^{-1}[AQ + D].$$

Substituting for R in the third equation results in

$$0 = FP^2 + GP + H - J\left[C^{-1}[AP + B]\right]P - K\left[C^{-1}[AP + B]\right],$$

and, after a bit of matrix algebra, this becomes the matrix quadratic equation

$$0 = \left[F - JC^{-1}A\right]P^2 - \left[JC^{-1}B - G + KC^{-1}A\right]P - KC^{-1}B + H.$$

Solving the matrix quadratic equation gives the matrix P, and once we have P, we use it in the above equation to find R.

The final expression is found by taking the fourth equation and substituting in for S. This gives

$$0 = FPQ + FQN + GQ + JRQ-$$

$$J\left[C^{-1}[AQ + D]\right]N - K\left[C^{-1}[AQ + D]\right] + LN + M,$$

which simplifies to

$$\left[\left(F - JC^{-1}A\right)Q\right]N + \left[FP + G + JR - KC^{-1}A\right]Q$$

$$= \left[JC^{-1}D - L\right]N + KC^{-1}D - M.$$

This equation presents a problem. We are interested in finding the matrix Q as a linear function of the known matrices of the system, but given where Q appears in the equation, there is no simple, direct matrix manipulation that will permit us to solve for it. In the first component of the first line of this equation, Q is the second from the last matrix and, in the second component of this line, it is the last element. To solve for Q, we make use of the following theorem from tensor algebra.[10]

THEOREM 6.1 *Let* **A**, **B**, *and* **C** *be matrices whose dimensions are such that the product* **ABC** *exists. Then*

$$\text{vec}(\mathbf{ABC}) = \left(\mathbf{C}' \otimes \mathbf{A}\right) \cdot \text{vec}(\mathbf{B})$$

where the symbol $\otimes$ *denotes the Kronecker product.*

The operator $\text{vec}(\mathbf{X})$ of a matrix $\mathbf{X}$ results in column-wise vectorization of the form

$$\text{vec}\left(\begin{bmatrix} a_{11} & a_{12} & a_{13} \\ a_{21} & a_{22} & a_{23} \end{bmatrix}\right) = \begin{bmatrix} a_{11} \\ a_{21} \\ a_{12} \\ a_{22} \\ a_{13} \\ a_{23} \end{bmatrix}.$$

The Kronecker product is defined (for the case where **A** is 2×2 and **B** is 3×2) as

$$\mathbf{A} \otimes \mathbf{B} = \begin{bmatrix} a_{11} & a_{12} \\ a_{21} & a_{22} \end{bmatrix} \otimes \begin{bmatrix} b_{11} & b_{12} \\ b_{21} & b_{22} \\ b_{31} & b_{32} \end{bmatrix} = \begin{bmatrix} a_{11}\mathbf{B} & a_{12}\mathbf{B} \\ a_{21}\mathbf{B} & a_{22}\mathbf{B} \end{bmatrix}$$

$$= \begin{bmatrix} a_{11}b_{11} & a_{11}b_{12} & a_{12}b_{11} & a_{12}b_{12} \\ a_{11}b_{21} & a_{11}b_{22} & a_{12}b_{21} & a_{12}b_{22} \\ a_{11}b_{31} & a_{11}b_{32} & a_{12}b_{31} & a_{12}b_{32} \\ a_{21}b_{11} & a_{21}b_{12} & a_{22}b_{11} & a_{22}b_{12} \\ a_{21}b_{21} & a_{21}b_{22} & a_{22}b_{21} & a_{22}b_{22} \\ a_{21}b_{31} & a_{21}b_{32} & a_{22}b_{31} & a_{22}b_{32} \end{bmatrix}.$$

A useful corollary to the above theorem is the special case where **B** has dimension $n \times r$, and **C** is an identity matrix of dimension n, $\mathbf{I}_n$.

COROLLARY 6.1

$$\text{vec}(\mathbf{AB}) = \left(\mathbf{I}_n \otimes \mathbf{A}\right) \text{vec}(\mathbf{B}).$$

---

10. The statement of this theorem comes from Hamilton [47], page 265.

The proof of the corollary comes from simply replacing C in the theorem by the identity matrix I_n.

Using this theorem and corollary, one can write $\left[\left(F - JC^{-1}A\right) Q\right] N$ as

$$\text{vec}\left(\left[\left(F - JC^{-1}A\right) Q\right] N\right) = \left(N' \otimes \left(F - JC^{-1}A\right)\right) \text{vec}\,(Q)$$

and $\left[FP + G + JR - KC^{-1}A\right] Q$ as

$$\text{vec}\left(\left[FP + G + JR - KC^{-1}A\right] Q\right)$$
$$= \left(I_k \otimes \left(FP + G + JR - KC^{-1}A\right)\right) \text{vec}\,(Q)\,,$$

where k is the number of columns in Q.

Using these results,

$$\left[\left(F - JC^{-1}A\right) Q\right] N + \left[FP + G + JR - KC^{-1}A\right] Q$$
$$= \left[JC^{-1}D - L\right] N + KC^{-1}D - M$$

can be solved for $\text{vec}(Q)$ by applying the vec operator to both sides of the equation and getting

$$\left(N' \otimes (F - JC^{-1}A) + I_k \otimes (FP + G + JR - KC^{-1}A)\right) \text{vec}(Q)$$
$$= \text{vec}\left(\left(JC^{-1}D - L\right) N + KC^{-1}D - M\right).$$

The matrix Q is constructed by separating the columns in $\text{vec}(Q)$, where

$$\text{vec}(Q)$$
$$= \left(N' \otimes (F - JC^{-1}A) + I_k \otimes (FP + G + JR - KC^{-1}A)\right)^{-1}$$
$$\times\ \text{vec}\left(\left(JC^{-1}D - L\right) N + KC^{-1}D - M\right).$$

Once Q is defined, so is the matrix S from

$$S = -C^{-1}\left[AQ + D\right].$$

6.8   APPENDIX 2: BLANCHARD AND KAHN'S SOLUTION METHOD

The method that we are using in this book for solving linear dynamic stochastic general equilibrium models is known as the undetermined coefficients method. It was originally presented by McCallum [60] and developed by Christiano [28]. What is probably the clearest exposition of the method is by Uhlig [86], although he used a solution technique different from that of Christiano. Basically, a linear form for the solution is assumed and the method finds the coefficients for the solution of this form. The assumption of a linear form for the solution is not a very great jump, since linear models generally provide linear solutions.

The undetermined coefficients solution method was not the first method in the literature for solving rational expectations models. The first method, in economics, for solving these linear rational expectations models comes from Blanchard and Kahn [14], who used techniques that were in the engineering literature (from Vaughan [88]) and applied them to macroeconomic models.[11] Christiano uses solution techniques similar to those of Blanchard and Kahn for solving his undetermined coefficients problems. A good expanded explanation of these methods can be found in Blake and Fernandez-Corugedo [12].

6.8.1   General Version

A linear model can be written (in what is known as a state space representation) as

$$B \begin{bmatrix} x_{t+1} \\ E_t y_{t+1} \end{bmatrix} = A \begin{bmatrix} x_t \\ y_t \end{bmatrix} + G \varepsilon_t, \tag{6.13}$$

where x_t is an $(n \times 1)$ vector of predetermined variables at date t, y_t is an $(m \times 1)$ vector of non-predetermined variables at time t, $E_t y_{t+1}$ is the $(m \times 1)$ vector of expectations for the non-predetermined variables at date $t + 1$, ε_t is a $(k \times 1)$ vector of stochastic shocks, A and B are $((n + m) \times (n + m))$ matrices, and G is an $((n + m) \times k)$ matrix. The difference between predetermined and non-predetermined variables is that the values of the predetermined variables at time $t + 1$ do not depend on the values of the time $t + 1$ shocks, while the values of the non-predetermined variables do depend on them. That is why, at time t, one can only think of the expectation of the value of a time $t + 1$ non-predetermined variable. Its realized value will depend on the (unknown) time $t + 1$ shock. The equations of the system that are used to make the matrices A, B, and G are ordered so that those with expectations in them are last (given by the bottom rows of the matrices).

If the matrix B is invertible, then the first-order difference system of equation 6.13 can be written as

11. I thank Andrew P. Blake and Emilio Fernandez-Corugedo for showing me the results given here.

$$\begin{bmatrix} x_{t+1} \\ E_t y_{t+1} \end{bmatrix} = B^{-1} A \begin{bmatrix} x_t \\ y_t \end{bmatrix} + B^{-1} G \varepsilon_t. \qquad (6.14)$$

The matrix, $Z = B^{-1}A$, can be decomposed into $Z = M \Lambda M^{-1}$, where Λ is a matrix with the eigenvalues of the matrix Z on its diagonal, and where M is a matrix of the right eigenvectors. Reorder the eigenvalues from smallest to largest (along the diagonal) as $\bar{\Lambda}$ and the corresponding matrix of eigenvectors as $\overline{M}$ (with the same reordering, so that each eigenvector is still associated with the same eigenvalue as before). The condition of Blanchard and Kahn for finding a solution to this problem is that the number of eigenvalues that are outside the unit circle (which have an absolute value greater than one) is equal to the number of expectational variables, m.

When the number of expectational equations is equal to the number of explosive roots (the number of eigenvalues outside the unit circle), one can impose conditions on the equilibrium to guarantee that there exists a stable solution to the economy.

To begin with, we consider just the deterministic part of the model and write equation 6.14 as

$$\begin{bmatrix} x_{t+1} \\ E_t y_{t+1} \end{bmatrix} = \overline{M} \bar{\Lambda} \overline{M}^{-1} \begin{bmatrix} x_t \\ y_t \end{bmatrix}$$

or, after multiplying both sides by $\overline{M}^{-1}$, as

$$\overline{M}^{-1} \begin{bmatrix} x_{t+1} \\ E_t y_{t+1} \end{bmatrix} = \bar{\Lambda} \overline{M}^{-1} \begin{bmatrix} x_t \\ y_t \end{bmatrix}. \qquad (6.15)$$

Partitioning the $\overline{M}^{-1}$ matrix as

$$\overline{M}^{-1} = \begin{bmatrix} \widehat{M}_{11} & \widehat{M}_{12} \\ \widehat{M}_{21} & \widehat{M}_{22} \end{bmatrix}$$

and the matrix $\bar{\Lambda}$ as

$$\bar{\Lambda} = \begin{bmatrix} \bar{\Lambda}_{11} & 0_{12} \\ 0_{21} & \bar{\Lambda}_{22} \end{bmatrix},$$

where a matrix X_{11} is $n \times n$, a matrix X_{12} is $n \times m$, a matrix X_{21} is $m \times n$, and a matrix X_{22} is $m \times m$. A matrix 0_{ij} is a matrix of zeros of the size that corresponds to ij. The matrix $\bar{\Lambda}_{11}$ is a diagonal matrix that contains all the stable eigenvalues of the model, and $\bar{\Lambda}_{22}$ is a diagonal matrix with all the unstable eigenvalues (those outside the unit circle). Using this partition, equation 6.15 can be written as the two matrix equations

$$\left[\widehat{M}_{11} x_{t+1} + \widehat{M}_{12} E_t y_{t+1} \right] = \bar{\Lambda}_{11} \left[\widehat{M}_{11} x_t + \widehat{M}_{12} y_t \right] \qquad (6.16)$$

and

$$\left[\widehat{M}_{21}x_{t+1} + \widehat{M}_{22}E_t y_{t+1} \right] = \bar{\Lambda}_{22} \left[\widehat{M}_{21}x_t + \widehat{M}_{22}y_t \right].$$

Given that the elements of the diagonal matrix $\bar{\Lambda}_{22}$ are all greater than one, if $[\widehat{M}_{21}x_t + \widehat{M}_{22}y_t]$ is ever nonzero, the model will explode. For there to be a stable solution to this problem, $[\widehat{M}_{21}x_t + \widehat{M}_{22}y_t] = 0$, always, and that implies that $[\widehat{M}_{21}x_{t+1} + \widehat{M}_{22}y_{t+1}] = 0$ as well. For all this to happen, in each period, the non-predetermined variables, y_t, need to be equal to

$$y_t = - \left(\widehat{M}_{22} \right)^{-1} \widehat{M}_{21}x_t.$$

This equation solves for the non-predetermined variables in each period as a linear function of the predetermined variables. Since this version of the model is deterministic,

$$E_t y_{t+1} = y_{t+1} = - \left(\widehat{M}_{22} \right)^{-1} \widehat{M}_{21}x_{t+1},$$

and substituting these two results into equation 6.16, after a bit of algebra, one gets

$$x_{t+1} = \left[\widehat{M}_{11} - \widehat{M}_{12} \left(\widehat{M}_{22} \right)^{-1} \widehat{M}_{21} \right]^{-1} \bar{\Lambda}_{11} \left[\widehat{M}_{11} - \widehat{M}_{12} \left(\widehat{M}_{22} \right)^{-1} \widehat{M}_{21} \right] x_t.$$

6.8.2   Stochastic Shocks

When the economy has stochastic shocks, the solution is a bit different. We still consider only the case where B is invertible, so we can write the model in its stochastic version as

$$\left[\begin{array}{c} x_{t+1} \\ E_t y_{t+1} \end{array} \right] = B^{-1}A \left[\begin{array}{c} x_t \\ y_t \end{array} \right] + B^{-1}G \left[\varepsilon_t \right].$$

Using the exact same eigenvalue-eigenvector decomposition as before, one gets

$$\overline{M}^{-1} \left[\begin{array}{c} x_{t+1} \\ E_t y_{t+1} \end{array} \right] = \bar{\Lambda} \overline{M}^{-1} \left[\begin{array}{c} x_t \\ y_t \end{array} \right] + \overline{M}^{-1}B^{-1}G \left[\varepsilon_t \right],$$

or

$$\left[\begin{array}{cc} \widehat{M}_{11} & \widehat{M}_{12} \\ \widehat{M}_{21} & \widehat{M}_{22} \end{array} \right] \left[\begin{array}{c} x_{t+1} \\ E_t y_{t+1} \end{array} \right] = \left[\begin{array}{cc} \bar{\Lambda}_{11} & 0_{12} \\ 0_{21} & \bar{\Lambda}_{22} \end{array} \right] \left[\begin{array}{cc} \widehat{M}_{11} & \widehat{M}_{12} \\ \widehat{M}_{21} & \widehat{M}_{22} \end{array} \right] \left[\begin{array}{c} x_t \\ y_t \end{array} \right] + \left[\begin{array}{c} \widehat{G}_1 \\ \widehat{G}_2 \end{array} \right] \left[\varepsilon_t \right],$$

where everything is as before except that we define the partition

$$\left[\begin{array}{c} \widehat{G}_1 \\ \widehat{G}_2 \end{array} \right] = \overline{M}^{-1}B^{-1}G,$$

with $\widehat{G}_1$ a $k \times n$ matrix and $\widehat{G}_2$ a $k \times m$ matrix. The lower partition, that associated with the eigenvalues outside the unit circle (the exploding ones), can be written as

$$\widehat{M}_{21}x_{t+1} + \widehat{M}_{22}E_t y_{t+1} = \bar{\Lambda}_{22}\left[\widehat{M}_{21}x_t + \widehat{M}_{22}y_t\right] + \widehat{G}_2\left[\varepsilon_t\right]$$

or, letting $\lambda_t = \widehat{M}_{21}x_t + \widehat{M}_{22}y_t$, as

$$E_t\lambda_{t+1} = \bar{\Lambda}_{22}\lambda_t + \widehat{G}_2\left[\varepsilon_t\right].$$

Since the $\bar{\Lambda}_{22}$ are all greater than one, this can be solved forward (see Sargent [71], for example) to get

$$\lambda_t = -\sum_{i=0}^{\infty} \bar{\Lambda}_{22}^{-i-1}\widehat{G}_2 E_t\left[\varepsilon_{t+i}\right].$$

Given the expectations on future shocks, the current value of λ_t is found from a converging sequence. If, as we normally set up a model, the expected future values of the shocks are zero, then this equation can be written as

$$\lambda_t = -\bar{\Lambda}_{22}^{-1}\widehat{G}_2\left[\varepsilon_t\right]$$

or, writing out λ_t, as

$$y_t = -\widehat{M}_{22}^{-1}\widehat{M}_{21}x_t - \widehat{M}_{22}^{-1}\bar{\Lambda}_{22}^{-1}\widehat{G}_2\left[\varepsilon_t\right].$$

The time $t + 1$ values for the predetermined variables are found just as above but using this equation for y_t and

$$E_t y_{t+1} = -\widehat{M}_{22}^{-1}\widehat{M}_{21}x_{t+1}$$

for the expected value of y_{t+1}. We use the stable part of the process and, after a bit of algebra, get the equation

$$x_{t+1} = \left[\widehat{M}_{11} - \widehat{M}_{12}\widehat{M}_{22}^{-1}\widehat{M}_{21}\right]^{-1}\bar{\Lambda}_{11}\left[\widehat{M}_{11} - \widehat{M}_{12}\widehat{M}_{22}^{-1}\widehat{M}_{21}\right]x_t$$
$$- \left[\widehat{M}_{11} - \widehat{M}_{12}\widehat{M}_{22}^{-1}\widehat{M}_{21}\right]^{-1}\left[\bar{\Lambda}_{11}\widehat{M}_{12}\widehat{M}_{22}^{-1}\bar{\Lambda}_{22}^{-1}\widehat{G}_2 - \widehat{G}_1\right]\left[\varepsilon_t\right].$$

The coefficient on x_t is exactly the same as in the deterministic case, and we add to that a fairly complicated term for the vector of shocks.

6.8.3   Hansen's Model and Blanchard-Kahn

We need to write out the log-linear version of Hansen's model with indivisible labor (ordered with the expectational variables last) in a state space version.

The model is

$$\bar{K}\tilde{K}_{t+1} = \bar{Y}\tilde{Y}_t - \bar{C}\tilde{C}_t + (1-\delta)\,\bar{K}\tilde{K}_t,$$

$$\tilde{\lambda}_t = \gamma\tilde{\lambda}_{t-1} + \varepsilon_t,$$

$$0 = \tilde{\lambda}_t - \theta\tilde{Y}_t + \theta\tilde{K}_t - (1-\theta)\,\tilde{C}_t,$$

$$0 = \tilde{K}_t + \tilde{r}_t - \tilde{Y}_t,$$

$$E_t\tilde{C}_{t+1} - \beta\bar{r}E_t\tilde{r}_{t+1} = \tilde{C}_t.$$

We have made the system somewhat smaller than the version at the beginning of section 6.4.2 by substituting out $\tilde{H}_t$. Write the vector of variables at time $t+1$ as

$$\begin{bmatrix} x_{t+1} \\ E_t y_{t+1} \end{bmatrix} = \begin{bmatrix} \tilde{K}_{t+1} \\ \tilde{\lambda}_t \\ \tilde{Y}_t \\ E_t\tilde{C}_{t+1} \\ E_t\tilde{r}_{t+1} \end{bmatrix},$$

where $\tilde{K}_{t+1}$, $\tilde{\lambda}_t$, and $\tilde{Y}_t$ are the predetermined variables and $\tilde{C}_t$ and $\tilde{r}_t$ are the jump (non-predetermined) variables. The model can be written in the state space form,

$$B\begin{bmatrix} x_{t+1} \\ E_t y_{t+1} \end{bmatrix} = A\begin{bmatrix} x_t \\ y_t \end{bmatrix} + G\left[\varepsilon_t\right], \qquad (6.17)$$

where

$$B = \begin{bmatrix} \bar{K} & 0 & -\bar{Y} & 0 & 0 \\ 0 & 1 & 0 & 0 & 0 \\ 0 & -1 & \theta & 0 & 0 \\ 0 & 0 & 1 & 0 & 0 \\ 0 & 0 & 0 & 1 & -\bar{r}\beta \end{bmatrix},$$

$$A = \begin{bmatrix} (1-\delta)\,\bar{K} & 0 & 0 & -\bar{C} & 0 \\ 0 & \gamma & 0 & 0 & 0 \\ \theta & 0 & 0 & -(1-\theta) & 0 \\ 1 & 0 & 0 & 0 & 1 \\ 0 & 0 & 0 & 1 & 0 \end{bmatrix},$$

and

$$G = \begin{bmatrix} 0 \\ 1 \\ 0 \\ 0 \\ 0 \end{bmatrix}.$$

The basic problem that we have with the model as it is written above is that the B matrix is not invertible. The method of Blanchard and Kahn using eigenvalues doesn't work for this version of Hansen's model.

6.8.4   The Generalized Schur Method

Luckily, there are ways of decomposing the matrices B and A that do let us solve the system. The generalized Schur decomposition gives us what we need. One can follow the same basic logic as in the Blanchard-Kahn problem described above, but using a different way of handling the matrices B and A. As an extra benefit, all of the matrices that one gets using the Schur decomposition are real matrices. In the method described above, it is completely possible that some of the eigenvalues and their corresponding eigenvectors are complex. While complex variables are not normally much of a problem for computer programs like Matlab, they do make things a bit more complicated. In this section, all matrices are real ones.

A generalized Schur decomposition takes a pair of square matrices (B and A) and decomposes them (usually using what is called a QZ algorithm) into the matrices T, S, Q, and Z, where

$$B = QTZ',$$
$$A = QSZ',$$

and Q and Z have the special properties that

$$QQ' = Q'Q = I = ZZ' = Z'Z$$

and where both T and S are upper triangular matrices.[12] The eigenvalues of the system are given by $\lambda_{ii} = s_{ii}/t_{ii}$, where s_{ii} and t_{ii} are the associated diagonal

---

12. An upper triangular matrix has all zero elements below the diagonal. For example,

$$A = \begin{bmatrix} a_{11} & a_{12} & a_{13} & a_{14} \\ 0 & a_{22} & a_{23} & a_{24} \\ 0 & 0 & a_{33} & a_{34} \\ 0 & 0 & 0 & a_{44} \end{bmatrix}$$

is an upper triangular matrix.

elements of matrices T and S, respectively. We assume that the program that finds the generalized Schur decomposition produces the output with the matrices Q, Z, S, and T ordered so that the absolute values of the eigenvalues increase for lower rows of the matrices[13].

The deterministic version[14] of the model of equation 6.17 can be written as

$$QTZ'\begin{bmatrix} x_{t+1} \\ E_t y_{t+1} \end{bmatrix} = QSZ'\begin{bmatrix} x_t \\ y_t \end{bmatrix}.$$

Premultiplying both sides by Q' (which removes Q, since $Q'Q = I$) and writing out Z' as a partitioned matrix gives

$$\begin{bmatrix} T_{11} & T_{12} \\ 0_{21} & T_{22} \end{bmatrix}\begin{bmatrix} Z'_{11} & Z'_{12} \\ Z'_{21} & Z'_{22} \end{bmatrix}\begin{bmatrix} x_{t+1} \\ E_t y_{t+1} \end{bmatrix} = \begin{bmatrix} S_{11} & S_{12} \\ 0_{21} & S_{22} \end{bmatrix}\begin{bmatrix} Z'_{11} & Z'_{12} \\ Z'_{21} & Z'_{22} \end{bmatrix}\begin{bmatrix} x_t \\ y_t \end{bmatrix},$$

or, concentrating just on the equations with explosive eigenvalues, the result is

$$T_{22}\left[Z'_{21}x_{t+1} + Z'_{22}E_t y_{t+1} \right] = S_{22}\left[Z'_{21}x_t + Z'_{22}y_t \right].$$

We use the notation that the submatrix Z'_{ij} is the ijth part of the partition of the Z' matrix. To keep this last equation from generating an explosive path, we need the condition

$$Z'_{21}x_t + Z'_{22}y_t = 0.$$

For this condition to hold, the jump variables at time t, y_t, must be equal to

$$y_t = -\left(Z'_{22} \right)^{-1} Z'_{21}x_t = -Nx_t,$$

where we define $N \equiv \left(Z'_{22} \right)^{-1} Z'_{21}$. Notice that the form of this result is identical to that in the original, eigenvalue-eigenvector version of Blanchard-Kahn that we did above, but here we use the submatrices that come from the Schur decomposition.

Going back to the original model, we write

$$\begin{bmatrix} B_{11} & B_{12} \\ B_{21} & B_{22} \end{bmatrix}\begin{bmatrix} x_{t+1} \\ -Nx_{t+1} \end{bmatrix} = \begin{bmatrix} A_{11} & A_{12} \\ A_{21} & A_{22} \end{bmatrix}\begin{bmatrix} x_t \\ -Nx_t \end{bmatrix}.$$

---

13. The schurg function in Scilab does this automatically, although it puts unit roots at the very bottom.

14. The stochastic version comes shortly.

The top half of this can be written as

$$\left[B_{11} - B_{12}N\right] x_{t+1} = \left[A_{11} - A_{12}N\right] x_t,$$

so one can solve this as

$$x_{t+1} = \left[B_{11} - B_{12}N\right]^{-1} \left[A_{11} - A_{12}N\right] x_t.$$

SOLVING THE DETERMINISTIC HANSEN MODEL

To find the linear solution of the jump variables as functions of the state variables for Hansen's model with indivisible labor, we use the stationary state values we found in the chapter and get

$$B = \begin{bmatrix} 12.6695 & 0 & -1.2353 & 0 & 0 \\ 0 & 1 & 0 & 0 & 0 \\ 0 & -1 & .36 & 0 & 0 \\ 0 & 0 & 1 & 0 & 0 \\ 0 & 0 & 0 & 1 & -.03475 \end{bmatrix}$$

and

$$A = \begin{bmatrix} 12.353 & 0 & 0 & -.9186 & 0 \\ 0 & .95 & 0 & 0 & 0 \\ .36 & 0 & 0 & -.64 & 0 \\ 1 & 0 & 0 & 0 & 1 \\ 0 & 0 & 0 & 1 & 0 \end{bmatrix}.$$

The generalized Schur decomposition[15] of the matrices A and B results in the four matrices S, T, Q, Z, where

$$S = \begin{bmatrix} 0 & -6.0713 & 2.5534 & -5.6797 & -0.4798 \\ 0 & 5.2880 & -3.3924 & 6.2982 & 0.1563 \\ 0 & 0 & 0.7200 & 0.6793 & -0.0954 \\ 0 & 0 & 0 & 0.9103 & 0.5953 \\ 0 & 0 & 0 & 0 & .8228 \end{bmatrix},$$

15. For a Matlab program that finds the ordered Schur decomposition, see Anderson et. al. [2]. This Matlab program can be downloaded from Evan Anderson's website at www.math.niu .edu/~anderson.

$$
T = \begin{bmatrix}
1.6296 & -6.5107 & 3.6395 & -6.0515 & -0.1748 \\
0 & 5.6147 & -2.9158 & 5.2866 & -0.2383 \\
0 & 0 & 0.7579 & 0.6832 & -0.9014 \\
0 & 0 & 0 & 0.8488 & 0.7907 \\
0 & 0 & 0 & 0 & 0
\end{bmatrix},
$$

$$
Q = \begin{bmatrix}
-0.758 & 0.6507 & 0.0124 & 0.0427 & 0 \\
0 & 0 & -0.6993 & 0.2034 & 0.6853 \\
0.2209 & 0.2562 & 0.624 & -0.1633 & 0.6853 \\
0.6137 & 0.7116 & -0.2093 & 0.1115 & -0.2467 \\
0 & 0.0682 & -0.2786 & -0.958 & 0
\end{bmatrix},
$$

and

$$
Z = \begin{bmatrix}
0 & 0.6779 & -0.3668 & 0.6371 & 0 \\
0 & 0 & -0.53 & -0.3051 & 0.7912 \\
1 & 0 & 0 & 0 & 0 \\
0 & 0.3604 & -0.4318 & -0.6321 & -0.533 \\
0 & -0.6407 & -0.631 & 0.3185 & -0.2998
\end{bmatrix}.
$$

Notice that S and T are upper triangular as required. The eigenvalues of the system are found by dividing the diagonal elements of S by the corresponding diagonal elements of T, so that,

$$
\text{eigenvalues} = \begin{bmatrix}
0/1.6296 \\
5.2880/5.6147 \\
0.7200/0.7579 \\
0.9103/0.8488 \\
0.8228/0
\end{bmatrix} = \begin{bmatrix}
0 \\
0.9418 \\
0.9500 \\
1.0725 \\
\infty
\end{bmatrix}.
$$

The first three elements in the eigenvalue vector have absolute values less than one, are inside the unit circle, and represent the stable roots of the system. The other two roots are greater than one, are outside the unit circle, and are unstable.

Using these matrices, the process for the values of the non-predetermined variables at time t is equal to

$$
\begin{bmatrix} \tilde{C}_t \\ \tilde{r}_t \end{bmatrix} = -N \begin{bmatrix} \tilde{K}_t \\ \tilde{\lambda}_{t-1} \\ Y_{t-1} \end{bmatrix} = \begin{bmatrix} 0.5317 & 0.4468 & 0 \\ -0.9452 & 1.8445 & 0 \end{bmatrix} \begin{bmatrix} \tilde{K}_t \\ \tilde{\lambda}_{t-1} \\ Y_{t-1} \end{bmatrix}.
$$

The deterministic process for the predetermined variables is

$$
[B_{11} - B_{12}N] \begin{bmatrix} \tilde{K}_{t+1} \\ \tilde{\lambda}_t \\ Y_t \end{bmatrix} = [A_{11} - A_{12}N] \begin{bmatrix} \tilde{K}_t \\ \tilde{\lambda}_{t-1} \\ Y_{t-1} \end{bmatrix}.
$$

Using the matrices from our model, we get

$$
\begin{bmatrix} \begin{bmatrix} 12.67 & 0 & -1.24 \\ 0 & 1 & 0 \\ 0 & -1 & .36 \end{bmatrix} - \begin{bmatrix} 0 & 0 \\ 0 & 0 \\ 0 & 0 \end{bmatrix} \begin{bmatrix} -0.53 & -0.447 & 0 \\ 0.945 & -1.845 & 0 \end{bmatrix} \end{bmatrix} \begin{bmatrix} \tilde{K}_{t+1} \\ \tilde{\lambda}_t \\ Y_t \end{bmatrix}
$$

$$
= \begin{bmatrix} 12.353 & 0 & 0 \\ 0 & .95 & 0 \\ .36 & 0 & 0 \end{bmatrix} - \begin{bmatrix} -.919 & 0 \\ 0 & 0 \\ -.64 & 0 \end{bmatrix} \begin{bmatrix} -0.532 & -0.447 & 0 \\ 0.9452 & -1.845 & 0 \end{bmatrix} \begin{bmatrix} \tilde{K}_t \\ \tilde{\lambda}_{t-1} \\ Y_{t-1} \end{bmatrix},
$$

or

$$
\begin{bmatrix} \tilde{K}_{t+1} \\ \tilde{\lambda}_t \\ Y_t \end{bmatrix} = \begin{bmatrix} 12.669 & 0 & -1.235 \\ 0 & 1 & 0 \\ 0 & -1 & .36 \end{bmatrix}^{-1} \begin{bmatrix} 11.865 & -0.410 & 0 \\ 0 & 0.95 & 0 \\ 0.0197 & -0.286 & 0 \end{bmatrix} \begin{bmatrix} \tilde{K}_t \\ \tilde{\lambda}_{t-1} \\ Y_{t-1} \end{bmatrix}
$$

$$
= \begin{bmatrix} 0.9418 & 0.1475 & 0 \\ 0 & 0.95 & 0 \\ 0.0548 & 1.8446 & 0 \end{bmatrix} \begin{bmatrix} \tilde{K}_t \\ \tilde{\lambda}_{t-1} \\ Y_{t-1} \end{bmatrix}.
$$

THE STOCHASTIC VERSION

The stochastic version of the model is

$$
\begin{bmatrix} B \begin{matrix} x_{t+1} \\ E_t y_{t+1} \end{matrix} \end{bmatrix} = A \begin{bmatrix} x_t \\ y_t \end{bmatrix} + G [\varepsilon_t].
$$

Using the Schur decomposition of B and A that we found above, we have

$$
QTZ' \begin{bmatrix} x_{t+1} \\ E_t y_{t+1} \end{bmatrix} = QSZ' \begin{bmatrix} x_t \\ y_t \end{bmatrix} + G [\varepsilon_t],
$$

and multiplying through by Q' gives

$$
\begin{bmatrix} T_{11} & T_{12} \\ 0_{21} & T_{22} \end{bmatrix} \begin{bmatrix} Z'_{11} & Z'_{12} \\ Z'_{21} & Z'_{22} \end{bmatrix} \begin{bmatrix} x_{t+1} \\ E_t y_{t+1} \end{bmatrix}
$$

$$
= \begin{bmatrix} S_{11} & S_{12} \\ 0_{21} & S_{22} \end{bmatrix} \begin{bmatrix} Z'_{11} & Z'_{12} \\ Z'_{21} & Z'_{22} \end{bmatrix} \begin{bmatrix} x_t \\ y_t \end{bmatrix} + \begin{bmatrix} Q'_{11} & Q'_{12} \\ Q'_{21} & Q'_{22} \end{bmatrix} \begin{bmatrix} G_1 \\ G_2 \end{bmatrix} [\varepsilon_t].
$$

These submatrices are ordered as above, and those associated with the explosive eigenvalues are in the bottom row. For the model to be nonexplosive, we need either

$$0 = S_{22}Z'_{21}x_t + S_{22}Z'_{22}y_t + \left[Q'_{21}G_1 + Q'_{22}G_2 \right] \left[\varepsilon_t \right],$$

or

$$y_t = -\left[S_{22}Z'_{22} \right]^{-1} S_{22}Z'_{21}x_t - \left[S_{22}Z'_{22} \right]^{-1} \left[Q'_{21}G_1 + Q'_{22}G_2 \right] \left[\varepsilon_t \right],$$

$$= -\left(Z'_{22} \right)^{-1} Z'_{21}x_t - \left(Z'_{22} \right)^{-1} S_{22}^{-1} \left[Q'_{21}G_1 + Q'_{22}G_2 \right] \left[\varepsilon_t \right].$$

The last line comes from the fact that $\left[S_{22}Z'_{22} \right]^{-1} = \left(Z'_{22} \right)^{-1} S_{22}^{-1}$. To keep notation simple, let $L = \left(Z'_{22} \right)^{-1} S_{22}^{-1} \left[Q'_{21}G_1 + Q'_{22}G_2 \right]$. The solution to the non-predetermined variables can be written as

$$y_t = -Nx_t - L \left[\varepsilon_t \right].$$

Because the expected value of the shocks are assumed to be zero, the expectational non-predetermined variables are equal to

$$E_t y_{t+1} = -\left(Z'_{22} \right)^{-1} Z'_{21}x_{t+1} = -Nx_{t+1},$$

and we write the model as

$$\begin{bmatrix} B_{11} & B_{12} \\ B_{21} & B_{22} \end{bmatrix} \begin{bmatrix} I \\ -N \end{bmatrix} x_{t+1} = \begin{bmatrix} A_{11} & A_{12} \\ A_{21} & A_{22} \end{bmatrix} \begin{bmatrix} x_t \\ y_t \end{bmatrix} + \begin{bmatrix} G_1 \\ G_2 \end{bmatrix} \left[\varepsilon_t \right].$$

Replacing y_t with $-Nx_t - L \left[\varepsilon_t \right]$ gives

$$\begin{bmatrix} B_{11} & B_{12} \\ B_{21} & B_{22} \end{bmatrix} \begin{bmatrix} I \\ -N \end{bmatrix} x_{t+1} = \begin{bmatrix} A_{11} & A_{12} \\ A_{21} & A_{22} \end{bmatrix} \begin{bmatrix} I \\ -N \end{bmatrix} x_t + \begin{bmatrix} G_1 - A_{12}L \\ G_2 - A_{22}L \end{bmatrix} \left[\varepsilon_t \right].$$

Using the stable part of the problem (the top half of the partitioned matrices) gives

$$\left[B_{11} - B_{12}N \right] x_{t+1} = \left[A_{11} - A_{12}N \right] x_t + \left[G_1 - A_{12}L \right] \left[\varepsilon_t \right],$$

or

$$x_{t+1} = \left[B_{11} - B_{12}N \right]^{-1} \left[A_{11} - A_{12}N \right] x_t + \left[B_{11} - B_{12}N \right]^{-1} \left[G_1 - A_{12}L \right] \left[\varepsilon_t \right],$$

$$= Cx_t + D \left[\varepsilon_t \right],$$

where $C = [B_{11} - B_{12}N]^{-1}[A_{11} - A_{12}N]$ and $D = [B_{11} - B_{12}N]^{-1}[G_1 - A_{12}L]$. This is the stable solution to the problem of finding the values for the predetermined variables as a function of the shock and the previous values of the predetermined variables.

SOLVING THE STOCHASTIC HANSEN MODEL

We are looking for two equations. The first gives the values of the non-predeterimined variables at time t as a function of the predetermined variables and the shocks at time t. This is the equation

$$y_t = -Nx_t - L\left[\varepsilon_t\right].$$

The second equation gives the values of the time $t + 1$ predetermined variables as a function of the time t predetermined variables and the shocks. This equation is

$$x_{t+1} = Cx_t + D\left[\varepsilon_t\right].$$

Using the results of the above section to find a solution for the specific version of Hansen's model gives the same result for $N = (Z'_{22})^{-1}Z'_{21}$ as was found in the deterministic solution,

$$N = \begin{bmatrix} -0.5317 & -0.4468 & 0 \\ 0.9452 & -1.8445 & 0 \end{bmatrix},$$

and a solution for $L = (Z'_{22})^{-1}S_{22}^{-1}[Q'_{21}G_1 + Q'_{22}G_2]$ of

$$L = \begin{bmatrix} -0.4704 \\ -1.9416 \end{bmatrix}.$$

The value for $C = [B_{11} - B_{12}N]^{-1}[A_{11} - A_{12}N]$ is the same as in the deterministic version of the model,

$$C = \begin{bmatrix} 0.9418 & 0.1474 & 0 \\ 0 & .95 & 0 \\ 0.0548 & 1.8445 & 0 \end{bmatrix},$$

and a solution of $D = [B_{11} - B_{12}N]^{-1}[G_1 - A_{12}L]$ results in

$$D = \begin{bmatrix} 0.1552 \\ 1 \\ 1.9416 \end{bmatrix}.$$

One can write the model as

$$\begin{bmatrix} x_{t+1} \\ y_t \end{bmatrix} = \widehat{R}x_t + \widehat{S}\varepsilon_t,$$

where

$$\widehat{R} = \begin{bmatrix} 0.9418 & 0.1474 \\ 0 & .95 \\ 0.0548 & 1.8445 \\ 0.5317 & 0.4468 \\ -0.9452 & 1.8445 \end{bmatrix}$$

and

$$\widehat{S} = \begin{bmatrix} 0.1552 \\ 1 \\ 1.9416 \\ 0.4704 \\ 1.9416 \end{bmatrix}.$$

Compare these to those found using the Uhlig methods. These are

$$\tilde{K}_{t+1} = .9418\tilde{K}_t + .1552\lambda_t,$$

and for $y_t = \left[\tilde{Y}_t, \tilde{C}_t, \tilde{H}_t, \tilde{r}_t \right]$,

$$y_t = R\tilde{K}_t + S\lambda_t,$$

where

$$R = \begin{bmatrix} 0.0550 \\ 0.5316 \\ -0.4766 \\ -0.9450 \end{bmatrix}$$

and

$$S = \begin{bmatrix} 1.9418 \\ 0.4703 \\ 1.4715 \\ 1.9417 \end{bmatrix}.$$

The coefficients on $\tilde{K}_t$ are the same for all shared variables. The coefficients for shared variables in $\widehat{S}$ are the same as those in S. The coefficients on λ_{t-1}

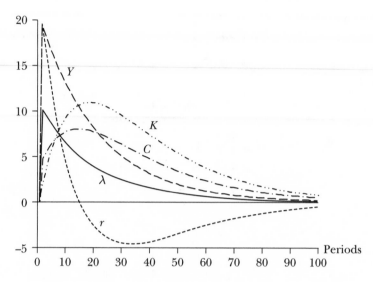

FIGURE 6.9   Responses for Hansen model solved using Schur

in $\widehat{R}$ are .95 times the value of the corresponding coefficients in $\widehat{S}$, taking into account the value of the coefficient γ in the technology shock process.

The impulse-response functions for a shock to technology of .01 are shown in Figure 6.9. Compare these impulse responses to those found using the model solution that comes from Uhlig's solution technique, Figure 6.6. Not surprisingly, they are identical for shared variables.

6.9   MATLAB CODE

Three programs are presented here. The first is a basic program for finding the solution to a linear model when there is only one state variable. The example given is for the basic Hansen model but it only requires changing the matrices to get it to solve Hansen's model with indivisible labor. The second program calculates model variances from the laws of motion. The third program is a function that solves a state space version of a linear model using the method of Blanchard and Kahn and is quite general.

6.9.1   Solution to Basic Hansen Model

The following code solves the basic Hansen model. The code for finding the solution to the model with indivisible labor is similar. The quadratic equation is scalar, so the solution does not require a matrix technique. The names of the

variables should be clear: kbar= $\bar{K}$. The stable root of the quadratic equation
(that with value less than one) is chosen for finding the linear policy functions.

```
% stationary state values are found in another program
A=[0 -kbar 0 0]';
B=[0 (1-delta)*kbar theta -1]';
C=[1 -1 -1/(1-hbar) 0
    ybar -cbar 0 0
    -1 0 1-theta 0
    1 0 0 -1];
D=[0 0 1 0]';
F=[0];
G=F;
H=F;
J=[0 -1 0 beta*rbar];
K=[0 1 0 0];
L=F;
M=F;
N=[.95];
Cinv=inv(C);
a=F-J*Cinv*A;
b=-(J*Cinv*B-G+K*Cinv*A);
c=-K*Cinv*B+H;
P1=(-b+sqrt(b^2-4*a*c))/(2*a);
P2=(-b-sqrt(b^2-4*a*c))/(2*a);
if abs(P1)<1
    P=P1;
else
    P=P2;
end
R=-Cinv*(A*P+B);
Q=(J*Cinv*D-L)*N+K*Cinv*D-M;
QD=kron(N',(F-J*Cinv*A))+(J*R+F*P+G-K*Cinv*A);
Q=Q/QD;
S=-Cinv*(A*Q+D);
```

6.9.2 Approximating the Variances

The following code gives the function for calculating the relative variances
from the laws of motion.

```
%function to approximate the ratio of the variance of a jump
%variable in the Hansen model to the variance of the shock
%to the technology process. The iteration limit is 1000.
function vr=varratio(a,b,c,d,roe,tol)
vr=0;
```

```
for i=1:1000
   shortsum=0;
   if i==1
      shortsum=1;
   else
      for j=1:(i+1)
         shortsum=shortsum+a^(j-1)*roe^(i+1-j);
      end
   end
   increment=c*b*shortsum+d*roe^i;
   vr=vr+increment*increment;
   if abs(increment)<tol
      'tol achieved'
      increment
      i
      break
   end
end
vr=vr+d*d;
```

6.9.3   Code for Appendix 2

The following code finds the N, L, C, and D matrices given the matrices A, B, and G and the number of expectactional variables, nx. The function, schurg, that solves the Schur decomposition is given to us from Anderson.[16] This program is a function that takes the output of Anderson's program and constructs the appropriate solution matrices.

```
function [N,L,C,D,alphabeta]=modelschur(A,B,G,nx)
%This program solves a model of the form
% [ xt+1 ] [xt]
% B[ ]=A[ ]+G[et]
% [Etyt+1] [yt]
%using a Schur decomposition of the matrices B and A
%nx is the number of expecational variables in Etyt+1
% if plotcode=1, impulse response is plotted
%solution is yt = -N xt - L et
%and xt+1 = C xt + D et
[Z,TT,SS,alpha,beta,info,Q] = schurg(B,A);
alphabeta=[alpha beta];
Zp=Z';
Qp=Q';
[a,b]=size(Z);
```

---

16. The program can be downloaded from www.math.niu.edu/~anderson.

```
N=inv(Zp(a-nx+1:a,a-nx+1:a))*Zp(a-nx+1:a,1:a-nx);
L=inv(Zp(a-nx+1:a,a-nx+1:a))*inv(SS(a-nx+1:a,a-nx+1:a));
L=L*(Qp(a-nx+1:a,1:a-nx)*G(1:a-nx,1)+Qp(a-nx+1:a,a-nx+1:a)
   *G(a-nx+1:a,1));
invBBN=inv(B(1:a-nx,1:a-nx)-B(1:a-nx,a-nx+1:a)*N);
C=invBBN*(A(1:a-nx,1:a-nx)-A(1:a-nx,a-nx+1:a)*N);
D=invBBN*(G(1:a-nx,1)-A(1:a-nx,a-nx+1:a)*L);
```

7

Linear Quadratic Dynamic Programming

In the previous chapter, we solved for the first-order conditions of Hansen's model and then used log linearization techniques to convert the general problem into a linear approximation. The first-order conditions were found for a non linear dynamic optimization problem and only then was the problem linearized.

In this chapter, we show an alternative approach. Here we derive a quadratic approximation for the objective function of the infinite horizon dynamic optimization problem and, using linear budget constraints, find a policy function that gives the optimizing values for the control variables as a linear function of the state variables. Note that there are two problems facing the modeler: the budget constraints need to be linear and the objective function needs to be quadratic. The original budget constraints can frequently be converted into linear ones by appropriate changes of variables and/or by putting all of the nonlinearity into the objective function.

Since we are interested in the dynamics of a system, we need to have, at least, a quadratic approximation of the objective function. A linear (first-order) approximation would result in constants for the first-order conditions, and these do not produce interesting dynamics. Higher-order approximations of the objective function are likely to do a better job of capturing the dynamics, but solving them is more difficult.

The discounted quadratic objective function we are looking for is of the form

$$\sum_{t=0}^{\infty} \beta^t \left[x_t' R x_t + y_t' Q y_t + 2 y_t' W x_t \right], \tag{7.1}$$

subject to the linear budget constraints

$$x_{t+1} = Ax_t + By_t,$$

where x_t is the $n \times 1$ vector of state variables, y_t is an $m \times 1$ vector of control variables, R and A are $n \times n$ matrices, Q is an $m \times m$ matrix, W is an $m \times n$, and B is an $n \times m$ matrix.

The method most commonly used for finding a quadratic approximation of the objective function is by taking second-order Taylor expansions.

7.1 TAYLOR APPROXIMATIONS OF THE OBJECTIVE FUNCTION

Brook Taylor (1685–1731) introduced the theorem that we use for approximating continuous and continuously differentiable functions by polynomials. What has become known as Taylor's Theorem is stated as follows:

Suppose that f is a function with domain D in $\mathbf{R}^p$ and range in $\mathbf{R}$, and suppose that f has continuous partial derivatives of order n in a neighborhood of every point on a line segment joining two points u, v in D. Then there exists a point $\tilde{u}$ on this line segment such that

$$f(v) = f(u) + \frac{1}{1!}Df(u)(v - u) + \frac{1}{2!}D^2f(u)(v - u)^2$$

$$+ \cdots + \frac{1}{(n-1)!}D^{n-1}f(u)(v - u)^{n-1} + \frac{1}{n!}D^n f(\tilde{u})(v - u)^n.$$

Because the error term in the polynomial,

$$\frac{1}{n!}D^n f(\tilde{u})(v - u)^n,$$

usually gets small quickly as n grows when the distance, $v - u$, is small, this polynomial is frequently used to approximate a function around a point with known value using only the first- or second-order expansion (up to the quadratic).

The *point of known value* that we use is that of the stationary state, which we calculate as in the previous chapter, using the Euler equations. Note that what we need is the value of the objective function at the stationary state. To get this value, we find the values of the state and control variables in the stationary state and plug these values into the objective function. In addition, we take the first and second derivatives of the objective function and, using the same values for the state and control variables, find the values of the derivatives. For example, if the discounted utility function is of the form

$$\sum_{t=0}^{\infty} \beta^t u(c_t, h_t) = \sum_{t=0}^{\infty} \beta^t \left[\ln c_t + A \ln(1 - h_t) \right],$$

the objective function is

$$\ln c_t + A \ln(1 - h_t),$$

the first derivative of the objective function is the vector,

$$[\tfrac{1}{c_t} \quad -\tfrac{A}{1-h_t}],$$

and the second derivative is the matrix,

$$\begin{bmatrix} -\frac{1}{c_t^2} & 0 \\ 0 & \frac{A}{(1-h_t)^2} \end{bmatrix}.$$

The approximation of the objective function that we get from the Taylor expansion, when we evaluate the function and its first and second derivatives at the stationary state, $\bar{c}$ and $\bar{h}$, is

$$u(c_t, h_t) \approx \ln \bar{c} + A \ln(1 - \bar{h}) + [\tfrac{1}{\bar{c}} \quad -\tfrac{A}{1-\bar{h}}] \begin{bmatrix} c_t - \bar{c} \\ h_t - \bar{h} \end{bmatrix}$$

$$+ \frac{1}{2} [c_t - \bar{c} \quad h_t - \bar{h}] \begin{bmatrix} -\frac{1}{\bar{c}^2} & 0 \\ 0 & \frac{A}{(1-\bar{h})^2} \end{bmatrix} \begin{bmatrix} c_t - \bar{c} \\ h_t - \bar{h} \end{bmatrix}.$$

Notice that the Taylor approximation has a component (the part associated with the second derivative) that is, as this is written, a matrix in the controls. This is a part of the S matrix of the quadratic version of the objective function as written in equation 7.1. However, there is a difficulty that needs to be confronted. The rest of the Taylor expansion is a constant, the $\ln \bar{c} + A \ln(1 - \bar{h})$ part, and a linear component, the

$$[\tfrac{1}{\bar{c}} \quad -\tfrac{A}{1-\bar{h}}] \begin{bmatrix} c_t - \bar{c} \\ h_t - \bar{h} \end{bmatrix}$$

part. We need to find a way to include these two components in the quadratic version of the objective function to be able to solve our model by linear dynamic programming techniques.

7.2 THE METHOD OF KYDLAND AND PRESCOTT

Kydland and Prescott [52] use a second-order Taylor series approximation as the discounted quadratic objective function for their model. To illustrate the technique they applied to include the constant and linear parts of the Taylor series, we use a Hansen model like the one discussed in Chapter 6.[1]

A general version of the problem is to maximize

$$\sum_{t=0}^{\infty} \beta^t F(x_t, y_t),$$

subject to the budget constraint

$$x_{t+1} = G(x_t, y_t) = Ax_t + By_t,$$

where x_t are the period t state variables and y_t are the period t control variables. Here we assume that the budget constraints, $G(x_t, y_t)$, are linear or have been made linear by putting all the nonlinear budget constraints into the objective function, $F(x_t, y_t)$.

The second-order Taylor expansion of the function $F(x_t, y_t)$ is

$$F(x_t, y_t) \approx F(\bar{x}, \bar{y}) + [\, F_x(\bar{x}, \bar{y})' \quad F_y(\bar{x}, \bar{y})'\,] \begin{bmatrix} x_t - \bar{x} \\ y_t - \bar{y} \end{bmatrix}$$

$$+ [\, (x_t - \bar{x})' \quad (y_t - \bar{y})'\,] \begin{bmatrix} \frac{F_{xx}(\bar{x}, \bar{y})}{2} & \frac{F_{xy}(\bar{x}, \bar{y})}{2} \\ \frac{F_{yx}(\bar{x}, \bar{y})}{2} & \frac{F_{yy}(\bar{x}, \bar{y})}{2} \end{bmatrix} \begin{bmatrix} x_t - \bar{x} \\ y_t - \bar{y} \end{bmatrix}.$$

To write this Taylor expansion in quadratic form, we define a vector z_t as

$$z_t = \begin{bmatrix} 1 \\ x_t \\ y_t \end{bmatrix}$$

and its value in the stationary state as

$$\bar{z} = \begin{bmatrix} 1 \\ \bar{x} \\ \bar{y} \end{bmatrix}.$$

Since the vector x_t is of length k and the vector y_t is of length l, the vector z_t is of length $1 + k + l$. Consider the $(1 + k + l) \times (1 + k + l)$ matrix

$$M = \begin{bmatrix} m_{11} & m_{12} & m_{13} \\ m_{21} & m_{22} & m_{23} \\ m_{31} & m_{32} & m_{33} \end{bmatrix}.$$

1. The actual model that Kydland and Prescott used is substantially more complicated. The techniques that they used are easier to explain in the basic Hansen model.

The matrix m_{11} is 1×1, m_{22} is $k \times k$, m_{33} is $l \times l$, and the rest of the matrices conform to make M square. The product

$$z'_t M z_t = m_{11} + (m_{12} + m'_{21})x_t + (m_{13} + m'_{31})y_t + x'_t m_{22} x_t$$

$$+ x'_t(m_{23} + m'_{32})y_t + y'_t m_{33} y_t. \tag{7.2}$$

Notice that there is a constant term and two linear terms in equation 7.2 as well as the quadratic terms. By defining

$$m_{11} = F(\bar{x}, \bar{y}) - \bar{x}' F_x(\bar{x}, \bar{y}) - \bar{y}' F_y(\bar{x}, \bar{y}) + \frac{\bar{x}' F_{xx}(\bar{x}, \bar{y})\bar{x}}{2} + \bar{x}' F_{xy}(\bar{x}, \bar{y})\bar{y}$$

$$+ \frac{\bar{y}' F_{yy}(\bar{x}, \bar{y})\bar{y}}{2},$$

all of the constant components of the Taylor expansion are included in m_{11}. Defining

$$m_{12} = m'_{21} = \frac{F_x(\bar{x}, \bar{y})' - \bar{x}' F_{xx}(\bar{x}, \bar{y}) - \bar{y}' F_{yx}(\bar{x}, \bar{y})}{2}$$

and

$$m_{13} = m'_{31} = \frac{F_y(\bar{x}, \bar{y})' - \bar{x}' F_{xy}(\bar{x}, \bar{y}) - \bar{y}' F_{yy}(\bar{x}, \bar{y})}{2},$$

all the linear components of the Taylor expansion are included in M and we are making M a symmetric matrix. The quadratic components of the Taylor expansion are found in

$$m_{22} = \frac{F_{xx}(\bar{x}, \bar{y})}{2},$$

$$m_{23} = m'_{32} = \frac{F_{xy}(\bar{x}, \bar{y})}{2},$$

and

$$m_{33} = \frac{F_{yy}(\bar{x}, \bar{y})}{2}.$$

In this way, we have constructed a matrix M that is symmetric and gives the complete quadratic Taylor expansion as $z'_t M z_t$. The quadratic discounted dynamic programming problem to be solved is now

$$\sum_{t=0}^{\infty} \beta^t z'_t M z_t,$$

with $z_t' = [\, 1 \quad x_t \quad y_t \,]$, subject to the budget constraints

$$\begin{bmatrix} 1 \\ x_{t+1} \end{bmatrix} = A \begin{bmatrix} 1 \\ x_t \end{bmatrix} + By_t.$$

7.2.1 An Example

A specific example of the problem to be solved is

$$\sum_{t=0}^{\infty} \beta^t u(c_t, h_t),$$

subject to the budget constraint

$$c_t = f(k_t, h_t) + (1 - \delta)k_t - k_{t+1}.$$

The budget constraint is not linear, given that the production function used is a Cobb-Douglas, so it can be substituted into the utility function to get a maximization problem of

$$\sum_{t=0}^{\infty} \beta^t u(f(k_t, h_t) + (1 - \delta)k_t - k_{t+1}, h_t),$$

where, in a deterministic version of the problem, k_t is the state variable and h_t and k_{t+1} are the controls. The linear budget constraint is simply

$$k_{t+1} = k_{t+1},$$

where the right-hand k_{t+1} is one of the controls in period t and the left-hand k_{t+1} is the state in period $t + 1$.

The exact function $u(c_t, h_t)$ is

$$u(c_t, h_t) = \ln c_t + A \ln(1 - h_t),$$

or, after substituting in the budget constraint, is

$$u(k_t, k_{t+1}, h_t) = \ln \left(f(k_t, h_t) + (1 - \delta)k_t - k_{t+1} \right) + A \ln(1 - h_t),$$

where k_t is the period t state variable and k_{t+1} and h_t are the control variables. The production function, $f(k_t, h_t)$, is Cobb-Douglas, so

$$f(k_t, h_t) = k_t^{\theta} h_t^{1-\theta}.$$

The second-order Taylor expansion of the objective function is

$$u(k_t, k_{t+1}, h_t) \approx \ln\left(f(\bar{k}, \bar{h}) - \delta\bar{k}\right) + A\ln(1 - \bar{h})$$

$$+ \frac{1}{\bar{c}}\left[\theta\frac{\bar{y}}{k} + (1 - \delta)\right](k_t - \bar{k}) - \frac{1}{\bar{c}}(k_{t+1} - \bar{k})$$

$$+ \left[(1 - \theta)\frac{1}{\bar{c}}\frac{\bar{y}}{h} - \frac{A}{1 - \bar{h}}\right](h_t - \bar{h})$$

$$+ \begin{bmatrix} (k_t - \bar{k}) \\ (k_{t+1} - \bar{k}) \\ (h_t - \bar{h}) \end{bmatrix}' \begin{bmatrix} a_{11} & a_{12} & a_{13} \\ a_{21} & a_{22} & a_{23} \\ a_{31} & a_{32} & a_{33} \end{bmatrix} \begin{bmatrix} (k_t - \bar{k}) \\ (k_{t+1} - \bar{k}) \\ (h_t - \bar{h}) \end{bmatrix},$$

where the constant elements of the matrix are

$$a_{11} = -\frac{1}{2\bar{c}^2}\left[\theta\frac{\bar{y}}{k} + (1 - \delta)\right]^2 - \frac{1}{2\bar{c}}\theta(1 - \theta)\frac{\bar{y}}{\bar{k}^2},$$

$$a_{12} = a_{21} = \frac{1}{2\bar{c}^2}\left[\theta\frac{\bar{y}}{k} + (1 - \delta)\right],$$

$$a_{13} = a_{31} = -\frac{1}{2\bar{c}^2}\left[\theta\frac{\bar{y}}{k} + (1 - \delta)\right](1 - \theta)\frac{\bar{y}}{h} + \frac{1}{2\bar{c}}\theta(1 - \theta)\frac{\bar{y}}{kh},$$

$$a_{22} = -\frac{1}{2\bar{c}^2},$$

$$a_{23} = a_{32} = \frac{1}{2\bar{c}^2}(1 - \theta)\frac{\bar{y}}{h},$$

and

$$a_{33} = -\frac{1}{2\bar{c}^2}\left[(1 - \theta)\frac{\bar{y}}{h}\right]^2 - \frac{1}{2\bar{c}}\theta(1 - \theta)\frac{\bar{y}}{h^2} - \frac{A}{2(1 - \bar{h})^2}.$$

To find the matrix M, we first define the four-element vector z_t as $z_t = [1 \quad k_t \quad k_{t+1} \quad h_t]'$. The 4×4 matrix M is

$$M = \begin{bmatrix} m_{11} & m_{12} & m_{13} & m_{14} \\ m_{21} & a_{11} & a_{12} & a_{13} \\ m_{31} & a_{21} & a_{22} & a_{23} \\ m_{41} & a_{31} & a_{32} & a_{33} \end{bmatrix},$$

where the a_{ij}'s are defined as above and

$$m_{11} = \ln\left(f(\bar{k}, \bar{h}) - \delta\bar{k}\right) + A\ln(1 - \bar{h})$$

$$-\frac{1}{c}\left[\theta\frac{\bar{y}}{\bar{k}} + (1 - \delta) - 1\right]\bar{k} - \left[(1 - \theta)\frac{1}{\bar{c}}\frac{\bar{y}}{\bar{h}} - \frac{A}{1 - \bar{h}}\right]\bar{h}$$

$$+ \begin{bmatrix} \bar{k} \\ \bar{k} \\ \bar{h} \end{bmatrix}' \begin{bmatrix} a_{11} & a_{12} & a_{13} \\ a_{21} & a_{22} & a_{23} \\ a_{31} & a_{32} & a_{33} \end{bmatrix} \begin{bmatrix} \bar{k} \\ \bar{k} \\ \bar{h} \end{bmatrix},$$

$$m_{12} = m_{21} = \frac{1}{c}\left[\theta\frac{\bar{y}}{\bar{k}} + (1 - \delta)\right] - \begin{bmatrix} \bar{k} & \bar{k} & \bar{h} \end{bmatrix}\begin{bmatrix} a_{11} \\ a_{21} \\ a_{31} \end{bmatrix},$$

$$m_{13} = m_{31} = -\frac{1}{c} - \begin{bmatrix} \bar{k} & \bar{k} & \bar{h} \end{bmatrix}\begin{bmatrix} a_{12} \\ a_{22} \\ a_{32} \end{bmatrix},$$

and

$$m_{14} = m_{41} = \left[(1 - \theta)\frac{1}{\bar{c}}\frac{\bar{y}}{\bar{h}} - \frac{A}{1 - \bar{h}}\right] - \begin{bmatrix} \bar{k} & \bar{k} & \bar{h} \end{bmatrix}\begin{bmatrix} a_{13} \\ a_{23} \\ a_{33} \end{bmatrix}.$$

The problem to be solved is to maximize

$$\sum_{t=0}^{\infty} \beta^t z_t' M z_t,$$

subject to the budget constraint

$$\begin{bmatrix} 1 \\ k_{t+1} \end{bmatrix} = A\begin{bmatrix} 1 \\ k_t \end{bmatrix} + B\begin{bmatrix} k_{t+1} \\ h_t \end{bmatrix},$$

where for this particular problem

$$A = \begin{bmatrix} 1 & 0 \\ 0 & 0 \end{bmatrix} \text{ and } B = \begin{bmatrix} 0 & 0 \\ 1 & 0 \end{bmatrix}.$$

Notice that the first rows of A and B and the inclusion of 1 in the first row of x_t means that the first row of x_{t+1} will also be 1. Before we solve this particular problem, we show how to solve the general discounted linear quadratic dynamic programming problem.

7.2.2   Solving the Bellman Equation

Define the vector

$$z_t \equiv \begin{bmatrix} x_t \\ y_t \end{bmatrix}.$$

To keep things consistent with the development up to now, let the first element of x_t be the constant 1. Consider the more general discounted optimization problem in which one wants to maximize

$$\sum_{t=0}^{\infty} \beta^t z_t' M z_t,$$

subject to the linear budget constraint

$$x_{t+1} = Ax_t + By_t.$$

$$x_{t+1} = A z_t + B u_t$$

In keeping with the definition of the first element of x_t as equal to 1, the first row of A is made up of a 1 in the first position and zeros in all the others and the first row of B is all zeros. Written this way, the matrix multiplication guarantees that the first element of x_{t+1} will always be equal to 1.

The objective function is of the form

$$z_t' M z_t = [\, x_t' \quad y_t' \,] \begin{bmatrix} R & W' \\ W & Q \end{bmatrix} \begin{bmatrix} x_t \\ y_t \end{bmatrix},$$

where x_t is a $1 \times n$ vector, y_t is a $1 \times m$ vector, and z_t is therefore a $1 \times (n+m)$ vector. The matrix R is $n \times n$, Q is $m \times m$, and W is $m \times n$. R and Q are positive, symmetric, and semidefinite. Since $x_t' W' y_t = y_t' W x_t$,[2] this objective function can be written as

$$x_t' Q x_t + u_t' R u_t + 2 y_t' u' x_t$$

$$x_t' R x_t + y_t' Q y_t + 2 y_t' W x_t. \tag{7.3}$$

What we are looking for is a value function for the model that can be expressed by a matrix P (positive, symmetric, and semidefinite), where $x_t' P x_t$ is the value of the solved discounted optimization problem given the state x_t. If such a matrix exists, the Bellman equation will be

$$x_t' P x_t = \max_{y_t} \left[z_t' M z_t + \beta x_{t+1}' P x_{t+1} \right],$$

Ricardi

2. A rule of transposition of matrices is that $(ABC)' = C'B'A'$. The products here result in scalars and the transpose of a scalar is equal to itself.

subject to the linear budget constraints

$$x_{t+1} = Ax_t + By_t.$$

(handwritten: u_c above y_t)

Using the version of the objective function in equation 7.3 and substituting in the budget constraint for x_{t+1}, the Bellman equation can be written as

$$x_t'Px_t = \max_{y_t} \left[x_t'Rx_t + y_t'Qy_t + 2y_t'Wx_t + \beta \left(Ax_t + By_t \right)' P \left(Ax_t + By_t \right) \right].$$

(handwritten expansion: $\left[x_t'Qx_t + u_t'Pu_t + 2u_t'U x_t + \beta(Ax_t + Bu_t)'P(Ax_t + Bu_t) \right]$)

The first-order conditions[3] for the problem are

$$\left[Q + \beta B'PB \right] y_t = -\left[W + \beta B'PA \right] x_t,$$

(handwritten: $-[Q + \beta B'xB]^{-1}[u' + \beta B'xA]'$)

which gives the policy function (matrix), F, where

$$y_t = Fx_t = -\left[Q + \beta B'PB \right]^{-1} \left[W + \beta B'PA \right] x_t. \tag{7.4}$$

(handwritten: $[R + \beta B'PB]u_t =$; $u = F'x_t = -[R + \beta B'PB]^{-1}[u' + \beta B'PA]$)

P is still undefined. Substitute this policy function into the Bellman equation in place of y_t and, after a fair amount of matrix algebra, one arrives at the expression *(handwritten: ← Riccati Matrix)*

$$P = R + \beta A'PA - \left(\beta A'PB + W' \right) \left[Q + \beta B'PB \right]^{-1} \left(\beta B'PA + W \right)$$

(handwritten: $P = Q + \beta A'PA - (\beta A'PB + u)[R + \beta B'PB]^{-1}(\beta B'PA + u')$)

The matrix P can be found from an initial guess for P, for example, P_0 equals the identity matrix, and iterating on the matrix Ricotti equation,

$$P_{k+1} = R + \beta A'P_kA - \left(\beta A'P_kB + W' \right) \left[Q + \beta B'P_kB \right]^{-1} \left(\beta B'P_kA + W \right). \tag{7.5}$$

The sequence of $\{ P_k \}$, $k \to \infty$, converges to the desired P. Once P is approximated, the policy function, F, is found using equation 7.4. The matrix F gives a linear approximation of the optimal plan in the neighborhood of the stationary state.

7.2.3 Calibrating the Example Economy

As above for the Hansen economy, we use an economy with $\beta = .99$, $\delta = .025$, $\theta = .36$, and $A = 1.72$. The stationary state that is associated with these parameters has $\bar{h} = .3335$, $\bar{k} = 12.6695$, $\bar{y} = 1.2353$, and $\bar{c} = .9186$. Using these

---

3. To get the first-order conditions, we used the rules for matrix differentiation given in Ljungqvist and Sargent [54], p. 71. These definitions are that $\frac{\partial x'Ax}{\partial x} = (A + A')x$, $\frac{\partial y'Bx}{\partial y} = Bx$, and $\frac{\partial y'Bx}{\partial x} = B'y$.

values, the matrix a is given by

$$a = \begin{bmatrix} -0.6056 & 0.5986 & -1.3823 \\ 0.5986 & -0.5926 & 1.4048 \\ -1.3823 & 1.4048 & -6.6590 \end{bmatrix},$$

and the matrix M is therefore

$$M = \begin{bmatrix} -1.6374 & 1.0996 & -1.0886 & 1.9361 \\ 1.0996 & -0.6056 & 0.5986 & -1.3823 \\ -1.0886 & 0.5986 & -0.5926 & 1.4048 \\ 1.9361 & -1.3823 & 1.4048 & -6.6590 \end{bmatrix}.$$

The matrices R, Q, and W come from the matrix M, where $M = \begin{bmatrix} R & W' \\ W & Q \end{bmatrix}$, so

$$R = \begin{bmatrix} -1.6374 & 1.0996 \\ 1.0996 & -0.6056 \end{bmatrix},$$

$$Q = \begin{bmatrix} -0.5926 & 1.4048 \\ 1.4048 & -6.6590 \end{bmatrix},$$

and

$$W = \begin{bmatrix} -1.0886 & 0.5986 \\ 1.9361 & -1.3823 \end{bmatrix}.$$

We begin iterating in equation 7.5 with the identity matrix,

$$P_0 = \begin{bmatrix} 1 & 0 \\ 0 & 1 \end{bmatrix},$$

and get

$$P_1 = \begin{bmatrix} -.7515 & .9987 \\ .9987 & -0.4545 \end{bmatrix},$$

$$P_2 = \begin{bmatrix} -1.6909 & .8247 \\ .8247 & -0.1924 \end{bmatrix}.$$

After 200 iterations, the values in P have settled down to

$$P = \begin{bmatrix} -96.3615 & .8779 \\ .8779 & -0.0259 \end{bmatrix}.$$

The policy function that is found using this P is

$$F = \begin{bmatrix} 0.5869 & 0.9537 \\ 0.4146 & -0.0064 \end{bmatrix} . = - \begin{bmatrix} R + \beta \, B' P B \end{bmatrix}^{-1} \begin{bmatrix} Q + \beta \, B' P A \end{bmatrix}$$

Recall that the control variables are $y_t = [\, k_{t+1} \quad h_t \,]'$ and the state variables are $x_t = [\, 1 \quad k_t \,]'$. Checking to see that this linear version of the model has been calculated correctly, we put in the value of the stationary state for k_t and use

$$\begin{bmatrix} k_{t+1} \\ h_t \end{bmatrix} = F \begin{bmatrix} 1 \\ k_t \end{bmatrix},$$

or

$$\begin{bmatrix} 12.6695 \\ .3335 \end{bmatrix} = \begin{bmatrix} 0.5869 & 0.9537 \\ 0.4146 & -0.0064 \end{bmatrix} \begin{bmatrix} 1 \\ 12.6695 \end{bmatrix}.$$

The values in the policy matrix, F, indicate that with amounts of time t capital above the stationary state, time $t + 1$ capital will be above the stationary state value and labor supply will be below the stationary state value.

In this section, we found a solution to a quadratic version of the simple Hansen model. To do this, we put the nonlinearity into the objective function and used very simple budget constraints, the same budget constraints that we used in earlier chapters to get simple Euler equations. This choice made the calculation of the derivatives of the objective function and the M matrix fairly burdensome. Other choices for the linear form of budget constraints and of the objective function for the same model are possible, and we will be using a different separation of objective function and budget constraint in the next section.

7.3 ADDING STOCHASTIC SHOCKS

The easiest way to solve models with stochastic shocks is to put all of the stochastic parts in the linear budget constraints. Since we are limiting ourselves to linear budget constraints, the shocks appear as

$$x_{t+1} = A x_t + B y_t + C \varepsilon_{t+1},$$

where ε_t is an independent and identically distributed random variable with $E_t(\varepsilon_{t+1}) = \vec{0}$,[4] and with a finite, diagonal variance matrix, Σ. C is a matrix that is $m \times n$, where m is the number of state variables and n is the length

---

4. Here, $\vec{0}$ is a vector of zeros the same dimension as ε_{t+1}.

of the vector of shocks, ε_{t+1}. As before, x_t is the time t state variable and y_t are the control variables. All of the nonlinearity of the model is put into the objective function, $F(x_t, y_t)$. Agents maximize the discounted expected value of the objective function,

$$\max_{y_t} E_0 \sum_{t=0}^{\infty} \beta^t F(x_t, y_t).$$

The expectations operator is included because future values of the objective function will depend on the realizations of the random shocks. Although the shocks will matter for future realizations of the objective function, the problem is written so that the stochastic variables do not appear directly in the objective function.

One first finds a quadratic approximation of the objective function so that in a neighborhood of the stationary state, $(\bar{x}, \bar{y})$,

$$F(x_t, y_t) = F(z_t) \approx z_t' M z_t = [\, 1 \quad x_t'\,] R \begin{bmatrix} 1 \\ x_t \end{bmatrix} + y_t' Q y_t + 2 y_t' W \begin{bmatrix} 1 \\ x_t \end{bmatrix},$$

where $z_t = [\, 1 \quad x_t \quad y_t\,]'$ and M is found from the second-order Taylor approximation of the function F. The model to be solved is

$$E_0 \sum_{t=0}^{\infty} \beta^t z_t' M z_t,$$

subject to the linear budget constraints

$$x_{t+1} = A x_t + B y_t + C \varepsilon_{t+1}.$$

The problem can be written in a recursive form by first defining a value matrix P so that $x_t' P x_t + c$ is the value function, where

$$x_t' P x_t + c = \max_{\{y_s\}_{s=t}^{\infty}} E_0 \sum_{s=t}^{\infty} \beta^{s-t} z_s' M z_s,$$

subject to the budget constraint. This value function is different from earlier versions in that it includes a potential constant term, c. The recursive form (the Bellman equation) is

$$x_t' P x_t + c = \max_{y_t} \left\{ z_t' M z_t + \beta E_0 \left[x_{t+1}' P x_{t+1} + c \right] \right\},$$

subject to

$$x_{t+1} = A x_t + B y_t + C \varepsilon_{t+1}.$$

Substituting the right-hand side of the budget constraint into the expectations part of the Bellman equation gives

$$x_t'Px_t + c = \max_{y_t} \left[z_t'Mz_t + \beta x_t'A'PAx_t + 2x_t'A'PBy_t + \beta y_t'B'PBy_t \right.$$

$$\left. + \beta E_0 \left[\varepsilon_{t+1}'C'PC\varepsilon_{t+1} \right] + \beta c \right]. \tag{7.6}$$

Define the square matrix $G = \left[g_{jk} \right] = C'PC$. Then

$$E_t \left[\varepsilon_{t+1}'C'PC\varepsilon_{t+1} \right] = \sum_j \sum_k E_t \left[\varepsilon_{t+1}^j g_{jk} \varepsilon_{t+1}^k \right] = \sum_j g_{jj} E_t \left[\varepsilon_{t+1}^j \varepsilon_{t+1}^j \right].$$

The last equality holds because $E_t \left[\varepsilon_{t+1}^k \varepsilon_{t+1}^j \right] = 0$, when $k \neq j$. Therefore,

$$E_t \left[\varepsilon_{t+1}'C'PC\varepsilon_{t+1} \right] = \text{trace} \left[C'PC\Sigma \right],$$

which is a constant.[5] Putting this into equation 7.6 gives

$$x_t'Px_t + c = \max_{y_t} \{ z_t'Mz_t + \beta x_t'A'PAx_t$$

$$+ 2x_t'A'PBy_t + \beta y_t'B'PBy_t + \beta \text{trace} \left[C'PC\Sigma \right] \} + \beta c,$$

so

$$c = \frac{\beta \text{trace} \left[C'PC\Sigma \right]}{1 - \beta}$$

and

$$x_t'Px_t = \max_{y_t} \left[z_t'Mz_t + \beta x_t'A'PAx_t + \beta y_t'B'PBy_t \right]$$

$$= \max_{y_t} \left[x_t'Rx_t + y_t'Qy_t + 2y_t'Wx_t + \beta x_t'A'PAx_t \right.$$

$$\left. + 2x_t'A'PBy_t + \beta y_t'B'PBy_t \right]. \tag{7.7}$$

The first-order conditions of this problem are

$$\left[Q + \beta B'PB \right] y_t = - \left[W + \beta B'PA \right] x_t,$$

which are exactly the same as in the nonstochastic problem. The policy function, F, where

$$y_t = Fx_t = - \left[Q + \beta B'PB \right]^{-1} \left[W + \beta B'PA \right] x_t,$$

5. The trace(A) of a square matrix A is the sum of its diagonal elements.

is also exactly the same as in the nonstochastic problem.

The matrix $P = \lim P_k$ as $k \to \infty$ is found by making an initial guess for P_0 and iterating on the matrix Ricotti equation,

$$P_{k+1} = R + \beta A' P_k A - \left(\beta A' P_k B + W'\right) \left[Q + \beta B' P_k B\right]^{-1} \left(\beta B' P_k A + W\right).$$

This Ricotti equation is found by substituting the policy function into equation 7.7 and is the same equation as in the nonstochastic case.

To simulate the time path for a stochastic economy of the kind we have been studying in this section, one begins with an initial value for the state variables x_0, and uses the policy function, F, to find the appropriate values for the control variables, y_0. Next, a set of observations of the random variable, ε_1, is taken from the appropriate distribution. The values of the state variables in period 1 are found from

$$x_1 = A x_0 + B y_0 + C \varepsilon_1.$$

The calculation is repeated to generate the time series. This process is equal to finding the process $\{x_t\}$ given a sequence of $\{\varepsilon_{t+1}\}$ using the laws of motion,

$$x_{t+1} = [A + BF] x_t + C \varepsilon_{t+1}.$$

7.3.1   The Example Economy

For the example economy of Chapter 6, the random process for technology is

$$\lambda_{t+1} = \gamma \lambda_t + \widehat{\varepsilon}_{t+1},$$

where $\widehat{\varepsilon}_{t+1}$ has a mean of $1 - \gamma$, and the production function is

$$y_t = \lambda_t k_t^\theta h_t^{1-\theta}.$$

Here we let k_t and λ_t be the state variables and k_{t+1} and h_t be the controls for the basic Hansen model. We would like the error, ε_{t+1}, to have a mean of zero, so we add a constant to the random process and can write it as

$$\lambda_{t+1} = (1 - \gamma) + \gamma \lambda_t + \varepsilon_{t+1},$$

where ε_{t+1} has a mean of zero and finite variance.

Agents maximize

$$u(k_t, \lambda_t, k_{t+1}, h_t) = \sum_{t=0}^{\infty} \beta^t \left[\ln(\lambda_t k_t^\theta h_t^{1-\theta} + (1 - \delta)k_t - k_{t+1}) + A\left(1 - h_t\right)\right],$$

subject to the budget constraints

$$k_{t+1} = k_{t+1}$$

and

$$\lambda_{t+1} = (1 - \gamma) + \gamma \lambda_t + \varepsilon_{t+1}.$$

Define $z_t = [\, x_t' \quad y_t' \,]'$, where the state variables are $x_t = [\, 1 \quad k_t \quad \lambda_t \,]'$ and the control variables are $y_t = [\, k_{t+1} \quad h_t \,]'$. The "1" is in the first row of x_t for two reasons. One is to allow a constant term in the matrix version of the budget constraint for λ_{t+1}, and the other is, as described above, to include the constant and linear terms of the Taylor approximation of the objective function. Using these definitions, the budget constraints are written as

$$x_{t+1} = Ax_t + By_t + C\varepsilon_{t+1},$$

or as

$$
\begin{bmatrix} 1 \\ k_{t+1} \\ \lambda_{t+1} \end{bmatrix} =
\begin{bmatrix} 1 & 0 & 0 \\ 0 & 0 & 0 \\ 1-\gamma & 0 & \gamma \end{bmatrix}
\begin{bmatrix} 1 \\ k_t \\ \lambda_t \end{bmatrix} +
\begin{bmatrix} 0 & 0 \\ 1 & 0 \\ 0 & 0 \end{bmatrix}
\begin{bmatrix} k_{t+1} \\ h_t \end{bmatrix} +
\begin{bmatrix} 0 \\ 0 \\ 1 \end{bmatrix} \varepsilon_{t+1}.
$$

The second-order Taylor series expansion of the objective function is

$$u(\cdot) \approx \ln \left(\bar{\lambda} \bar{k}^\theta \bar{h}^{1-\theta} - \delta \bar{k} \right) + A \ln(1 - \bar{h})$$

$$+ \frac{1}{\bar{c}} \left[\theta \frac{\bar{y}}{\bar{k}} + (1 - \delta) \right] (k_t - \bar{k})$$

$$+ \frac{\bar{y}}{\bar{c}} (\lambda_t - \bar{\lambda}) - \frac{1}{\bar{c}} (k_{t+1} - \bar{k})$$

$$+ \left[(1 - \theta) \frac{1}{\bar{c}} \frac{\bar{y}}{\bar{h}} - \frac{A}{1 - \bar{h}} \right] (h_t - \bar{h})$$

$$+ \begin{bmatrix} (k_t - \bar{k}) \\ (\lambda_t - \bar{\lambda}) \\ (k_{t+1} - \bar{k}) \\ (h_t - \bar{h}) \end{bmatrix}'
\begin{bmatrix} a_{11} & \widehat{a}_{1\lambda} & a_{12} & a_{13} \\ \widehat{a}_{\lambda 1} & \widehat{a}_{\lambda\lambda} & \widehat{a}_{\lambda 2} & \widehat{a}_{\lambda 3} \\ a_{21} & \widehat{a}_{2\lambda} & a_{22} & a_{23} \\ a_{31} & \widehat{a}_{3\lambda} & a_{32} & a_{33} \end{bmatrix}
\begin{bmatrix} (k_t - \bar{k}) \\ (\lambda_t - \bar{\lambda}) \\ (k_{t+1} - \bar{k}) \\ (h_t - \bar{h}) \end{bmatrix},$$

where the elements of the matrix, a_{ij}, are the same as in the previous example from section 7.2.1 (and their subindices are the same as in that example) and the elements $\widehat{a}_{ij}$, where either i or $j = \lambda$ as part of the subindex, are the new ones related to the new variable, λ_t. The difference between this Taylor expansion and the previous one is the addition of the $\left(\lambda_t - \bar{\lambda}\right)$ terms. The "$\widehat{a}_{ij}$" terms are

$$\widehat{a}_{1\lambda} = \widehat{a}_{\lambda 1} = -\frac{\bar{y}}{\bar{c}^2}\left[\theta\frac{\bar{y}}{\bar{k}} + (1 - \delta)\right] + \theta\frac{1}{\bar{c}}\frac{\bar{y}}{\bar{k}},$$

$$\widehat{a}_{\lambda\lambda} = -\frac{\bar{y}^2}{\bar{c}^2},$$

$$\widehat{a}_{2\lambda} = \widehat{a}_{\lambda 2} = \frac{\bar{y}}{\bar{c}^2},$$

and

$$\widehat{a}_{3\lambda} = \widehat{a}_{\lambda 3} = -(1 - \theta)\frac{1}{\bar{c}^2}\frac{\bar{y}^2}{\bar{h}} + (1 - \theta)\frac{1}{\bar{c}}\frac{\bar{y}}{\bar{h}}.$$

The matrix quadratic version of the objective function is $z_t' M z_t$. The dynamic programming problem to be solved is

$$\max_{\{y_t\}}\sum_{t=0}^{\infty} z_t' M z_t,$$

subject to the budget constraints

$$x_{t+1} = Ax_t + By_t + C\varepsilon_{t+1}.$$

The 5×5 matrix M in the quadratic version of the objective function is

$$M = \begin{bmatrix} m_{11} & m_{12} & m_{13} & m_{14} & m_{15} \\ m_{21} & a_{11} & \widehat{a}_{1\lambda} & a_{12} & a_{13} \\ m_{31} & \widehat{a}_{\lambda 1} & \widehat{a}_{\lambda\lambda} & \widehat{a}_{\lambda 2} & \widehat{a}_{\lambda 3} \\ m_{41} & a_{21} & \widehat{a}_{2\lambda} & a_{22} & a_{23} \\ m_{51} & a_{31} & \widehat{a}_{3\lambda} & a_{32} & a_{33} \end{bmatrix},$$

where the a_{ij} and $\widehat{a}_{ij}$ elements are defined as above and

$$m_{11} = \ln\left(f(\bar{k}, \bar{h}) - \delta\bar{k}\right) + A\ln(1 - \bar{h})$$

$$-\frac{1}{\bar{c}}\left[\theta\frac{\bar{y}}{\bar{k}} + (1 - \delta) - 1\right]\bar{k} - \frac{\bar{y}}{\bar{c}}\bar{\lambda}$$

$$-\left[(1-\theta)\frac{1}{\bar{c}}\frac{\bar{y}}{\bar{h}}-\frac{A}{1-\bar{h}}\right]\bar{h}$$

$$+\begin{bmatrix}\bar{k}\\\bar{\lambda}\\\bar{k}\\\bar{h}\end{bmatrix}'\begin{bmatrix}a_{11}&\widehat{a}_{1\lambda}&a_{12}&a_{13}\\\widehat{a}_{\lambda1}&\widehat{a}_{\lambda\lambda}&\widehat{a}_{\lambda2}&\widehat{a}_{\lambda3}\\a_{21}&\widehat{a}_{2\lambda}&a_{32}&a_{32}\\a_{31}&\widehat{a}_{3\lambda}&a_{32}&a_{33}\end{bmatrix}\begin{bmatrix}\bar{k}\\\bar{\lambda}\\\bar{k}\\\bar{h}\end{bmatrix},$$

$$m_{12}=m_{21}=\frac{1}{\bar{c}}\left[\theta\frac{\bar{y}}{\bar{k}}+(1-\delta)\right]-[\,\bar{k}\quad\bar{\lambda}\quad\bar{k}\quad\bar{h}\,]\begin{bmatrix}a_{11}\\\widehat{a}_{\lambda1}\\a_{21}\\a_{31}\end{bmatrix},$$

$$m_{13}=m_{31}=\frac{\bar{y}}{\bar{c}}-[\,\bar{k}\quad\bar{\lambda}\quad\bar{k}\quad\bar{h}\,]\begin{bmatrix}\widehat{a}_{1\lambda}\\\widehat{a}_{\lambda\lambda}\\\widehat{a}_{2\lambda}\\\widehat{a}_{3\lambda}\end{bmatrix},$$

$$m_{14}=m_{41}=-\frac{1}{\bar{c}}-[\,\bar{k}\quad\bar{\lambda}\quad\bar{k}\quad\bar{h}\,]\begin{bmatrix}a_{12}\\\widehat{a}_{\lambda2}\\a_{22}\\a_{32}\end{bmatrix},$$

and

$$m_{15}=m_{51}=\left[(1-\theta)\frac{1}{\bar{c}}\frac{\bar{y}}{\bar{h}}-\frac{A}{1-\bar{h}}\right]-[\,\bar{k}\quad\bar{\lambda}\quad\bar{k}\quad\bar{h}\,]\begin{bmatrix}a_{13}\\\widehat{a}_{\lambda3}\\a_{23}\\a_{33}\end{bmatrix}.$$

7.3.2 Calibrating the Example Economy

We calibrate this economy with the same values for the parameters as was used in section 7.2.3, adding the parameter $\gamma=.95$. The stationary states are the same as in that section, since in a stationary state for this economy the shocks are zero and the stationary state value for the technology parameter is $\bar{\lambda}=1$.

We iterate using the equation

$$P_{k+1}=R+\beta A'P_kA-\left(\beta A'P_kB+W'\right)\left[Q+\beta B'P_kB\right]^{-1}\left(\beta B'P_kA+W\right),$$

to find the matrix P as

$$P = \begin{bmatrix} -124.0532 & 1.0657 & 15.6762 \\ 1.0657 & -0.0259 & -0.1878 \\ 15.6762 & -0.1878 & -1.9963 \end{bmatrix}$$

and then use

$$y_t = Fx_t = -\left[Q + \beta B'PB\right]^{-1}\left[W + \beta B'PA\right]x_t,$$

to find the policy function F,

$$F = \begin{bmatrix} -0.8470 & 0.9537 & 1.4340 \\ 0.1789 & -0.0064 & 0.2357 \end{bmatrix}.$$

Combining this policy function with the budget constraints, one gets

$$\begin{bmatrix} 1 \\ k_{t+1} \\ \lambda_{t+1} \end{bmatrix} = \begin{bmatrix} 1 & 0 & 0 \\ 0 & 0 & 0 \\ .05 & 0 & .95 \end{bmatrix}\begin{bmatrix} 1 \\ k_t \\ \lambda_t \end{bmatrix}$$

$$+ \begin{bmatrix} 0 & 0 \\ 1 & 0 \\ 0 & 0 \end{bmatrix}\begin{bmatrix} -0.8470 & 0.9537 & 1.4340 \\ 0.1789 & -0.0064 & 0.2357 \end{bmatrix}\begin{bmatrix} 1 \\ k_t \\ \lambda_t \end{bmatrix}$$

$$+ \begin{bmatrix} 0 \\ 0 \\ 1 \end{bmatrix}\varepsilon_{t+1},$$

or, a simple form for the laws of motion is

$$\begin{bmatrix} 1 \\ k_{t+1} \\ \lambda_{t+1} \end{bmatrix} = \begin{bmatrix} 1 & 0 & 0 \\ -0.8470 & 0.9537 & 1.4340 \\ .05 & 0 & .95 \end{bmatrix}\begin{bmatrix} 1 \\ k_t \\ \lambda_t \end{bmatrix} + \begin{bmatrix} 0 \\ 0 \\ 1 \end{bmatrix}\varepsilon_{t+1}.$$

One can think of this last equation in terms of

$$x_{t+1} = \Psi x_t + C\varepsilon_{t+1},$$

and recursively replacing lagged versions of this equation in the right-hand side gives a moving average representation of x_{t+1} as

$$x_{t+1} = \sum_{i=0}^{\infty} \Psi^i C\varepsilon_{t-i} + \Psi^{\infty}x_{-\infty},$$

where we define Ψ^∞ as the limit of Ψ^i as $i \to \infty$. It turns out that

$$\Psi^\infty = \begin{bmatrix} 1 & 0 & 0 \\ \bar{k} & 0 & 0 \\ \bar{\lambda} & 0 & 0 \end{bmatrix} = \begin{bmatrix} 1 & 0 & 0 \\ 12.6695 & 0 & 0 \\ 1 & 0 & 0 \end{bmatrix},$$

which, when multiplied by any $x_{-\infty}$, is equal to $\bar{x}$. This occurs because the first element of every x_t is the constant 1. Using this equation, one can calculate the covariance matrix of x as

$$\text{var}(x) = E(x_{t+1} - \bar{x})(x_{t+1} - \bar{x})'$$

$$= E\left[x_{t+1}x'_{t+1} - x_{t+1}\bar{x}' - \bar{x}x'_{t+1} + \bar{x}\bar{x}' \right]$$

$$= E\left[x_{t+1}x'_{t+1} \right] - \bar{x}\bar{x}'.$$

Substituting in the moving average representation of x_{t+1} gives

$$\text{var}(x) = E\left[\left(\sum_{i=0}^\infty \Psi^i C\varepsilon_{t-i} \right) \left(\sum_{i=0}^\infty \varepsilon'_{t-i} C' \left(\Psi'\right)^i \right) + \Psi^\infty x_{-\infty} x'_{-\infty} \left(\Psi^\infty\right)' \right] - \bar{x}\bar{x}'$$

$$= \sum_{i=0}^\infty \Psi^i C \text{var}(\varepsilon_t) C' \left(\Psi'\right)^i,$$

where $E\left[\Psi^\infty x_{-\infty} x'_{-\infty} \left(\Psi^\infty\right)' \right] = \bar{x}\bar{x}'$. Because ε_t is a 1×1 vector, $\text{var}(\varepsilon_t)$ is a scalar. Then the $\text{var}(x)$ can be written as

$$\text{var}(x) = \text{var}(\varepsilon_t) \sum_{i=0}^\infty \Psi^i CC' \left(\Psi'\right)^i.$$

Using the Ψ and C matrices as defined above,

$$\text{var}(x) = \text{var}\begin{bmatrix} 1 \\ k_{t+1} \\ \lambda_{t+1} \end{bmatrix} = \text{var}(\varepsilon_t)\begin{bmatrix} 0 & 0 & 0 \\ 0 & 4728.5 & 148.7 \\ 0 & 148.7 & 10.3 \end{bmatrix}.$$

Since $y_t = Fx_t$, one can find the variance of the control variables (in this case one is really only adding the variance of hours worked), as

$$\text{var}(y) = \text{var}\begin{bmatrix} k_{t+1} \\ h_t \end{bmatrix} = F\text{var}(x)F' = \begin{bmatrix} 4728.2 & 6.7 \\ 6.7 & 0.3 \end{bmatrix}.$$

Finding the variance for other variables in this model is more difficult, since the relationships are not linear. Output is equal to $y_t = \lambda_t k_t^\theta h_t^{1-\theta}$, and even a

Table 7.1   Statistics from simulations

	Output	Consumption	Invest.	Hours	Capital	Tech.
Standard error	1.42%	0.91%	3.60%	0.54%	1.20%	0.88%
Correl. with y	100%	84%	93%	82%	63%	90%

second-order Taylor approximation of the production function results in a quadratic function.

> **EXERCISE 7.1**   Find the second-order Taylor expansion of the Cobb-Douglas production function with stochastic technology, $y_t = \lambda_t k_t^\theta h_t^{1-\theta}$. Use the values for the stationary state that we have been using in this chapter.

In order to find the variances for the other variables, we run simulations. Hansen reports data from a sample of 115 observations, so we will run 100 simulations of length 115 using the parameters given above. The one parameter that is yet to be defined is $\text{var}(\varepsilon)$. The value we choose for this parameter is .0000105, so that the standard error of the shock is .0032. This value is chosen so that in the section that follows, on the Hansen model with indivisible labor, the standard error of output is 1.76 percent of its average value. Running the simulations (the shocks come from a normal distribution), the average standard errors of output, consumption, investment, labor hours, capital, and the technology process are given in Table 7.1. Standard errors given are as a percentage of the stationary state value.

7.4   HANSEN WITH INDIVISIBLE LABOR

In his paper, Hansen used the techniques we are describing in this chapter to solve both the basic model and the one with indivisible labor. The model with indivisible labor assumes that an individual who is working provides a predetermined amount of labor, h_0, in a period in which he/she works but only an α_t fraction of the population is working in each period. The process of deciding who works and who does not is perfectly random so that each person has an expected utility function of

$$E \sum_{t=0}^{\infty} \beta^t \left[\ln(c_t) + \alpha_t A \ln(1 - h_0) \right].$$

The total amount of labor that is provided to the firms in period t is $\alpha_t h_0$, and given the amount of capital carried over from the previous period, k_t, production in period t is

$$y_t = \lambda_t f(k_t, \alpha_t h_0) = \lambda_t k_t^\theta \left(\alpha_t h_0\right)^{1-\theta}.$$

The budget constraints in period t are

$$c_t = y_t + (1 - \delta)k_t - k_{t+1}$$

and

$$\lambda_{t+1} = (1 - \gamma) + \gamma\lambda_t + \varepsilon_{t+1}.$$

The model assumes that there is a mutual insurance program that guarantees every individual the same consumption whether he/she is one of those who must work or not. The only change between this model and the basic model is in the part of the subutility function that is associated with the disutility of labor. Here, the expected disutility of work is what matters, and changes in the amount of work provided shows up in the utility function in a linear form (caused by changes in the variable a_t while $A \ln(1 - h_0)$ is a constant). In the basic version of this model, changes in the amount of labor provided by an individual change utility as the logarithm of the change in labor.

Since we want to use the linear quadratic dynamic programming that we developed above to solve this model, we need to put all the nonlinearity into the objective function and have linear budget constraints. We choose $x_t = [\,1 \quad k_t \quad \lambda_t\,]'$ as the state variables (the constant, 1, will serve the same purpose as it did above; it will help with the inclusion of the constant and linear terms of the second-order Taylor expansion) and $y_t = [\,k_{t+1} \quad \alpha_t\,]'$ as the control variables. The objective function we use is

$$E \sum_{t=0}^{\infty} \beta^t \left[\ln(\lambda_t k_t^\theta \left(\alpha_t h_0\right)^{1-\theta} + (1 - \delta)k_t - k_{t+1}) + \alpha_t A \ln(1 - h_0)\right],$$

subject to the budget constraints

$$k_{t+1} = k_{t+1},$$
$$\lambda_{t+1} = (1 - \gamma) + \gamma\lambda_t + \varepsilon_{t+1}.$$

The second-order Taylor expansion of the objective function is

$$u(\cdot) \approx \ln\left(\bar{\lambda}\bar{k}^\theta\left(\bar{\alpha}h_0\right)^{1-\theta} - \delta\bar{k}\right) + \bar{\alpha}A\ln(1-h_0)$$

$$+ \frac{1}{\bar{c}}\left[\theta\frac{\bar{y}}{\bar{k}} + (1-\delta)\right](k_t - \bar{k})$$

$$+ \frac{\bar{y}}{\bar{c}}\left(\lambda_t - \bar{\lambda}\right) - \frac{1}{\bar{c}}\left(k_{t+1} - \bar{k}\right)$$

$$+ \left[(1-\theta)\frac{1}{\bar{c}}\frac{\bar{y}}{\bar{\alpha}} + A\ln(1-h_0)\right](\alpha_t - \bar{\alpha})$$

$$+ \begin{bmatrix} (k_t - \bar{k}) \\ (\lambda_t - \bar{\lambda}) \\ (k_{t+1} - \bar{k}) \\ (\alpha_t - \bar{\alpha}) \end{bmatrix}' \begin{bmatrix} a_{11} & \widehat{a}_{1\lambda} & a_{12} & a_{13} \\ \widehat{a}_{\lambda 1} & \widehat{a}_{\lambda\lambda} & \widehat{a}_{\lambda 2} & \widehat{a}_{\lambda 3} \\ a_{21} & \widehat{a}_{2\lambda} & a_{32} & a_{32} \\ a_{31} & \widehat{a}_{3\lambda} & a_{32} & a_{33} \end{bmatrix} \begin{bmatrix} (k_t - \bar{k}) \\ (\lambda_t - \bar{\lambda}) \\ (k_{t+1} - \bar{k}) \\ (\alpha_t - \bar{\alpha}) \end{bmatrix},$$

where all parameters are the same as in the basic version of the model, except $\alpha = 0.5721$, $h_0 = 5.83$, and these elements of the a matrix are changed:

$$a_{13} = a_{31} = -\frac{1}{\bar{c}^2}\left[\theta\frac{\bar{y}}{\bar{k}} + (1-\delta)\right]\left[(1-\theta)\frac{\bar{y}}{\bar{\alpha}}\right] + \frac{1}{\bar{c}}\theta(1-\theta)\frac{\bar{y}}{\bar{k}\bar{\alpha}},$$

$$\widehat{a}_{\lambda 3} = \widehat{a}_{3\lambda} = -\frac{\bar{y}}{\bar{c}^2}\left[(1-\theta)\frac{\bar{y}}{\bar{\alpha}}\right] + (1-\theta)\frac{\bar{y}}{\bar{c}\bar{\alpha}},$$

$$a_{32} = a_{23} = \frac{1}{\bar{c}^2}\left[(1-\theta)\frac{\bar{y}}{\bar{\alpha}}\right],$$

and

$$a_{33} = -\frac{1}{\bar{c}^2}\left[(1-\theta)\frac{\bar{y}}{\bar{\alpha}}\right]^2 - \frac{1}{\bar{c}}\theta(1-\theta)\frac{\bar{y}}{\bar{\alpha}^2}.$$

Using the technique of Kydland and Prescott, we define the matrix M for the quadratic approximation of the objective function, $z_t'Mz_t$, where $z_t = [\,x_t \quad y_t\,]$, as

$$M = \begin{bmatrix} m_{11} & m_{12} & m_{13} & m_{14} & m_{15} \\ m_{21} & a_{11} & \widehat{a}_{1\lambda} & a_{12} & a_{13} \\ m_{31} & \widehat{a}_{\lambda 1} & \widehat{a}_{\lambda\lambda} & \widehat{a}_{\lambda 2} & \widehat{a}_{\lambda 3} \\ m_{41} & a_{21} & \widehat{a}_{2\lambda} & a_{22} & a_{23} \\ m_{51} & a_{31} & \widehat{a}_{3\lambda} & a_{32} & a_{33} \end{bmatrix},$$

where

$$m_{11} = \ln\left(f(\bar{k}, \bar{h}) - \delta\bar{k}\right) + \bar{\alpha}A\ln(1 - h_0)$$

$$- \frac{1}{\bar{c}}\left[\theta\frac{\bar{y}}{\bar{k}} + (1 - \delta) - 1\right]\bar{k} - \frac{\bar{y}}{\bar{c}}\bar{\lambda}$$

$$- \left[(1 - \theta)\frac{1}{\bar{c}}\frac{\bar{y}}{\bar{\alpha}} + A\left(1 - h_0\right)\right]\bar{\alpha}$$

$$+ \begin{bmatrix} \bar{k} \\ \bar{\lambda} \\ \bar{k} \\ \bar{\alpha} \end{bmatrix}' \begin{bmatrix} a_{11} & \widehat{a}_{1\lambda} & a_{12} & a_{13} \\ \widehat{a}_{\lambda 1} & \widehat{a}_{\lambda\lambda} & \widehat{a}_{\lambda 2} & \widehat{a}_{\lambda 3} \\ a_{21} & \widehat{a}_{2\lambda} & a_{22} & a_{23} \\ a_{31} & \widehat{a}_{3\lambda} & a_{32} & a_{33} \end{bmatrix} \begin{bmatrix} \bar{k} \\ \bar{\lambda} \\ \bar{k} \\ \bar{\alpha} \end{bmatrix},$$

$$m_{12} = m_{21} = \frac{1}{\bar{c}}\left[\theta\frac{\bar{y}}{\bar{k}} + (1 - \delta)\right] - [\,\bar{k} \quad \bar{\lambda} \quad \bar{k} \quad \bar{\alpha}\,]\begin{bmatrix} a_{11} \\ \widehat{a}_{\lambda 1} \\ a_{21} \\ a_{31} \end{bmatrix},$$

$$m_{13} = m_{31} = \frac{\bar{y}}{\bar{c}} - [\,\bar{k} \quad \bar{\lambda} \quad \bar{k} \quad \bar{\alpha}\,]\begin{bmatrix} \widehat{a}_{1\lambda} \\ \widehat{a}_{\lambda\lambda} \\ \widehat{a}_{2\lambda} \\ \widehat{a}_{3\lambda} \end{bmatrix},$$

$$m_{14} = m_{41} = -\frac{1}{\bar{c}} - [\,\bar{k} \quad \bar{\lambda} \quad \bar{k} \quad \bar{\alpha}\,]\begin{bmatrix} a_{12} \\ \widehat{a}_{\lambda 2} \\ a_{22} \\ a_{32} \end{bmatrix},$$

and

$$m_{15} = m_{51} = \left[(1 - \theta)\frac{1}{\bar{c}}\frac{\bar{y}}{\bar{\alpha}} + A\left(1 - h_0\right)\right] - [\,\bar{k} \quad \bar{\lambda} \quad \bar{k} \quad \bar{h}\,]\begin{bmatrix} a_{13} \\ \widehat{a}_{\lambda 3} \\ a_{23} \\ a_{33} \end{bmatrix}.$$

Given this definition of M, one wants to choose a sequence of $\{y_t\}$ to maximize

$$E_0 \sum_{t=0}^{\infty} \beta^t z_t' M z_t = E_0 \sum_{t=0}^{\infty} \beta^t [\,x_t' \quad y_t'\,]\begin{bmatrix} R & W' \\ W & Q \end{bmatrix}\begin{bmatrix} x_t \\ y_t \end{bmatrix},$$

subject to the budget constraints

$$
\begin{bmatrix} 1 \\ k_{t+1} \\ \lambda_{t+1} \end{bmatrix} = A \begin{bmatrix} 1 \\ k_t \\ \lambda_t \end{bmatrix} + B \begin{bmatrix} k_{t+1} \\ \alpha_t \end{bmatrix} + C\varepsilon_{t+1},
$$

where

$$
A = \begin{bmatrix} 1 & 0 & 0 \\ 0 & 0 & 0 \\ 1-\gamma & 0 & \gamma \end{bmatrix},
$$

$$
B = \begin{bmatrix} 0 & 0 \\ 1 & 0 \\ 0 & 0 \end{bmatrix},
$$

and

$$
C = \begin{bmatrix} 0 \\ 0 \\ 1 \end{bmatrix}.
$$

We look for a policy function, F, that solves the value function, P, where

$$
x_t' P x_t = \max_{k_{t+1}, \alpha_t} \left[z_t' M z_t + \beta E_t \left(A x_t + B y_t + C\varepsilon_t \right)' P \left(A x_t + B y_t + C\varepsilon_t \right) \right].
$$

As before, P is found by making an initial guess, P_0, and iterating on

$$
P_{k+1} = R + \beta A' P_k A - \left(\beta A' P_k B + W' \right) \left[Q + \beta B' P_k B \right]^{-1} \left(\beta B' P_k A + W \right).
$$

Once P is known, the policy function is found from

$$
y_t = F x_t = - \left[Q + \beta B' P B \right]^{-1} \left[W + \beta B' P A \right] x_t.
$$

We want the stationary state to be the same as in the basic example, so we use the same values we found at the end of Chapter 6: $\bar{\alpha} = 572$, and $h_0 = 583$. All other stationary state values are the same as above. Using these values for the stationary state variables, we get

$$
P = \begin{bmatrix} -139.5224 & 1.0816 & 14.9763 \\ 1.0816 & -0.0245 & -0.2215 \\ 14.9763 & -0.2215 & -0.8695 \end{bmatrix}
$$

and

$$F = \begin{bmatrix} -1.2295 & 0.9418 & 1.9667 \\ 0.0029 & -0.0215 & 0.8418 \end{bmatrix}.$$

We get the laws of motion for this economy by substituting Fx_t for y_t in the budget constraints. This gives

$$\begin{bmatrix} 1 \\ k_{t+1} \\ \lambda_{t+1} \end{bmatrix} = \begin{bmatrix} 1 & 0 & 0 \\ -1.2295 & 0.9418 & 1.9667 \\ .05 & 0 & .95 \end{bmatrix} \begin{bmatrix} 1 \\ k_t \\ \lambda_t \end{bmatrix} + \begin{bmatrix} 0 \\ 0 \\ 1 \end{bmatrix} \varepsilon_{t+1}.$$

We want to compare the results of simulation of this economy with those of the basic model. As with the basic model we used a value for $\mathrm{var}(\varepsilon) = .0000105$, which gives a standard error for the error term of .0032. This standard error results in a standard error for output of 1.76 percent, the same value as Hansen found from his 115 quarterly observations for output from the United States (from third quarter of 1955 to first quarter of 1984). The variance of the error term is calibrated so that the simulations have this standard error for output. The standard errors (and the correlation of the variable with output) for output, consumption, investment, hours worked, capital, and the technology process are given in Table 7.2.

Using the model with indivisible labor improves the results with respect to the data in investment and hours worked and reduces the importance of the technology in explaining movements in output. Table 7.3 shows the standard errors (as a fraction of the standard error of output) in the basic model and in the model with indivisible labor. Note the results for investment, hours worked, and technology.

We can get some insight into why this relatively minor change of adding indivisible labor would result in such a large change in the relative standard error of hours by looking at the two Taylor expansions of the objective function and calculating how much utility would change as a result of a small change in the variable related to hours worked. Define the two vectors, χ_h as $\chi_h = \bar{z}_h + [\, 0 \quad 0 \quad 0 \quad 0 \quad .01 * \bar{h} \,]$, and χ_α as $\chi_\alpha = \bar{z}_\alpha + [\, 0 \quad 0 \quad 0 \quad 0 \quad .01 * \bar{\alpha} \,]$. The

Table 7.2   Standard errors and correlations from U.S. data

	Output	Consumption	Invest.	Hours	Capital	Tech.
Standard error	1.76%	1.06%	4.69%	1.08%	1.45%	0.88%
As % of Y	100%	60%	266%	61%	82%	50%
Correl with Y	100%	82%	93%	84%	61%	91%

Table 7.3   Standard errors from the models

	Output	Consumption	Invest.	Hours	Capital	Tech.
Basic model	100%	63.91%	253.06%	38.06%	84.45%	62.10%
Indivisible labor	100%	60.31%	265.89%	61.11%	82.28%	50.14%

vector χ_i represents a one percent movement in the hours worked variable from the stationary state. The two stationary states are represented by different vectors (with $\bar{h}$ in the basic model and $\bar{\alpha}$ in the indivisible labor model). The one percent increase in labor supplied in the basic model results in a change in utility of -7.3691×10^{-5} units, which is a decline of .0094613 percent in utility from the stationary state. A one percent increase in labor supplied in the indivisible labor model results in a change of utility of -5.2556×10^{-5} units, which is a decline of .0055559 percent from the stationary state. The incorporation of indivisible labor into the model has made utility less sensitive to change in labor and therefore encourages agents to change the labor supplied (or expected labor supplied) more than they would have in the basic model.

7.5   IMPULSE RESPONSE FUNCTIONS

Using the linear policy function, F, and a vector of technology that incorporates a one-time shock to technology in period 2, $\varepsilon_2 = .01$, and the technology law of motion,

$$\lambda_t = (1 - \gamma) + \gamma \lambda_{t-1} + \varepsilon_t,$$

one can find the time path of capital and hours worked (the state variables), and, using the production function and the budget constraints, one can then calculate the path of output and consumption. The solution technique used in this chapter finds the values of the variables in levels, and the resulting impulse response functions are those shown in Figure 7.1. To be able to compare the response functions to those in the previous chapter, one needs to find the log differences around the stationary state values of the variables. Figure 7.2 shows the resulting response functions for the basic Hansen model.

    These response functions should look familiar. These are very close to the response functions we found using the log-linear method of Chapter 6. Figure 7.3 shows the response functions above compared to those for the same model using Uhlig's log-linear method. The 45 degree line has a little width to it, so the two solution methods don't give exactly the same impulse response functions, but they are very close. One should expect a little

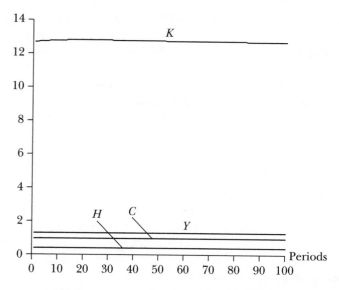

FIGURE 7.1   Impulse response function in levels

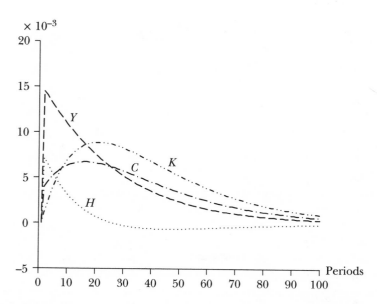

FIGURE 7.2   Responses found using the linear quadratic solution method

difference because of the order in which we took the approximations, but Figure 7.3 shows that, for most purposes, the results are the same.

A graph that is essentially identical to Figure 7.3 is found if one graphs the impulse response functions found using the two different techniques for Hansen's model with indivisible labor. For models as simple as those we have developed here, with logarithmic utility functions and Cobb-Douglas production functions, either of the methods produces results that are, given the uncertainties we have about the parameters of the model, the same.

7.5.1   Vector Autoregressions

Comparing the impulse reponse functions generated by the model to those observed in the data is one way of evaluating how well a model is capturing important characteristics of the economy. While comparing covariances of simulations of the model to those of the data is a form of evaluating models that is frequently used, comparing impulse response functions demands more of a model and is a finer measure of success.

The impulse response functions from the data are usually found by estimating vector autoregressions (VARs). The method is well known. One estimates linear equations of the form

$$y_t = A(L)y_{t-1} + \varepsilon_t = A_1 y_{t-1} + A_2 y_{t-2} + \cdots + A_n y_{t-n} + \varepsilon_t,$$

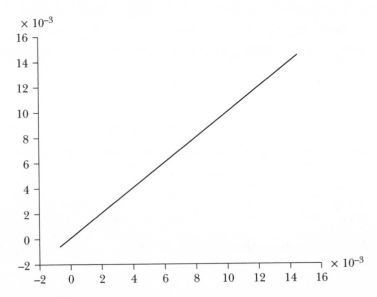

FIGURE 7.3   Comparing the two solution techniques using Hansen's model

where y_t is a vector of variables, $A(L)$ is an nth order matrix polynomial in the lag operator, and ε_t is a vector of error terms that we usually want to have zero mean and a diagonal variance matrix. A lag operator, L, applied to a variable X_t results in

$$LX_t = X_{t-1}.$$

Applied twice gives

$$L^2 X_t = LX_{t-1} = X_{t-2}.$$

The polynomial in the lag operator, $A(L)$, can be written

$$A(L) = A_1 L + A_2 L^2 + \cdots + A_n L^n.$$

In a VAR, current values of each of a set of variables are a function of past values of all the variables in the set. VARs are good for forecasting, since one can find predictions for tomorrow's values for the set of variables using current and past values and then recursively solve for predictions further into the future. In doing these forecasts, the shocks are usually set to zero.

Define $B(L) = 1 - A(L)$. One can rewrite the above equation as

$$B(L)y_t = \varepsilon_t.$$

Let $C(L) = (B(L))^{-1}$ be the inverse of the matrix polynomial $B(L)$. Applying this inverse to both sides of the above equation gives the moving average representation of the vector autoregression,

$$y_t = (B(L))^{-1}B(L)y_t = C(L)B(L)y_t = C(L)\varepsilon_t,$$

or $y_t = C(L)\varepsilon_t$. One can use the matrix polynomial $C(L)$ to find the impulse response functions for the vector autoregressive system. Set all of the error terms to zero except for the one that you wish to study; for example, if we wish to study the results of a shock to the second variable in y_t, we apply

$$\widehat{y_1} = C(L) \begin{bmatrix} 0 \\ \varepsilon_1 \\ 0 \\ \vdots \\ 0 \end{bmatrix}$$

to get the response of the variables in y_t in the first period. Since all shocks return to zero in periods 2 and beyond, we find the rest of the response function by recursively applying the matrix $A(L)$ to get

$$\widehat{y}_2 = A(L)\widehat{y}_1,$$

$$\widehat{y}_3 = A(L)\widehat{y}_2,$$

$$\vdots$$

Finding the inverse of the $B(L)$ matrix polynomial is not always easy, and the interested reader is encouraged to consult texts in time series such as Hamilton [47] for details.

Unfortunately, for a particular economy, it is sometimes (as is the case here) difficult to identify the shocks from the real world that one is using in a model. What constitute shocks to technology in the real world, how big these shocks are, and what the process of their persistence looks like are all difficult questions. If one cannot find a shock in the economy that approximates well the shock used in the model, then comparing impulse response functions is not possible. If possible, one should try to choose stochastic shocks for the models that have a natural counterpart in the data. For example, some models that include money consider unpredictable changes in short-term interest rates as representing monetary shocks. The residuals of the vector autoregression equation for short-term interest rates provide the required data on this shock.

Sims [77] suggests an alternative method for using VARs to compare impulse response functions. One can find the impulse response functions for the data as described above. Using the model, generate a large number of time series for the simulated economy (using appropriately calibrated variances for the model's shocks). Estimate VARs using this simulated time series and compare them to those generated from the data. Since the times series from the data and those from the simulated economies should have the same variables, the impulse response functions are comparable.

7.6 AN ALTERNATIVE PROCESS FOR TECHNOLOGY

It is sometimes desirable to use a stochastic process that will not go negative. For example, a stochastic process for technology of the form that we have been using,

$$\lambda_{t+1} = (1 - \gamma) + \gamma \lambda_t + \varepsilon_{t+1},$$

with $\varepsilon_{t+1} \sim N(0, \sigma_\varepsilon^2)$, can end up with some values for λ_t that are negative. Since the normal distribution is unbounded below (and above), there is a very small but finite probability that some ε_{t+1} will have a value sufficiently negative so that the associated λ_{t+1} is also negative. There is no economic (nor engineering) sense to a negative level of technology.

A simple way to ensure that technology will not go negative is to use a different stochastic process, one where the λ_{t+1} will never be negative. One stochastic process that has this characteristic, along with the characteristic that the unconditional expectation of λ_{t+1}, $E\lambda_{t+1}$ is equal to one, is

$$\ln\left(\lambda_{t+1}\right) = \gamma \ln\left(\lambda_t\right) + \varepsilon_{t+1},$$

with $\varepsilon_{t+1} \sim N(0, \sigma_\varepsilon^2)$. With this process, a very large negative realization for ε_{t+1} implies that λ_{t+1} will be close to zero but positive. The entire sequence of $\{\lambda_t\}$ is guaranteed to be positive. One can check that the mean of λ_{t+1} is 1. Take unconditional expectations of both sides of the process, so that

$$E \ln\left(\lambda_{t+1}\right) = \gamma E \ln\left(\lambda_t\right) + E\varepsilon_{t+1} = \gamma E \ln\left(\lambda_t\right) + 0.$$

Simple manipulation gives

$$E \ln\left(\lambda_{t+1}\right) - \gamma E \ln\left(\lambda_t\right) = (1 - \gamma) \ln\left(\lambda\right) = 0,$$

so, in a stationary state, $E \ln(\lambda) = 0$. This occurs when $\lambda = 1$.

If we would like to use this process in our basic Hansen model, there is a problem: the budget constraint that we have is not linear in technology, so we cannot immediately use the linear quadratic dynamic programming techniques that we have developed in this section. We need to modify the model slightly to be able to continue using these techniques.

Define the variable $\widehat{\lambda}_t = \ln(\lambda_t)$ and the vector of state variables as $x_t = [1 \ \ k_t \ \ \widehat{\lambda}_t]'$. Then one can write the budget constraints, the laws of motion, as

$$\begin{bmatrix} 1 \\ k_{t+1} \\ \widehat{\lambda}_{t+1} \end{bmatrix} = \begin{bmatrix} 1 & 0 & 0 \\ 0 & 0 & 0 \\ 0 & 0 & \gamma \end{bmatrix} \begin{bmatrix} 1 \\ k_t \\ \widehat{\lambda}_t \end{bmatrix} + \begin{bmatrix} 0 & 0 \\ 1 & 0 \\ 0 & 0 \end{bmatrix} \begin{bmatrix} k_{t+1} \\ h_t \end{bmatrix} + \begin{bmatrix} 0 \\ 0 \\ 1 \end{bmatrix} \varepsilon_{t+1}.$$

This way, the budget constraints are linear, although the variable in which they are linear is a variable in logs.

One needs to make a change in the objective function to incorporate this stochastic process. In the objective function,

$$u\left(c_t, h_t\right) = \ln(e^{\widehat{\lambda}_t} k_t^\theta h_t^{1-\theta} + (1 - \delta)k_t - k_{t+1}) + A \ln(1 - h_t),$$

we replace λ_t with $e^{\widehat{\lambda}_t}$, since $e^{\ln(\lambda_t)} = \lambda_t$. This has the effect of complicating a bit the second-order Taylor expansion, but it is normally quite manageable.

7.7 REPRISE

Linear quadratic dynamic programming methods provide an alternative to the linear approximation of the model that we presented in Chapter 6. They have their advantages and limitations. Solving linear quadratic problems is relatively simple once they are formulated. The difficulties arise in the need for being careful in taking the many derivatives that are required for the Taylor approximation and in including economy-wide variables in the problem. Most of the earlier papers in Real Business Cycle theory used this method for finding solutions.

A more extensive development of linear quadratic dynamic programming methods, along with numerous applications, can be found in Ljungqvist and Sargent [54]. Another general reference on dynamic programming with applications to linear quadratic problems is Bertsekas [10].

7.8 MATLAB CODE

The following Matlab program finds the solution to the linear quadratic problem for a standard version of the basic Hansen model. Most of the program involves setting up the matrices. The loop at the end of the program finds the value matrix, and this is used to find the policy function.

```
%this program finds the value function (P matrix) for the linear
%quadratic optimal regulator problem and also calculates the
%resulting policy function
theta=.36;
beta=.99;
delta=.025;
A=1.72;
kbar=12.6695;
hbar=.3335;
ybar=kbar^theta*hbar^(1-theta);
cbar=ybar-delta*kbar;
aa=(theta*ybar/kbar+1-delta);
a(1,1)=-1/(2*cbar*cbar)*aa*aa-1/(2*cbar)*theta*(1-theta)*ybar/
    (kbar*kbar);
a(1,2)=1/(2*cbar*cbar)*aa;
a(2,1)=1/(2*cbar*cbar)*aa;
a(1,3)=-1/(2*cbar*cbar)*aa*(1-theta)*ybar/hbar;
a(1,3)=a(1,3)+1/(2*cbar)*theta*(1-theta)*ybar/(kbar*hbar);
a(3,1)=a(1,3);
a(2,2)=-1/(2*cbar*cbar);
a(2,3)=1/(2*cbar*cbar)*(1-theta)*ybar/hbar;
a(3,2)=a(2,3);
a(3,3)=-1/(2*cbar*cbar)*(1-theta)*ybar/hbar*(1-theta)*ybar/hbar;
```

```
a(3,3)=a(3,3)-1/(2*cbar)*theta*(1-theta)*ybar/(hbar*hbar);
a(3,3)=a(3,3)-A/(2*(1-hbar)*(1-hbar));
x=[kbar kbar hbar]';
m(1,1)=log(kbar^theta*hbar^(1-theta)-delta*kbar)+A*log(1-hbar);
mm1=1/cbar*(theta*ybar/kbar+1-delta);
mm2=(1-theta)*ybar/(cbar*hbar)-A/(1-hbar);
m(1,1)=m(1,1)-mm1*kbar+kbar/cbar-mm2*hbar;
m(1,1)=m(1,1)+(x')*a*x;
m(1,2)=mm1/2-1*a(1:3,1)'*x;
m(2,1)=m(1,2);
m(1,3)=-1/(2*cbar)-1*a(1:3,2)'*x;
m(3,1)=m(1,3);
m(1,4)=mm2/2-1*a(1:3,3)'*x;
m(4,1)=m(1,4);
m(2:4,2:4)=a;
AA=[1 0
    0 0];
B=[0 0
   1 0];
R=m(1:2,1:2);
Q=m(3:4,3:4);
W=m(1:2,3:4)';
P=[1 0
   0 1];
% iterating the Ricotti equation
for i=1:1000
    zinv=inv(Q+beta*B'*P*B);
    z2=beta*AA'*P*B+W';
    P=R+beta*AA'*P*AA-z2*zinv*z2'
end
% finding the policy function
F=-zinv*(W+beta*B'*P*AA)
```

PART TWO

EXTENSIONS OF THE BASIC RBC MODEL

Money: Cash in Advance

Cooley and Hansen [36] introduce money into Hansen's model [48] with indivisible labor. The model of money they present is one with cash in advance (Clower [35] or Lucas and Stokey [58], for example) but where the use of cash is restricted to the purchase of consumption goods. The purchase of investment goods does not require the use of money held over from the previous period but is restricted by an overall, flow budget constraint. Consumption is purchased using money that is held over from the previous period, but capital can be purchased using this period's income. This model adds two new features to our models: money and economy-wide variables. Some changes in techniques are required to handle models with these new features.

Cash-in-advance models require agents to have carried over from the previous period the money they will use in this period to make purchases or to make a subset of their purchases. The story that is often used to describe a cash-in-advance model has a family with two members, one called the shopper and the other the worker. In the beginning of each period, the two members of the family separate. The shopper takes the money the family has (along with any transfer received from the government) and goes to market. Sometimes there is a sequence of markets, first a market in financial assets and then a market in goods. The producer goes to the family factory, uses capital and her/his labor to produce goods, and sells them to shoppers who are not members of the same family. Families cannot consume the good they produce. At the end of the period, the members of the family rejoin and consume the goods that were purchased for consumption. The worker brings home the money from that period's sales and gives it to the shopper who will use it in the next period, along with any money that remains from this day's shopping.

The requirement that money be used to purchase goods, or at least some goods, is simply imposed. Nothing in the model explains why money is used or what particular benefit comes from using money. However, for most practical purposes, the same can be said about how most of us use money day to day. There is nothing in daily life that much explains why we use money except that it is what our employer gives us for the labor we provide and what the grocer accepts in exchange for the food we want to consume. This is usually a good enough reason for using money day by day and the reason we use it in this chapter.[1]

Cash-in-advance models normally have only one good. That is the reason for the taboo on consuming goods produced by the same family. Most families in the real world produce only one market good or service, and the particular good or service that they produce is only an extremely small part of the basket of goods they consume. The prohibition of consuming the family's own production is a way of making a one-good model behave like one with many diversified goods without the complications. Money is buying us the basket of goods we normally consume but do not produce for ourselves.

Adding money to the model creates an additional complication in solving the models. The presence of money puts a friction into the economy so that the equilibrium will not necessarily be that of a frictionless competitive equilibrium. The second welfare theorem allowed us to use a Robinson Crusoe (representative agent) type model to solve for a multi-agent competitive equilibrium because, without frictions, the equilibria would be the same. Here, we need to work explicitly with multiple agents, with markets, and with the friction of money. Each family in the economy will be responding to market variables (the price level) or economy-wide expectations variables (the next period's aggregate capital stock). In each period, each family bases its decisions on these variables. In an equilibrium, the values that the families use for these variables need to be the actual ones (in the case of prices) or the expected value of the economy-wide realization (in the case of the next period's capital). This complication adds a new step to the solution of an equilibrium, one that makes the solution process a bit more difficult, but not excessively so.

8.1 COOLEY AND HANSEN'S MODEL

A number of changes are required in the basic Hansen model to include money. One of the most important is that the model can no longer be solved

---

1. In some countries this issue is less than clear. One money, pesos, for example, is used for small transactions and another money, dollars, for example, is used for large transactions. There is an extensive and very interesting literature on endogenous money that tries to deal with such issues using search models for money. For some recent papers on this topic, see Lagos and Wright [53] and Zhu and Wallace [91].

by using a representative agent of the style of Robinson Crusoe. We now need to explicitly include markets for labor and capital, with wages and rentals determined by the aggregate labor and capital provided. Individual agents (families or households) take these wages and rentals as given and do not believe that their actions can influence either current or future wages and rentals. Although in equilibrium, the amount of labor provided and the stock of capital are determined by these family decisions, this feedback is not taken into account when the optimization decisions are made. All families are identical and all will end up doing the same thing, but each family is so small that if it chooses to do something else it will not have an effect on aggregate labor or capital. It is useful to think of the economy as being comprised of a continuum of agents indexed by i, where $i = [0, 1]$. There is a unit mass of agents (all points from zero to one) and each agent is simply a point. All agents are identical, so when we sum them (take the integral over i from 0 to 1, since there is a continuum of them), the aggregate behaves like any one of them. Points have measure zero, so if one agent behaves differently from the rest, the aggregate is not affected.

Each family, i, wants to maximize the discounted expected utility function,

$$E_0 \sum_{t=0}^{\infty} \beta^t u(c_t^i, h_t^i).$$

Utility increases with consumption and declines with labor supplied. As before, families have a maximum of 1 unit of labor in each period, so the leisure they consume, which does give positive utility, is equal to $1 - h_t^i$. Following Cooley and Hansen, the subutility function we use has indivisible labor, where each family signs a contract to provide with probability α_t^i an amount of h_0 units of labor.[2] The amount of indivisible labor, h_0, is the same for all families. Defining h_t^i as the expected labor to be provided in period t, $h_t^i = \alpha_t^i h_0$, the subutility function can be written as

$$u(c_t^i, h_t^i) = \ln c_t^i + \left[A \frac{\ln(1 - h_0)}{h_0} \right] h_t^i.$$

Production in the economy occurs with a Cobb-Douglas aggregate production function,

$$y_t = \lambda_t K_t^\theta H_t^{1-\theta}.$$

Technology follows a stochastic process,

---

2. In Chapter 6, we discussed how this assumption makes convex the set over which one is finding the optimum.

$$\ln(\lambda_{t+1}) = \gamma \ln(\lambda_t) + \varepsilon_{t+1},$$

where the error term is independently and identically distributed as $\varepsilon_{t+1} \sim N(0, \sigma_\varepsilon^2)$. This assumption implies that the unconditional expectation of $\ln(\lambda_t) = 0$. In a stationary state stochastic variables are equal to their unconditional expectation, so $\ln(\bar{\lambda}) = 0$, and the stationary state value of the level of technology is $\bar{\lambda} = 1$.

Under conditions of perfect competition, the wage rate at time t equals

$$w_t = (1 - \theta) \lambda_t K_t^\theta H_t^{-\theta},$$

and the rental rate is

$$r_t = \theta \lambda_t K_t^{\theta-1} H_t^{1-\theta}.$$

Notice that it is the amounts of aggregate labor and capital that determine wage and rental rates. Given that the production function displays constant returns to scale, all income to the firm gets paid out in wages and rentals: there are no excess profits to be distributed. The aggregate amount of labor available at time t is equal to

$$H_t = \int_0^1 h_t^i di,$$

and the aggregate amount of capital available at time t is

$$K_t = \int_0^1 k_t^i di.$$

Family i carries over an amount of money from the previous period, m_{t-1}^i, and receives a transfer of money from the government equal to $(g_t - 1) M_{t-1}$, where M_{t-1} is the per capita money stock at time $t - 1$. In this model, since there is a unit mass of families, the per capita variables are equal to the aggregate of the same variable.[3] Notice that, in this model, a family's holdings of money do not determine how much they will receive from the government as a transfer. The cash-in-advance constraint on consumption purchases implies that

$$p_t c_t^i \leq m_{t-1}^i + (g_t - 1) M_{t-1},$$

---

3. This because there is a mass 1 of individuals, so dividing the aggregate amount of some variable by 1 gives the per capita, which is also the aggregate. This is the benefit of defining the population as being a continuum of mass = 1,

where p_t is the price level in period t, and g_t is the time t gross growth rate of money (equal to 1 plus the net growth rate of money). One can consider cases where the growth rate of money is constant and one is in a stationary state or where it follows a stochastic process and the dynamics are of interest. We will consider an example of each case.

Notice that money transfers to families are a function of the aggregate money supply and not of the family's own money holdings. The results of the model would be different if the money transfer were based on the family's own holdings, since they would take into account how their decision to hold money would affect the transfer.

To keep the solution technique simple, we want a condition under which the cash-in-advance constraint always holds. Cooley and Hansen give this condition as follows: the expected gross growth rate of money, g_t, must be greater than the discount factor, β. If the expected gross growth rate of money were less than β, keeping some of the money acquired last period into the next period would increase consumption more than the discount rate and raise discounted welfare. Therefore, we will limit ourselves to cases where $g_t \geq \beta$. This implies that, in every period t, the shopper spends all the family's money holdings on time t consumption goods.

Families enter a period with holdings of capital, k_t^i, and money, m_{t-1}^i. In addition to the cash-in-advance constraint on consumption purchases, family i faces the flow budget constraint,

$$c_t^i + k_{t+1}^i + \frac{m_t^i}{p_t} = w_t h_t^i + r_t k_t^i + (1-\delta)k_t^i + \frac{m_{t-1}^i + (g_t - 1)M_{t-1}}{p_t}.$$

The right-hand side of the budget constraint sums income from labor (from the labor contract where they get paid whether they work or not) and capital holdings, the capital that remains after depreciation, and the real value of money held at the beginning of the period (but after the government transfer has been made). On the left-hand side of the budget constraint are consumption, the new capital holdings, and the real value of money to be held into the next period. Notice that everything in this budget constraint is measured in real terms (in terms of the one good in the economy).

To be able to solve this model, we need to be able to define a stationary state. When $\bar{g} = 1$, for all t, the stock of money is constant and there exists a natural concept for a stationary state. When $\bar{g} \neq 1$, the stock of money is either growing or shrinking continually over time and we will not, in general, be able to find stationary state values for p_t, m_t^i, or M_t. There are two ways of handling this problem.

One way, that of Cooley and Hansen, is to normalize the three nominal variables in each period by dividing them by M_t, and to define $\hat{p}_t = p_t/M_t$,

$\hat{m}_t^i = m_t^i / M_t$, and $M_t / M_t = 1$. Using these definitions, the cash-in-advance constraint is equal to

$$\frac{p_t}{M_t} c_t^i = \frac{m_{t-1}^i + (g_t - 1) M_{t-1}}{M_t},$$

which can be written as

$$\hat{p}_t c_t^i = \frac{m_{t-1}^i + (g_t - 1) M_{t-1}}{g_t M_{t-1}}$$

$$\hat{p}_t c_t^i = \frac{\hat{m}_{t-1}^i + (g_t - 1)}{g_t}.$$

Dividing each nominal variable by M_t, the household budget constraint can be written as

$$c_t^i + k_{t+1}^i + \frac{\hat{m}_t^i}{\hat{p}_t} = w_t h_t^i + r_t k_t^i + (1 - \delta) k_t^i + \frac{\hat{m}_{t-1}^i + (g_t - 1)}{g_t \hat{p}_t}.$$

Writing the model this way allows the nominal variables to have stationary values in an economy with nonzero net money growth. It will also allow us to find a stable solution to the dynamic version of the model.

A second way of normalizing the nominal variables in a stationary state is to divide them by prices and write everything in terms of real balances. In that case, we define the family's real balances as

$$\overline{m/p} = \frac{m_t^i}{p_t}$$

and the economy's real balances as

$$\overline{M/p} = \frac{M_t}{p_t}.$$

Some care needs to be taken with the lagged money variables. In a stationary state, money growth and (as we will show later) inflation are constant through time and equal to each other, $\bar{g} = \bar{\pi}$. Defining the gross inflation from period $t - 1$ to period t as π_{t-1}, the stationary state value of a family's money holdings at the beginning of period t are

$$\frac{m_{t-1}^i}{p_t} = \frac{m_{t-1}^i}{\pi_{t-1} p_{t-1}} = \frac{\overline{m/p}}{\bar{\pi}} = \frac{\overline{m/p}}{\bar{g}}.$$

A similar condition holds for M_{t-1}.

Since we are developing the model of Cooley and Hansen, we will use their method in this chapter. In future chapters, it will be more convenient (and possibly more natural for an economist) to write the model in terms of real balances.

With these variables, the equilibrium we want can be found by solving the maximization problem,

$$\max E_0 \sum_{t=0}^{\infty} \left(\beta^t \ln c_t^i + \left[A \frac{\ln(1-h_0)}{h_0} \right] h_t^i \right),$$

subject to the budget constraints

$$c_t^i = \frac{\hat{m}_{t-1}^i + (g_t - 1)}{g_t \hat{p}_t}$$

and

$$c_t^i + k_{t+1}^i + \frac{\hat{m}_t^i}{\hat{p}_t} = \left((1-\theta) \lambda_t K_t^\theta H_t^{-\theta} \right) h_t^i + \left(\theta \lambda_t K_t^{\theta-1} H_t^{1-\theta} \right) k_t^i$$

$$+ (1-\delta) k_t^i + \frac{\hat{m}_{t-1}^i + (g_t - 1)}{g_t \hat{p}_t}.$$

The law of motion for the stochastic shock is

$$\ln \lambda_{t+1} = \gamma \ln \lambda_t + \varepsilon_{t+1}^\lambda,$$

and the growth rate for money is either a stationary state rule,

$$g_t = \bar{g},$$

or a stochastic rule

$$\ln g_{t+1} = (1-\pi) \ln \bar{g} + \pi \ln g_t + \varepsilon_{t+1}^g.$$

This last expression is the law of motion for money growth. The inclusion of the term $(1-\pi) \ln \bar{g}$ causes this g_t process to have a stationary state value of $\bar{g}$. This can be seen by setting the shocks, ε_{t+1}^g, to zero and solving for $g_t = g_{t+1}$.

The aggregation conditions for an equilibrium are

$$K_t = k_t^i,$$

$$H_t = h_t^i,$$

$$C_t = c_t^i,$$

and

$$\hat{M}_t = \hat{m}_t^i = 1.$$

Before solving for the dynamic version of the model, we need to find the stationary state.

> **EXERCISE 8.1** Write out the equations for an economy identical to the one above but where the government makes money transfers to each family as a fraction of the money that family is holding when it enters the period.

8.2 FINDING THE STATIONARY STATE

For the two methods we have for approximating the dynamic version of the model, we first need to find the stationary state. As mentioned earlier, variational methods[4] are adequate for finding a stationary state, so we can use these methods here to find the first-order conditions for the families. In addition, since we will later be solving a log-linear approximation of the model (the first-order constraints, the budget constraints, and the equilibrium conditions), the conditions we get here will be used in that part as well. One could get exactly the same first-order conditions using a Bellman equation approach.

The problem that the households solve can be written as the Lagrangian,

$$
L = \max_{\left\{ c_t^i, k_{t+1}^i, h_t^i, \hat{m}_t^i \right\}} E_0 \sum_{t=0}^{\infty} \beta^t \left[\ln c_t^i + B h_t^i + \chi_t^1 \left(\hat{p}_t c_t^i - \frac{\hat{m}_{t-1}^i + g_t - 1}{g_t} \right) \right.
$$

$$
\left. + \chi_t^2 \left(k_{t+1}^i + \frac{\hat{m}_t^i}{\hat{p}_t} - (1-\delta) k_t^i - w_t h_t^i - r_t k_t^i \right) \right].
$$

Since the stochastic variables, g_t and λ_t, will be held constant in a stationary state, the expectations operator will drop out. However, we keep it because we will be using these first order-conditions later in the log-linear solution to the model. Solving this Lagrangian yields the first-order conditions

$$\frac{\partial L}{\partial c_t^i} = \frac{1}{c_t^i} + \chi_t^1 \hat{p}_t = 0,$$

$$\frac{\partial L}{\partial h_t^i} = B - \chi_t^2 w_t = 0,$$

---

4. While not explicitly written here, a transversality condition must hold.

$$\frac{\partial L}{\partial k_{t+1}^i} = \chi_t^2 - \beta E_t \chi_{t+1}^2 \left[(1-\delta) + r_{t+1}\right] = 0,$$

and

$$\frac{\partial L}{\partial \hat{m}_t^i} = \chi_t^2 \frac{1}{\hat{p}_t} - \beta E_t \chi_{t+1}^1 \frac{1}{g_{t+1}} = 0.$$

The first two first-order conditions can be solved for the Lagrangian multipliers,

$$\chi_t^1 = -\frac{1}{\hat{p}_t c_t^i}$$

and

$$\chi_t^2 = \frac{B}{w_t}.$$

We use these to remove the multipliers from the last two first-order conditions. These two equations plus the two budget constraints of the families give the following four equations of the model:

$$\frac{1}{\beta} = E_t \frac{w_t}{w_{t+1}} \left[(1-\delta) + r_{t+1}\right],$$

$$\frac{B}{w_t \hat{p}_t} = -\beta E_t \frac{1}{\hat{p}_{t+1} c_{t+1}^i g_{t+1}},$$

$$\hat{p}_t c_t^i = \frac{\hat{m}_{t-1}^i + g_t - 1}{g_t},$$

and

$$k_{t+1}^i + \frac{\hat{m}_t^i}{\hat{p}_t} = (1-\delta) k_t^i + w_t h_t^i + r_t k_t^i$$

In addition, the factor market conditions, from the assumption of perfect competition in the factor markets, are

$$w_t = (1-\theta) \lambda_t \left[\frac{K_t}{H_t}\right]^\theta$$

and

$$r_t = \theta \lambda_t \left[\frac{K_t}{H_t} \right]^{\theta - 1}.$$

In a stationary state, the stochastic technology parameter, λ_t, will be equal to 1 and drop out of the equations.

Since all families are the same, in equilibrium, the individual values will be the same as the aggregate, so

$$C_t = c_t^i,$$

$$H_t = h_t^i,$$

$$K_{t+1} = k_{t+1}^i,$$

and

$$\hat{M}_t = \hat{m}_t^i.$$

In the stationary state, $\bar{K} = K_t = K_{t+1}$, $\bar{H} = H_t = H_{t+1}$, $\bar{C} = C_t = C_{t+1}$, $\bar{w} = w_t = w_{t+1}$, $\bar{r} = r_t = r_{t+1}$, $\hat{p}_t = \hat{p}_{t+1} = \hat{p}$, and $\hat{M}_t = \hat{M}_{t+1} = 1$. The six equations of the model in a stationary state are

$$\frac{1}{\beta} = (1 - \delta) + \bar{r},$$

$$\frac{B}{\bar{w}} = -\frac{\beta}{\bar{g}\bar{C}},$$

$$\hat{p}\bar{C} = 1,$$

$$\frac{1}{\hat{p}} = (\bar{r} - \delta)\,\bar{K} + \bar{w}\bar{H},$$

$$\bar{w} = (1 - \theta) \left[\frac{\bar{K}}{\bar{H}} \right]^{\theta},$$

and

$$\bar{r} = \theta \left[\frac{\bar{K}}{\bar{H}} \right]^{\theta - 1}.$$

The first equation gives us the rental rate on capital as

$$\bar{r} = \frac{1}{\beta} - (1 - \delta).$$

We can then find the real wage in terms of the rental rate from the two factor market equations and get

$$\bar{w} = (1 - \theta) \left[\frac{\bar{K}}{\bar{H}} \right]^{\theta} = (1 - \theta) \left[\frac{\bar{r}}{\theta} \right]^{\frac{\theta}{\theta - 1}}.$$

Consumption is

$$\bar{C} = -\frac{\beta \bar{w}}{\bar{g} B}, \tag{8.1}$$

and the price level is

$$\hat{p} = \frac{1}{\bar{C}}.$$

Using the factor market equations, we can write

$$\bar{H} = \left(\frac{\bar{r}}{\theta} \right)^{\frac{1}{1 - \theta}} \bar{K}$$

and, using the family's budget constraint, get

$$\bar{K} = \frac{\bar{C}}{\frac{\bar{r}}{\theta} - \delta}.$$

Since stationary state consumption is known, so is equilibrium capital stock and the labor supply. Output can be found from the household budget constraint as

$$\bar{Y} = \bar{C} + \delta \bar{K}.$$

For our normal, quarterly economy, we have been using the parameter values $\beta = .99$, $\delta = .025$, $\theta = .36$, $A = 1.72$, and $h_0 = .583$, so $B = -2.5805$. Using these parameter values, the stationary state values for the variables are those shown in Table 8.1. Notice that real wages and rentals do not depend on the rate of growth of the money supply, but stationary state consumption, price level, capital stock, hours worked, and output do depend on it.

In their paper, Cooley and Hansen have a table that shows how different levels of inflation in the stationary state can result in different values for the real variables. They also calculate the welfare loss that comes from inflation. Since in the stationary state discounted utility is

$$\sum_{i=0}^{\infty} \beta^i \left(\ln \bar{C} + B \bar{H} \right) = \frac{\ln \bar{C} + B \bar{H}}{1 - \beta},$$

we can easily use our results on the stationary state to construct the table they have (Cooley and Hansen [36], page 743). Table 8.2 shows these results.

The level of utility when the inflation rate is equal to the discount rate is used as the basis from which to measure welfare losses from inflation. The loss is measured as the percentage decline in discounted lifetime utility from the case where the gross growth rate of money is equal to β. Recall that for the cash-in-advance constraint to hold with equality, one needs $\bar{g} \geq \beta$. This is why -4% (where $\bar{g} = .99$) is the lowest inflation rate shown in the table.

One interesting characteristic of this table is that the stationary state values for the case where inflation is -4 percent are almost exactly equal to those of the Hansen model with indivisible labor but without money (the second model in Chapter 6; see Table 6.3). The equilibria are subtly different. Compare the Hansen model with indivisible labor to the Cooley-Hansen model without

Table 8.1   Stationary state as a function of g

Variable	Value in stationary state
$\bar{r}$	.0351
$\bar{w}$	2.3706
$\bar{C}$	$\frac{0.9095}{\bar{g}}$
$\hat{p}$	$1.0995\bar{g}$
$\bar{K}$	$\frac{12.544}{\bar{g}}$
$\bar{H}$	$\frac{0.3302}{\bar{g}}$
$\bar{Y}$	$\frac{1.2231}{\bar{g}}$

Table 8.2   Table as in Cooley and Hansen

Annual inflation	-4%	0%	10%	100%	400%
Corresponding g	β	1	1.024	1.19	1.41
Output	1.2355	1.2231	1.1944	1.0278	0.8674
Consumption	0.9187	0.9095	0.8882	0.7643	0.6450
Investment	0.3168	0.3136	0.3063	0.2635	0.2224
Capital stock	12.6707	12.544	12.2500	10.541	8.8965
Hours worked	0.3335	0.3302	0.3225	0.2775	0.2342
Welfare loss, %	0	.15%	.55%	4.16%	10.29%

inflation. In the Cooley-Hansen model, money is acquired in period t to pay for consumption in period $t + 1$, so this time $t + 1$ consumption is reduced by the factor β. This shows up in the first-order conditions, where the only difference (with zero inflation) is the addition of a β in the equation relating consumption to inflation (see equations 6.7 and 8.1 for the versions in the stationary state).

> **EXERCISE 8.2**   Find the stationary states as a function of the growth rate of money for the economy, where the government makes money transfers to each family as a fraction of the money that family is holding when it enters the period.

8.3   SOLVING THE MODEL USING LINEAR QUADRATIC METHODS

Cooley and Hansen solve their model using linear quadratic techniques, so we will show these methods first. The methods are somewhat more complicated than those given in Chapter 7 because the choices of the families depend on the values of some economy-wide variables, K_t and $\hat{p}_t$. The optimization problem for each family in each period must take these values as given (because each family is too small to have a direct effect on the values of these variables), but the aggregate behavior of the families determines the values of these variables. The optimization problem needs to be separated from the aggregation problem. In this section, we set up this problem and show how to find the approximation to the dynamic model but do not actually calculate the solution.

A second, and normally simpler, method of finding a solution is by using the log linearization techniques shown in Chapter 6. This solution is normally very similar to that found by using linear quadratic methods. In the next section, we use this method to find the dynamic properties of this model.

Given the values for the stationary state of this economy, we look for a solution to an approximate, quadratic version of the model. There are two stages to finding an equilibrium. First, one needs to find the optimal behavior for a family given the aggregate variables for the economy. Then, one uses the decision rules of the families and aggregates them (given that all families in the economy are identical and there is a mass $= 1$ of families) to find the values of the aggregate variables in the economy. Using aggregate versions of the policy functions for families, one needs to find a fixed point for time $t + 1$ aggregate capital so that the amount of time $t + 1$ aggregate capital that families expect is equal to the sum of capital that all the families in the economy actually hold into time $t + 1$. The market variable, the price level, is found simultaneously with the fixed point for capital.

The optimization problem and the aggregation problem need to be separated, with the optimization done before the aggregation. If one were to do the aggregation first, the results of the optimization problem would not be the same as that of an economy of small, atomic families. The second welfare theorem does not hold here because the addition of money creation means that the equilibrium is not that of a pure competitive equilibrium.

8.3.1   Finding a Quadratic Objective Function

The method we have available to us solves a quadratic objective function with linear budget constraints. To make sure that we can use that method, we need to put all the nonlinear restrictions into the objective function. Using the restriction that

$$c_t^i = \frac{\hat{m}_{t-1}^i + (g_t - 1)}{g_t \hat{p}_t},$$

one first eliminates the variable c_t from both the objective function and from the second budget constraint. That makes the objective function

$$\max E_0 \sum_{t=0}^{\infty} \left(\beta^t \ln \left[\frac{\hat{m}_{t-1}^i + (g_t - 1)}{g_t \hat{p}_t} \right] + \left[A \frac{\ln(1 - h_0)}{h_0} \right] h_t^i \right),$$

and the remaining budget constraint

$$k_{t+1}^i + \frac{\hat{m}_t^i}{\hat{p}_t} = \left((1 - \theta) \lambda_t K_t^\theta H_t^{-\theta} \right) h_t^i + \left(\theta \lambda_t K_t^{\theta-1} H_t^{1-\theta} \right) k_t^i + (1 - \delta) k_t^i.$$

This budget constraint can be simplified to get

$$k_{t+1}^i - (1 - \delta) k_t^i + \frac{\hat{m}_t^i}{\hat{p}_t} = \left(\lambda_t K_t^\theta H_t^{1-\theta} \right) \left[(1 - \theta) \frac{h_t^i}{H_t} + \theta \frac{k_t^i}{K_t} \right]. \quad (8.2)$$

Summing across families, the individual variables are replaced by the aggregate, and the budget constraint becomes

$$K_{t+1} + \frac{1}{\hat{p}_t} = \lambda_t K_t^\theta H_t^{1-\theta} + (1 - \delta) K_t,$$

which can be solved for aggregate labor as

$$H_t = \left[\frac{K_{t+1} - (1-\delta)K_t + \frac{1}{\hat{p}_t}}{\lambda_t K_t^\theta} \right]^{\frac{1}{1-\theta}}.$$

Putting this definition for aggregate labor into the individual budget constraint, equation 8.2, gives individual labor supply as

$$h_t^i = \frac{k_{t+1}^i - (1-\delta)k_t^i + \frac{\hat{m}_t^i}{\hat{p}_t} - \theta\left[K_{t+1} - (1-\delta)K_t + \frac{1}{\hat{p}_t}\right]\frac{k_t^i}{K_t}}{(1-\theta)\left[K_{t+1} - (1-\delta)K_t + \frac{1}{\hat{p}_t}\right]^{-\frac{\theta}{1-\theta}}\left[\lambda_t K_t^\theta\right]^{\frac{1}{1-\theta}}}.$$

Using this equation to remove labor from the objective function gives

$$\max_{k_{t+1}^i,\hat{m}_t^i} E_0 \sum_{t=0}^{\infty} \left(\beta^t \ln\left[\frac{\hat{m}_{t-1}^i + (g_t - 1)}{g_t \hat{p}_t} \right] \right. \tag{8.3}$$

$$\left. + \left[A\frac{\ln(1-h_0)}{h_0} \right]\left[\frac{k_{t+1}^i - (1-\delta)k_t^i + \frac{\hat{m}_t^i}{\hat{p}_t} - \theta\left[K_{t+1} - (1-\delta)K_t + \frac{1}{\hat{p}_t}\right]\frac{k_t^i}{K_t}}{(1-\theta)\left[K_{t+1} - (1-\delta)K_t + \frac{1}{\hat{p}_t}\right]^{-\frac{\theta}{1-\theta}}\left[\lambda_t K_t^\theta\right]^{\frac{1}{1-\theta}}} \right] \right).$$

The state variables at time t are $x_t = [\,1 \quad \lambda_t \quad k_t^i \quad \hat{m}_{t-1}^i \quad g_t \quad K_t\,]'$. A family maximizes its objective function over $y_t = [\,k_{t+1}^i \quad \hat{m}_t^i\,]'$, subject to the budget constraints

$$\ln(\lambda_{t+1}) = \gamma \ln(\lambda_t) + \varepsilon_{t+1}^\lambda,$$

$$k_{t+1}^i = k_{t+1}^i,$$

$$\hat{m}_t^i = \hat{m}_t^i,$$

and

$$\ln g_{t+1} = (1-\pi)\,\bar{g} + \pi \ln g_t + \varepsilon_{t+1}^g.$$

In addition, the set of aggregate or market variables is $Z_t = [\,K_{t+1} \quad \hat{p}_t\,]'$, where

$$K_{t+1} = \int_0^1 k_{t+1}^i di,$$

and $\hat{p}_t$ is the time t price level divided by the time t money supply.

The first step is to take the second-order Taylor expansion of equation 8.3 and, using the method of Kydland and Prescott described in Chapter 7, to write the approximate objective function as

$$
[x_t' \quad y_t' \quad Z_t'] Q \begin{bmatrix} x_t \\ y_t \\ Z_t \end{bmatrix}.
$$

Given this objective function, we want to solve a Bellman equation of the form

$$
x_t' P x_t = \max_{y_t} \left[[x_t' \quad y_t' \quad Z_t'] Q \begin{bmatrix} x_t \\ y_t \\ Z_t \end{bmatrix} + \beta E_0 \left[x_{t+1}' P x_{t+1} \right] \right],
$$

subject to the budget constraints

$$
x_{t+1} = A x_t + B y_t + C Z_t + D \varepsilon_{t+1}.
$$

We can rewrite the matrix Q as

$$
Q = \begin{bmatrix} R & W' & X' \\ W & T & N' \\ X & N & S \end{bmatrix},
$$

and write

$$
[x_t' \quad y_t' \quad Z_t'] Q \begin{bmatrix} x_t \\ y_t \\ Z_t \end{bmatrix}
$$

as

$$
x_t' R x_t + y_t' T y_t + Z_t' S Z_t + 2 y_t' W x_t + 2 Z_t' X x_t + 2 Z_t' N y_t.
$$

The second half of the right-hand side of the Bellman equation can be written as

$$
\beta E_0 \left[x_{t+1}' P x_{t+1} \right]
$$

$$
= \beta E_0 \left[\left(A x_t + B y_t + C Z_t + D \varepsilon_{t+1} \right)' P \left(A x_t + B y_t + C Z_t + D \varepsilon_{t+1} \right) \right].
$$

Taking the derivative of the first half (written out) with respect to y_t gives

$$
\left(T + T' \right) y_t + 2 W x_t + 2 N' Z_t,
$$

and the second half gives

$$\beta \left[2B'PAx_t + 2B'PBy_t + 2B'PCZ_t \right].$$

Combining, and recalling that T is symmetric, we get the first-order condition (the 2's drop out),

$$0 = Ty_t + Wx_t + N'Z_t + \beta \left[B'PAx_t + B'PBy_t + B'PCZ_t \right],$$

or

$$(T + \beta B'PB)\, y_t = - (W + \beta B'PA)\, x_t - (N + \beta B'PC)\, Z_t.$$

When $(T + \beta B'PB)$ is invertible, this gives

$$y_t = - (T + \beta B'PB)^{-1} (W + \beta B'PA)\, x_t - (T + \beta B'PB)^{-1} (N + \beta B'PC)\, Z_t,$$

as the *linear* policy function, which we can write as

$$y_t = F_1 x_t + F_2 Z_t,$$

with

$$F_1 = - (T + \beta B'PB)^{-1} (W + \beta B'PA)$$

and

$$F_2 = - (T + \beta B'PB)^{-1} (N + \beta B'PC).$$

When $(T + \beta B'PB)$ is not invertible, somewhat different methods need to be used to get a solution. One way to do this is by using the generalized Schur decomposition described in section 6.8.4.

The value function matrix P fulfills

$$x_t'Px_t = [\, x_t' \quad (F_1 x_t + F_2 Z_t)' \quad Z_t'\,]\, Q \begin{bmatrix} x_t \\ F_1 x_t + F_2 Z_t \\ Z_t \end{bmatrix}$$

$$+ \beta \left((A + BF_1)\, x_t + (BF_2 + C)\, Z_t \right)' P \left((A + BF_1)\, x_t + (BF_2 + C)\, Z_t \right).$$

8.3.2 Finding the Economy Wide Variables

The above expression of the value function matrix still contains the aggregate variable $Z_t = [\, K_{t+1} \quad \hat{p}_t \,]'$. We want to find an expression that will give Z_t as a function of x_t. We start by noting that integrating the policy variable, y_t, over the unit mass of families gives us the aggregate values for the time t money stock and the time $t+1$ capital. Given that $y_t^i = [\, k_{t+1}^i \quad \hat{m}_t^i \,]'$, the aggregate capital and money stock can be found by integrating over the unit mass of families,

$$\int_0^1 y_t^i di = \left[\begin{array}{c} \int_0^1 k_{t+1}^i di \\ \int_0^1 \hat{m}_t^i di \end{array} \right] = \left[\begin{array}{c} K_{t+1} \\ 1 \end{array} \right],$$

where $1 = M_t / M_t$, the aggregate value of the $\hat{m}_t^i$ variable. If a policy function,

$$y_t = F_1 x_t + F_2 Z_t,$$

exists, F_1 and F_2 are both linear functions, and the policy function holds in aggregate when we integrate both sides over the unit mass of families. Doing this gives

$$\left[\begin{array}{c} K_{t+1} \\ 1 \end{array} \right] = F_1 \int_0^1 x_{t+1}^i di + F_2 Z_t. \tag{8.4}$$

Recalling that

$$x_t^i = [\, 1 \quad \lambda_t \quad k_t^i \quad \hat{m}_{t-1}^i \quad g_t \quad K_t \,]',$$

and that the integral of this vector is

$$\hat{x}_t = \int_0^1 x_{t+1}^i di = [\, 1 \quad \lambda_t \quad K_t \quad 1 \quad g_t \quad K_t \,],$$

we can construct a matrix

$$G = \begin{bmatrix} 1 & 0 & 0 & 0 & 0 & 0 \\ 0 & 1 & 0 & 0 & 0 & 0 \\ 0 & 0 & 0 & 0 & 0 & 1 \\ 1 & 0 & 0 & 0 & 0 & 0 \\ 0 & 0 & 0 & 0 & 1 & 0 \\ 0 & 0 & 0 & 0 & 0 & 1 \end{bmatrix}$$

that will give us $\hat{x}_t = G x_t^i$, for all i. The matrix G is a diagonal matrix except in rows 3 and 4, where it takes k_t^i into K_t and m_t^i into 1, respectively.

Using this aggregation matrix, G, equation 8.4 can be written as

$$\left[\begin{array}{c} K_{t+1} \\ 1 \end{array} \right] = F_1 G x_t^i + F_2 \left[\begin{array}{c} K_{t+1} \\ \hat{p}_t \end{array} \right].$$

If the matrix, F_2, is invertible, we can find the values of the aggregate variables as

$$\begin{bmatrix} K_{t+1} \\ \hat{p}_t \end{bmatrix} = F_2^{-1} \begin{bmatrix} K_{t+1} \\ 1 \end{bmatrix} - F_2^{-1} F_1 G x_t^i,$$

or as

$$\begin{bmatrix} K_{t+1} \\ \hat{p}_t \end{bmatrix} = J \begin{bmatrix} K_{t+1} \\ 1 \end{bmatrix} + H x_t^i,$$

where $J = [J_{ij}]$ is a 2×2 matrix and $H = [H_{ij}]$ is a 2×6 matrix. Recalling that the first element of x_t^i is always 1, and working through the matrix algebra of the above equation, we can find K_{t+1} and $\hat{p}_t$ as

$$Z_t = F_3 x_t^i,$$

where

$$F_3 = \begin{bmatrix} \frac{H_{11}+J_{12}}{1-J_{11}} & \frac{H_{12}}{1-J_{11}} & \frac{H_{13}}{1-J_{11}} & \frac{H_{14}}{1-J_{11}} \\ H_{21}+J_{22}+\frac{J_{21}(H_{11}+J_{12})}{1-J_{11}} & H_{22}+\frac{J_{21}H_{12}}{1-J_{11}} & H_{23}+\frac{J_{21}H_{13}}{1-J_{11}} & H_{24}+\frac{J_{21}H_{14}}{1-J_{11}} \end{bmatrix}$$

$$\begin{bmatrix} \frac{H_{15}}{1-J_{11}} & \frac{H_{16}}{1-J_{11}} \\ H_{25}+\frac{J_{21}H_{15}}{1-J_{11}} & H_{26}+\frac{J_{21}H_{16}}{1-J_{11}} \end{bmatrix}.$$

While the expression for the F_3 matrix is messy, it simply describes a way of solving for the two variables, K_{t+1} and $\hat{p}_t$, in a system of two linear equations when, given x_t^i, $H x_t^i$ is taken as a constant and where J_{12} and J_{22} are constants in their respective equations.

Given this matrix for finding the aggregate variables, we can write

$$P = [\, I_x \quad F_1' + F_3'F_2' \quad F_3'\,] Q \begin{bmatrix} I_x \\ F_1 + F_2 F_3 \\ F_3 \end{bmatrix}$$

$$+ \beta \left((A + BF_1) + (BF_2 + C) F_3 \right)' P \left((A + BF_1) + (BF_2 + C) F_3 \right),$$

where I_x is an identity matrix with dimensions equal to the size of the state variable x_t.

To find P, we use an iterative process. One begins with an initial guess for the value matrix, P_0, calculates initial policy functions, F_1^0 and F_2^0, using that P_0, and then uses these F_1^0 and F_2^0 to calculate the function for finding the economy-wide variables, F_3^0. Once these three matrices are found, they are put into the above equation, along with P_0 on the right-hand side, and the result is the value matrix for the next iteration, P_1. Using this P_1, new calculations are made for F_1^1, F_2^1, and F_3^1, and using P_1, the above equation is used to calculate P_2. The iterations continue until the difference between P_j and P_{j+1} are within the desired tolerances. As one finds the value matrix P, one also finds the linear approximations of the policy functions, F_1 and F_2, and of the function for calculating the economy-wide variables, F_3.

8.4 SOLVING THE MODEL USING LOG LINEARIZATION

The process for finding the equilibrium using second-order Taylor expansions is very intensive in differentiation, since one has to work out by hand the second partial derivatives of an objective function that contains all the non-linearity of the system. The existence of economy-wide variables adds another level of complexity. A frequently simpler alternative (that we introduced in Chapter 6) is to find a linear version of the model using the method of log linearization on the first-order conditions of the model, the budget constraints, the stochastic processes, and the aggregation rules. One can then solve this linear system for the linear policy functions. That is what we do in this section.

8.4.1 The Log Linearization

To find the log-linear version of this model, we can use the first-order conditions, the budget constraints, and the equilibrium conditions that we found when we calculated the stationary state. The equations for the household decisions are the two first-order conditions,

$$\frac{1}{\beta} = E_t \frac{w_t}{w_{t+1}} \left[(1 - \delta) + r_{t+1} \right]$$

and

$$\frac{B}{w_t \hat{p}_t} = -\beta E_t \frac{1}{\hat{p}_{t+1} c_{t+1}^i g_{t+1}},$$

the cash-in-advance constraint,

$$\hat{p}_t c_t^i = \frac{\hat{m}_{t-1}^i + g_t - 1}{g_t},$$

and the flow budget constraint,

$$k_{t+1}^i + \frac{\hat{m}_t^i}{\hat{p}_t} = (1 - \delta) k_t^i + w_t h_t^i + r_t k_t^i.$$

The competitive factor market gives us the two equations

$$w_t = (1 - \theta)\,\lambda_t \left[\frac{K_t}{H_t}\right]^{\theta}$$

and

$$r_t = \theta\lambda_t \left[\frac{K_t}{H_t}\right]^{\theta - 1}.$$

The equilibrium and aggregation conditions are

$$C_t = c_t^i,$$

$$H_t = h_t^i,$$

$$K_{t+1} = k_{t+1}^i,$$

and

$$\hat{M}_t = \hat{m}_t^i = 1.$$

Recall that we have normalized this economy so that $\hat{M}_t = 1$. In addition, we have the two stochastic processes,

$$\ln \lambda_{t+1} = \gamma \ln \lambda_t + \varepsilon_{t+1}^{\lambda}$$

and

$$\ln g_{t+1} = (1 - \pi)\ln \bar{g} + \pi \ln g_t + \varepsilon_{t+1}^{g}.$$

Taking log linearizations of the two first-order conditions gives

$$-\tilde{w}_t = \beta E_t \left[\bar{r}\left(\tilde{r}_{t+1} - \tilde{w}_{t+1}\right) - (1 - \delta)\,\tilde{w}_{t+1}\right] \qquad (8.5)$$

and

$$-\frac{B}{\bar{C}\bar{w}}\left[\tilde{p}_t + \tilde{w}_t\right] = \beta E_t \left[\frac{1}{\bar{g}}\tilde{g}_{t+1}\right], \qquad (8.6)$$

having used the cash-in-advance constraint in the form

$$g_t \hat{p}_t c_t^i = \hat{m}_{t-1}^i + g_t - 1.$$

The log-linear version of the cash-in-advance constraint in aggregate gives the conditions that $\tilde{p}_t + \tilde{C}_t = 0$, for all t, and this lets us remove these two variables from the above equation. The real budget constraint is written as

$$\bar{k}\tilde{k}_{t+1} + \frac{\bar{m}}{\bar{p}}\left[\tilde{m}_t - \tilde{p}_t\right] = \bar{w}\bar{h}\left[\tilde{w}_t + \tilde{h}_t\right] + \bar{r}\bar{k}\left[\tilde{r}_t + \tilde{k}_t\right] + (1 - \delta)\bar{k}\tilde{k}_t. \quad (8.7)$$

Log-linear versions of the competitive factor market conditions are

$$\bar{r}\tilde{r}_t = \theta \bar{K}^{\theta-1} \bar{H}^{1-\theta} \left[\tilde{\lambda}_t + (\theta - 1) \left[\tilde{K}_t - \tilde{H}_t \right] \right] \qquad (8.8)$$

and

$$\bar{w}\tilde{w}_t = (1-\theta) \, \bar{K}^{\theta} \bar{H}^{-\theta} \left[\tilde{\lambda}_t + \theta \left[\tilde{K}_t - \tilde{H}_t \right] \right] . \qquad (8.9)$$

The stochastic processes of the technology and money supply shocks[5] are

$$\tilde{\lambda}_{t+1} = \gamma \tilde{\lambda}_t + \varepsilon^{\lambda}_{t+1} \qquad (8.10)$$

and

$$\tilde{g}_{t+1} = \pi \tilde{g}_t + \varepsilon^{g}_{t+1}. \qquad (8.11)$$

The aggregation conditions are

$$\tilde{K}_t = \tilde{k}_t, \qquad (8.12)$$

$$\tilde{H}_t = \tilde{h}_t, \qquad (8.13)$$

and

$$\tilde{m}_t = 0. \qquad (8.14)$$

This last restriction holds because $\hat{M}_t = 1 = \bar{m} \left(1 + \tilde{m}_t \right) = 1 \left(1 + \tilde{m}_t \right)$.

It is useful to eliminate some variables from the model and to reduce the number of expectational variables. One can remove the expectations from the equation

$$-\frac{B}{\bar{C}\bar{w}} \left[\tilde{p}_t + \tilde{w}_t \right] = \beta E_t \left[\frac{1}{\bar{g}} \tilde{g}_{t+1} \right]$$

by using the process for money growth,

$$\tilde{g}_{t+1} = \pi \tilde{g}_t + \varepsilon^{g}_{t+1}.$$

Since the expectation of the error is zero, one can eliminate the expectations operator and get

$$-\frac{B}{\bar{C}\bar{w}} \left[\tilde{p}_t + \tilde{w}_t \right] = \frac{\beta \pi}{\bar{g}} \tilde{g}_t. \qquad (8.15)$$

---

5. The money process, $\ln g_{t+1} = (1 - \pi) \ln \bar{g} + \pi \ln g_t + \varepsilon^{g}_{t+1}$, can be written as $\ln g_{t+1} - \ln \bar{g} = \pi \left(\ln g_t - \ln \bar{g} \right) + \varepsilon^{g}_{t+1}$, which, since $\tilde{g}_t = \ln g_t - \ln \bar{g}$, is equal to $\tilde{g}_{t+1} = \pi \tilde{g}_t + \varepsilon^{g}_{t+1}$.

We can remove the individual variables by replacing them with the aggregate variables that they equal in equilibrium, replacing $\tilde{k}_t$ with $\tilde{K}_t$ and $\tilde{h}_t$ with $\tilde{H}_t$. We can also remove the money stock variable since aggregate money must always equal 1 and that implies that $\tilde{m}_t = 0$, always. After these adjustments, we have a system with four equations without expectations,

$$0 = \bar{K}\tilde{K}_{t+1} - \frac{1}{\bar{p}}\tilde{p}_t - \bar{w}\bar{H}\tilde{w}_t - \bar{w}\bar{H}\tilde{H}_t - \bar{r}\bar{K}\tilde{r}_t - \bar{r}\bar{K}\tilde{K}_t - (1-\delta)\bar{K}\tilde{K}_t,$$

$$0 = \tilde{r}_t - \tilde{\lambda}_t - (\theta - 1)\tilde{K}_t + (\theta - 1)\tilde{H}_t,$$

$$0 = \tilde{w}_t - \tilde{\lambda}_t - \theta\tilde{K}_t + \theta\tilde{H}_t,$$

and

$$0 = \tilde{p}_t + \tilde{w}_t - \pi\tilde{g}_t$$

one equation with expectations,

$$0 = \tilde{w}_t + \beta\bar{r}E_t\tilde{r}_{t+1} - E_t\tilde{w}_{t+1},$$

and the two stochastic processes for the shocks to technology and money growth,

$$\tilde{\lambda}_{t+1} = \gamma\tilde{\lambda}_t + \varepsilon^{\lambda}_{t+1}$$

and

$$\tilde{g}_{t+1} = \pi\tilde{g}_t + \varepsilon^{g}_{t+1}.$$

8.4.2   Solving the Log-Linear System

First, write out the system in the form

$$0 = Ax_t + Bx_{t-1} + Cy_t + Dz_t,$$

$$0 = E_t\left[Fx_{t+1} + Gx_t + Hx_{t-1} + Jy_{t+1} + Ky_t + Lz_{t+1} + Mz_t\right],$$

$$z_{t+1} = Nz_t + \varepsilon_{t+1},$$

where $x_t = [\tilde{K}_{t+1}]'$, $y_t = [\tilde{r}_t \quad \tilde{w}_t \quad \tilde{H}_t \quad \tilde{p}_t]'$, and $z_t = [\tilde{\lambda}_t \quad \tilde{g}_t]'$, and where

$$A = \begin{bmatrix} \bar{K} \\ 0 \\ 0 \\ 0 \end{bmatrix},$$

$$B = \begin{bmatrix} -(\bar{r} + 1 - \delta)\,\bar{K} \\ (1 - \theta) \\ -\theta \\ 0 \end{bmatrix},$$

$$C = \begin{bmatrix} -\bar{r}\bar{K} & -\bar{w}\bar{H} & -\bar{w}\bar{H} & -\frac{1}{p} \\ 1 & 0 & (\theta - 1) & 0 \\ 0 & 1 & \theta & 0 \\ 0 & -1 & 0 & -1 \end{bmatrix},$$

$$D = \begin{bmatrix} 0 & 0 \\ -1 & 0 \\ -1 & 0 \\ 0 & \pi \end{bmatrix},$$

$$F = [0],$$

$$G = [0],$$

$$H = [0],$$

$$J = [\,\beta\bar{r} \quad -1 \quad 0 \quad 0\,],$$

$$K = [\,0 \quad 1 \quad 0 \quad 0\,],$$

$$L = [\,0 \quad 0\,],$$

$$M = [\,0 \quad 0\,],$$

and

$$N = \begin{bmatrix} \gamma & 0 \\ 0 & \pi \end{bmatrix}.$$

The linear laws of motion that we are looking for are given by the matrices P, Q, R, and S, where

$$x_{t+1} = Px_t + Qz_t$$

and

$$y_t = Rx_t + Sz_t.$$

From Uhlig [86] and Appendix 1 of Chapter 6, we know that P solves the quadratic equation (matrix equation in general but a simple quadratic in this case, since capital is the only state variable)

$$(F - JC^{-1}A)P^2 - (JC^{-1}B - G + KC^{-1}A)P - KC^{-1}B + H = 0,$$

and that

$$R = -C^{-1}(AP + B),$$

vec(Q)

$$= \left(N' \otimes (F - JC^{-1}A) + I_k \otimes (FP + G + JR - KC^{-1}A)\right)^{-1}$$

$$\times \text{vec}\left(\left(JC^{-1}D - L\right)N + KC^{-1}D - M\right),$$

and

$$S = -C^{-1}(AQ + D).$$

The results for the model are $P = [0.9418]$, $Q = [\,0.1552 \quad 0.0271\,]$,

$$R = \begin{bmatrix} -0.9450 \\ 0.5316 \\ -0.4766 \\ -0.5316 \end{bmatrix},$$

$$S = \begin{bmatrix} 1.9418 & -0.0555 \\ 0.4703 & 0.0312 \\ 1.4715 & -0.0867 \\ -0.4703 & 0.4488 \end{bmatrix}.$$

The results of the simulations are given in Tables 8.3 and 8.4. In this run, the stationary state inflation rate was set to zero ($\bar{g} = 1$). For the simulations, the standard economy was used except that the standard error of the error terms was set to $\sigma_\lambda = .0036$, and either $\sigma_g = .00, .01$, or $.02$. In these tables one can see that the increasing money growth shocks have relatively little effect on the production-related variables ($\tilde{Y}$, $\tilde{K}$, $\tilde{H}$, $\tilde{r}$, and $\tilde{w}$) and relatively more on consumption and investment. Not surprisingly, the standard error of prices grows rapidly with the growth in the standard eror of money growth. Since output reacts so little to the money growth shock, it should not be surprising that correlations with output decline across the board as the money growth shock increases.

A particular characteristic of this model is that the dynamics do not depend on the stationary state inflation rate. A brief look at the A to M matrices of the model shows that the level of $\bar{g}$ does not show up explicitly anywhere. It does show up through the stationary state values of $\bar{K}$, $\bar{H}$, and $1/\bar{p}$, since $\bar{K}$ and $\bar{H}$ are determined by a constant divided by $\bar{g}$ and $\bar{p}$ by a constant multiplied by $\bar{g}$, but these stationary state variables all show up in only one equation and every coefficient in that equation gets divided by $\bar{g}$. Therefore, the relationship between variables described by that equation does not change as $\bar{g}$ changes. The log-linear model is the same for all permissible values of $\bar{g}$.

Table 8.3 Standard errors of variables in cash-in-advance model

Variable	$\sigma_\lambda = .0036$ $\sigma_g = 0$	$\sigma_\lambda = .0036$ $\sigma_g = .01$	$\sigma_\lambda = .0036$ $\sigma_g = .02$
$\tilde{Y}$	0.0176	0.0176	0.0178
$\tilde{C}$	0.0098	0.0119	0.0168
$\tilde{I}$	0.0478	0.0496	0.0535
$\tilde{K}$	0.0130	0.0129	0.0130
$\tilde{r}$	0.0147	0.0147	0.0148
$\tilde{w}$	0.0098	0.0098	0.0098
$\tilde{H}$	0.0110	0.0110	0.0112
$\tilde{p}$	0.0098	0.0109	0.0138

Table 8.4 Correlations with output in the CIA economy

Variable	$\sigma_\lambda = .0036$ $\sigma_g = 0$	$\sigma_\lambda = .0036$ $\sigma_g = .01$	$\sigma_\lambda = .0036$ $\sigma_g = .02$
$\tilde{Y}$	1.0000	1.0000	1.0000
$\tilde{C}$	0.8234	0.6666	0.5094
$\tilde{I}$	0.9472	0.9060	0.8030
$\tilde{K}$	0.6166	0.6106	0.5966
$\tilde{r}$	0.7149	0.7173	0.7161
$\tilde{w}$	0.8234	0.8186	0.8045
$\tilde{H}$	0.8753	0.8758	0.8715
$\tilde{p}$	−0.8234	−0.7291	−0.5993

> **EXERCISE 8.3**   Write out a cash-in-advance model in which money is used by the families to purchase consumption goods and by the firms to pay wages. In each case, it is time $t-1$ money, adjusted by any government transfer or tax in period t that is used to make the payments in period t.

8.4.3   Impulse Response Functions

The impulse response functions make very clear some characteristics of this model. The response of the economy to a technology shock is exactly the same as that of the Hansen indivisible labor model of Chapter 6. Figure 8.1 shows the impulse response function (given a .01 shock) from the earlier Hansen model (this is the same as Figure 6.5). Figure 8.2 shows the response of the Cooley-Hansen model to the same shock. The difference in the figures is in the variables that each model is finding. The Hansen indivisible labor model shows the responses of $\tilde{K}$, $\tilde{Y}$, $\tilde{C}$, $\tilde{H}$, and $\tilde{r}$ while the Cooley-Hansen model shows the responses of $\tilde{K}$, $\tilde{r}$, $\tilde{w}$, $\tilde{H}$, and $\tilde{p}$.

In the Cooley-Hansen model, when there is only a technology shock, log-linear version of the cash-in-advance constraint gives us prices and consumption that move exactly opposite from one another. With only a technology shock, the log-linear version of the second first-order condition (equation

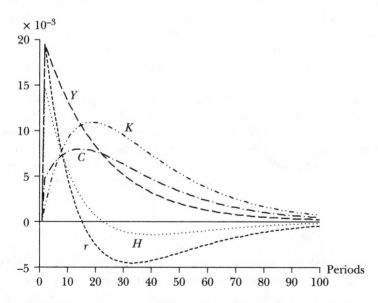

FIGURE 8.1   Response of Hansen's model to technology shock

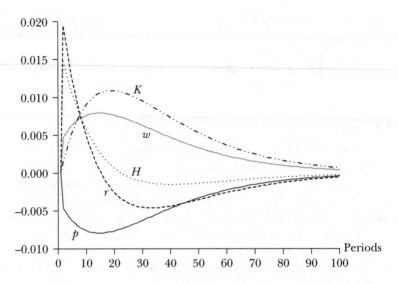

FIGURE 8.2 Response of Cooley-Hansen model to technology shock

8.15) gives us prices and wages that move exactly opposite from one another. This implies that wages and consumption respond in exactly the same way to a technology shock.

The response of the Cooley-Hansen model to a .01 money growth shock is shown in Figure 8.3. The very clear reaction is that of prices, which responds very quickly and almost in the same amount as the money growth shock. Since we have assumed that money growth is less serially correlated than technology (the coefficient on the first lag term is .48 for the money process and .95 for the technology process), the shock dies off much faster than in the case of the technology shock. This is caused almost entirely by the serial correlation in the stochastic process and says little about the propagation characteristics of the model itself. Monetary shocks do have real effects, as can be seen from the responses of capital and labor, but these are relatively small. This is consistent with the relatively small changes that one observes in the standard errors of the real variables as the money shock increases. In particular, output changes are quite small.

8.5 SEIGNIORAGE

A monetary policy that operates in the manner described above is not very common. Governments do make transfers directly to citizens, in the form of unemployment insurance payments, social security payments, and, in less well organized countries, by direct payments by politicians to their friends

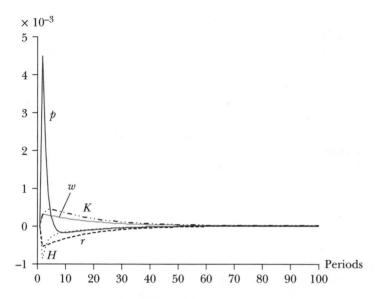

FIGURE 8.3   Response of Cooley-Hansen model to money growth shock

and family. While these payments can make up a relatively large part of the government budget, it is not common that they are financed directly with money issue. In addition, these payments are different from the lump sum monetary transfer that we used in the above model.

In this section we will assume that, instead of simply giving money to the families in the economy, the government runs a fiscal deficit that it finances with the issue of new money. The real value of the goods that the government purchases with the new money is called *seigniorage*. Introducing new money via seigniorage involves two changes in the model.

First, there needs to be a government budget constraint. The government deficit in each period needs to be defined so that the amount of new money that is issued can be determined. The government is consuming goods and these goods reduce those available for private consumption, so in this way seigniorage functions like a tax. To keep the government budget constraint simple, we assume that seigniorage is the only way the government can pay for its goods. Normally, a government uses a wide range of taxes to provide revenue for its expenditures and only resorts to seigniorage when the revenue from other taxes is inadequate. Here we eliminate other taxes and consider government expenditures to be just the deficit that remains, and this deficit is covered by seigniorage.

The second change to the model is that there is no longer a need for the sometimes-difficult-to-justify fiction of direct transfers of money to families. Here the government spends, and the amount of money that enters the economy each period depends on how much the government spends. As mentioned above, it is difficult to find a real-world policy that mimics the direct transfers of money to all the families in the economy, and it is not difficult to find governments that use seigniorage to cover a part of their expenditures. By the way, seigniorage is a taxing method that is particularly effective when there is a large informal sector in the economy. By its very nature, the informal sector can escape normal taxes but tends to use cash extensively. Seigniorage, which operates as a tax on the use of cash, is a way that governments can tax the informal sector. Nicolini [66] shows that countries with larger informal sectors tend to use seigniorage more than those with small informal sectors.

8.5.1   The Model

The budget constraint for the government is

$$g_t = \hat{g}_t \bar{g} = \frac{M_t - M_{t-1}}{p_t},$$

where $g_t = \hat{g}_t \bar{g}$ is the amount of real goods that the government consumes in period t. The amount $\bar{g}$ is the average government deficit, and the shock to the government deficit, $\hat{g}_t$, follows a stochastic process of the form

$$\ln \hat{g}_t = \pi \ln \hat{g}_{t-1} + \varepsilon_t^g,$$

where ε_t^g has the distribution $\varepsilon_t^g \sim N(0, \sigma_g^2)$. This stochastic process implies a stationary state value of 1 for $\hat{g}_t$. $M_t - M_{t-1}$ is the amount of new money that the government issues in period t to finance that period's deficit.

The techniques that we use for solving the model require that there exists a stationary state. As written so far, money and prices can grow without bound if $\bar{g}$ is positive. This is because, on average, the government will have to issue additional new money every period. It is helpful to normalize money and prices by dividing time t money and prices by M_t and by defining φ_t as the time t growth rate of money[6] so that $M_t = \varphi_t M_{t-1}$. Let $\hat{m}_t^i = m_t^i / M_t$, and $\hat{p}_t = p_t / M_t$. Given these definitions, the government budget constraint is written as

$$g_t = \hat{g}_t \bar{g} = \frac{\frac{M_t}{M_t} - \frac{M_{t-1}}{M_t}}{\frac{p_t}{M_t}} = \frac{1 - \frac{1}{\varphi_t}}{\hat{p}_t}.$$

---

6. The variable φ_t now fills the role that the variable g_t had in the previous sections.

The rest of the model is similar to the previous cash-in-advance model. Families chose a sequence of $\left\{c_t^i, h_t^i, k_{t+1}^i, \hat{m}_t^i\right\}_{t=0}^{\infty}$ to maximize

$$E_0 \sum_{t=0}^{\infty} \beta^t u(c_t^i, 1 - h_t^i),$$

subject to the sequence of cash-in-advance constraints,

$$\hat{p}_t c_t^i \leq \frac{\hat{m}_{t-1}^i}{\varphi_t},$$

and the sequence of family real budget constraints,

$$k_{t+1}^i + \frac{\hat{m}_t^i}{\hat{p}_t} = w_t h_t^i + r_t k_t^i + (1 - \delta)k_t^i.$$

Since money enters the economy through government expenditures, we no longer have the monetary transfers in the family's cash-in-advance constraint. We will assume that the necessary conditions are met so that the cash-in-advance constraint holds with equality.

Since money is used only to purchase goods for consumption by the families or for the deficit of the government, the economy-wide cash-in-advance constraints (at equality) are

$$p_t C_t + p_t g_t = p_t C_t + p_t \hat{g}_t \bar{g} = M_t,$$

or

$$\hat{p}_t C_t + \hat{p}_t \hat{g}_t \bar{g} = 1$$

and

$$p_t C_t = M_{t-1},$$

or, dividing both sides of this equation by M_t,

$$\hat{p}_t C_t = \frac{1}{\varphi_t},$$

where aggregate consumption is defined as $C_t = \int_0^1 c_t^i di$. The real budget constraint for the economy is

$$C_t + K_{t+1} + \hat{g}_t \bar{g} = w_t H_t + r_t K_t + (1 - \delta)K_t.$$

The first economy-wide cash-in-advance constraint says that aggregate consumption and government expenditures are paid for with money. The second says that aggregate consumption is paid for with money that families carried over from the previous period. At the end of a period, all the money is in the hands of families (since the workers bring home all the money received from the sale of goods). The third constraint says that real aggregate output,

$$Y_t = \lambda_t K_t^\theta H_t^{1-\theta} = w_t H_t + r_t K_t,$$

is equal to the sum of aggregate consumption, aggregate investment (which equals $K_{t+1} - (1 - \delta)K_t$), and real value of government expenditure. This third constraint comes from the assumption of competitive factor markets and a Cobb-Douglas production function. The conditions of competitive factor markets imply that

$$r_t = \theta \lambda_t K_t^{\theta-1} H_t^{1-\theta}$$

and

$$w_t = (1 - \theta) \lambda_t K_t^\theta H_t^{-\theta},$$

and that firms make zero profits.

Production, wages, and rentals in each period depend on the aggregate capital stock and aggregate amount of hours worked and are taken as given by individual families. In our economy, where all the unit mass of families are identical, the aggregation conditions for capital and hours worked are

$$K_{t+1} = k_{t+1}^i$$

and

$$H_t = h_t^i.$$

Families take wages, w_t, rentals, r_t, prices, $\hat{p}_t$, and their capital stock from the previous period, k_t^i, as given. As in other models with indivisible labor, the subutility function for period t is

$$u(c_t^i, 1 - h_t^i) = \ln c_t^i + B h_t^i,$$

where $B = A \ln(1 - h_0)/h_0$. Substituting the family budget constraints into the subutility function, one can write family i's optimization problem as

$$\max_{\{\hat{m}_t^i, k_{t+1}^i\}} E_0 \sum_{t=0}^{\infty} \beta^t \left[\ln \left(\frac{\hat{m}_{t-1}^i}{\varphi_t \hat{p}_t} \right) + B \left(\frac{k_{t+1}^i + \frac{\hat{m}_t^i}{\hat{p}_t} - r_t k_t^i - (1 - \delta)k_t^i}{w_t} \right) \right].$$

This problem can be written in recursive form as

$$V\left(k_t^i, \hat{m}_{t-1}^i, \lambda_t, \hat{g}_t, K_t\right) = \max_{\hat{m}_t^i, k_{t+1}^i} \left[\ln\left(\frac{\hat{m}_{t-1}^i}{\varphi_t \hat{p}_t}\right)\right.$$

$$+ B\left(\frac{k_{t+1}^i + \frac{\hat{m}_t^i}{\hat{p}_t} - r_t k_t^i - (1-\delta)k_t^i}{w_t}\right)$$

$$\left. + \beta E_t V\left(k_{t+1}^i, \hat{m}_t^i, \lambda_{t+1}, \hat{g}_{t+1}, K_{t+1}\right)\right],$$

subject to the (degenerate) budget constraints[7]

$$k_{t+1}^i = k_{t+1}^i$$

and

$$\hat{m}_t^i = \hat{m}_t^i.$$

The first-order conditions that come from this problem are

$$\frac{1}{w_t} = \beta E_t\left[\frac{r_{t+1} + 1 - \delta}{w_{t+1}}\right]$$

and

$$-\frac{B}{\hat{p}_t w_t} = \frac{\beta}{\hat{m}_t}.$$

8.5.2 The Stationary State

The stationary state is found by setting $\hat{g}_t = 1$, $\lambda_t = 1$, and φ_t and taking all other real and normalized nominal variables, $\hat{p}$ and $\hat{m}$, as constants. The stationary state versions of the first-order conditions are

$$\frac{1}{\beta} = \bar{r} + (1-\delta)$$

and

$$-\frac{\beta \bar{w}}{B} = \frac{\hat{m}}{\hat{p}}.$$

---

7. We write the problem this way so that we can get the first-order conditions using the Benveniste-Scheinkman envelope theorem condition.

This last condition may seem strange intuitively. As we shall see shortly, the real wage does not depend on the inflation rate, so the family's desired real money balances at the end of each period are a constant; in particular, desired real money balances do not depend on the inflation rate. This feature of the model comes from the use of a logarithmic utility function.[8] In Appendix 1 of this chapter we find the stationary state for an economy with constant elasticity of substitution subutility for consumption and in that model inflation does have an effect on desired real money balances.

Since in aggregate $\int_0^1 \hat{m} di = 1$, the second condition gives

$$-\frac{B}{\beta \bar{w}} = \hat{p}.$$

From the conditions for competitive factor markets and the capital first-order condition, we can find the real wage rate as the constant

$$\bar{w} = (1 - \theta) \left[\frac{\theta}{\frac{1}{\beta} - (1 - \delta)} \right]^{\frac{\theta}{1-\theta}},$$

so the ratio of prices to money in this model is constant (and independent of the inflation rate). The government budget constraint is written as

$$\bar{g}\hat{p} = 1 - \frac{1}{\varphi}.$$

Replace $\hat{p}$ in this version of the government budget constraint with the constant $-B/\beta \bar{w}$ ($= 1.0995$ given the values of the parameters that we have been using), and we get the expression for the growth rate of money (and the inflation rate since $\hat{p}$, the ratio of prices to the money stock, is a constant),

$$\varphi = \frac{\beta \bar{w}}{B\bar{g} + \beta \bar{w}}.$$

For our standard calibrated economy, $\beta = .99$, $B = -2.5805$, $\delta = .025$, and $\theta = .36$, so $\bar{w} = 2.3706$, and

$$\varphi = \frac{2.3469}{2.3469 - 2.5805\bar{g}}.$$

8. When one takes the derivative of $\ln \left(\frac{\hat{m}_{t-1}^i}{\varphi_t \hat{p}_t} \right)$ with respect to money, the result is $\frac{\varphi_t \hat{p}_t}{\hat{m}_{t-1}^i} \frac{1}{\varphi_t \hat{p}_t} = \frac{1}{\hat{m}_{t-1}^i}$, and both the price level and the growth rate of money drop out. Logarithmic utility functions have the property that they allocate fixed fractions of income to each good, independent of prices.

The maximum stationary state seigniorage that the government can obtain in this economy is 0.90947. When the government is collecting this much seigniorage, it does so by creating infinite money growth every period and taxing away all of the consumption of individuals. When $g = 0.90947$, the denominator of the above equation equals zero and φ equals infinity. A Bailey curve, named for Martin Bailey, who first applied this kind of curve to seigniorage in Bailey [5], shows the real seigniorage as a function of the different stationary state inflation rates. The Bailey curve for the economy in this section is shown in Figure 8.4.

We will need the values of $\bar{C}$, $\bar{K}$, and $\bar{H}$ as coefficients in the log-linear version of the model. From above, we know that

$$\hat{p}_t C_t + \hat{p}_t \hat{g}_t \bar{g} = 1,$$

or in a stationary state that

$$\bar{C} + \bar{g} = \frac{1}{\hat{p}}$$

or

$$\bar{C} = -\frac{\beta \bar{w}}{B} - \bar{g} = .90947 - \bar{g}.$$

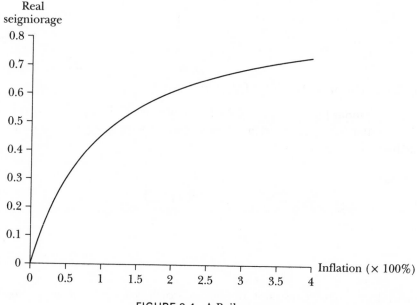

FIGURE 8.4   A Bailey curve

This corresponds with the calculation of maximum seigniorage, since the largest that $\bar{g}$ can be is .90947. It also shows why it is reasonable to speak of seigniorage as a tax on consumption, since in stationary states with higher government deficits, consumption is correspondingly lower. From the competitive factor market condition in a stationary state, we know that

$$\bar{r} = \frac{1}{\beta} - (1 - \delta) = \theta \left[\frac{\bar{K}}{\bar{H}} \right]^{\theta - 1}.$$

For our standard economy, $\bar{r} = .035101$, and $\bar{K}/\bar{H} = (\theta/\bar{r})^{1/(1-\theta)} = 37.99$. From the aggregate version of the family's real budget constraint in a stationary state, we have

$$\bar{K} + \frac{1}{\hat{p}} = \bar{w}\bar{H} + \bar{r}\bar{K} + (1 - \delta)\bar{K},$$

or

$$\frac{1}{\hat{p}} = \left[\bar{w} + (\bar{r} - \delta) \frac{\bar{K}}{\bar{H}} \right] \bar{H}.$$

Therefore,

$$\bar{H} = \frac{\beta \bar{w}}{-B \left[\bar{w} + (\bar{r} - \delta) \frac{\bar{K}}{\bar{H}} \right]} = 0.33020,$$

and $\bar{K} = (\bar{K}/\bar{H}) \bar{H} = 12.544$.

8.5.3   Log-Linear Version of the Model

The 9 equations for the model in the 9 variables, w_t, r_t, p_t, C_t, K_t, H_t, φ_t, $\hat{g}_t$, and λ_t (after having replaced $\hat{m}_t^i$, k_t^i, and h_t^i with their aggregate values), are the first-order conditions

$$\frac{1}{w_t} = \beta E_t \left[\frac{r_{t+1} + 1 - \delta}{w_{t+1}} \right]$$

and

$$-\frac{B}{\beta w_t} = \hat{p}_t,$$

the cash-in-advance constraint for families, which we eliminate from the log-linear version of the model because it only determines consumption as a function of the other variables,

$$\hat{p}_t C_t = \frac{1}{\varphi_t},$$

and the cash-in-advance constraint for the government,

$$\hat{p}_t \hat{g}_t \bar{g} = 1 - \frac{1}{\varphi_t},$$

the real budget constraint for the families,

$$K_{t+1} + \frac{1}{\hat{p}_t} = w_t H_t + r_t K_t + (1 - \delta) K_t,$$

the equilibrium condition for competitive factor markets,

$$r_t = \theta \lambda_t K_t^{\theta-1} H_t^{1-\theta}$$

and

$$w_t = (1 - \theta) \lambda_t K_t^{\theta} H_t^{-\theta},$$

and the laws of motion for the stochastic variables,

$$\ln \hat{g}_t = \pi \ln \hat{g}_{t-1} + \varepsilon_t^g$$

and

$$\ln \lambda_t = \gamma \ln \lambda_{t-1} + \varepsilon_t^{\lambda}.$$

Defining a log difference variable $\tilde{X}_t = \ln X_t - \ln \bar{X}$, this system can be written in log-linear form around a stationary state (indicated by a bar over the variable)[9] as

---

9. Stationary state values for $\hat{g}_t$ and λ_t are 1, so these disappear from the equations.

$$0 = \tilde{w}_t + \bar{r}\beta E_t \tilde{r}_{t+1} - E_t \tilde{w}_{t+1},$$

$$0 = \tilde{w}_t + \tilde{p}_t,$$

$$0 = \bar{p}\bar{g}\left[\tilde{p}_t + \tilde{g}_t\right] - \frac{1}{\bar{\varphi}}\tilde{\varphi}_t,$$

$$0 = \bar{K}\tilde{K}_{t+1} - \frac{1}{\bar{p}}\tilde{p}_t - \bar{w}\bar{H}\left[\tilde{w}_t + \tilde{H}_t\right] - \bar{r}\bar{K}\left[\tilde{r}_t + \tilde{K}_t\right] - (1-\delta)\bar{K}\tilde{K}_t,$$

$$0 = \tilde{r}_t - \tilde{\lambda}_t - (\theta - 1)\tilde{K}_t - (1-\theta)\tilde{H}_t,$$

and

$$0 = \tilde{w}_t - \tilde{\lambda}_t - \theta\tilde{K}_t + \theta\tilde{H}_t.$$

Letting $x_t = \left[\tilde{K}_{t+1}\right]$, $y_t = \left[\tilde{r}_t, \tilde{w}_t, \tilde{p}_t, \tilde{\varphi}_t, \tilde{H}_t\right]'$, and $z_t = \left[\tilde{\lambda}_t, \tilde{g}_t\right]'$, one can write the model as we did earlier in the form

$$0 = Ax_t + Bx_{t-1} + Cy_t + Dz_t,$$

$$0 = E_t\left[Fx_{t+1} + Gx_t + Hx_{t-1} + Jy_{t+1} + Ky_t + Lz_{t+1} + Mz_t\right],$$

$$z_{t+1} = Nz_t + \varepsilon_{t+1},$$

where

$$A = \begin{bmatrix} 0 \\ 0 \\ \bar{K} \\ 0 \\ 0 \end{bmatrix},$$

$$B = \begin{bmatrix} 0 \\ 0 \\ -\bar{K}(\bar{r}+1-\delta) \\ (1-\theta) \\ -\theta \end{bmatrix},$$

$$C = \begin{bmatrix} 0 & 1 & 1 & 0 & 0 \\ 0 & 0 & \bar{p}\bar{g} & -\frac{1}{\bar{\varphi}} & 0 \\ -\bar{r}\bar{K} & -\bar{w}\bar{H} & -\frac{1}{\bar{p}} & 0 & -\bar{w}\bar{H} \\ 1 & 0 & 0 & 0 & -(1-\theta) \\ 0 & 1 & 0 & 0 & \theta \end{bmatrix},$$

$$D = \begin{bmatrix} 0 & 0 \\ 0 & \bar{p}\bar{g} \\ 0 & 0 \\ -1 & 0 \\ -1 & 0 \end{bmatrix},$$

$$F = [0], \ G = [0], \ H = [0],$$

$$J = [\beta\bar{r} \quad -1 \quad 0 \quad 0 \quad 0],$$

$$K = [0 \quad 1 \quad 0 \quad 0 \quad 0],$$

$$L = [0 \quad 0], M = [0 \quad 0],$$

and

$$N = \begin{bmatrix} \gamma & 0 \\ 0 & \pi \end{bmatrix}.$$

The calculation of the laws of motion are the same as before: the matrix C is invertible and the vector of state variables (minus the stochastic variables) has only one element. The linear laws of motion that we are looking for are given by the matrices P, Q, R, and S, where

$$x_{t+1} = Px_t + Qz_t$$

and

$$y_t = Rx_t + Sz_t.$$

Using the parameter values for our standard economy and solving the linear system described above, we get the matrices shown in Table 8.5. The results shown are for the cases where stationary state seigniorage is equal to $\bar{g} = \{0, .01, .1\}$.

The shocks to seigniorage only affect the growth rate of money. The endogenous variables modeled here, including the holdings of real balances, do not respond to the shocks on seigniorage. The economy-wide cash-in-advance constraint implies that consumption will change in response to shocks on seigniorage. Since $\hat{p}_t C_t + \hat{p}_t \hat{g}_t \bar{g} = 1$, increasing $\hat{p}_t$ means that C_t must decline for this equation to hold. Seigniorage functions as a tax on consumption. The only other variable that responds is the growth rate of money, φ_t. Changes in money growth pass through to changes in the price level since the ratio of prices to money does not respond to seigniorage.

Table 8.5   Values for matrices in standard economy

$\bar{g}$	0	.01	.1
P	$\begin{bmatrix} .9697 \end{bmatrix}$	$\begin{bmatrix} .9697 \end{bmatrix}$	$\begin{bmatrix} .9697 \end{bmatrix}$
Q	$\begin{bmatrix} .07580 & 0 \end{bmatrix}$	$\begin{bmatrix} .07580 & 0 \end{bmatrix}$	$\begin{bmatrix} .07580 & 0 \end{bmatrix}$
R	$\begin{bmatrix} -0.4300 \\ 0.4781 \\ -0.4782 \\ 0 \\ -0.3282 \end{bmatrix}$	$\begin{bmatrix} -0.4300 \\ 0.4781 \\ -0.4782 \\ -0.0053 \\ -0.3282 \end{bmatrix}$	$\begin{bmatrix} -0.4300 \\ 0.4781 \\ -0.4782 \\ -0.0591 \\ -0.3282 \end{bmatrix}$
S	$\begin{bmatrix} 0.2536 & 0 \\ 0.5802 & 0 \\ -0.5802 & 0 \\ 0 & 0 \\ 1.1662 & 0 \end{bmatrix}$	$\begin{bmatrix} 0.2536 & 0 \\ 0.5802 & 0 \\ -0.5802 & 0 \\ -0.0065 & 0.0111 \\ 1.1662 & 0 \end{bmatrix}$	$\begin{bmatrix} 0.2536 & 0 \\ 0.5802 & 0 \\ -0.5802 & 0 \\ -0.0717 & 0.1235 \\ 1.1662 & 0 \end{bmatrix}$

8.6   REPRISE

Adding cash-in-advance money to Hansen's indivisible labor model has its complications. Because of the importance of aggregate variables and the price level, one cannot, in general, iterate to find the value function and a nonlinear policy function. Linear quadratic methods give a linear policy function, but finding these are relatively complicated. The most direct method for approxiating the model is to take log-linear approximations of the first-order conditions, the budget constraints, and the equilibrium conditions. There are a variety of methods for solving the linear model; here we use Uhlig's version of the undetermined coefficients method.

The results show that higher stationary state levels of inflation function as a tax, implying lower output, consumption, and utility. The dynamics of the model are independent of the stationary state inflation rate. There is only one equation in the log-linear version of the model where stationary state values of the variables enter, and all the parameters of this equation are divided by the stationary state inflation rate, leaving the relative effect of each parameter unchanged. The responses to real shocks are exactly the same as those in the Hansen model without money. The responses to money growth shocks are smaller, with prices showing the biggest response.

The cash-in-advance model is one of the workhorses of monetary theory. While it has its problems (money is exchanged only one time per period, for example), it is quite easy to use. Excellent expositions of the theory behind this model can be found in standard graduate macroeconomic texts such as Sargent [72], Blanchard and Fischer [13], or Walsh [89].

8.7 APPENDIX 1: CES UTILITY FUNCTIONS

Instead of the subutility function

$$u(c_t^i, 1 - h_t^i) = \ln c_t^i + Bh_t^i,$$

in this appendix we use the constant elasticity of substitution (in consumption), or CES, function,

$$u(c_t^i, 1 - h_t^i) = \frac{\left(c_t^i\right)^{1-\eta} - 1}{1 - \eta} + Bh_t^i,$$

to consider the stationary states in an economy with seigniorage. This function is equal to the logarithmic case when $\eta = 1$. Here we assume that $\eta \neq 1$. The elasticity of substitution is equal to $1/\eta$, so when $\eta > 1$, the indifference curves for consumption between two adjacent periods are flatter than those in the logarithmic case (where the indifference curves are rectangular hyperbolas) and when $\eta < 1$, they are more curved than in the logarithmic case.

The model is the same as before except that the function that families optimize is now

$$\max_{\left\{\hat{m}_t^i, k_{t+1}^i\right\}} E_0 \sum_{t=0}^{\infty} \beta^t \left[\frac{\left(\frac{\hat{m}_{t-1}^i}{\varphi_t \hat{p}_t}\right)^{1-\eta} - 1}{1 - \eta} + B\left(\frac{k_{t+1}^i + \frac{\hat{m}_t^i}{\hat{p}_t} - r_t k_t^i - (1 - \delta)k_t^i}{w_t}\right) \right],$$

where we used the cash-in-advance constraint,

$$\hat{p}_t c_t^i = \frac{\hat{m}_{t-1}^i}{\varphi_t},$$

to remove consumption and the real budget constraint,

$$k_{t+1}^i + \frac{\hat{m}_t^i}{\hat{p}_t} = w_t h_t^i + r_t k_t^i + (1 - \delta)k_t^i,$$

to eliminate hours worked. The first-order conditions are

$$\frac{1}{w_t} = \beta E_t \left[\frac{r_{t+1}}{w_{t+1}} + \frac{1 - \delta}{w_{t+1}} \right],$$

as before, and

$$\beta E_0 \frac{\left(\varphi_{t+1}\hat{p}_{t+1}\right)^{\eta-1}}{\left(\hat{m}_t^i\right)^{\eta}} = -\frac{B}{w_t\hat{p}_t}.$$

In a stationary state, the first condition is

$$\frac{1}{\beta} = \bar{r} + (1-\delta),$$

and the second is

$$\left(-\frac{\bar{w}\beta}{B}\right)^{\frac{1}{\eta}} \bar{\varphi}^{1-\frac{1}{\eta}} = \frac{\hat{m}^i}{\hat{p}}.$$

In the aggregate, the second condition becomes

$$\left(-\frac{\bar{w}\beta}{B}\right)^{\frac{1}{\eta}} \bar{\varphi}^{1-\frac{1}{\eta}} = \frac{1}{\hat{p}},$$

or

$$\hat{p} = \left(-\frac{B}{\bar{w}\beta}\right)^{\frac{1}{\eta}} \bar{\varphi}^{\frac{1}{\eta}-1}.$$

One can see from this last equation how when $\eta = 1$ and only when $\eta = 1$, the rate of growth of the money supply drops out of the equation and the price level is independent of the rate of growth of money. The stationary state real wage is as before,

$$\bar{w} = (1-\theta) \left[\frac{\theta}{\frac{1}{\beta} - (1-\delta)} \right]^{\frac{\theta}{1-\theta}},$$

and depends only on a set of parameters of the economy that excludes the growth rate of money.

The relationship between the growth rate of money and seigniorage in a stationary state comes from the government's budget constraint,

$$\hat{p}\bar{g} = 1 - \frac{1}{\varphi},$$

and, substituting in $\hat{p}$ from above, the relationship is

$$\left(-\frac{B}{\bar{w}\beta}\right)^{\frac{1}{\eta}} \bar{\varphi}^{\frac{1}{\eta}}\bar{g} = \varphi - 1,$$

or

$$\bar{g} = \left(-\frac{\bar{w}\beta}{B}\right)^{\frac{1}{\eta}} \bar{\varphi}^{-\frac{1}{\eta}} (\varphi - 1) .$$

The relationship between seigniorage and the growth rate of money (the Bailey curve) is shown in Figure 8.5 for stationary state economies where $\eta = .5$, $\eta = 1$, and $\eta = 2$.

With the rental on capital fixed at $\bar{r} = \frac{1}{\beta} - (1 - \delta)$, the stationary state capital-labor ratio is fixed at

$$\frac{\bar{K}}{\bar{H}} = \left[\frac{\theta}{\frac{1}{\beta} - (1 - \delta)}\right]^{\frac{1}{1-\theta}} .$$

Aggregating the real budget constraints

$$k_{t+1}^i + \frac{\hat{m}_t^i}{\hat{p}_t} = w_t h_t^i + r_t k_t^i + (1 - \delta)k_t^i$$

in a stationary state gives

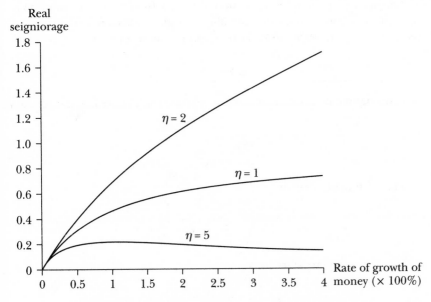

FIGURE 8.5   Bailey curves for a CES utility economy

$$\frac{1}{\hat{p}} = \left[\bar{w} + (\bar{r} - \delta)\, \frac{\bar{K}}{\bar{H}} \right] \bar{H}.$$

The items in the square brackets are all constant in a stationary state and equal

$$\Upsilon = \left[\bar{w} + (\bar{r} - \delta)\, \frac{\bar{K}}{\bar{H}} \right]$$

$$= \left[(1-\theta) \left[\frac{\theta}{\frac{1}{\beta} - (1-\delta)} \right]^{\frac{\theta}{1-\theta}} + \left(\frac{1}{\beta} - 1 \right) \left[\frac{\theta}{\frac{1}{\beta} - (1-\delta)} \right]^{\frac{1}{1-\theta}} \right]$$

$$= 2.7543.$$

Then

$$\bar{H} = \frac{1}{\Upsilon} \frac{1}{\hat{p}} = \frac{1}{\Upsilon} \left(-\frac{\bar{w}\beta}{B} \right)^{\frac{1}{\eta}} \bar{\varphi}^{1 - \frac{1}{\eta}} = \bar{H}_0(\eta) \bar{\varphi}^{1 - \frac{1}{\eta}}$$

$$= \frac{(0.9095)^{\frac{1}{\eta}}}{2.7543} \bar{\varphi}^{1 - \frac{1}{\eta}},$$

where $\bar{H}_0(\eta)$ is the hours worked in a stationary state with no money growth (and no seigniorage) and is a function of the coefficient on consumption in the utility function, η. Since the capital-labor ratio is constant and output is of constant returns to scale, we know that output follows the rule

$$\bar{Y} = \bar{Y}_0(\eta) \bar{\varphi}^{1 - \frac{1}{\eta}}.$$

Using the aggregated cash-in-advance constraint for families in the stationary state,

$$\bar{C} = \frac{1}{\hat{p}\bar{\varphi}},$$

and eliminating prices with

$$\hat{p} = \left(-\frac{B}{\bar{w}\beta} \right)^{\frac{1}{\eta}} \bar{\varphi}^{\frac{1}{\eta} - 1},$$

one gets the stationary state consumption as

$$\bar{C} = \left(-\frac{\bar{w}\beta}{B} \right)^{\frac{1}{\eta}} \bar{\varphi}^{-\frac{1}{\eta}} = \bar{C}_0 \bar{\varphi}^{-\frac{1}{\eta}}.$$

Utility in the stationary state is

$$\frac{\left[\frac{\bar{C}_0^{1-\eta}}{1-\eta} + B\bar{H}_0(\eta)\right]\bar{\varphi}^{1-\frac{1}{\eta}} - \frac{1}{1-\eta}}{1-\beta}.$$

Figure 8.6 shows how utility changes in stationary states with different rates of growth of money and with $\eta = .5$ and $\eta = 2$.

The full model is comprised of the first-order conditions

$$\frac{1}{w_t} = \beta E_t\left[\frac{r_{t+1}}{w_{t+1}} + \frac{1-\delta}{w_{t+1}}\right]$$

and

$$\beta E_0 \frac{\left(\varphi_{t+1}\hat{p}_{t+1}\right)^{\eta-1}}{(1)^\eta} = -\frac{B}{w_t\hat{p}_t},$$

the cash-in-advance constraint for families and the government, which we will not use in the log-linear version of the model since it only determines consumption as a function of the other variables,

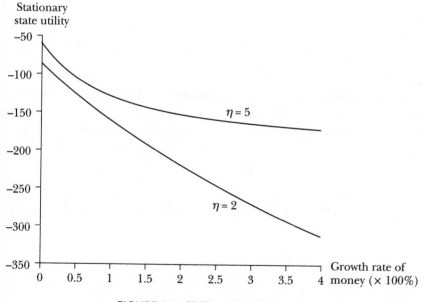

FIGURE 8.6 Utility with seigniorage

$$\hat{p}_t C_t = \frac{1}{\varphi_t}$$

and

$$\hat{p}_t \hat{g}_t \bar{g} = 1 - \frac{1}{\varphi_t},$$

the real budget constraint for the families,

$$K_{t+1} + \frac{1}{\hat{p}_t} = w_t H_t + r_t K_t + (1 - \delta) K_t,$$

the equilibrium condition for competitive factor markets,

$$r_t = \theta \lambda_t K_t^{\theta-1} H_t^{1-\theta}$$

and

$$w_t = (1 - \theta) \lambda_t K_t^{\theta} H_t^{-\theta},$$

and the laws of motion for the stochastic variables,

$$\ln \hat{g}_t = \pi \ln \hat{g}_{t-1} + \varepsilon_t^g$$

and

$$\ln \lambda_t = \gamma \ln \lambda_{t-1} + \varepsilon_t^\lambda.$$

All of these equations are the same as in the version of this model with logarithmic utility of consumption except for one of the first-order conditions. Likewise, the log-linear version is the same except that the log-linear version of the aggregate version of the second equation is the expectational equation

$$(\eta - 1) (\bar{\varphi}\bar{p})^{\eta-1} \beta E_t \left(\tilde{\varphi}_{t+1} + \tilde{p}_{t+1} \right) = \frac{B}{\bar{w}\bar{p}} \left(\tilde{w}_t + \tilde{p}_t \right).$$

Letting $x_t = \left[\tilde{K}_{t+1}, \tilde{\varphi}_t \right]$, $y_t = \left[\tilde{r}_t, \tilde{w}_t, \tilde{p}_t, \tilde{H}_t \right]'$, and $z_t = \left[\tilde{\lambda}_t, \tilde{g}_t \right]$, one can write the model as we did above,

$$0 = Ax_t + Bx_{t-1} + Cy_t + Dz_t,$$

$$0 = E_t \left[Fx_{t+1} + Gx_t + Hx_{t-1} + Jy_{t+1} + Ky_t + Lz_{t+1} + Mz_t \right],$$

$$z_{t+1} = Nz_t + \varepsilon_{t+1},$$

but now

$$A = \begin{bmatrix} 0 & -\frac{1}{\bar{\varphi}} \\ \bar{K} & 0 \\ 0 & 0 \\ 0 & 0 \end{bmatrix},$$

$$B = \begin{bmatrix} 0 & 0 \\ -\bar{K}\,(\bar{r}+1-\delta) & 0 \\ (1-\theta) & 0 \\ -\theta & 0 \end{bmatrix},$$

$$C = \begin{bmatrix} 0 & 0 & \bar{p}\bar{g} & 0 \\ -\bar{r}\bar{K} & -\bar{w}\bar{H} & -\frac{1}{\bar{p}} & -\bar{w}\bar{H} \\ 1 & 0 & 0 & -(1-\theta) \\ 0 & 1 & 0 & \theta \end{bmatrix},$$

$$D = \begin{bmatrix} 0 & \bar{p}\bar{g} \\ 0 & 0 \\ -1 & 0 \\ -1 & 0 \end{bmatrix},$$

$$F = \begin{bmatrix} 0 & 0 \\ 0 & (\eta-1)\,(\bar{\varphi}\bar{p})^{\eta-1}\beta \end{bmatrix}, \; G = \begin{bmatrix} 0 & 0 \\ 0 & 0 \end{bmatrix}, \; H = \begin{bmatrix} 0 & 0 \\ 0 & 0 \end{bmatrix},$$

$$J = \begin{bmatrix} \beta\bar{r} & -1 & 0 & 0 \\ 0 & 0 & (\eta-1)\,(\bar{\varphi}\bar{p})^{\eta-1}\beta & 0 \end{bmatrix},$$

$$K = \begin{bmatrix} 0 & 1 & 0 & 0 \\ 0 & -\frac{B}{\bar{w}\bar{p}} & -\frac{B}{\bar{w}\bar{p}} & 0 \end{bmatrix},$$

$$L = \begin{bmatrix} 0 & 0 \\ 0 & 0 \end{bmatrix}, \; M = \begin{bmatrix} 0 & 0 \\ 0 & 0 \end{bmatrix},$$

and

$$N = \begin{bmatrix} \gamma & 0 \\ 0 & \pi \end{bmatrix}.$$

The system was written with the variable $\tilde{\varphi}_t$ as a state variable (part of x_t) so that the matrix C would be square and invertible. Solving the quadratic equation for P is somewhat more complicated because P is now a 2×2 matrix. A method for doing this is from Uhlig [86] and is described in Appendix 2.

Table 8.6   Values for matrices in a CES economy

$\bar{g} = .2$	$\eta = .8, \varphi = 1.3180$	$\eta = 1.8, \varphi = 1.2373$
P	$\begin{bmatrix} 0.9418 & 0 \\ -0.2049 & 0 \end{bmatrix}$	$\begin{bmatrix} 0.9418 & 0 \\ -0.0761 & 0 \end{bmatrix}$
Q	$\begin{bmatrix} 0.1723 & 0.0020 \\ -0.1628 & 0.3282 \end{bmatrix}$	$\begin{bmatrix} 0.1305 & -0.0035 \\ -0.0773 & 0.2232 \end{bmatrix}$
R	$\begin{bmatrix} -0.8612 & 0 \\ 0.4844 & 0 \\ -0.6444 & 0 \\ -0.3456 & 0 \end{bmatrix}$	$\begin{bmatrix} -1.1018 & 0 \\ 0.6198 & 0 \\ -0.3208 & 0 \\ -0.7216 & 0 \end{bmatrix}$
S	$\begin{bmatrix} 2.1478 & -0.0037 \\ 0.3544 & 0.0021 \\ -0.5118 & 0.0322 \\ 1.7934 & -0.0058 \end{bmatrix}$	$\begin{bmatrix} 1.5802 & 0.0083 \\ 0.6736 & -0.0047 \\ -0.3258 & -0.0593 \\ 0.9066 & 0.0130 \end{bmatrix}$

The results for the case where $\bar{g} = .2$ and $\eta = .8$ and $\eta = 1.8$ are given in Table 8.6.

8.8   APPENDIX 2: MATRIX QUADRATIC EQUATIONS

Following Uhlig [86], we look for a solution to a matrix quadratic equation,

$$AP^2 - BP - C = 0,$$

of $P = \Psi\Lambda\Psi^{-1}$, where Λ is a matrix of eigenvalues on the diagonal of the form

$$\Lambda = \begin{bmatrix} \lambda_1 & 0 & \cdots & \cdots & 0 \\ 0 & \lambda_2 & 0 & \cdots & \vdots \\ \vdots & 0 & \ddots & \ddots & \vdots \\ \vdots & \cdots & \ddots & \lambda_{n-1} & 0 \\ 0 & \cdots & \cdots & 0 & \lambda_n \end{bmatrix},$$

and Ψ is a matrix with the corresponding eigenvectors. Notice that this form of writing P implies that $P^2 = \Psi\Lambda\Psi^{-1}\Psi\Lambda\Psi^{-1} = \Psi\Lambda^2\Psi^{-1}$, where Λ^2 is a diagonal matrix with the squares of the eigenvalues along the diagonal. Uhlig's method for solving the matrix quadratic equation exploits this feature of the decomposition of P into eigenvalues and eigenvectors.

The matrices A, B, and C are all $n \times n$. Construct the $2n \times 2n$ matrices

$$D = \begin{bmatrix} B & C \\ I & \vec{0} \end{bmatrix}$$

and

$$E = \begin{bmatrix} A & \vec{0} \\ \vec{0} & I \end{bmatrix},$$

where I is an $n \times n$ identity matrix and $\vec{0}$ is an $n \times n$ matrix of zeros. Find the solution to the generalized eigenvalue problem for the matrix pair (D, E). The solution to this problem is a set of $2n$ eigenvalues λ_k and corresponding eigenvectors x_k, such that

$$D x_k = E x_k \lambda_k$$

for $k = 1, \ldots, 2n$. Let X be the matrix of all eigenvectors. Assume that there are at least n stable eigenvectors, those whose absolute value is less than one. Order the eigenvalues and their corresponding eigenvectors so that the n stable eigenvalues come first. The eigenvectors are columns, so that the matrix X is

$$X = \begin{bmatrix} x_{1,1} & x_{2,1} & \cdots & \cdots & x_{2n,1} \\ x_{1,2} & x_{2,2} & \vdots & \vdots & x_{2n,2} \\ \vdots & \vdots & \vdots & \vdots & \vdots \\ \vdots & \vdots & \vdots & \vdots & \vdots \\ x_{1,2n} & x_{2,2n} & \cdots & \cdots & x_{2n,2n} \end{bmatrix}.$$

The matrix X can be broken into four parts, each $n \times n$, of the form

$$X = \begin{bmatrix} X^{11} & X^{21} \\ X^{12} & X^{22} \end{bmatrix}$$

$$= \begin{bmatrix} x_{1,1} & x_{2,1} & \cdots & x_{n,1} & x_{n+1,1} & x_{n+2,1} & \cdots & x_{2n,1} \\ x_{1,2} & x_{2,2} & \cdots & x_{n,2} & x_{n+1,2} & x_{n+2,2} & \cdots & x_{2n,2} \\ \vdots & \vdots & \cdots & \vdots & \vdots & \vdots & \cdots & \vdots \\ x_{1,n} & x_{2,n} & \cdots & x_{n,n} & x_{n+1,n} & x_{n+2,n} & \cdots & x_{2n,n} \\ x_{1,n+1} & x_{2,n+1} & \cdots & x_{n,n+1} & x_{n+1,n+1} & x_{n+2,1} & \cdots & x_{2n,n+1} \\ x_{1,n+2} & x_{2,n+2} & \cdots & x_{n,n+2} & x_{n+1,n+2} & x_{n+2,2} & \cdots & x_{2n,n+2} \\ \vdots & \vdots & \cdots & \vdots & \vdots & \vdots & \cdots & \vdots \\ x_{1,2n} & x_{2,2n} & \cdots & x_{n,2n} & x_{n+1,2n} & x_{n+2,2n} & \cdots & x_{2n,2n} \end{bmatrix}.$$

The matrix X^{11} contains the first half of the generalized eigenvectors that correspond to the n stable eigenvalues. The structure of the matrices that were constructed for the generalized eigenvalue problem tell us something about the matrix X^{21}. Solutions to the generalized eigenvalue problem are

$$DX = EX\Delta,$$

where Δ is the diagonal matrix of generalized eigenvalues with the n stable eigenvalues coming first. Using the descriptions of the matrices given above, this corresponds to

$$\begin{bmatrix} B & C \\ I & \vec{0} \end{bmatrix} \begin{bmatrix} X^{11} & X^{21} \\ X^{12} & X^{22} \end{bmatrix} = \begin{bmatrix} A & \vec{0} \\ \vec{0} & I \end{bmatrix} \begin{bmatrix} X^{11} & X^{21} \\ X^{12} & X^{22} \end{bmatrix} \begin{bmatrix} \Delta^1 & \vec{0} \\ \vec{0} & \Delta^2 \end{bmatrix},$$

where Δ^1 contains the stable eigenvalues along the diagonal and zeros everywhere else. Multiplying out the matrices on each side gives

$$\begin{bmatrix} BX^{11} + CX^{12} & BX^{21} + CX^{22} \\ X^{11} & X^{21} \end{bmatrix} = \begin{bmatrix} AX^{11}\Delta^1 & AX^{21}\Delta^2 \\ X^{12}\Delta^1 & X^{22}\Delta^2 \end{bmatrix}.$$

Each of the four $n \times n$ matrices on the left-hand side of the equals sign must be equal to the corresponding matrix on the right-hand side. In particular,

$$X^{11} = X^{12}\Delta^1$$

and

$$BX^{11} + CX^{12} = AX^{11}\Delta^1.$$

Substituting in $X^{12}\Delta^1$ for X^{11} in the second equation gives

$$BX^{12}\Delta^1 + CX^{12} = AX^{12}\Delta^1\Delta^1,$$

and postmultiplying both sides by $\left(X^{12}\right)^{-1}$ gives

$$BX^{12}\Delta^1 \left(X^{12}\right)^{-1} + C = AX^{12}\Delta^1\Delta^1 \left(X^{12}\right)^{-1}.$$

Define $P = X^{12}\Delta^1 \left(X^{12}\right)^{-1}$. Then $P^2 = X^{12}\Delta^1\Delta^1 \left(X^{12}\right)^{-1}$ and

$$BP + C = AP^2.$$

Therefore, the solution to the matrix quadratic equation can be found by constructing the matrices D and E and finding the solution to the generalized eigenvalue problem for those matrices as the generalized eigenvector matrix X and the generalized eigenvalue matrix Δ (ordered appropriately, with the stable eigenvalues first). The matrix Δ^1 contains the eigenvalues, and the matrix X^{12} contains the eigenvectors that we use to construct

$$P = X^{12}\Delta^1 \left(X^{12}\right)^{-1}.$$

8.9 MATLAB CODE FOR SOLVING THE CES MODEL WITH SEIGNIORAGE

This program finds the solution to a matrix quadratic polynomial in order to solve for the dynamics of the seigniorage model in an economy with CES utility.

```
%solution to the cash in advance model with a CES utility function
%set the parameters and find the stationary state
theta=.36;
beta=.99;
gamma=.95;
delta=.025;
pie=.48;
varphi=1.3180;
eta=.8;
BB=-2.5805;
rbar=1/beta-(1-delta);
wbar=(1-theta)*(theta/rbar)^(theta/(1-theta));
gbar=(-wbar*beta/(BB*varphi))^(1/eta)*(varphi-1);
KoverH=(theta/rbar)^(1/(1-theta));
pbar=(-BB/(wbar*beta))^(1/eta)*(varphi)^(1/eta-1);
hibar=1/(pbar*(wbar+(rbar-delta)*KoverH));
Hbar=hibar;
kibar=KoverH*Hbar;
Kbar=kibar;
cbar=1/(pbar*varphi);
mbar=1;
%build the required matrices A through N
A=[0 -1/varphi
   Kbar 0
   0 0
   0 0];
B=[0 0
   -(rbar+1-delta)*Kbar 0
   1-theta 0
   -theta 0];
C=[0 0 pbar*gbar 0
   -rbar*Kbar -wbar*Hbar -1/pbar -wbar*Hbar
   1 0 0 -(1-theta)
   0 1 0 theta];
```

```
D=[0 pbar*gbar
   0 0
   -1 0
   -1 0];
F=[0 0
   0 (eta-1)];
G=[0 0
   0 0];
H=[0 0
   0 0];
J=[beta*rbar -1 0 0
   0 0 (eta-1) 0];
K=[0 1 0 0
   0 1 1 0];
L=[0 0
   0 0];
M=[0 0
   0 0];
N=[gamma 0
   0 pie];
%Set up and find the solution to the matrix quadratic
polynomial
I1=[1 0
    0 1];
Z1=zeros(2);
invC=inv(C);
psy=F-J*invC*A;
lambda=J*invC*B-G+K*invC*A;
T=K*invC*B-H;
AA1=[lambda T
     I1 Z1];
AA2=[psy Z1
     Z1 I1];
%find the generalized eigenvalues and eigenvectors
[eigvec eigval]=eig(AA1,AA2);
diageigval=diag(eigval)
%select the stable eigenvalues and the corresponding
eigenvalues
iz=find(abs(diageigval)<1);
DD=diag(diageigval(iz));
ei=size(eigvec);
EE=eigvec(ei/2+1:ei,iz);
% find the matrices P, R, Q, and S
P=EE*DD*inv(EE)
R=-invC*(A*P+B)
```

```
I2=[1 0
    0 1];
QQ=kron(N',(F-J*invC*A))+kron(I2,(J*R+F*P+G-K*invC*A));
invQQ=inv(QQ);
QQQ=((J*invC*D-L)*N+K*invC*D-M);
[aa,bb]=size(QQQ);
Qfindvert=[];
for ij=1:bb
    Qfindvert=vertcat(Qfindvert,QQQ(:,ij));
end
Qvert=invQQ*Qfindvert;
Q=[];
for ij=1:bb
    begini=(ij-1)*aa+1;
    endi=ij*aa;
    Q=[Q Qvert(begini:endi,1)];
end
Q
S=-invC*(A*Q+D)
```

9

Money in the Utility Function

Putting money into a general microfoundations model is not easy. In the cash-in-advance model, it was simply assumed that money had to be used to make certain types of purchases, in our case, consumption goods. There was no real theoretical rationale for that assumption other than the empirical observation that we seem to find money being used on one side of most transactions. If one takes this empirical observation as a given, then the cash-in-advance models are fine.

A second way of introducing money into a model, introduced by Sidrauski [76], is to assume that money provides some service to the economy and that the benefits of that service can be expressed in the utility function. If one assumes that having more real balances means that one will be able to reduce the time and energy spent making transactions, for example, one might include real balances in the utility function as a way of representing these utility gains.[1] There are other ways to rationalize putting money in the utility function. Additional holdings of real balances might provide insurance against certain individual or economy-wide shocks and might permit transactions with unknown individuals (with whom credit transactions might not be feasible nor wise). Whatever the reason for the benefits derived from the holding of real balances, we assume we can approximate them in the utility function.

In this chapter we will use a utility function in which increased holdings of real balances directly increases welfare. Utility that individuals wish to maxi-

---

1. Of course, another way to do this would be to include transactions costs in the budget constraint and have these costs be a declining function of real balances held at the beginning of the period.

mize is still the present value of an infinite sequence of additively separable subutilities. The subutility function in period t for individual i is of the form

$$u(c_t^i, \frac{m_t^i}{P_t}, l_t^i) = u(c_t^i, \frac{m_t^i}{P_t}, 1 - h_t^i),$$

where the only important change is that we now add real balances of the individual, m_t^i / P_t, as a variable. The rationale for adding real balances to the utility function is the presumption that additional real balances reduce the cost of making transactions or reduce search (since they solve the noncoincidence-of-wants problem that arises in barter trade). One of the benefits of putting money in the utility function is that if there are other assets that individuals can hold, capital, for instance, the model will produce a real rate of return for money that is less than that of the other assets.

This benefit does not come without costs. The model doesn't explain which money should be in the utility function (dollars or pesos, for example). In addition, there is no clear use for money in the model: it doesn't do anything. Just keeping the money in your possession creates the utility. In economies with one good in which all agents are identical, no trades ever take place and money really is not ever used for anything. Nevertheless, as a rough approximation of the gains from using money, and in particular, for giving money value when there are interest-earning assets available, money-in-the-utility-function models are useful.

9.1 THE MODEL

A unit mass of identical households each choose sequences of $\{c_t^i, m_t^i, k_{t+1}^i, h_t^i\}_{t=0}^{\infty}$ to maximize the infinite horizon discounted utility function,

$$E_0 \sum_{t=0}^{\infty} \beta^t u(c_t^i, \frac{m_t^i}{P_t}, 1 - h_t^i),$$

subject to the sequence of period t budget constraints,

$$c_t^i + k_{t+1}^i + \frac{m_t^i}{P_t} = w_t h_t^i + r_t k_t^i + (1 - \delta)k_t^i + \frac{m_{t-1}^i}{P_t} + (g_t - 1)\frac{M_{t-1}}{P_t}, \quad (9.1)$$

where $(g_t - 1)M_{t-1}$ is a lump sum transfer of money from the monetary authority to the household in period t. All other variables are defined as in previous chapters. The subutility function $u(\cdot)$ is

$$u(c_t^i, \frac{m_t^i}{P_t}, 1 - h_t^i) = \ln c_t^i + D \ln \left(\frac{m_t^i}{P_t} \right) + B h_t^i,$$

where D is the positive coefficient on the log of real balances. Assuming indivisible labor of h_0 and an insurance system that provides labor income in period t, whether or not the household is one of those chosen to work in period t, the coefficient B on labor in the subutility function is equal to $B = A \ln(1 - h_0)/h_0$. Here there is only one budget constraint for the households since a cash-in-advance constraint no longer applies. With these assumptions, the first-order conditions for the household are

$$\frac{1}{c_t^i} = \beta E_t \frac{P_t}{c_{t+1}^i P_{t+1}} + \frac{D P_t}{m_t^i}, \tag{9.2}$$

$$\frac{1}{c_t^i} = \beta E_t \frac{1}{c_{t+1}^i} \left[r_{t+1} + (1 - \delta) \right], \tag{9.3}$$

$$\frac{1}{c_t^i} = -\frac{B}{w_t}. \tag{9.4}$$

Note that in a representative agent economy or an economy where all of a mass $= 1$ of agents are identical, the first-order condition, equation 9.2, can be written in aggregate terms as

$$\frac{1}{P_t C_t} = \beta E_t \frac{1}{C_{t+1} P_{t+1}} + D \frac{1}{M_t}.$$

One can write this equation for the expected values one period into the future as

$$E_t \frac{1}{P_{t+1} C_{t+1}} = \beta E_t \frac{1}{C_{t+2} P_{t+2}} + D \frac{1}{M_{t+1}},$$

and substituting this into the first equation gives

$$\frac{1}{P_t C_t} = \beta E_t \left[\beta E_t \frac{1}{C_{t+2} P_{t+2}} + D \frac{1}{M_{t+1}} \right] + D \frac{1}{M_t}$$

$$= \beta^2 E_t \frac{1}{C_{t+2} P_{t+2}} + \beta E_t D \frac{1}{M_{t+1}} + D \frac{1}{M_t}.$$

Applying this substitution repeatedly, one gets a solution for this first-order difference equation of

$$\frac{1}{P_t} = D C_t \sum_{j=0}^{\infty} \beta^j E_t \frac{1}{M_{t+j}}.$$

One can apply the money growth rule,

$$M_{t+1} = g_{t+1} M_t,$$

to get the above equation in terms of a sequence of growth rates of money,

$$\frac{1}{P_t} = \frac{DC_t}{M_t} \sum_{j=0}^{\infty} \beta^j E_t \prod_{k=1}^{j} \frac{1}{g_{t+k}}. \tag{9.5}$$

The price level is forward looking and depends on the current consumption, the amount of money with which people begin the period t, and the entire sequence of expected future growth rates of money.

Since all firms have the same Cobb-Douglas production function, one can aggregate production and treat the economy as if it had the aggregate production function

$$Y_t = \lambda_t K_t^{\theta} H_t^{1-\theta},$$

with

$$\text{costs} = w_t H_t + r_t K_t.$$

This results in the competitive factor market conditions of

$$r_t = \theta \lambda_t K_t^{\theta-1} H_t^{1-\theta}$$

and

$$w_t = (1 - \theta) \lambda_t K_t^{\theta} H_t^{-\theta}.$$

As before, we assume that the stochastic shocks for technology, λ_t, and for money growth, g_t, follow the processes

$$\ln \lambda_t = \gamma \ln \lambda_{t-1} + \varepsilon_t^{\lambda}$$

and

$$\ln g_t = (1 - \pi) \ln \bar{g} + \pi \ln g_{t-1} + \varepsilon_t^g,$$

where $\varepsilon_t^i \sim N(0, \sigma^i)$ for $i = \lambda, g$, and $\bar{g}$ is the stationary state growth rate of money.

Since all of the unit mass of households are alike and the insurance system provides the same income whether the household works or not, aggregation conditions for this economy are

$$C_t = c_t^i,$$

$$M_t = m_t^i,$$

$$H_t = h_t^i,$$

and

$$K_t = k_t^i,$$

for all $t \geq 0$.

9.2 STATIONARY STATES

A stationary state for an economy with a constant rate of money growth $\bar{g}$ is given by a set of constant real variables, $\{\bar{Y}, \bar{C}, \bar{H}, \bar{K}, \bar{w}, \bar{r}\}$, and constant real balances, $\overline{M/P}$, where all the first-order conditions of the households and firms hold, the budget constraint of households holds, and the production function defines output. Since $\overline{M/P}$ is constant in a stationary state, if the money supply grows at the rate $\bar{g}$ in a stationary state, so must prices. Therefore, the stationary state gross inflation rate, $\bar{\pi}$, must be equal to the stationary state gross growth rate of money, $\bar{g}$. The stationary state version of the first-order conditions are

$$\frac{1}{\bar{C}} = \beta \frac{P_t}{\bar{C} P_{t+1}} + D \frac{P_t}{M_t},$$

$$\bar{r} = \frac{1}{\beta} - (1 - \delta),$$

and

$$\bar{C} = -\frac{\bar{w}}{B}.$$

The stationary state budget constraint is simply

$$\bar{Y} = \bar{C} + \delta \bar{K}.$$

The factor market conditions in a stationary state are

$$\bar{r} = \theta \bar{K}^{\theta - 1} \bar{H}^{1 - \theta}$$

and

$$\bar{w} = (1 - \theta) \, \bar{K}^{\theta} \bar{H}^{-\theta}.$$

The rental rate on capital is given by the second first-order condition. From the equilibrium conditions for the factor markets, we get

$$\bar{w} = (1 - \theta) \left[\frac{\theta}{\bar{r}} \right]^{\frac{\theta}{1 - \theta}}.$$

Once the stationary state wage is known, consumption is immediate from the third first-order condition. Since in the stationary state the gross inflation rate, $\pi = P_{t+1}/P_t$, equals the gross growth rate of money, $\bar{g}$, the first first-order condition can be written as

$$1 = \frac{\beta}{\bar{g}} + D\frac{\bar{C}}{M/P}.$$

This expression can be rearranged to give

$$\overline{M/P} = D\frac{\bar{g}\bar{C}}{\bar{g} - \beta}. \tag{9.6}$$

Combining the household budget constraint with the expression we get from the production function and the factor market condition,

$$\bar{Y} = \bar{K}\left[\frac{\bar{r}(1-\theta)}{\bar{w}\theta}\right]^{1-\theta}, \tag{9.7}$$

gives

$$\bar{K} = \frac{\bar{C}}{\left[\frac{\bar{r}(1-\theta)}{\bar{w}\theta}\right]^{1-\theta} - \delta}.$$

With this value of $\bar{K}$, one finds hours worked as

$$\bar{H} = \left[\frac{\bar{r}(1-\theta)}{\bar{w}\theta}\right]\bar{K},$$

and output from the above expression, equation 9.7.

In stationary states for this model of money in the utility function, the growth rate of money is completely neutral with respect to the real variables in the economy. This kind of neutrality is sometimes called *superneutrality* since, in the long run, the growth rate of money has no effect at all on the real variables.

Equation 9.6 says that stationary state real money holdings are smaller in economies with higher stationary state growth rates of money. In fact, utility is maximized in a stationary state when the growth rate of money is equal to the discount factor β. This result is well known, for example, Friedman [41] was the first to conjecture this optimality condition. In the model as written here, this is somewhat problematic since equation 9.6 tells us that desired real balances are infinite when $\bar{g} = \beta$. That the desired real balances are infinite come from our use of a separable subutility function with log utility for real balances and does not necessarily hold for other formulations of the subutility

Table 9.1   Stationary state values

Variable	Stationary state value
$\bar{r}$	.035101
$\bar{w}$	2.3706
$\bar{C}$	.9187
$\bar{K}$	12.6707
$\bar{H}$	.3335
$\bar{Y}$	1.2354
$\overline{M/P}$	$\dfrac{.009187\bar{g}}{\bar{g}-.99}$

function. This problem with desiring an infinite amount of money has been observed before by Brock [17], using a model similar to the one here, and by Bewley [11], using a stochastic model.

For the standard economy with $\beta = .99$, $\delta = .025$, $\theta = .36$, and $B = -2.5805$, the stationary state values for the variables are given in Table 9.1. In order to get the same values when $\bar{g} = 1$ for $\overline{M/P}$ as one would have had in the cash-in-advance model (where $\bar{C} = \overline{M/P}$), we use a value for the parameter in the utility function on real balances of $D = .01$.

9.3   LOG-LINEAR VERSION OF THE MODEL

We find a version of the model in the log-linear values of the variables around their stationary state, $\tilde{X}_t = \ln X_t - \ln \bar{X}$. The set of variables of the system are the eight variables, $\tilde{K}_t$, $\tilde{M}_t$, $\tilde{P}_t$, $\tilde{r}_t$, $\tilde{w}_t$, $\tilde{C}_t$, $\tilde{Y}_t$, $\tilde{H}_t$, and the two stochastic shock variables, $\tilde{\lambda}_t$ and $\tilde{g}_t$. The log-linear version of the model, found using Uhlig's method, is given in the eight equations,

$$0 = \tilde{C}_t + \left[\frac{\beta}{\bar{g}} + \frac{D\bar{C}}{M/P} \right] \tilde{P}_t - \frac{\beta}{\bar{g}} E_t \tilde{C}_{t+1} - \frac{\beta}{\bar{g}} E_t \tilde{P}_{t+1} - \frac{D\bar{C}}{M/P} \tilde{M}_t,$$

$$0 = \tilde{w}_t + \beta \bar{r} E_t \tilde{r}_{t+1} - \beta \left[\bar{r} + (1-\delta) \right] E_t \tilde{w}_{t+1},$$

$$0 = \tilde{w}_t - \tilde{C}_t,$$

$$0 = \bar{C}\tilde{C}_t + \bar{K}\tilde{K}_{t+1} - \bar{w}\bar{H}\tilde{w}_t - \bar{w}\bar{H}\tilde{H}_t - \bar{r}\bar{K}\tilde{r}_t - \left[\bar{r} + (1-\delta) \right] \bar{K}\tilde{K}_t, \qquad (9.8)$$

$$0 = \tilde{Y}_t - \tilde{\lambda}_t - \theta \tilde{K}_t - (1 - \theta)\tilde{H}_t,$$

$$0 = \tilde{r}_t - \tilde{\lambda}_t - (\theta - 1)\, \tilde{K}_t - (1 - \theta)\tilde{H}_t,$$

$$0 = \tilde{w}_t - \tilde{\lambda}_t - \theta \tilde{K}_t + \theta \tilde{H}_t,$$

$$0 = \tilde{M}_t - \tilde{g}_t - \tilde{M}_{t-1}. \tag{9.9}$$

In addition, we have the two processes for the log-linear form of the stochastic variables,

$$\tilde{\lambda}_t = \gamma \tilde{\lambda}_{t-1} + \varepsilon_t^\lambda$$

and

$$\tilde{g}_t = \gamma \tilde{g}_{t-1} + \varepsilon_t^g.^2$$

The system can be written in terms of three "state" variables,[3] $x_t = [\tilde{K}_{t+1}, \tilde{M}_t, \tilde{P}_t]$, the five "jump" variables, $y_t = [\tilde{r}_t, \tilde{w}_t, \tilde{C}_t, \tilde{Y}_t, \tilde{H}_t]$, and the stochastic variables, $z_t = [\tilde{\lambda}_t, \tilde{g}_t]$, as

$$0 = Ax_t + Bx_{t-1} + Cy_t + Dz_t,$$

$$0 = E_t \left[Fx_{t+1} + Gx_t + Hx_{t-1} + Jy_{t+1} + Ky_t + Lz_{t+1} + Mz_t \right],$$

$$z_{t+1} = Nz_t + \varepsilon_{t+1},$$

where

$$A = \begin{bmatrix} 0 & 0 & 0 \\ \bar{K} & 0 & 0 \\ 0 & 0 & 0 \\ 0 & 0 & 0 \\ 0 & 0 & 0 \end{bmatrix},$$

$$B = \begin{bmatrix} 0 & 0 & 0 \\ -[\bar{r} + (1 - \delta)]\,\bar{K} & 0 & 0 \\ -\theta & 0 & 0 \\ (1 - \theta) & 0 & 0 \\ -\theta & 0 & 0 \end{bmatrix},$$

2. Recall that $\ln g_t = (1 - \pi) \ln \bar{g} + \pi \ln g_{t-1} + \varepsilon_t^g$ can be written as $\ln g_t - \ln \bar{g} = \pi \left[\ln g_{t-1} - \ln \bar{g} \right] + \varepsilon_t^g$, which is equal to $\tilde{g}_t = \gamma \tilde{g}_{t-1} + \varepsilon_t^g$ by the definition of $\tilde{g}_t$.

3. As we will see below, $\tilde{P}_t$ is not really a state variable.

$$
C = \begin{bmatrix}
0 & 1 & -1 & 0 & 0 \\
-\bar{r}\bar{K} & -\bar{w}\bar{H} & \bar{C} & 0 & -\bar{w}\bar{H} \\
0 & 0 & 0 & 1 & -(1-\theta) \\
1 & 0 & 0 & 0 & -(1-\theta) \\
0 & 1 & 0 & 0 & \theta
\end{bmatrix},
$$

$$
D = \begin{bmatrix}
0 & 0 \\
0 & 0 \\
-1 & 0 \\
-1 & 0 \\
-1 & 0
\end{bmatrix},
$$

$$
F = \begin{bmatrix}
0 & 0 & -\frac{\beta}{g} \\
0 & 0 & 0 \\
0 & 0 & 0
\end{bmatrix},
$$

$$
G = \begin{bmatrix}
0 & -\frac{D\bar{C}}{M/P} & \frac{\beta}{g} + \frac{D\bar{C}}{M/P} \\
0 & 0 & 0 \\
0 & 1 & 0
\end{bmatrix},
$$

$$
H = \begin{bmatrix}
0 & 0 & 0 \\
0 & 0 & 0 \\
0 & -1 & 0
\end{bmatrix},
$$

$$
J = \begin{bmatrix}
0 & 0 & -\frac{\beta}{g} & 0 & 0 \\
\beta\bar{r} & -\beta\left[\bar{r} + (1-\delta)\right] & 0 & 0 & 0 \\
0 & 0 & 0 & 0 & 0
\end{bmatrix},
$$

$$
K = \begin{bmatrix}
0 & 0 & 1 & 0 & 0 \\
0 & 1 & 0 & 0 & 0 \\
0 & 0 & 0 & 0 & 0
\end{bmatrix},
$$

$$
L = \begin{bmatrix}
0 & 0 \\
0 & 0 \\
0 & 0
\end{bmatrix},
$$

$$
M = \begin{bmatrix}
0 & 0 \\
0 & 0 \\
0 & -1
\end{bmatrix},
$$

and

$$N = \begin{bmatrix} \gamma & 0 \\ 0 & \pi \end{bmatrix}.$$

Solving the above system gives matrix policy equations of the form

$$x_{t+1} = Px_t + Qz_t$$

and

$$y_t = Rx_t + Sz_t.$$

When $\bar{g} = 1$, the P, Q, R, and S matrices are

$$P = \begin{bmatrix} 0.9418 & 0 & 0 \\ 0 & 1 & 0 \\ -0.5316 & 1 & 0 \end{bmatrix},$$

$$Q = \begin{bmatrix} 0.1552 & 0 \\ 0 & 1 \\ -0.4703 & 1.6648 \end{bmatrix},$$

$$R = \begin{bmatrix} -0.9450 & 0 & 0 \\ 0.5316 & 0 & 0 \\ 0.5316 & 0 & 0 \\ 0.0550 & 0 & 0 \\ -0.4766 & 0 & 0 \end{bmatrix},$$

and

$$S = \begin{bmatrix} 1.9417 & 0 \\ 0.4703 & 0 \\ 0.4703 & 0 \\ 1.9417 & 0 \\ 1.4715 & 0 \end{bmatrix}.$$

The policy matrices show a pair of interesting characteristics of the model. First, prices are not really a state variable and, for that reason, the coefficients on prices in the matrices P and R are all zero. Second, the real variables of the economy are not affected by money growth shocks in this model. The only variables that respond to the money growth shocks are M and P. Interestingly, they do not respond in exactly the same way. As was shown earlier, equation 9.5, the current price level is determined by expected future growth in the money

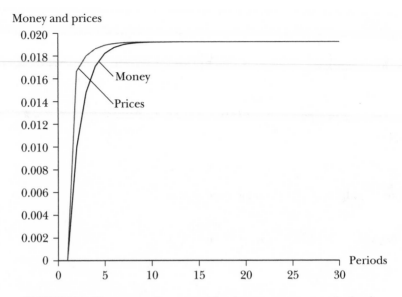

FIGURE 9.1 Response of money and prices to money growth shock

supply. A single shock to the gross growth rate of money continues to cause the money supply to grow for some time. This occurs because of the π parameter on the lagged shock in the money stock growth equation. Prices take this into account and adjust immediately, although not completely because of the β discount factor, to the single shock. Figure 9.1 shows the response functions for the money supply and for forward-looking prices in response to a single shock (impulse) to the growth rate of money. Because prices adjust much more rapidly than does the money stock, real balances decline in response to a money supply growth shock.

The responses of the real variables to a technology shock are the same in this model as they have been in previous models. Figure 9.2 shows these responses. Compare this figure to the Cooley-Hansen model in Figure 8.2. They are identical. The real sides of these two economies are exactly the same.

9.4 SEIGNIORAGE

Consider the same model as above but where the government finances a stochastic real expenditure g_t by issuing new money in period t. The budget constraint for the government is

$$g_t = \widehat{g}_t \bar{g} = \frac{M_t - M_{t-1}}{P_t}.$$

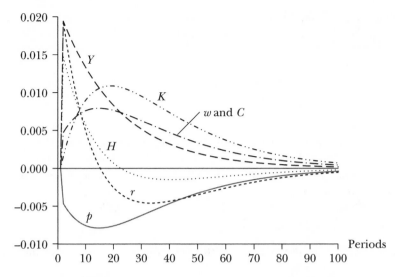

FIGURE 9.2　Responses to a .01 impulse in technology

As in the chapter on cash-in-advance money, we let $\bar{g}$ be the average government deficit financed with money issue and the random variable $\widehat{g}_t$ follows the process

$$\ln \widehat{g}_t = \pi \ln \widehat{g}_{t-1} + \varepsilon_t^g,$$

where $\varepsilon_t^g \sim N(0, \sigma_g)$, with σ_g as the standard error.[4] Define φ_t as the gross growth rate of money that is required to finance the budget deficit in period t. With this definition, $M_t = \varphi_t M_{t-1}$, and

$$g_t = \widehat{g}_t \bar{g} = \frac{(\varphi_t - 1) M_{t-1}}{P_t} = \frac{(\varphi_t - 1)}{\varphi_t} \frac{M_t}{P_t}.$$

This equation will be useful for finding the expression for a stationary state.

The only other change, compared to the previous model, is in the household flow budget constraint, equation 9.1. Households no longer receive direct transfers of money from the government. Instead, the flow of new money into the economy occurs through government purchases of goods. These purchases compete with those of the households. An important assumption here

---

4. We are committing something of a notational sin here. Before, g_t was the gross growth rate of money; here it stands for real government consumption and is related to the growth rate of money, φ_t, through the government's budget constraint.

is that the government's consumption of goods does not enter directly into household utility. With these considerations, household i's flow budget constraint is

$$c_t^i + k_{t+1}^i + \frac{m_t^i}{P_t} = w_t h_t^i + r_t k_t^i + (1 - \delta) k_t^i + \frac{m_{t-1}^i}{P_t}.$$

The first-order conditions for the household are the same as in the earlier version of the money in the utility function model. The only differences in the model are the change in the household budget constraint and in the government's budget constraint. The extra equation, the government's budget constraint, relates money supply growth to government consumption.

9.4.1 The Full Model

The full model for the economy with seigniorage, after the aggregation has been done, is given by

$$\frac{1}{C_t} = \beta E_t \frac{P_t}{C_{t+1} P_{t+1}} + \frac{D P_t}{M_t},$$

$$\frac{1}{w_t} = \beta E_t \frac{1}{w_{t+1}} \left[r_{t+1} + (1 - \delta) \right],$$

$$w_t = -B C_t,$$

$$C_t + K_{t+1} + \frac{M_t}{P_t} = w_t H_t + r_t K_t + (1 - \delta) K_t + \frac{M_{t-1}}{P_t},$$

$$Y_t = \lambda_t K_t^\theta H_t^{1-\theta},$$

$$r_t = \theta \lambda_t K_t^{\theta-1} H_t^{1-\theta},$$

$$w_t = (1 - \theta) \lambda_t K_t^\theta H_t^{-\theta},$$

$$\widehat{g_t} \bar{g} = \frac{M_t - M_{t-1}}{P_t}.$$

This model is the same as the first except for the fourth equation, which does not contain the transfers of money from the government, and the last equation, which can be thought of as either the government's budget constraint or the seigniorage equation.

9.4.2 Stationary States

Stationary states are defined by constant government deficit financed by a constant growth rate of money, constant values for the rest of the real variables, and constant real balances, M_t/P_t. Given an average government deficit, $\bar{g}$, the government budget constraint can be written as

$$\bar{g} = \left(1 - \frac{1}{\bar{\varphi}}\right) \overline{M/P},$$

where, as before, a bar over a variable is its stationary state value. In a stationary state, the household flow budget constraint is

$$\bar{C} + \left[1 - \frac{1}{\bar{\varphi}}\right] \overline{M/P} = \bar{w}H + (\bar{r} - \delta)\,\bar{K}.$$

This flow budget constraint implies the feasibility constraint

$$\bar{C} + \bar{g} + \delta\bar{K} = \bar{Y}$$

that output in the stationary states goes to consumption, to government consumption, and to replace the depreciated capital stock.

As before, we find that rentals, wages, and consumption are independent of the rate of growth of the money supply. In particular,

$$\bar{r} = \frac{1}{\beta} - (1 - \delta),$$

$$\bar{w} = (1 - \theta) \left[\frac{\theta}{\bar{r}}\right]^{\frac{\theta}{1-\theta}},$$

and

$$\bar{C} = -\frac{\bar{w}}{B}.$$

From the first-order condition for money holdings, one gets

$$\overline{M/P} = D \frac{\bar{\varphi}\bar{C}}{\bar{\varphi} - \beta},$$

and from the government budget constraint

$$\bar{g} = \left(1 - \frac{1}{\bar{\varphi}}\right) D \frac{\bar{\varphi}\bar{C}}{\bar{\varphi} - \beta} = \frac{(\bar{\varphi} - 1)\,D}{\bar{\varphi} - \beta}\bar{C}.$$

From the factor market conditions,

$$\bar{Y} = \left[\frac{(1 - \theta)\bar{r}}{\theta\bar{w}}\right]^{1-\theta}\bar{K}.$$

Putting these into the feasibility constraint gives

$$\left[1 + \frac{(\bar{\varphi} - 1)\, D}{\bar{\varphi} - \beta}\right] \bar{C} = \left(\left[\frac{(1-\theta)\bar{r}}{\theta \bar{w}}\right]^{1-\theta} - \delta\right) \bar{K},$$

or

$$\bar{K} = \frac{\left[1 + \frac{(\bar{\varphi}-1)D}{\bar{\varphi}-\beta}\right]}{\left[\frac{(1-\theta)\bar{r}}{\theta\bar{w}}\right]^{1-\theta} - \delta} \bar{C}.$$

Once $\bar{K}$ is determined, from the equilibrium condition for the labor market, one gets

$$\bar{H} = \left(\frac{1-\theta}{\bar{w}}\right)^{\frac{1}{\theta}} \bar{K},$$

and from the production function,

$$\bar{Y} = \bar{K}^\theta \bar{H}^{1-\theta}.$$

For our standard economy, with $D = .01$, the Bailey curve, the relationship between the stationary state money growth rate (which equals the inflation rate in stationary states) and seigniorage, is shown in Figure 9.3. The stationary state values of variables for this economy at annual inflation rates of 0 percent, 10 percent, 100 percent, and 400 percent are given in Table 9.2.

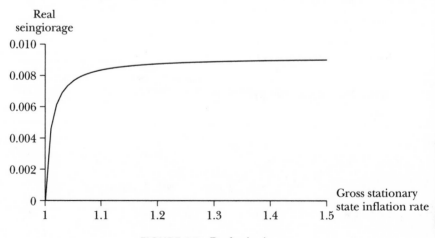

FIGURE 9.3   Real seigniorage

The structure of the model makes consumption constant in stationary states. The rental on capital is determined by the "Fisher" equation. The factor market equations then give us the real wage (since $\bar{r}$ determines the capital-labor ratio). Consumption is determined by the real wage. All three of these variables were determined without any information about the rate of money creation, so they are independent of the rate of money growth. Since consumption is the same in every stationary state, higher seigniorage must come from higher output (which requires more labor and capital at fixed wage-rental ratios). Therefore, seigniorage is generated by higher levels of capital stock and of hours worked that produce additional output to cover the seigniorage and the additional depreciation that must be replaced to be in a stationary state with higher capital stock.

9.4.3   Log Linearization

The log-linear version of this model is the same as that of the previous except for three changes. The household flow budget constraint, equation 9.8, is replaced by

$$0 = \bar{C}\tilde{C}_t + \bar{K}\tilde{K}_{t+1} + \overline{M/P}\tilde{M}_t - \overline{M/P}\left(1 - \frac{1}{\bar{\varphi}}\right)\tilde{P}_t$$

$$- \bar{w}\bar{H}\tilde{w}_t - \bar{w}\bar{H}\tilde{H}_t - \bar{r}\bar{K}\tilde{r}_t - [\bar{r} + (1-\delta)]\bar{K}\tilde{K}_t - \frac{\overline{M/P}}{\bar{\varphi}}\tilde{M}_{t-1}.$$

One replaces the money growth rule, equation 9.9, with the seigniorage equation

Table 9.2   Stationary states for different inflation rates

Annual inflation	0%	10%	100%	400%
Corresponding $\bar{\varphi}$	1	1.024	1.19	1.41
Rental	0.0351	0.0351	0.0351	0.0351
Wages	2.3706	2.3706	2.3706	2.3706
Consumption	0.9187	0.9187	0.9187	0.9187
Real balances $=\overline{M/P}$	0.9187	0.2767	0.0547	0.0308
Output	1.2354	1.2441	1.2472	1.2475
Capital	12.6707	12.7601	12.7910	12.7943
Hours worked	0.3335	0.3359	0.3367	0.3368
Seigniorage = $\bar{g}$	0	0.0065	0.0087	0.0090

$$0 = \bar{g}\tilde{g}_t + \overline{M/P}\left(1 - \frac{1}{\bar{\varphi}}\right)\tilde{P}_t - \overline{M/P}\tilde{M}_t + \frac{\overline{M/P}}{\bar{\varphi}}\tilde{M}_{t-1},$$

where $\tilde{g}_t \equiv \ln \hat{g}_t - \ln 1 = \ln \hat{g}_t$ is the log of the shock to the government deficit that is financed by seigniorage. The stationary state value of $\hat{g}_t$ is 1.

Defining x_t, y_t, and z_t as before, so $x_t = [\tilde{K}_{t+1}, \tilde{M}_t, \tilde{P}_t]$, $y_t = [\tilde{r}_t, \tilde{w}_t, \tilde{C}_t, \tilde{Y}_t, \tilde{H}_t]$, and $z_t = [\tilde{\lambda}_t, \tilde{g}_t]$, one can write the model in matrix form,

$$0 = Ax_t + Bx_{t-1} + Cy_t + Dz_t,$$

$$0 = E_t\left[Fx_{t+1} + Gx_t + Hx_{t-1} + Jy_{t+1} + Ky_t + Lz_{t+1} + Mz_t\right],$$

$$z_{t+1} = Nz_t + \varepsilon_{t+1},$$

where

$$A = \begin{bmatrix} 0 & 0 & 0 \\ \bar{K} & \overline{M/P} & -\overline{M/P}\left(1 - \frac{1}{\bar{\varphi}}\right) \\ 0 & 0 & 0 \\ 0 & 0 & 0 \\ 0 & 0 & 0 \end{bmatrix},$$

$$B = \begin{bmatrix} 0 & 0 & 0 \\ -\left[\bar{r} + (1-\delta)\right]\bar{K} & -\frac{\overline{M/P}}{\bar{\varphi}} & 0 \\ -\theta & 0 & 0 \\ (1-\theta) & 0 & 0 \\ -\theta & 0 & 0 \end{bmatrix},$$

$$C = \begin{bmatrix} 0 & 1 & -1 & 0 & 0 \\ -\bar{r}\bar{K} & -\bar{w}\bar{H} & \bar{C} & 0 & -\bar{w}\bar{H} \\ 0 & 0 & 0 & 1 & -(1-\theta) \\ 1 & 0 & 0 & 0 & -(1-\theta) \\ 0 & 1 & 0 & 0 & \theta \end{bmatrix},$$

$$D = \begin{bmatrix} 0 & 0 \\ 0 & 0 \\ -1 & 0 \\ -1 & 0 \\ -1 & 0 \end{bmatrix},$$

$$F = \begin{bmatrix} 0 & 0 & -\frac{\beta}{\varphi} \\ 0 & 0 & 0 \\ 0 & 0 & 0 \end{bmatrix},$$

$$G = \begin{bmatrix} 0 & -\frac{D\bar{C}}{M/P} & \frac{\beta}{\varphi} + \frac{D\bar{C}}{M/P} \\ 0 & 0 & 0 \\ 0 & -\overline{M/P} & \left[1 - \frac{1}{\varphi}\right]\overline{M/P} \end{bmatrix},$$

$$H = \begin{bmatrix} 0 & 0 & 0 \\ 0 & 0 & 0 \\ 0 & \frac{\overline{M/P}}{\varphi} & 0 \end{bmatrix},$$

$$J = \begin{bmatrix} 0 & 0 & -\frac{\beta}{\varphi} & 0 & 0 \\ \beta\bar{r} & -\beta\left[\bar{r} + (1-\delta)\right] & 0 & 0 & 0 \\ 0 & 0 & 0 & 0 & 0 \end{bmatrix},$$

$$K = \begin{bmatrix} 0 & 0 & 1 & 0 & 0 \\ 0 & 1 & 0 & 0 & 0 \\ 0 & 0 & 0 & 0 & 0 \end{bmatrix},$$

$$L = \begin{bmatrix} 0 & 0 \\ 0 & 0 \\ 0 & 0 \end{bmatrix},$$

$$M = \begin{bmatrix} 0 & 0 \\ 0 & 0 \\ 0 & \bar{g} \end{bmatrix},$$

and

$$N = \begin{bmatrix} \gamma & 0 \\ 0 & \pi \end{bmatrix}.$$

As before, the solution is a set of policy matrices of the form

$$x_{t+1} = Px_t + Qz_t$$

and

$$y_t = Rx_t + Sz_t.$$

For the policy matrices, it matters what the stationary state is. In the case where $\bar{\varphi} = 1$, there is no seigniorage in the stationary state and the P, Q, R, and S matrices are

$$
P = \begin{bmatrix} 0.9418 & 0 & 0 \\ 0 & 1 & 0 \\ -0.5316 & 1 & 0 \end{bmatrix},
$$

$$
Q = \begin{bmatrix} 0.1552 & 0 \\ 0 & 0 \\ -0.4703 & 0 \end{bmatrix},
$$

$$
R = \begin{bmatrix} -0.9450 & 0 & 0 \\ 0.5316 & 0 & 0 \\ 0.5316 & 0 & 0 \\ 0.0550 & 0 & 0 \\ -0.4766 & 0 & 0 \end{bmatrix},
$$

and

$$
S = \begin{bmatrix} 1.9417 & 0 \\ 0.4703 & 0 \\ 0.4703 & 0 \\ 1.9417 & 0 \\ 1.4715 & 0 \end{bmatrix}.
$$

Around a stationary state with no seigniorage, the economy is completely neutral to seigniorage shocks.

In the case where $\bar{\varphi} = 1.19$, these matrices are

$$
P = \begin{bmatrix} 0.9418 & 0 & 0 \\ -0.3243 & 1 & 0 \\ -2.0213 & 1 & 0 \end{bmatrix},
$$

$$
Q = \begin{bmatrix} 0.1547 & -0.0005 \\ -0.9330 & 0.2178 \\ -5.8433 & 0.3644 \end{bmatrix},
$$

$$R = \begin{bmatrix} -0.9477 & 0 & 0 \\ 0.5331 & 0 & 0 \\ 0.5331 & 0 & 0 \\ 0.0523 & 0 & 0 \\ -0.4807 & 0 & 0 \end{bmatrix},$$

and

$$S = \begin{bmatrix} 1.9359 & 0.0011 \\ 0.4735 & -0.0006 \\ 0.4735 & -0.0006 \\ 1.9359 & 0.0011 \\ 1.4624 & 0.0017 \end{bmatrix}.$$

The response function for a seigniorage impulse when $\bar{\varphi} = 1$ is flat except for money and prices. For the case where $\bar{\varphi} = 1.19$, the response of the real variables to a seigniorage shock is shown in Figure 9.4. While the responses are small (the shock is .01), real variables do respond to seigniorage shocks through their effects on government expenditures. The persistence observed in the figure comes from the fact that the coefficient on one period lagged

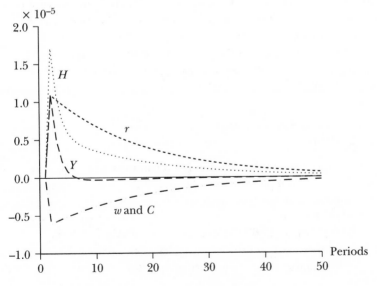

FIGURE 9.4 Response to seigniorage shock, $\bar{\varphi} = 1.19$

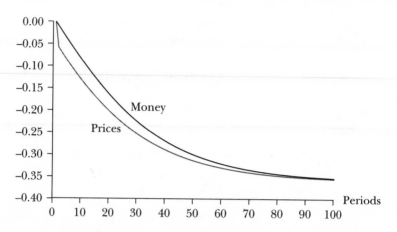

FIGURE 9.5   Responses of money and prices to a technology shock when seignior-age is collected in the stationary state, $\bar{\varphi} = 1.19$

government expenditure is $\pi = .48$ in the stochastic process for government expenditures financed by seigniorage.

Another interesting characteristic of this model is how prices and money respond to a technology shock in the case where the stationary state is one with seigniorage. The responses of money and prices to a .01 technology shock when $\bar{\varphi} = 1.19$ are shown in Figure 9.5. Notice how both money and prices fall to a new level (although the ratio returns to the stationary state value). As before, prices fall faster than does money. What happens here is that the technology shock causes prices to fall (relative to the stationary state inflation) and this means that the government needs to issue less money to cover the constant expenditures that it is purchasing with seigniorage. Both money and prices eventually have the same relative change, and their ratio returns to the stationary state value.

9.5   REPRISE

Putting money in the utility function is a second way of getting money into a macro model. It is simple, and the idea that holding real balances gives util-ity (possibly by reducing transactions costs) is appealing to many. It creates a demand for money in the most basic way possible; money gives utility. The basic model produces both a stationary state and a dynamic superneutrality of money with respect to the real variables of the system. The dynamic su-perneutrality persists even when there is a positive inflation in the stationary state.

Putting seigniorage into the model is quite straightforward. With seigniorage, dynamic superneutrality depends on the stationary state. In cases where there is no stationary state financing of government expenditures by seigniorage, the log-linear model displayes dynamic neutrality. When the stationary state is one where stationary state seigniorage financing is positive, then monetary shocks (which are equivalent to changes in the government deficit financed by seigniorage) are not neutral.

More on models with money in the utility function can be found in Sargent [72] and Blanchard and Fischer [13]. A careful critique of money in the utility function models can be found in Karaken and Wallace [49].

Staggered Pricing Model

In general, models of the type we have been constructing adjust too fast to shocks and return too quickly to stationary states, at least when compared to the evidence in the data. This is especially true with respect to prices. We want to add a mechanism that will slow up the return of prices to their stationary state and increase the temporal persistence of the effects of a shock. To do this, we use a model of Calvo [19] in which only a randomly chosen fraction of the firms are allowed to adjust their prices in any given period.

The model is similar to the cash-in-advance model, but we change the production sector so that firms have some market power that they can exploit to let them charge prices higher than their marginal costs. This is done by separating the production sector into two parts, one that makes differentiated intermediate goods and a second, competitive, final goods sector that bundles these intermediate goods into a final good that is used for consumption and investment. Firms in the intermediate goods sector are allowed to choose prices, but not every period. Each period, a randomly and independently chosen fraction $(1 - \rho)$ of the intermediate goods firms can set their prices. The rest of the intermediate goods sector firms either keep the price from the last fixing or are able to adjust according to a rule of thumb (such as adjusting for average or lagged inflation, depending on the model). This kind of pricing rule is called *staggered pricing*.

The staggered pricing rule of Calvo is not the only one in use. Taylor [84] has recommended models where firms get to optimize their prices every N periods, where the value of N is a given for the economy. This means that a fraction, $1/N$, of the firms get to optimize each period and all firms know that they will get to optimize every N period.

The intermediate goods are bundled into a final good by a competitive final goods firm. To keep things as simple as possible, we assume that this firm can do this bundling costlessly, in the sense that it uses neither labor nor capital. It is the nature of the bundling function, one of constant elasticity of substitution, that gives the intermediate goods firms their market power.

The model in which we imbed intermediate goods firms with a staggered pricing rule is a simple cash-in-advance model. Families are identical and need to use money to make their consumption purchases. One minor adaptation of the family's budget constraint is necessary: since firms have and exploit market power, they will make excess profits. These profits are distributed as lump sum dividend payments to the families, who are all assumed to be equal shareholders in the firms.

Models of staggered pricing are sometimes used to justify equations such as the Phillips curve that occur in Keynesian type models. Galí [44] and Galí, Gertler, and López-Salido [45] are examples of this approach. Although this is a useful characteristic of these models, it is not one that we particularly emphasize here, and we do not put our model into a traditional Keynesian context. Instead, we maintain the structure of earlier chapters, adding this feature of staggered pricing. Our hope is to show how adding staggered pricing can make our original model richer and better able to match data.

10.1 THE BASIC MODEL

We need to consider separately the household and firm decisions. The families behave as before, but the intermediate goods firms will be able to exploit their market power, so the outcome of the intermediate goods firms optimization will change the way prices behave and the relationship between marginal costs and prices. We begin with the problem of the final goods firm and then proceed to that of the intermediate goods firms since this is the new element of this chapter. We then review the problem of the family and build the complete model.

10.1.1 The Final Goods Firms

We assume that there is a continuum of intermediate firms (of unit mass indexed by $k \in [0, 1]$) and that each firm produces an intermediate good that is different from that of other firms. The continuum of intermediate goods in period t, $Y_t(k)$, $k \in [0, 1]$, gets bundled by a final goods firm, or by a group of final goods firms, that behaves competitively, into the time t final goods, Y_t. The final goods production technology (rule, if one wishes to think of it that way) is

$$Y_t = \left[\int_0^1 Y_t(k)^{\frac{\psi-1}{\psi}} dk \right]^{\frac{\psi}{\psi-1}}$$

for $\psi > 1$. This type of production technology is called a constant elasticity of substitution (CES) bundler. Recall the CES subutility function, $C_t^{1-\eta} / (1-\eta)$, where $1/\eta$ was the elasticity of substitution. Here, $(\psi - 1)/\psi = 1 - 1/\psi$, so that ψ is the elasticity of substitution in production. The integral is raised to the power $\psi/(\psi - 1)$ to make the production function display constant returns to scale.

A profit-maximizing final goods firm chooses to maximize

$$\text{profits}_t = P_t Y_t - \int_0^1 P_t(k) Y_t(k) dk,$$

subject to the above production technology. Of course, since the firm is competitive, profits will end up being equal to zero. The problem the final goods firms solve in period t is

$$\max_{\{Y_t(k)\}} P_t \left[\int_0^1 Y_t(k)^{\frac{\psi-1}{\psi}} dk \right]^{\frac{\psi}{\psi-1}} - \int_0^1 P_t(k) Y_t(k) dk,$$

and this results in the first-order condition of

$$P_t \left[\int_0^1 Y_t(k)^{\frac{\psi-1}{\psi}} dk \right]^{\frac{1}{\psi-1}} Y_t(k)^{\frac{-1}{\psi}} = P_t(k),$$

which simplifies to a demand function for good k of

$$Y_t(k) = Y_t \left(\frac{P_t}{P_t(k)} \right)^{\psi}. \tag{10.1}$$

Putting this demand for sector k's output into the bundler function gives

$$Y_t = \left[\int_0^1 \left[Y_t \left(\frac{P_t}{P_t(k)} \right)^{\psi} \right]^{\frac{\psi-1}{\psi}} dk \right]^{\frac{\psi}{\psi-1}} = Y_t \left[\int_0^1 \left(\frac{P_t}{P_t(k)} \right)^{\psi-1} dk \right]^{\frac{\psi}{\psi-1}},$$

which can be written as

$$\frac{1}{P_t} = \left[\int_0^1 \left(\frac{1}{P_t(k)} \right)^{\psi-1} dk \right]^{\frac{1}{\psi-1}},$$

or as a final goods pricing rule of

$$P_t = \left[\int_0^1 P_t(k)^{1-\psi} dk \right]^{\frac{1}{1-\psi}}. \tag{10.2}$$

10.1.2   The Intermediate Goods Firms

Intermediate goods firms maximize the market value of the firm subject to the demand for their output by the final goods firm. Their demand curve is given above in equation 10.1. Intermediate goods firms get to choose how much to produce in every period, but following a Calvo rule (Calvo [19]) they do not get to choose the price of their good every period. In each period t, a fraction $0 < 1 - \rho < 1$ of firms are randomly selected and are permitted to choose their price for period t, $P_t^*(k)$.

The rest of the firms (the ρ fraction of the firms who are not allowed to choose their prices optimally) follow a rule of thumb for updating their prices. Different rules of thumb are possible, depending on the assumptions of the model. We give three of the many possible updating schemes for a firm k that was *not* selected as a part of the fraction ρ that can choose prices optimally in period t. These three commonly used rules are: 1) keeping prices the same as the last updating,

$$P_t(k) = P_{t-1}(k),$$

2) updating prices by a stationary state gross inflation rate $\bar{\pi}$,

$$P_t(k) = \bar{\pi} P_{t-1}(k),$$

or 3) updating prices by the one-period lagged realized gross inflation rate, $\pi_{t-1} = P_{t-1}/P_{t-2}$,

$$P_t(k) = \pi_{t-1} P_{t-1}(k).$$

Which rule is chosen to model those firms that cannot optimally choose their prices has important consequences on the dynamics of the model. For most of this chapter, we will assume that for the ρ fraction of the firms who cannot adjust their prices, their prices remain at the price of the last fixing, so that for these firms,

$$P_t(k) = P_{t-1}(k).$$

The markets for both labor and capital are perfectly competitive, so each infinitesimally small intermediate goods firm takes wages and rentals as given.

The production function for intermediate goods firm k is

$$Y_t(k) = \lambda_t K_t^\theta(k) H_t^{1-\theta}(k),$$

where all firms are subject to the same technology shock, λ_t. Each firm has a ρ probability that it will keep the price of the period before and a $1 - \rho$ probability that it will be able to choose its price optimally. Once a price is fixed in period t, there is a probability ρ that this price will continue into period $t + 1$, a probability ρ^2 that this price will continue into period $t + 2$, and so on. The intermediate goods firm takes into account these probabilities when it chooses the price it will set in a period when it can set its price.

An intermediate goods firm, k, which can choose prices in period t, chooses the price, $P_t^*(k)$, to maximize[1]

$$E_t \sum_{i=0}^{\infty} \beta^i \rho^i \left[P_t^*(k) Y_{t+i} \left(\frac{P_{t+i}}{P_t^*(k)} \right)^\psi - P_{t+i} r_{t+i} K_{t+i}(k) - P_{t+i} w_{t+i} H_{t+i}(k) \right],$$

(10.3)

subject to the production technology

$$Y_{t+i} \left(\frac{P_{t+i}}{P_t^*(k)} \right)^\psi = \lambda_{t+i} K_{t+i}^\theta(k) H_{t+i}^{1-\theta}(k).$$

Notice that the production restiction says that, in each period, the firm will produce all of its good that is demanded at the current price.

Expression 10.3 is *not* the market value of the firm. It is the discounted present value of profits of the firms during the period over which the price $P_t^*(k)$ is in effect. The market value of the firm includes the expected profits generated when the firm can reset its prices in the future times the probability that it can reset prices. However, the price that the firm will choose in some future period $t + n$ depends on the realization of the economy from period t to period $t + n$ and the expectations about the future with information available in period $t + n$. The price that the firm will choose in period $t + n$ is independent of the price it chooses today, so future price fixings are not part of today's maximization problem. After these are removed, what remains is the expected profits in each future period under which the price $P_t^*(k)$ continues to hold, weighed by the probability that the firm will still have that

---

1. Notice how this maximization problem would change with a Taylor staggered pricing rule (Taylor [84]). The sum would only be for the N periods during which the firm cannot optimize its prices. In addition, the discount factor would be simply β^i since the probability of changing prices, ρ, is no longer relevant.

price. Following a strategy of maximizing expression 10.3 each time the firm has the opportunity to choose prices will cause the firm to maximize its market value.

A firm that is maximizing the above expression is simultaneously minimizing, in each period, total costs. These are not necessarily the same problem, but a firm that maximizes expression 10.3 will also have to be minimizing costs in each period. We can find the conditions for cost minimization and replace the costs in expression 10.3. The real cost minimization problem for intermediate goods firm k in period $t + i$ is

$$\min_{K_{t+i}(k), H_{t+i}(k)} r_{t+i} K_{t+i}(k) + w_{t+i} H_{t+i}(k),$$

subject to the production technology

$$Y_{t+i}(k) = \lambda_{t+i} K_{t+i}^{\theta}(k) H_{t+i}^{1-\theta}(k).$$

Eliminating the Lagrangian multiplier from the two first-order conditions that come from this minimization results in the expression

$$\frac{(1 - \theta) r_{t+i}}{\theta w_{t+i}} = \frac{H_{t+i}(k)}{K_{t+i}(k)}.$$

This is one of the equations that will be used to resolve the model. The other that comes from the minimization problem is the production function. Combining these two equations, one can arrive at firm k's demand for labor,

$$H_{t+i}(k) = \frac{Y_{t+i}(k)}{\lambda_{t+i}} \left[\frac{r_{t+i}(1 - \theta)}{w_{t+i}\theta} \right]^{\theta},$$

and its demand for capital,

$$K_{t+i}(k) = \frac{Y_{t+i}(k)}{\lambda_{t+i}} \left[\frac{r_{t+i}(1 - \theta)}{w_{t+i}\theta} \right]^{\theta - 1}.$$

Substituting these factor demands into the cost equation gives

$$r_{t+i} \frac{Y_{t+i}(k)}{\lambda_{t+i}} \left[\frac{r_{t+i}(1 - \theta)}{w_{t+i}\theta} \right]^{\theta - 1} + w_{t+i} \frac{Y_{t+i}(k)}{\lambda_{t+i}} \left[\frac{r_{t+i}(1 - \theta)}{w_{t+i}\theta} \right]^{\theta},$$

which can be written as the expression for the real costs of intermediate goods firm k when it produces the quantity of goods $Y_{t+i}(k)$,

$$\frac{w_{t+i}}{(1-\theta)\lambda_{t+i}} \left[\frac{r_{t+i}(1-\theta)}{w_{t+i}\theta} \right]^{\theta} Y_{t+i}(k).$$

Since in any period, all firms face the same wages, rentals, and technology, the period $t+i$ real marginal unit costs are the same for all firms and are equal to

$$MC_{t+i} = \frac{w_{t+i}}{(1-\theta)\lambda_{t+i}} \left[\frac{r_{t+i}(1-\theta)}{w_{t+i}\theta} \right]^{\theta}.$$

Total costs for firm k can be substituted into expression 10.3. The result is that an intermediate goods firm k, which can set its price in period t, wants to solve

$$\max_{P_t^*(k)} E_t \sum_{i=0}^{\infty} (\beta\rho)^i \left[P_t^*(k) Y_{t+i} \left(\frac{P_{t+i}}{P_t^*(k)} \right)^{\psi} \right.$$

$$\left. - P_{t+i} \frac{w_{t+i}}{(1-\theta)\lambda_{t+i}} \left[\frac{r_{t+i}(1-\theta)}{w_{t+i}\theta} \right]^{\theta} Y_{t+i} \left(\frac{P_{t+i}}{P_t^*(k)} \right)^{\psi} \right], \qquad (10.4)$$

or

$$\max_{P_t^*(k)} E_t \sum_{i=0}^{\infty} (\beta\rho)^i Y_{t+i} \left(\frac{P_{t+i}}{P_t^*(k)} \right)^{\psi} \left[P_t^*(k) - \frac{P_{t+i}w_{t+i}}{(1-\theta)\lambda_{t+i}} \left[\frac{r_{t+i}(1-\theta)}{w_{t+i}\theta} \right]^{\theta} \right].$$

The first-order condition for this problem is

$$0 = E_t \sum_{i=0}^{\infty} (\beta\rho)^i Y_{t+i}(k) \left[1 - \psi + \frac{\psi P_{t+i}w_{t+i}}{P_t^*(k)(1-\theta)\lambda_{t+i}} \left[\frac{r_{t+i}(1-\theta)}{w_{t+i}\theta} \right]^{\theta} \right].$$

The important result that we get from this is that an intermediate goods firm k that can set its price in period t wants to set its price to

$$P_t^*(k) = \frac{\psi}{\psi-1} \frac{E_t \sum_{i=0}^{\infty} (\beta\rho)^i P_{t+i} Y_{t+i}(k) \frac{w_{t+i}}{(1-\theta)\lambda_{t+i}} \left[\frac{r_{t+i}(1-\theta)}{w_{t+i}\theta} \right]^{\theta}}{E_t \sum_{i=0}^{\infty} (\beta\rho)^i Y_{t+i}(k)}. \qquad (10.5)$$

Recalling that $\psi > 1$, the expression $\psi/(\psi-1) > 1$ is the gross markup of the intermediate goods firm k's price over the ratio of the discounted stream of nominal total costs divided by the discounted stream of real output. This equation for the price setting behavior of the intermediate goods firms will be used to get the equation for price dynamics of the model.

Notice that all intermediate goods firms that can fix their prices have the same markup over the same marginal costs, so in every period t, $P_t^*(k)$ is the same for all of the $1 - \rho$ firms that adjust their prices. Combining the final goods pricing rule, equation 10.2, the fact that all the adjusting firms set the same price, and our assumption that all nonadjusting firms keep their price as it was in the previous period, one gets the price level updating expression of

$$P_t^{1-\psi} = \rho P_{t-1}^{1-\psi} + (1 - \rho) \left(P_t^* \right)^{1-\psi} . \tag{10.6}$$

Recall that there is a continuum of firms and the group that can change their prices is randomly chosen and is independent of when each one last changed their prices. This means that the distribution of prices among those who could not change their prices is identical to the distribution of prices in the economy of the previous period. Since the distribution does not change, the integral of the prices of the firms that cannot change their prices is equal to the price level of period $t - 1$.

Equation 10.6 says something interesting about the stationary state of an economy without money growth: the final good price and the intermediate goods prices will be the same. One can see this by substituting stationary state prices into equation 10.6. This gives

$$\bar{P}^{1-\psi} = \rho \bar{P}^{1-\psi} + (1 - \rho) \left(\bar{P}^* \right)^{1-\psi} ,$$

or simply that $\bar{P} = \bar{P}^*$.

Given the assumption of this model, a somewhat unrealistic event can occur for some intermediate goods firms. Suppose that the model has a rule of thumb where prices stay at the price they were set to at the last fixing but the economy has a positive stationary state inflation rate. Intermediate goods firm produce the quantity of their good that the final goods firms demand at the going price. If the intermediate goods firm has not been able to set its price for a long time, its price will be very low compared to the aggregate price because of inflation. The demand for this good will therefore be high and the firm must hire substantial labor and capital to meet this demand. Since these costs are high relative to the firm's price, the firm will be making losses until it can reset its price. These losses are the opposite of dividends and must be covered, indefinitely, by the firm's shareholders. Given the rule for updating prices, for some small fraction of firms a large number of periods will pass before they can reset their prices and their shareholders will have to be covering these losses for many periods. Such behavior is not much observed in the real world. With rules of thumb that update prices each period by either the stationary state inflation rate or a lagged inflation rate, these long-term losses are much less likely to occur.

10.1.3   The Family

We put money in the model with a cash-in-advance constraint and we continue to have indivisible labor, so family i, one of a continuum of a unit mass of households, maximizes

$$E_0 \sum_{t=0}^{\infty} \beta^t \left[\ln c_t^i + B h_t^i \right],$$

subject to a cash-in-advance constraint (written at equality),

$$P_t c_t^i = m_{t-1}^i + (g_t - 1) M_{t-1},$$

where $(g_t - 1) M_{t-1}$ is a stochastic lump sum monetary transfer or tax (when $g_t < 1$), and a real budget constraint,

$$k_{t+1}^i + \frac{m_t^i}{P_t} = w_t h_t^i + r_t k_t^i + \xi_t^i + (1 - \delta) k_t^i.$$

All the notation is as before except for the new term, ξ_t^i, which is the excess profits of the intermediate goods firms that are paid to family i in period t. We assume that each family owns the same fraction or share of the intermediate firms and the payment of excess profits is viewed by the family as a lump sum transfer. This term is necessary since, in general, the intermediate goods firms will make excess profits because of their market power and these excess profits need to be accounted for in the model.

Money is assumed to have a stationary state gross growth rate of 1, $\bar{g} = 1$, and the realization of g_t follows the process

$$\ln g_{t+1} = \pi \ln g_t + \varepsilon_{t+1}^g,$$

where ε_{t+1}^g has a normal distribution with zero mean. The market clearing condition for the money market is

$$\int_0^1 m_t^i = M_t,$$

and the aggregate money stock follows the process

$$M_t = g_t M_{t-1}.$$

Notice that we are not normalizing the stock of money to be equal to one as we did in the Cooley-Hansen model. This change has implications when we solve the log-linear version of the model.

First-order conditions for family i are

$$\frac{B}{w_t} = E_t\left[\frac{B\beta}{w_{t+1}}\left(r_{t+1} + (1-\delta)\right)\right]$$

and

$$-E_t\left[\frac{\beta}{c_{t+1}^i P_{t+1}}\right] = \frac{B}{w_t P_t}.$$

The four equations of the model that come from the family's decisions are these two first-order conditions, the cash-in-advance constraint, and the family's real budget constraint.

10.1.4 Equilibrium Conditions

Since all families are identical and there is a unit mass of families, in equilibrium the economy must fulfill the conditions

$$C_t = c_t^i,$$

$$K_t = k_t^i,$$

$$H_t = h_t^i,$$

and

$$M_t = m_t^i.$$

In these expressions, consumption and money represent the aggregate demands of the families, and capital and labor represent the aggregate supplies.

Equilibrium in the factor markets implies that supply equals demand for both labor and capital. In the labor market, equilibrium requires that

$$H_t = \int_0^1 H_t(k)dk.$$

Since the demand for labor of an intermediate firm in period t is given by

$$H_t(k) = \frac{Y_t(k)}{\lambda_t}\left[\frac{r_t(1-\theta)}{w_t\theta}\right]^\theta,$$

the equilibrium condition for the labor market in period t is

$$H_t = \int_0^1 H_t(k)dk = \frac{1}{\lambda_t}\left[\frac{r_t(1-\theta)}{w_t\theta}\right]^\theta \int_0^1 Y_t(k)dk.$$

This condition will not be used directly in the final model since it is found by using the first-order condition for the intermediate goods firms and the production function, both of which we will use in aggregate form in the final model.

In the market for capital,

$$K_t = \int_0^1 K_t(k)dk.$$

Since the demand for capital of an intermediate firm in period t is given by

$$K_t(k) = \frac{Y_t(k)}{\lambda_t}\left[\frac{r_t(1-\theta)}{w_t\theta}\right]^{\theta-1},$$

the equilibrium condition for the capital market in period t is

$$K_t = \int_0^1 K_t(k)dk = \frac{1}{\lambda_t}\left[\frac{r_t(1-\theta)}{w_t\theta}\right]^{\theta-1}\int_0^1 Y_t(k)dk.$$

As with the labor market condition, this will not appear directly in the model since the two equations from which it is found are already used there.

Notice that the aggregation of output in these two market conditions is not the CES bundler and that, in general, it is not equal to that bundler,

$$Y_t = \left[\int_0^1 Y_t(k)^{\frac{\psi-1}{\psi}}dk\right]^{\frac{\psi}{\psi-1}} \neq \int_0^1 Y_t(k)dk.$$

Since all families are equal shareholders in the intermediate firms, aggregate excess profits paid to the families in period t are

$$P_t\xi_t = P_t\int_0^1 \xi_t^i di = P_t\int_0^1 \text{profits}(k)dk$$

$$= \int_0^1 P_t(k)Y_t(k)dk - P_t\frac{w_t}{(1-\theta)\lambda_t}\left[\frac{r_t(1-\theta)}{w_t\theta}\right]^{\theta}\int_0^1 Y_t(k)dk.$$

Since the final goods firms are perfectly competitive and make no profits,

$$P_tY_t = \int_0^1 P_t(k)Y_t(k)dk.$$

Substituting this into the total profits equation for period t, and removing the price level P_t gives excess profits as

$$\xi_t = Y_t - \frac{w_t}{(1-\theta)\lambda_t} \left[\frac{r_t(1-\theta)}{w_t\theta} \right]^\theta \int_0^1 Y_t(k)dk.$$

10.1.5 The Full Model

In what follows, the simpler equilibrium conditions have already been substituted into the other equations. The full staggered pricing model with cash-in-advance money is found by combining the aggregated family first-order conditions and budget constraints, the intermediate goods firms first-order condition and budget constraint, the final goods pricing rule, the aggregation conditions, and the money growth rule. These equations are the family's aggregated first-order conditions,

$$\frac{1}{w_t} = E_t \left[\frac{\beta}{w_{t+1}} \left(r_{t+1} + (1-\delta) \right) \right]$$

and

$$-E_t \left[\frac{\beta}{C_{t+1}P_{t+1}} \right] = \frac{B}{w_t P_t},$$

the aggregated cash-in-advance constraint,

$$P_t C_t = g_t M_{t-1},$$

and the aggregated family's real budget constraint,

$$K_{t+1} + \frac{M_t}{P_t} = w_t H_t + r_t K_t + \xi_t + (1-\delta)K_t.$$

In the model, we use the fact that all income goes to the families and sums to output

$$Y_t = w_t H_t + r_t K_t + \xi_t,$$

so the family's real budget constraint will be used as

$$K_{t+1} + \frac{M_t}{P_t} = Y_t + (1-\delta)K_t.$$

From the intermediate goods firm decisions, we get the price setting equation for those firms that can set their price in period t,

$$P_t^*(k) = \frac{\psi}{\psi-1} \frac{E_t \sum_{i=0}^{\infty} (\beta\rho)^i P_{t+i} Y_{t+i}(k) \frac{w_{t+i}}{(1-\theta)\lambda_{t+i}} \left[\frac{r_{t+i}(1-\theta)}{w_{t+i}\theta} \right]^\theta}{E_t \sum_{i=0}^{\infty} (\beta\rho)^i Y_{t+i}(k)},$$

the first-order condition for cost minimization,

$$\frac{(1-\theta)\, r_t}{\theta\, w_t} = \frac{H_t(k)}{K_t(k)},$$

and the aggregate production equation,

$$\int_0^1 Y_t(k)\, dk = \lambda_t K_t^{\theta} H_t^{1-\theta}.$$

From the final goods firms, we get the rule determining the final good price in period t,

$$P_t^{1-\psi} = \rho P_{t-1}^{1-\psi} + (1-\rho)\left(P_t^*\right)^{1-\psi}.$$

The money supply growth rule is

$$M_t = g_t M_{t-1}.$$

Lastly, we have the stochastic process for money growth and technology,

$$\ln \lambda_t = \gamma \ln \lambda_{t-1} + \varepsilon_t^{\lambda}$$

and

$$\ln g_t = \pi \ln g_{t-1} + \varepsilon_t^{\lambda}.$$

10.2   THE STATIONARY STATE

In a stationary state, the stochastic shocks are zero, so $\lambda_t = \bar{\lambda} = 1$ and $g_t = \bar{g} = 1$. As before, the first-order conditions for the family are

$$\frac{1}{\beta} = \bar{r} + (1 - \delta) \tag{10.7}$$

and

$$\beta \bar{w} = -B\bar{C}. \tag{10.8}$$

The cash-in-advance condition gives

$$\bar{C} = \frac{\overline{M}}{\overline{P}}, \tag{10.9}$$

and the real budget constraint is

$$\frac{\overline{M}}{\overline{P}} = \overline{w}\bar{H} + \bar{\xi} + (\bar{r} - \delta)\,\bar{K} = \bar{Y} - \delta\bar{K}. \tag{10.10}$$

The rule for determining the final goods price becomes

$$\bar{P}^{1-\psi} = \rho\bar{P}^{1-\psi} + (1-\rho)\left(\bar{P}^*(k)\right)^{1-\psi},$$

or

$$\bar{P} = \bar{P}^*(k) = \bar{P}(k).$$

Putting this into the demand function for the intermediate good k gives

$$\bar{Y}(k) = \bar{Y}\left(\frac{\bar{P}}{\bar{P}(k)}\right)^{\psi} = \bar{Y}.$$

The price setting function for a firm that can fix its prices in period t becomes

$$\bar{P}^*(k) = \frac{\psi}{\psi-1}\frac{\frac{1}{1-\beta\rho}\bar{P}\bar{Y}\frac{\bar{w}}{(1-\theta)\bar{\lambda}}\left[\frac{\bar{r}(1-\theta)}{\bar{w}\theta}\right]^{\theta}}{\frac{1}{1-\beta\rho}\bar{Y}} = \frac{\psi}{\psi-1}\bar{P}\frac{\bar{w}}{(1-\theta)\bar{\lambda}}\left[\frac{\bar{r}(1-\theta)}{\bar{w}\theta}\right]^{\theta},$$

or

$$\frac{\psi}{\psi-1} = \frac{1}{\frac{\bar{w}}{(1-\theta)}\left[\frac{\bar{r}(1-\theta)}{\bar{w}\theta}\right]^{\theta}}. \tag{10.11}$$

This last equation says that the markup is equal to one over the real marginal cost. Since $\bar{r}$ is defined by the first-order condition, equation 10.7, this markup equation gives the real wage in the stationary state as

$$\bar{w} = \left[\frac{(\psi-1)(1-\theta)^{1-\theta}\theta^{\theta}}{\psi\bar{r}^{\theta}}\right]^{\frac{1}{1-\theta}}.$$

Once wages are given, the first-order condition of equation 10.8 determines consumption. With consumption given, equation 10.9 determines real balances. With real balances determined, the quantity of money $\overline{M}$ determines the price level in the stationary state by $\bar{P} = \overline{M}/\bar{C}$. Given rentals and wages, the stationary state demands for labor and capital are

$$\bar{H} = \left[\frac{\bar{r}(1-\theta)}{\bar{w}\theta}\right]^{\theta}\bar{Y}$$

and

$$\bar{K} = \left[\frac{\bar{r}(1-\theta)}{\bar{w}\theta}\right]^{\theta-1}\bar{Y}.$$

Real excess profits, after substituting in from equation 10.11, are

$$\bar{\xi} = \bar{Y}\left(1 - \frac{\bar{w}}{(1-\theta)}\left[\frac{\bar{r}(1-\theta)}{\bar{w}\theta}\right]^{\theta}\right) = \frac{\bar{Y}}{\psi}.$$

Output is not yet determined. Using the real budget constraint, equation 10.10, the first-order condition for consumption, equation 10.8, and the results above, one gets

$$-\frac{\beta\bar{w}}{B} = \bar{w}\left[\frac{\bar{r}(1-\theta)}{\bar{w}\theta}\right]^{\theta}\bar{Y} + \frac{\bar{Y}}{\psi} + (\bar{r}-\delta)\left[\frac{\bar{r}(1-\theta)}{\bar{w}\theta}\right]^{\theta-1}\bar{Y}, \quad (10.12)$$

or

$$\bar{Y} = \frac{-\beta\bar{w}}{B\left(\bar{w}\left[\frac{\bar{r}(1-\theta)}{\bar{w}\theta}\right]^{\theta} + \frac{1}{\psi} + (\bar{r}-\delta)\left[\frac{\bar{r}(1-\theta)}{\bar{w}\theta}\right]^{\theta-1}\right)}.$$

Using this value for $\bar{Y}$, one can determine the stationary state values for $\bar{H}$, $\bar{K}$, and $\bar{\xi}$.

The standard values for the deep parameters that we have been using for calibration are $\beta = .99$, $B = -2.5805$, $\delta = .025$, and $\theta = .36$. In addition, Galí [44] argues that appropriate values for the remaining parameters are $\rho = .75$ and $\psi = 11$, a value that gives a 10 percent markup in the stationary state. With these values for the underlying parameters and with $\bar{g} = 1$, we get stationary state values for the variables of the model, as shown in Table 10.1.

The stationary state value for real balances is the same as that for consumption. However, $\overline{M}$ is not determined in this model, which in the stationary state displays neutrality with respect to money. Given any positive stationary state value for the money supply, $\overline{M}$, then the price level in the stationary state is determined by

$$\bar{P} = \overline{M}/\bar{C}.$$

Notice that the stationary state we are showing here is one where the stationary state gross rate of growth of the money supply (and therefore, stationary state rate of inflation) is 1. The money stock is constant in stationary states for this economy.

Table 10.1 Stationary state values for staggered pricing model

Variable	$\bar{r}$	$\bar{w}$	$\bar{Y}$	$\bar{H}$	$\bar{K}$	$\bar{\xi}$	$\bar{C}$
Stationary state value	.0351	2.0426	1.0218	.2901	9.5271	.0929	.7836

> **EXERCISE 10.1** Does a stationary state exist for this economy for the case where $\bar{g} > 1$? Explain.

10.3 LOG LINEARIZATION

The interesting part of the log linearization problem is in the equations of the firms. A quasi differencing technique is used to simplify an infinite sum.

10.3.1 Log Linearization of the Firm's Problem

Here we use Uhlig's method to find the results of log linearization for the final and intermediate goods firm problems. A number of complications in the general model will become much simpler after log linearization. First we find a simple expression for the final goods firm's pricing rule. Then we simplify the intermediate goods firm's pricing rules. Lastly, we combine these to get a rule for price-level movement. This last expression is often viewed as a version of a Phillips curve.

10.3.2 The Final Goods Pricing Rule

Begin with the final goods pricing rule,

$$P_t^{1-\psi} = \rho P_{t-1}^{1-\psi} + (1-\rho)P_t^*(k)^{1-\psi}.$$

Using Uhlig's method for log linearization gives

$$\bar{P}^{1-\psi}e^{(1-\psi)\tilde{P}_t} = \rho\bar{P}^{1-\psi}e^{(1-\psi)\tilde{P}_{t-1}} + (1-\rho)\bar{P}^{1-\psi}e^{(1-\psi)\tilde{P}_t^*(k)},$$

where in the last term we can replace $\bar{P}^*(k)$ with $\bar{P}$. In a stationary state without trend inflation, all firms have the same price, $\bar{P}^*(k)$, and applying the price bundler results in $\bar{P} = \bar{P}^*(k)$. Using the standard approximation rule gives

$$1 + (1-\psi)\,\tilde{P}_t \approx \rho\left(1 + (1-\psi)\,\tilde{P}_{t-1}\right) + (1-\rho)\left(1 + (1-\psi)\,\tilde{P}_t^*(k)\right),$$

or

$$\tilde{P}_t \approx \rho\tilde{P}_{t-1} + (1-\rho)\tilde{P}_t^*(k).$$

10.3.3 The Intermediate Goods Pricing Rule

The result for the intermediate firm is the pricing rule

$$P_t^*(k) = \frac{\psi}{\psi - 1}\frac{E_t\sum_{i=0}^{\infty}(\beta\rho)^i\,P_{t+i}Y_{t+i}(k)\frac{w_{t+i}}{(1-\theta)\lambda_{t+i}}\left[\frac{r_{t+i}}{w_{t+i}}\right]^\theta}{E_t\sum_{i=0}^{\infty}(\beta\rho)^i\,Y_{t+i}(k)}.$$

Multiplying out the denominator gives

$$P_t^*(k)E_t\sum_{i=0}^{\infty}(\beta\rho)^i\, Y_{t+i}\,(k) = \frac{\psi}{\psi-1}E_t\sum_{i=0}^{\infty}(\beta\rho)^i\, P_{t+i}Y_{t+i}\,(k)\,\frac{w_{t+i}}{(1-\theta)\lambda_{t+i}}\left[\frac{r_{t+i}}{w_{t+i}}\right]$$

Uhlig's method of log linearization of the left-hand side of the above equation gives

$$E_t\sum_{i=0}^{\infty}(\beta\rho)^i\, P_t^*(k)Y_{t+i}\,(k) = E_t\sum_{i=0}^{\infty}(\beta\rho)^i\,\bar{P}^*(k)\bar{Y}\,(k)\, e^{\tilde{P}_t^*(k)+\tilde{Y}_{t+i}(k)}$$

$$\approx \bar{P}^*(k)\bar{Y}\,(k)\, E_t\sum_{i=0}^{\infty}(\beta\rho)^i\left(1+\tilde{P}_t^*(k)+\tilde{Y}_{t+i}\,(k)\right)$$

$$= \frac{\bar{P}^*(k)\bar{Y}\,(k)}{1-\beta\rho}\left(1+\tilde{P}_t^*(k)\right)$$

$$+\;\bar{P}^*(k)\bar{Y}\,(k)\, E_t\sum_{i=0}^{\infty}(\beta\rho)^i\left(\tilde{Y}_{t+i}\,(k)\right).$$

Log linearization of the right side of the pricing rule gives

$$\frac{\psi}{\psi-1}E_t\sum_{i=0}^{\infty}(\beta\rho)^i\, P_{t+i}Y_{t+i}\,(k)\,\frac{w_{t+i}}{(1-\theta)\lambda_{t+i}}\left[\frac{r_{t+i}(1-\theta)}{w_{t+i}\theta}\right]^{\theta}$$

$$=\frac{\psi}{\psi-1}\bar{P}\bar{Y}\,(k)\,\frac{\bar{w}}{(1-\theta)\bar{\lambda}}\left[\frac{(1-\theta)\bar{r}}{\theta\bar{w}}\right]^{\theta}$$

$$\times\; E_t\sum_{i=0}^{\infty}(\beta\rho)^i\, e^{\tilde{P}_{t+i}+\tilde{Y}_{t+i}(k)+(1-\theta)\tilde{w}_{t+i}-\tilde{\lambda}_{t+i}+\theta\tilde{r}_{t+i}}$$

$$\approx\frac{\psi}{\psi-1}\bar{P}\bar{Y}\,(k)\,\frac{\bar{w}}{(1-\theta)\bar{\lambda}}\left[\frac{(1-\theta)\bar{r}}{\theta\bar{w}}\right]^{\theta}$$

$$\times\; E_t\sum_{i=0}^{\infty}(\beta\rho)^i\left[1+\tilde{P}_{t+i}+\tilde{Y}_{t+i}\,(k)+(1-\theta)\,\tilde{w}_{t+i}-\tilde{\lambda}_{t+i}+\theta\tilde{r}_{t+i}\right].$$

In the stationary state

$$\frac{\psi}{\psi-1}=\frac{1}{\dfrac{\bar{w}}{(1-\theta)\bar{\lambda}}\left[\dfrac{(1-\theta)\bar{r}}{\theta\bar{w}}\right]^{\theta}},$$

so the right side becomes simply

$$\approx \bar{P}\bar{Y}(k) \, E_t \sum_{i=0}^{\infty} (\beta\rho)^i \left[1 + \tilde{P}_{t+i} + \tilde{Y}_{t+i}(k) + (1-\theta)\,\tilde{w}_{t+i} - \tilde{\lambda}_{t+i} + \theta\tilde{r}_{t+i} \right].$$

In addition, we have shown that $\bar{P} = \bar{P}^*$, so stationary state prices and $\bar{Y}(k)$ cancel out on both sides of the equation. Finally, both sides contain $E_t \sum_{i=0}^{\infty} (\beta\rho)^i \, \tilde{Y}_{t+i}(k)$, which we can eliminate.

After these simplifications, we get the log-linear pricing rule for the intermediate goods firm,

$$\tilde{P}_t^*(k) = (1-\beta\rho) \, E_t \sum_{i=0}^{\infty} (\beta\rho)^i \left[\tilde{P}_{t+i} + (1-\theta)\,\tilde{w}_{t+i} - \tilde{\lambda}_{t+i} + \theta\tilde{r}_{t+i} \right].$$

This equation is different from the one often encountered in the literature because everything here is measured in changes around the stationary state and the traditional one is measured in levels. In the traditional version, one finds a constant markup term of $\ln \frac{\psi}{\psi-1}$, which drops out here using conditions from the stationary state.

10.3.4 Inflation Equation (Phillips Curve)

Putting

$$\tilde{P}_t^*(k) = (1-\beta\rho) \, E_t \sum_{i=0}^{\infty} (\beta\rho)^i \left[\tilde{P}_{t+i} + (1-\theta)\,\tilde{w}_{t+i} - \tilde{\lambda}_{t+i} + \theta\tilde{r}_{t+i} \right]$$

into

$$\tilde{P}_t \approx \rho\tilde{P}_{t-1} + (1-\rho)\tilde{P}_t^*(k)$$

to remove $\tilde{P}_t^*(k)$, we get

$$\tilde{P}_t \approx \rho\tilde{P}_{t-1} + (1-\rho)(1-\beta\rho) \, E_t \sum_{i=0}^{\infty} (\beta\rho)^i \left[\tilde{P}_{t+i} + (1-\theta)\,\tilde{w}_{t+i} - \tilde{\lambda}_{t+i} + \theta\tilde{r}_{t+i} \right].$$

The right side of this equation contains an infinite sum of expected future values of the shocks to prices, wages, rents, and technology. One needs to find a way to remove most of these terms from the equation. We can do this by what is known as *quasi differencing*. Quasi differencing entails multiplying both sides of the equation by the polynomial in the lag operator $1 - \beta\rho L^{-1}$, where L stands for the lag operator. A lag operator L applied to a variable X_t results in that variable lagged one period, or

$$LX_t = X_{t-1},$$

and the lead operator L^{-1} applied to a variable results in that variable one period in the future, or

$$L^{-1}X_t = X_{t+1}.$$

Applying the operator polynomial to the left side of the equation gives

$$\left(1 - \beta\rho L^{-1}\right) \tilde{P}_t = \tilde{P}_t - \beta\rho \tilde{P}_{t+1},$$

and applying it to the right side gives

$$\left(1 - \beta\rho L^{-1}\right) \left(\rho \tilde{P}_{t-1} + (1 - \rho)(1 - \beta\rho)\right.$$

$$\times \left. E_t \sum_{i=0}^{\infty} (\beta\rho)^i \left[\tilde{P}_{t+i} + (1 - \theta)\tilde{w}_{t+i} - \tilde{\lambda}_{t+i} + \theta\tilde{r}_{t+i}\right]\right)$$

$$= \rho \tilde{P}_{t-1} + (1 - \rho)(1 - \beta\rho)$$

$$\times E_t \sum_{i=0}^{\infty} (\beta\rho)^i \left[\tilde{P}_{t+i} + (1 - \theta)\tilde{w}_{t+i} - \tilde{\lambda}_{t+i} + \theta\tilde{r}_{t+i}\right]$$

$$- \beta\rho\rho \tilde{P}_t + \beta\rho(1 - \rho)(1 - \beta\rho)$$

$$\times E_t \sum_{i=0}^{\infty} (\beta\rho)^i \left[\tilde{P}_{t+1+i} + (1 - \theta)\tilde{w}_{t+1+i} - \tilde{\lambda}_{t+1+i} + \theta\tilde{r}_{t+1+i}\right].$$

As the quasi differencing is explicitly designed to make happen, most terms from period $t + 1$ and after cancel out. One is left with the expression

$$\tilde{P}_t - \beta\rho E_t \tilde{P}_{t+1} \approx \rho \tilde{P}_{t-1} - \beta\rho\rho \tilde{P}_t$$

$$+ (1 - \rho)(1 - \beta\rho)\left[\tilde{P}_t + (1 - \theta)\tilde{w}_t - \tilde{\lambda}_t + \theta\tilde{r}_t\right].$$

A little algebra yields the "Phillips curve" of

$$\left[\tilde{P}_t - \tilde{P}_{t-1}\right] \approx \beta\left[E_t\tilde{P}_{t+1} - \tilde{P}_t\right] + \frac{(1 - \rho)(1 - \beta\rho)}{\rho}\left[(1 - \theta)\tilde{w}_t - \tilde{\lambda}_t + \theta\tilde{r}_t\right].$$

$$(10.13)$$

Note that $(1 - \theta)\tilde{w}_t - \tilde{\lambda}_t + \theta\tilde{r}_t$ is the log difference of the real marginal costs from their stationary state value and is sometimes written as $\ln \widehat{RMC}_t$.

This Phillips curve equation is commonly seen (Galí [44], for example) written in terms of inflation as

$$\ln \pi_t \approx \beta E_t \ln \pi_{t+1} + \frac{(1-\rho)(1-\beta\rho)}{\rho} \ln \widehat{RMC}_t.$$

In deriving the expression given in equation 10.13, we removed $\tilde{P}_t^*(k)$ from the model and have an expression for the evolution of prices in terms of the differences from the stationary state of aggregate prices, wages, rentals, and technology.

10.3.5 Log Linear Version of the Model

The log-linear version of the full model is found by applying Uhlig's techniques to the equations given in section 10.1.5, utilizing the log-linear versions of the final and intermediate goods firms' equations that we found above. There are ten variables in this model: $\tilde{r}_t$, $\tilde{w}_t$, $\tilde{C}_t$, $\tilde{P}_t$, $\tilde{g}_t$, $\tilde{M}_t$, $\tilde{K}_t$, $\tilde{H}_t$, $\tilde{Y}_t$, and $\tilde{\lambda}_t$. The log-linear versions of the first-order conditions are

$$-\tilde{w}_t = \beta \bar{r} E_t \tilde{r}_{t+1} - E_t \tilde{w}_{t+1}$$

and

$$E_t \tilde{C}_{t+1} + E_t \tilde{P}_{t+1} = \tilde{w}_t + \tilde{P}_t.$$

The cash-in-advance and budget constraints become

$$(\tilde{P}_t + \tilde{C}_t) = (\tilde{g}_t + \tilde{M}_{t-1})$$

and

$$\bar{K} \tilde{K}_{t+1} + \frac{\overline{M}}{\bar{P}}(\tilde{M}_t - \tilde{P}_t) = \bar{Y} \tilde{Y}_t + (1-\delta)\bar{K}\tilde{K}_t.$$

One gets this last equation by substituting output for total costs. This lets us remove the term $\tilde{\xi}_t$ from the model. The second first-order condition and the cash-in-advance constraint can be combined to get

$$E_t \left[\tilde{g}_{t+1} + \tilde{M}_t \right] = \tilde{w}_t + \tilde{P}_t,$$

and using the law of motion for $\tilde{g}_{t+1}$ that is shown below, this can be written as

$$\pi \tilde{g}_t + \tilde{M}_t = \tilde{w}_t + \tilde{P}_t.$$

From the price setting equations, we have the result for the pricing rule that we found above,

$$\left[\tilde{P}_t - \tilde{P}_{t-1} \right] \approx \beta \left[E_t \tilde{P}_{t+1} - \tilde{P}_t \right] + \frac{(1-\rho)(1-\beta\rho)}{\rho} \left[(1-\theta)\tilde{w}_t - \tilde{\lambda}_t + \theta\tilde{r}_t \right].$$

The first-order condition for the intermediate goods firm is

$$\tilde{H}_t + \tilde{w}_t = \tilde{r}_t + \tilde{K}_t.$$

The aggregate production function gives

$$\tilde{Y}_t = \tilde{\lambda}_t + \theta \tilde{K}_t + (1 - \theta)\,\tilde{H}_t.$$

The process for the aggregate money stock is

$$\tilde{M}_t = \tilde{M}_{t-1} + \tilde{g}_t.$$

The two stochastic process equations are

$$\tilde{\lambda}_t = \gamma \tilde{\lambda}_{t-1} + \varepsilon_t^\lambda$$

and

$$\tilde{g}_t = \pi \tilde{g}_{t-1} + \varepsilon_t^g.$$

One interesting characteristic of the model after log linearization is that the two definitions of output, the one with the bundler and the other integrating directly, turn out to be the same. Using the bundler technology of the final firm,

$$Y_t^{\frac{\psi-1}{\psi}} = \int_0^1 Y_t(k)^{\frac{\psi-1}{\psi}}\,dk,$$

and writing it in log-linear form gives

$$\bar{Y}^{\frac{\psi-1}{\psi}}\left(1 + \frac{\psi-1}{\psi}\tilde{Y}_t\right) \approx \bar{Y}^{\frac{\psi-1}{\psi}}\left[\int_0^1\left(1 + \frac{\psi-1}{\psi}\tilde{Y}_t(k)\right)dk\right],$$

or

$$\tilde{Y}_t \approx \left[\int_0^1 \tilde{Y}_t(k)dk\right].$$

The full set of log-linear equations that we use for the model is

$$0 = \tilde{w}_t + \beta\bar{r}E_t\tilde{r}_{t+1} - E_t\tilde{w}_{t+1},$$

$$0 = \tilde{M}_t - \tilde{M}_{t-1} - \tilde{g}_t,$$

$$0 = \beta E_t \tilde{P}_{t+1} + \frac{(1-\theta)(1-\rho)(1-\beta\rho)}{\rho}\tilde{w}_t - \frac{(1-\rho)(1-\beta\rho)}{\rho}\tilde{\lambda}_t$$

$$+ \frac{\theta(1-\rho)(1-\beta\rho)}{\rho}\tilde{r}_t - (1+\beta)\tilde{P}_t + \tilde{P}_{t-1},$$

$$0 = \tilde{g}_t + \tilde{M}_{t-1} - \tilde{P}_t - \tilde{C}_t,$$

$$0 = \bar{Y}\tilde{Y}_t + (1-\delta)\bar{K}\tilde{K}_t - \bar{K}\tilde{K}_{t+1} - \frac{\overline{M}}{\overline{P}}\tilde{M}_t + \frac{\overline{M}}{\overline{P}}\tilde{P}_t,$$

$$0 = \tilde{w}_t + \tilde{P}_t - \tilde{M}_t - \pi\tilde{g}_t,$$

$$0 = \tilde{\lambda}_t + (1-\theta)\tilde{H}_t + \theta\tilde{K}_t, -\tilde{Y}_t,$$

$$0 = \tilde{H}_t + \tilde{w}_t - \tilde{K}_t - \tilde{r}_t.$$

The order of the equations given here is that which we use below in the solution process.

10.4 SOLVING THE LOG LINEAR MODEL

Because past, current, and expected future prices show up in the model, we need to make prices a state variable. Notice that with prices in the x_t variable, they show up in the second, expectational, block of equations in our solution method. This should be expected since, with staggered price setting, past prices are part of what determines the current state of the economy. Letting $x_t = [\tilde{K}_{t+1}, \tilde{M}_t, \tilde{P}_t]'$, $y_t = [\tilde{r}_t, \tilde{w}_t, \tilde{C}_t, \tilde{Y}_t, \tilde{H}_t]'$, and $z_t = [\tilde{\lambda}_t, \tilde{g}_t]'$, one can write the model as we did earlier in the form

$$0 = Ax_t + Bx_{t-1} + Cy_t + Dz_t,$$

$$0 = E_t\left[Fx_{t+1} + Gx_t + Hx_{t-1} + Jy_{t+1} + Ky_t + Lz_{t+1} + Mz_t\right],$$

$$z_{t+1} = Nz_t + \varepsilon_{t+1},$$

where

$$A = \begin{bmatrix} 0 & 0 & -1 \\ -\bar{K} & -\bar{C} & \bar{C} \\ 0 & -1 & 1 \\ 0 & 0 & 0 \\ 0 & 0 & 0 \end{bmatrix},$$

$$B = \begin{bmatrix} 0 & 1 & 0 \\ (1-\delta)\,\bar{K} & 0 & 0 \\ 0 & 0 & 0 \\ \theta & 0 & 0 \\ -1 & 0 & 0 \end{bmatrix},$$

$$C = \begin{bmatrix} 0 & 0 & -1 & 0 & 0 \\ 0 & 0 & 0 & \bar{Y} & 0 \\ 0 & 1 & 0 & 0 & 0 \\ 0 & 0 & 0 & -1 & 1-\theta \\ -1 & 1 & 0 & 0 & 1 \end{bmatrix},$$

$$D = \begin{bmatrix} 0 & 1 \\ 0 & 0 \\ 0 & -\pi \\ 1 & 0 \\ 0 & 0 \end{bmatrix},$$

$$F = \begin{bmatrix} 0 & 0 & 0 \\ 0 & 0 & 0 \\ 0 & 0 & \beta \end{bmatrix},$$

$$G = \begin{bmatrix} 0 & 0 & 0 \\ 0 & 1 & 0 \\ 0 & 0 & -(1+\beta) \end{bmatrix},$$

$$H = \begin{bmatrix} 0 & 0 & 0 \\ 0 & -1 & 0 \\ 0 & 0 & 1 \end{bmatrix},$$

$$J = \begin{bmatrix} \beta\bar{r} & -1 & 0 & 0 & 0 \\ 0 & 0 & 0 & 0 & 0 \\ 0 & 0 & 0 & 0 & 0 \end{bmatrix},$$

$$K = \begin{bmatrix} 0 & 1 & 0 & 0 & 0 \\ 0 & 0 & 0 & 0 & 0 \\ \frac{\theta(1-\rho)(1-\beta\rho)}{\rho} & \frac{(1-\theta)(1-\rho)(1-\beta\rho)}{\rho} & 0 & 0 & 0 \end{bmatrix},$$

$$L = \begin{bmatrix} 0 & 0 \\ 0 & 0 \\ 0 & 0 \end{bmatrix},$$

$$M = \begin{bmatrix} 0 & 0 \\ 0 & -1 \\ \frac{-(1-\rho)(1-\beta\rho)}{\rho} & 0 \end{bmatrix},$$

and

$$N = \begin{bmatrix} \gamma & 0 \\ 0 & \pi \end{bmatrix}.$$

A certain amount of care was taken in constructing the model with the set of variables and equations that are given above. One of the criteria that we used was to choose the variables in x_t and in y_t and the equations to include in the expectational part so that the matrix C can be inverted. This is why we explicitly substituted out the expectations from one of the family's first-order conditions and why the equation for the aggregate money stock process is included in the expectational equation set.

A solution to this model is a pair of policy equations of the form

$$x_{t+1} = Px_t + Qz_t$$

and

$$y_t = Rx_t + Sz_t.$$

Using the parameters given in section 10.2 but for four values of $\rho = \{.1, .3, .5, .75\}$, we calculate the policy matrices given in Tables 10.2 and 10.3.

One of the first things to note about these policy matrices is that for low values of ρ they are quite similar to the ones found for the Cooley-Hansen cash-in-advance model (the coefficients are given in Table 8.3). As the value of ρ increases, the coefficients of the policy matrices change in a number of important ways. As ρ increases, capital is less determined by past capital and more by money and prices and by the two stochastic variables. Prices are less determined by capital and money and more by past prices. This last is consistent with the fact that fewer intermediate firms can adjust their prices when ρ is larger. The importance of the stochastic variables for determining prices declines as ρ increases. For the jump variables, rental on capital, output, and labor supply all show substantial increases in the absolute value of their coefficients on capital, money, and prices. For wages and consumption, the coefficient on capital declines while those for money and prices increase in absolute value. The coefficients on the stochastic variables with respect to

Table 10.2   Table of policy matrices for $\rho = .1$ and $.3$

ρ	.1	.3
P	$\begin{bmatrix} .931 & .020 & -.020 \\ 0 & 1 & 0 \\ -.509 & .989 & .011 \end{bmatrix}$	$\begin{bmatrix} .889 & .096 & -.096 \\ 0 & 1 & 0 \\ -.486 & .948 & .052 \end{bmatrix}$
Q	$\begin{bmatrix} .151 & .055 \\ 0 & 1 \\ -.501 & 1.433 \end{bmatrix}$	$\begin{bmatrix} .117 & .147 \\ 0 & 1 \\ -.483 & 1.383 \end{bmatrix}$
R	$\begin{bmatrix} -1.088 & .318 & -.318 \\ .509 & .011 & -.011 \\ .509 & .011 & -.011 \\ -.022 & .197 & -.197 \\ -.597 & .308 & -.308 \end{bmatrix}$	$\begin{bmatrix} -1.735 & 1.507 & -1.507 \\ .486 & .052 & -.052 \\ .486 & .052 & -.052 \\ -.421 & .931 & -.931 \\ -1.221 & 1.455 & -1.455 \end{bmatrix}$
S	$\begin{bmatrix} 1.735 & .328 \\ .501 & .047 \\ .501 & -.433 \\ 1.789 & .180 \\ 1.233 & .281 \end{bmatrix}$	$\begin{bmatrix} 1.200 & 1.783 \\ .483 & .098 \\ .483 & -.383 \\ 1.459 & 1.079 \\ .717 & 1.685 \end{bmatrix}$

Table 10.3   Table of policy matrices for $\rho = .5$ and $.75$

ρ	.5	.75
P	$\begin{bmatrix} .792 & .276 & -.276 \\ 0 & 1 & 0 \\ -.433 & .849 & .151 \end{bmatrix}$	$\begin{bmatrix} .446 & .915 & -.915 \\ 0 & 1 & 0 \\ -.244 & .500 & .500 \end{bmatrix}$
Q	$\begin{bmatrix} .035 & .372 \\ 0 & 1 \\ -.438 & 1.260 \end{bmatrix}$	$\begin{bmatrix} -.258 & 1.216 \\ 0 & 1 \\ -.278 & .799 \end{bmatrix}$
R	$\begin{bmatrix} -3.283 & 4.355 & -4.355 \\ .433 & .151 & -.151 \\ .433 & .151 & -.151 \\ -1.378 & 2.691 & -2.691 \\ -2.716 & 4.204 & -4.204 \end{bmatrix}$	$\begin{bmatrix} -8.738 & 14.427 & -14.427 \\ .244 & .499 & -.499 \\ .244 & .499 & -.499 \\ -4.748 & 8.913 & -8.913 \\ -7.982 & 13.927 & -13.927 \end{bmatrix}$
S	$\begin{bmatrix} -.087 & 5.323 \\ .438 & .220 \\ .438 & -.260 \\ .664 & 3.266 \\ -.525 & 5.102 \end{bmatrix}$	$\begin{bmatrix} -4.718 & 18.629 \\ .278 & .681 \\ .278 & .201 \\ -2.197 & 11.487 \\ -4.996 & 17.948 \end{bmatrix}$

technology shocks decline and those with respect to money growth shocks increase as ρ increases.

Notice that the coefficients on prices and money in the equations that determine real variables are of equal but opposite signs. This characteristic of the model is nothing more than the expression of the long run neutrality of money in the economy. Changes in money result in (eventually) equal changes in prices, and these cancel each other out on the real side of the economy.

The following three tables present the results of simulations. In all the examples, $\rho = .75$. As in the cash-in-advance basic model, 50 runs of 115 periods each were used to generate estimates of the relative standard errors and the correlations with output. For Table 10.4, the standard errors used for the technology and money growth shocks were the same as those used in the basic cash-in-advance model.

The results shown in Table 10.4 clearly indicate that the new model is much more responsive to shocks than the standard cash-in-advance model. This result is consistent with the increasing values in the matrices Q and S of the absolute values of the coefficients on the money growth shock. Since the major change in this model was the introduction of a friction to the correction of prices, one might well suspect that the increased variance is coming from the way the money growth shock is affecting the economy. One can ask how much the money shock needs to be reduced, keeping the technology shock unchanged, so that the relative standard error of output comes in line with that observed in the data for the United States. The standard error for the money growth shock needs to be reduced to .00135 (15 percent of the original standard error) before the relative standard error for output shrinks to the standard that comes from the data, 1.76 percent. Table 10.5 shows the relative standard errors and correlations with output for this economy.

Table 10.4   Staggered pricing model with shocks from Cooley-Hansen ($\rho = .75$)

$\sigma_\lambda = .00178$ $\sigma_g = .009$	Relative standard error	Corrrelation with output
Output	10.24%	100.00%
Consumption	1.58%	12.48%
Investment	43.55%	99.30%
Capital	3.16%	37.51%
Hours	16.04%	99.29%
Prices	5.97%	4.87%

Notice that as the size of the monetary shock declines relative to the technology shock, the correlation of consumption and prices (among other variables) with output changes dramatically. Table 10.6 shows the correlations with output in two economies, one with a pure monetary shock and one with a pure technology shock. In both economies, $\rho = .75$. Since our dynamic economies are linear, economies with independent mixed shocks are linear combinations of these two economies. That a monetary shock and a technology shock have such different effects on the correlations of variables with output means that some freedom in choosing the size of these relative shocks gives a model with staggered pricing an advantage in matching the variance-covariance characteristics of an economy.

Table 10.5   Economy with smaller monetary shock ($\rho = .75$)

$\sigma_\lambda = .00178$ $\sigma_g = .00135$	Relative standard error	Corrrelation with output
Output	1.76%	100.00%
Consumption	0.45%	32.43%
Investment	7.17%	98.19%
Capital	0.69%	40.73%
Hours	2.60%	95.15%
Prices	0.98%	−9.24%

Table 10.6   Correlations with output from pure shocks ($\rho = .75$)

	Technology shock	Monetary shock
Output	1.0000	1.0000
Consumption	0.6640	0.1175
Investment	0.9512	0.9931
Capital	0.5171	0.3732
Prices	−0.6640	0.0503
Rentals	0.7988	0.9805
Wages	0.6640	0.3809
Hours	0.8042	0.9939

10.4.1 Impulse Response Functions

We can use impulse response functions to make clearer some of the points made above about how the economy responds to technology and money growth shocks as ρ changes. A higher ρ means that a smaller fraction of the intermediate firms can change their prices in any period, and one would expect that this would result in smaller and slower movements of prices to either technology or money growth shocks. It also implies that other variables will need to respond more to compensate for the inability of prices to respond to these shocks.

Figure 10.1 seems a bit complicated. It shows the response of all variables of the model to a .01 shock to the technology variable. It shows these responses for three different values of ρ: $\rho = .3, .5, .75$. So for each variable of the model, the graph has three lines. The three lines for each variable are relatively close together, so there should not be much confusion. For example, look at the three lines that are indicated by the letter K. Two of these lines are close together and the third, following a similar path, is somewhat further away. The furthest one corresponds to the response for the economy with $\rho = .75$. Of the two other K curves, the one closest to the .75 line is the response for the economy with $\rho = .5$. The remaining line is for the economy with $\rho = .3$. For each set of three lines, the same pattern holds: the line furthest from the others is the one for the economy with $\rho = .75$. Similar lines further from

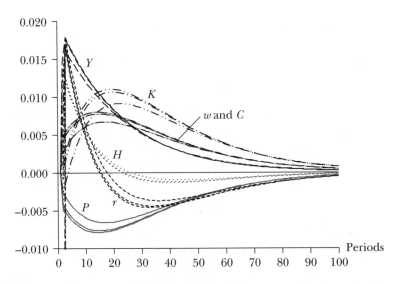

FIGURE 10.1 Responses of the model's variables to a technology shock: $\rho = .3, .5, .75$

this line represent the responses for economies with $\rho = .5$ and $\rho = .3$, in that order. There is a certain confusion of lines during the first few periods of the figure. These will be examined shortly.

For every variable, higher values of ρ correspond to smaller responses over most of the 100 periods shown in the figure. These medium-term responses are similar to those of the Cooley-Hansen model, only with a somewhat smaller and slightly slower response. In general, it is after the third period that the responses are similar to those of the model without staggered prices. The part that is quite different is how the model responds in period 2.

The impulse response functions shown in Figure 10.1 have been set up so that the shock to the stochastic process occurs in period 2. The response of the economy in period 2 comes entirely from the Q and S matrices of the policy function. In period 2, the lagged values of the state variables (measured in log differences) are their stationary state values of 0. It is only in period 3 that the P and R matrices of the policy functions begin to have their effects. From period 3 on, the response functions are a combination of the residual effect of the shock on the stochastic variables (working through Q and S) and the effects coming from the state variables (working through P and R).

Figure 10.2 shows the first ten periods of the responses to a .01 technology shock for the variables $\tilde{C}$, $\tilde{Y}$, and $\tilde{H}$ for values of $\rho = .3, .5, .75$. Figure 10.3 shows the same thing for the variables $\tilde{r}$, $\tilde{K}$, and $\tilde{P}$. What is of interest here

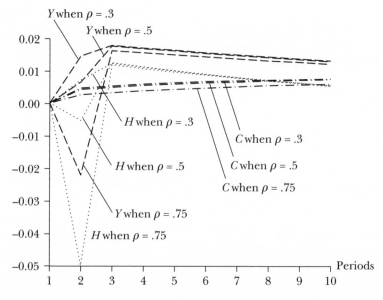

FIGURE 10.2   Responses of $\tilde{C}$, $\tilde{Y}$, and $\tilde{H}$ to a technology shock

is the period 2 response of the variables. For all variables except prices, the second-period response is more negative, the higher ρ. In some cases, for example, $\tilde{H}$, $\tilde{Y}$, and $\tilde{r}$, the negative response is very large for $\rho = .75$. For prices, the response is negative in all three cases, but it is smaller in absolute value for larger values of ρ. By period 3, all the variables are on response paths that look like the standard one (that of the Cooley-Hansen model) for that variable.

The large (usually negative) second-period responses of real variables to a positive technology shock can add substantial variance to the time paths of these variables in simulated economies when ρ is large.

Figures 10.4 and 10.5 show the responses of the staggered pricing economy to a .01 money growth shock. The difference between the two economies is the value of ρ, the fraction of intermediate goods firms who cannot change their prices in a given period. In Figure 10.4 the value of ρ is .75 and in Figure 10.5 it is .5. Notice that these figures are directly comparable since the vertical axes are identical. As is very clear from the figures, increasing the fraction of intermediate goods firms who cannot change their prices has a very large impact on the way the economy responds, especially in the first period of the shock.

A good part of the substantial change in output and labor supply when ρ = .75 can be explained by looking at the household budget constraint,

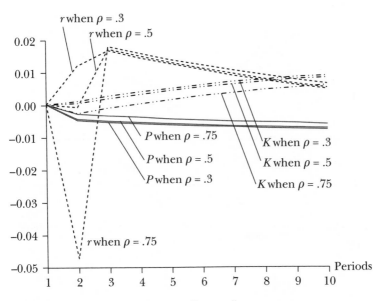

FIGURE 10.3   Responses of $\tilde{r}$, $\tilde{K}$, and $\tilde{P}$ to a technology shock

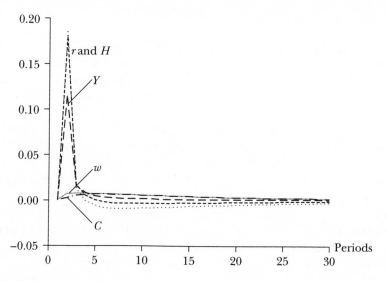

FIGURE 10.4   Response to a .01 money growth shock for economy where $\rho = .75$

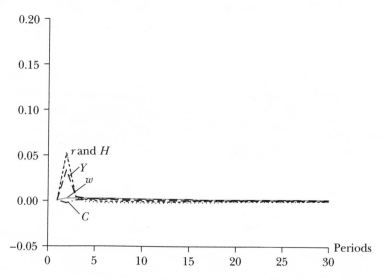

FIGURE 10.5   Response to a .01 money growth shock for economy where $\rho = .5$

$$0 = \bar{Y}\tilde{Y}_t + (1-\delta)\bar{K}\tilde{K}_t - \bar{K}\tilde{K}_{t+1} - \frac{\bar{M}}{\bar{P}}\tilde{M}_t + \frac{\bar{M}}{\bar{P}}\tilde{P}_t.$$

A positive shock to $\tilde{M}_t$, with prices sticky and with $\tilde{K}_t$ given, implies that output, $\tilde{Y}_t$, must rise for this equation to hold. For output to increase, since period t's capital is fixed, wages must rise to attract additional labor. Additional labor raises the marginal product of capital and raises rentals. Increased rentals (and the expectation that this increase will continue) causes an increase in capital accumulation. Gradually, prices catch up with the money growth, and the real side of the economy returns to the stationary state. The same process occurs when $\rho = .5$, but the reactions are much smaller because more intermediate goods firms can change their prices in period t.

Figure 10.6 shows how money, prices, and the capital stock respond to a money growth shock for staggered pricing economies where ρ takes on the values of .3, .5, and .75. Money follows a predictable growth path based on the stochastic process that $\tilde{g}_t$ follows, given a one-time shock to ε_t^g. Given that $\tilde{g}_t = \pi\tilde{g}_{t-1} + \varepsilon_t^g$, that $\pi = .48$, and that $\tilde{M}_t = \tilde{g}_t + \tilde{M}_{t-1}$, $\tilde{M}_t$ will eventually rise to a new level, that is,

$$\lim_{T\to\infty}\tilde{M}_T = \tilde{M}_{t-1} + \frac{\varepsilon_t^g}{1-\pi}.$$

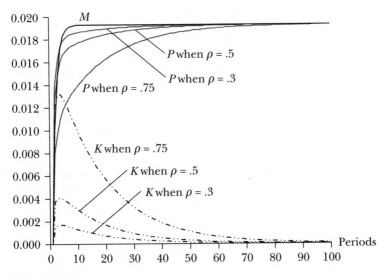

FIGURE 10.6 Responses of money, prices, and capital to a money growth shock for economies with $\rho = .3$, .5, and .75

What is particularly interesting about Figure 10.6 is how the response of prices changes with the value of ρ. At low values of ρ, prices initially respond faster than money, but as the value of ρ increases, the reaction of prices becomes much slower. At $\rho = .75$, some 80 periods are required for the change in prices to become essentially indistinguishable from that of money. A money shock results in a change in real balances that is sustained for a long time.

The reaction of the capital stock (the state variable measured in real terms) is much more dramatic with higher values of ρ.

10.5   INFLATION ADJUSTMENT FOR NONOPTIMIZING FIRMS

Consider the case where the rule of thumb for those firms that cannot set their prices in period t is that their prices are adjusted by the gross inflation rate of the previous period, $\pi_{t-1} = P_{t-1}/P_{t-2}$. Our expectation is that this rule will increase persistence of money growth shocks in the economy because we are adding additional lagged terms (a P_{t-2}) to the model.

A randomly selected group of firms of size $1 - \rho$ set their prices to $P_t^*(k)$ in period t. All other ρ firms adjust their time t price to

$$P_t(k) = \frac{P_{t-1}}{P_{t-2}} P_{t-1}(k),$$

where aggregate prices in period s are equal to

$$P_s = \left[\int_0^1 P_s(k)^{1-\psi} dk \right]^{\frac{1}{1-\psi}}.$$

The price setting rule for the final goods firms implies that prices evolve according to the rule

$$P_t^{1-\psi} = \rho \left(\frac{P_{t-1}}{P_{t-2}} P_{t-1} \right)^{1-\psi} + (1-\rho) P_t^{*1-\psi}, \tag{10.14}$$

where P_t^* is the identical price that is chosen by all firms who can set their price. An intermediate firm that set its price in period t to $P_t^*(k)$ and has not been able to reset it optimally since will have a price in period $t + n$ of

$$P_{t+n}(k) = \prod_{i=1}^{n} \frac{P_{t-1+i}}{P_{t-2+i}} P_t^*(k) = \frac{P_{t+n-1}}{P_{t-1}} P_t^*(k).$$

The problem that the optimizing intermediate goods firms face when setting their price $P_t^*(k)$ in period t is to maximize

$$\max_{P_t^*(k)} E_t \sum_{i=0}^{\infty} (\beta\rho)^i \left[\frac{P_{t+i-1}}{P_{t-1}} P_t^*(k) Y_{t+i} \left(\frac{P_{t+i}}{\frac{P_{t+i-1}}{P_{t-1}} P_t^*(k)} \right)^{\psi} \right.$$

$$\left. - P_{t+i} \frac{w_{t+i}}{(1-\theta)\lambda_{t+i}} \left[\frac{r_{t+i}(1-\theta)}{w_{t+i}\theta} \right]^{\theta} Y_{t+i} \left(\frac{P_{t+i}}{\frac{P_{t+i-1}}{P_{t-1}} P_t^*(k)} \right)^{\psi} \right],$$

which is the discounted sequence of expected income minus costs. This simplifies to

$$\max_{P_t^*(k)} E_t \sum_{i=0}^{\infty} (\beta\rho)^i \, Y_{t+i} \left(\frac{P_{t+i}}{\frac{P_{t+i-1}}{P_{t-1}} P_t^*(k)} \right)^{\psi}$$

$$\times \left[\frac{P_{t+i-1}}{P_{t-1}} P_t^*(k) - \frac{P_{t+i} w_{t+i}}{(1-\theta)\lambda_{t+i}} \left[\frac{r_{t+i}(1-\theta)}{w_{t+i}\theta} \right]^{\theta} \right].$$

The first-order condition for this problem is

$$0 = E_t \sum_{i=0}^{\infty} (\beta\rho)^i \, Y_{t+i}(k) \left[1 - \psi + \frac{\psi P_{t-1} P_{t+i} w_{t+i}}{P_{t+i-1} P_t^*(k)(1-\theta)\lambda_{t+i}} \left[\frac{r_{t+i}(1-\theta)}{w_{t+i}\theta} \right]^{\theta} \right],$$

which gives the pricing rule

$$P_t^*(k) = \frac{\psi}{\psi - 1} \frac{E_t \sum_{i=0}^{\infty} (\beta\rho)^i \frac{P_{t-1}P_{t+i}}{P_{t+i-1}} Y_{t+i}(k) \frac{w_{t+i}}{(1-\theta)\lambda_{t+i}} \left[\frac{r_{t+i}(1-\theta)}{w_{t+i}\theta} \right]^{\theta}}{E_t \sum_{i=0}^{\infty} (\beta\rho)^i \, Y_{t+i}(k)}. \quad (10.15)$$

Equations 10.14 and 10.15 are the only equations of the model that need to be modified because of the change in the rule of thumb used by the firms that cannot fix their prices optimally.

10.5.1   The Stationary State

Only two equations have changed in this model compared to the earlier: the intermediate goods firms' pricing rule and the final goods firms' pricing rule. We still have the same cash-in-advance constraint as before, so the stationary state version of that equation is still

$$\bar{C} = \overline{M/P}.$$

Here we write the constant stationary state real balances as $\overline{M/P}$. If consumption is to be constant in a stationary state, then so must be real balances. This implies that for any period t,

$$\frac{M_t}{P_t} = \overline{M/P} = \frac{M_{t-1}}{P_{t-1}},$$

and after a bit of algebra, this implies that

$$\frac{P_t}{P_{t-1}} = \frac{M_t}{M_{t-1}} = \bar{g}.$$

In a stationary state, the inflation rate must be the same as the growth rate of money.

The final goods firms' pricing rule can be written as

$$\left(P_t\right)^{1-\psi} = \rho \left(\bar{g} P_{t-1}\right)^{1-\psi} + (1 - \rho) \left(P_t^*\right)^{1-\psi},$$

and since $\bar{g} P_{t-1} = P_t$, this equation becomes

$$(1 - \rho) \left(P_t\right)^{1-\psi} = (1 - \rho) \left(P_t^*\right)^{1-\psi}.$$

In a stationary state where the rule-of-thumb firms have their prices adjusted by $\bar{g}$, the optimizing firms adjust their prices by exactly the same amount so that their prices are the same as the general price level.

Applying this result about optimal prices to the intermediate firms' pricing rule gives the same result that we found in the previous section,

$$\frac{\psi}{\psi - 1} = \frac{1}{\frac{\bar{w}}{(1-\theta)} \left[\frac{\bar{r}(1-\theta)}{\bar{w}\theta}\right]^{\theta}}.$$

This markup equation gives the same equation for salaries as before,

$$\bar{w} = \left[\frac{(\psi - 1)(1 - \theta)^{1-\theta} \theta^{\theta}}{\psi \bar{r}^{\theta}}\right]^{\frac{1}{1-\theta}}.$$

From the first-order conditions of the households, we have

$$-\frac{\beta}{\bar{C}} = \frac{B\bar{g}}{\bar{w}},$$

or

$$\bar{C} = -\frac{\beta \bar{w}}{\bar{g} B}.$$

The rest of the solution of the stationary state follows the same argument as before, except that when it comes to determining $\bar{Y}$, the result of substituting the above first-order condition into the household's budget constraint (equation 10.12) is now

$$-\frac{\beta\bar{w}}{\bar{g}B} = \bar{w}\left[\frac{\bar{r}(1-\theta)}{\bar{w}\theta}\right]^{\theta}\bar{Y} + \frac{\bar{Y}}{\psi} + (\bar{r}-\delta)\left[\frac{\bar{r}(1-\theta)}{\bar{w}\theta}\right]^{\theta-1}\bar{Y},$$

or

$$\bar{Y} = \frac{-\beta\bar{w}}{\bar{g}B\left(\bar{w}\left[\frac{\bar{r}(1-\theta)}{\bar{w}\theta}\right]^{\theta} + \frac{1}{\psi} + (\bar{r}-\delta)\left[\frac{\bar{r}(1-\theta)}{\bar{w}\theta}\right]^{\theta-1}\right)}.$$

This is the same expression as before, except that the old value of $\bar{Y}$ is divided by the gross rate of money growth, $\bar{g}$. Since the values of $\bar{K}$, $\bar{H}$, and $\bar{\xi}$ are all constants times Y, the growth rate of money matters in all of them. Table 10.7 shows the values of the variables in a stationary state with inflation adjustment in the rule of thumb.

The result of Table 10.7 is very similar to that we found in the Cooley-Hansen model of Chapter 8. Stationary state inflation reduces the values of all the real variables in a proportional way. The levels of the variables are somewhat lower here because of the effects of the markups of the intermediate goods firms.

| **EXERCISE 10.2**   Work out all the stationary state conditions.

10.5.2   Log Linearization

Log linearization of equation 10.14 gives

$$\bar{g}^{1-\psi}e^{(1-\psi)\tilde{P}_t-(1-\psi)\tilde{P}_{t-1}} = \rho\bar{g}^{1-\psi}e^{(1-\psi)\left(\tilde{P}_{t-1}-\tilde{P}_{t-2}\right)}$$

$$+ (1-\rho)\bar{g}^{1-\psi}e^{(1-\psi)\tilde{P}_t^*(k)-(1-\psi)\tilde{P}_{t-1}},$$

or

$$\tilde{P}_t = \rho\left(2\tilde{P}_{t-1} - \tilde{P}_{t-2}\right) + (1-\rho)\tilde{P}_t^*(k).$$

The log linearization of equation 10.15 results in

Table 10.7   Stationary states for standard economy with inflation rule of thumb

Variable	$\bar{r}$	$\bar{w}$	$\bar{Y}$	$\bar{H}$	$\bar{K}$	$\bar{\xi}$	$\bar{C}$
Stationary state value	.0351	2.0426	$\dfrac{1.0218}{\bar{g}}$	$\dfrac{.2901}{\bar{g}}$	$\dfrac{9.5271}{\bar{g}}$	$\dfrac{.0929}{\bar{g}}$	$\dfrac{.7836}{\bar{g}}$

$$\bar{P}^*(k)e^{\tilde{P}_t^*(k)} = \frac{\psi}{\psi - 1}\bar{P}\frac{\bar{w}}{(1-\theta)\lambda}\left[\frac{\bar{r}(1-\theta)}{\bar{w}\theta}\right]^{\theta}$$

$$\times \frac{E_t \sum_{i=0}^{\infty}(\beta\rho)^i\, e^{\tilde{P}_{t-1}+\tilde{P}_{t+i}-\tilde{P}_{t+i-1}+\tilde{Y}_{t+i}(k)+(1-\theta)\tilde{w}_{t+i}-\tilde{\lambda}_{t+i}+\theta\tilde{r}_{t+i}}}{E_t \sum_{i=0}^{\infty}(\beta\rho)^i\, e^{\tilde{Y}_{t+i}(k)}},$$

$$E_t \sum_{i=0}^{\infty}(\beta\rho)^i\, e^{\tilde{Y}_{t+i}(k)+\tilde{P}_t^*(k)}$$

$$= E_t \sum_{i=0}^{\infty}(\beta\rho)^i\, e^{\tilde{P}_{t-1}+\tilde{P}_{t+i}-\tilde{P}_{t+i-1}+\tilde{Y}_{t+i}(k)+(1-\theta)\tilde{w}_{t+i}-\tilde{\lambda}_{t+i}+\theta\tilde{r}_{t+i}},$$

or

$$\tilde{P}_t^*(k) = (1-\beta\rho)\, E_t \sum_{i=0}^{\infty}(\beta\rho)^i$$

$$\times \left[\tilde{P}_{t-1} + \tilde{P}_{t+i} - \tilde{P}_{t+i-1} + (1-\theta)\tilde{w}_{t+i} - \tilde{\lambda}_{t+i} + \theta\tilde{r}_{t+i}\right].$$

Substituting this into the log-linear version of the condition of the final goods firms gives

$$\tilde{P}_t = \rho\left(2\tilde{P}_{t-1} - \tilde{P}_{t-2}\right)$$

$$+\ (1-\rho)(1-\beta\rho)\, E_t \sum_{i=0}^{\infty}(\beta\rho)^i$$

$$\times \left[\tilde{P}_{t-1} + \tilde{P}_{t+i} - \tilde{P}_{t+i-1} + (1-\theta)\tilde{w}_{t+i} - \tilde{\lambda}_{t+i} + \theta\tilde{r}_{t+i}\right].$$

Now one needs to quasi difference this equation in order to reduce the infinite sum to something more manageable, so we operate on both sides by the polynomial in the lag operator, $1 - \beta\rho L^{-1}$, and get

$$\tilde{P}_t - \rho\left(2\tilde{P}_{t-1} - \tilde{P}_{t-2}\right) - \beta\rho\left(E_t\tilde{P}_{t+1} - \rho\left(2\tilde{P}_t - \tilde{P}_{t-1}\right)\right)$$

$$= (1-\rho)(1-\beta\rho)\, E_t \sum_{i=0}^{\infty}(\beta\rho)^i$$

$$\times \left[\tilde{P}_{t-1} + \tilde{P}_{t+i} - \tilde{P}_{t+i-1} + (1-\theta)\tilde{w}_{t+i} - \tilde{\lambda}_{t+i} + \theta\tilde{r}_{t+i}\right]$$

$$- \beta\rho(1-\rho)(1-\beta\rho) E_t \sum_{i=0}^{\infty} (\beta\rho)^i$$

$$\times \left[\tilde{P}_t + \tilde{P}_{t+i+1} - \tilde{P}_{t+i-1+1} + (1-\theta)\tilde{w}_{t+1+i} - \tilde{\lambda}_{t+1+i} + \theta\tilde{r}_{t+1+i} \right],$$

which simplifies to

$$\tilde{P}_t - \rho\left(2\tilde{P}_{t-1} - \tilde{P}_{t-2}\right) - \beta\rho\left(E_t\tilde{P}_{t+1} - \rho\left(2\tilde{P}_t - \tilde{P}_{t-1}\right)\right)$$

$$= (1-\rho)(1-\beta\rho)\left[(1-\theta)\tilde{w}_t - \tilde{\lambda}_t + \theta\tilde{r}_t\right]$$

$$+ (1-\rho)\left[(1-2\beta\rho) P_t + \beta\rho P_{t-1}\right]$$

and finally to

$$(1+2\beta)\,\tilde{P}_t - \beta E_t\tilde{P}_{t+1} - (2+\beta) P_{t-1} + \tilde{P}_{t-2} \qquad (10.16)$$

$$= \frac{(1-\rho)(1-\beta\rho)}{\rho}\left[(1-\theta)\tilde{w}_t - \tilde{\lambda}_t + \theta\tilde{r}_t\right].$$

This equation contains prices from four periods: $t-2$, $t-1$, t, and the expected prices in period $t+1$. To accommodate the addition of P_{t-2}, we will need to make some minor changes in the solution technique.

10.5.3 Solving the Model

The only change from the basic model with staggered prices is in replacing the third equation of the basic model with equation 10.16. However, this change necessitates a change in the way the model is written in its matrix form and a change in the definition of the state variables. The solution method we use requires that one is able to write the model in the form

$$0 = Ax_t + Bx_{t-1} + Cy_t + Dz_t,$$

$$0 = E_t\left[Fx_{t+1} + Gx_t + Hx_{t-1} + Jy_{t+1} + Ky_t + Lz_{t+1} + Mz_t\right],$$

$$z_{t+1} = Nz_t + \varepsilon_{t+1},$$

where x_t is the set of state variables at date t and y_t is the set of "jump" variables, the other variables of the model whose values one wants to determine. In the expectational equations, which is where the price setting equations went in the basic model, only x_{t+1}, x_t, and x_{t-1} appear, but this was enough so that the model with a price setting equation that included P_{t+1}, P_t, and P_{t-1} could be solved. In this model, the price setting equation contains P_{t+1}, P_t, P_{t-1}, and P_{t-2}, and it is this last element that causes the problem.

The technique for handling problems of this nature involves increasing the set of state variables and adding equations or identities so that the new variables will be appropriately defined. The new variable that is added to the state variable set is, in the case that we are treating here, prices lagged one period. We define x_t so that

$$x_t = \left[K_{t+1}, M_t, P_t, P_{t-1} \right]'.$$

With this definition of x_t, x_{t-1} is now

$$x_{t-1} = \left[K_t, M_{t-1}, P_{t-1}, P_{t-2} \right]',$$

and we have been able to include P_{t-2} among the variables of the model. The set of variables in y_t is unchanged. The new equation that we need to add is the identity $P_{t-1} = P_{t-1}$. It is added, in this case, so that the fourth element of x_t is always equal to the third element of x_{t-1}. In particular, we add an extra equation to the expectational set of equations, as represented by the block of matrices from F to M. In matrices F, J, K, L, and M, the fourth row, representing this new equation, is all zeros. In matrix G, the matrix associated with x_t, the fourth row is all zeros except for the fourth element, which is set equal to 1. In matrix H, the matrix associated with x_{t-1}, the fourth row is all zeros except for the third element, which is set equal to -1. This new equation imposes the condition that the fourth element of x_t, P_{t-1}, will always be equal to the third element of x_{t-1}, P_{t-1}. This equation generates what we need, that the last element of x_{t-1} will be equal to P_{t-2}, since it was set to that value in the period $t - 1$.

In the new version of our model, the matrices for the expectational equations are

$$F = \begin{bmatrix} 0 & 0 & 0 & 0 \\ 0 & 0 & 0 & 0 \\ 0 & 0 & \beta & 0 \\ 0 & 0 & 0 & 0 \end{bmatrix},$$

$$G = \begin{bmatrix} 0 & 0 & 0 & 0 \\ 0 & 1 & 0 & 0 \\ 0 & 0 & -1 - 2\beta & 0 \\ 0 & 0 & 0 & 1 \end{bmatrix},$$

$$H = \begin{bmatrix} 0 & 0 & 0 & 0 \\ 0 & -1 & 0 & 0 \\ 0 & 0 & 2+\beta & -1 \\ 0 & 0 & -1 & 0 \end{bmatrix},$$

$$J = \begin{bmatrix} \beta\bar{r} & -1 & 0 & 0 & 0 \\ 0 & 0 & 0 & 0 & 0 \\ 0 & 0 & 0 & 0 & 0 \\ 0 & 0 & 0 & 0 & 0 \end{bmatrix},$$

$$K = \begin{bmatrix} 0 & 1 & 0 & 0 & 0 \\ 0 & 0 & 0 & 0 & 0 \\ \frac{\theta(1-\rho)(1-\beta\rho)}{\rho} & \frac{(1-\theta)(1-\rho)(1-\beta\rho)}{\rho} & 0 & 0 & 0 \\ 0 & 0 & 0 & 0 & 0 \end{bmatrix},$$

$$L = \begin{bmatrix} 0 & 0 \\ 0 & 0 \\ 0 & 0 \\ 0 & 0 \end{bmatrix},$$

and

$$M = \begin{bmatrix} 0 & 0 \\ 0 & -1 \\ \frac{-(1-\rho)(1-\beta\rho)}{\rho} & 0 \\ 0 & 0 \end{bmatrix}.$$

Since the new state variable does not show up in the equations that are expressed by matrices A to D, these are simply

$$A = \begin{bmatrix} 0 & 0 & -1 & 0 \\ -\bar{K} & -\bar{C} & \bar{C} & 0 \\ 0 & -1 & 1 & 0 \\ 0 & 0 & 0 & 0 \\ 0 & 0 & 0 & 0 \end{bmatrix},$$

$$B = \begin{bmatrix} 0 & 1 & 0 & 0 \\ (1-\delta)\bar{K} & 0 & 0 & 0 \\ 0 & 0 & 0 & 0 \\ \theta & 0 & 0 & 0 \\ -1 & 0 & 0 & 0 \end{bmatrix},$$

$$C = \begin{bmatrix} 0 & 0 & -1 & 0 & 0 \\ 0 & 0 & 0 & \bar{Y} & 0 \\ 0 & 1 & 0 & 0 & 0 \\ 0 & 0 & 0 & -1 & 1-\theta \\ -1 & 1 & 0 & 0 & 1 \end{bmatrix},$$

and

$$D = \begin{bmatrix} 0 & 1 \\ 0 & 0 \\ 0 & -\pi \\ 1 & 0 \\ 0 & 0 \end{bmatrix},$$

where a column of zeros is added to matrices A and B and no changes at all occur to matrices C and D. N is also as before. $N = \begin{bmatrix} \gamma & 0 \\ 0 & \pi \end{bmatrix}$.

Using the model above, we solve for policy matrices of the form

$$x_{t+1} = Px_t + Qz_t$$

and

$$y_t = Rx_t + Sz_t.$$

We find, for the case where $\rho = .75$, that

$$P = \begin{bmatrix} 0.3450 & 1.1358 & -1.8440 & 0.7082 \\ 0 & 1 & 0 & 0 \\ -0.1881 & 0.3788 & 1.0073 & -0.3862 \\ 0 & 0 & 1 & 0 \end{bmatrix},$$

$$Q = \begin{bmatrix} -0.3926 & 1.5977 \\ 0 & 1 \\ -0.2040 & 0.5893 \\ 0 & 0 \end{bmatrix},$$

$$R = \begin{bmatrix} -10.3266 & 17.9123 & -29.0784 & 11.1662 \\ 0.1881 & 0.6212 & -1.0073 & 0.3862 \\ 0.1881 & 0.6212 & -1.0073 & 0.3862 \\ -5.7294 & 11.0663 & -17.9655 & 6.8992 \\ -9.5147 & 17.2911 & -28.0711 & 10.7800 \end{bmatrix},$$

and

$$S = \begin{bmatrix} -6.8340 & 24.6587 \\ 0.2040 & 0.8907 \\ 0.2040 & 0.4107 \\ -3.5044 & 15.2115 \\ -7.0381 & 23.7679 \end{bmatrix}.$$

Notice the "1" in the fourth row of the P matrix. This sets the fourth element of x_t, P_{t-1}, equal to the third element of x_{t-1}, also P_{t-1}. When this x_t becomes the state variable in period $s = t + 1$, $P_{s-2} = P_{t-1}$ is well defined.

The dynamic process for this model exhibits the same property that we observed in the Cooley-Hansen model. The coefficients of P, Q, R, and S do not change with the value of the stationary state growth rate of money. This occurs for the same reason as it did in the Cooley-Hansen model. The second line of the A to D matrices are the only part of the linear version model that contain stationary state values of the real variables. Every parameter of this equation is the value of a real variable whose value in the stationary state is a constant divided by the stationary state growth rate of money. All the parameters of this equation change proportionally, so the relationship among variables does not change.

The model was run for 50 simulations of 115 periods each. The estimates for relative standard errors and correlations with output are given in Table 10.8. Since prices respond to past inflation, there is less variance in consumption and capital. Notice that a slightly smaller standard error in the money supply shock (compared to the model with fixed prices for the nonoptimizing firms) was used to get this table, since this smaller value generated the relative standard error in output that we use as our benchmark. In this version of the model, output is even more sensitive to shocks in money growth.

Table 10.8   Staggered pricing model with inflation adjustment

$\sigma_\lambda = .00178$ $\sigma_g = .00116$	Relative standard error	Corrrelation with output
Output	1.76%	100.00%
Consumption	0.16%	16.72%
Investment	7.48%	99.75%
Capital	0.35%	39.67%
Hours	2.78%	99.72%
Prices	0.80%	-3.75%

10.5.4   Impulse Response Functions

In general, the impulse response functions for an economy with lagged inflation adjusted prices for the nonoptimizing firms show two differences when
compared to those of an economy with fixed prices for the nonoptimizing
firms. First, the medium-term responses are close to those of a similar model
without staggered pricing. This is because, in this newer model, technology
and monetary shocks do enter into the setting of the rule-of-thumb prices, but
with a lag. In the fixed price model, they never entered. Second, the short-term
responses are generally larger than in the fixed price model. The parameters
on the two lagged prices in the P and R matrices of the policy functions are
of opposite signs, and the second lagged price removes some of the effects
of the first. In period 2 when the shock occurs, both $\tilde{P}_{t-1}$ and $\tilde{P}_{t-2}$ are zero,
and only the effects of the Q and S matrices are seen. In period 3, $\tilde{P}_{t-1}$ is no
longer zero, but $\tilde{P}_{t-2}$ is, and the impacts of the large parameters on $\tilde{P}_{t-1}$ in
the policy matrices are not mitigated by the parameters, with opposite signs,
on $\tilde{P}_{t-2}$.

Responses to a technological or monetary growth shock for this model with
lagged inflation adjustment can be compared to those of the previous model
with fixed prices. In all cases, the economies being compared have $\bar{g} = 1$.

Figure 10.7 shows the response of prices and capital under both rules of
thumb to a technology shock of .01. The economy with the lagged inflation

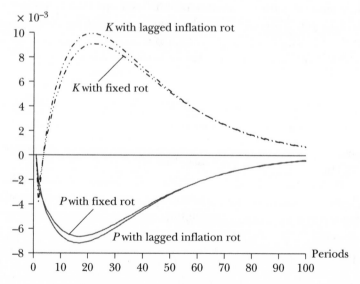

FIGURE 10.7   Response of $\tilde{K}$ and $\tilde{P}$ to a technology shock for two rules of thumb
(rot)

adjustment for nonoptimizing intermediate goods firms shows a larger initial negative response of capital and then a larger, positive medium-term response. Prices react more in the lagged inflation economy as well. Except for the initial response of capital, the responses of prices and capital are quite similar to those of the standard Cooley-Hansen model.

Figure 10.8 shows the medium-term responses of the real variables to the same shock for the two economies. The initial shocks are cut off so that one can better observe how the responses work out over the medium term. Both economies follow pretty much the same pattern, with the economy with lagged inflation adjustment producing slightly larger responses, responses closer to those of an economy without staggered pricing. The short-term responses of the two economies are shown in Figure 10.9. The economy with lagged inflation adjustment produces much larger negative initial responses for $\tilde{r}$, $\tilde{Y}$, and $\tilde{H}$, followed by larger positive responses for the same variables. This short-term response is a bit odd, especially if one considers the short-term effects of a negative technology shock. The initial response to a negative technology shock is for output to increase, rentals to increase, and labor supply to increase. Consumption declines and $\tilde{K}_{t+1}$ goes up. This is all quickly reverted, but these initial responses are difficult to explain.

The response of the model with a rule of thumb of lagged inflation adjustment to a money growth shock differs from the model with a rule of thumb of fixed prices in two ways. Figure 10.10 shows the responses of $\tilde{M}$, $\tilde{P}$, and $\tilde{K}$

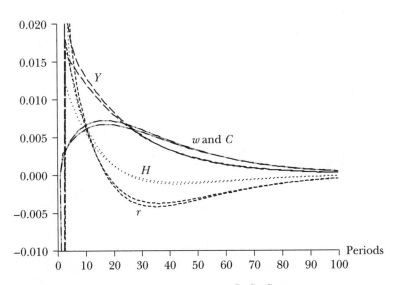

FIGURE 10.8 The medium-term responses of $\tilde{Y}$, $\tilde{C}$, $\tilde{H}$, $\tilde{r}$, and $\tilde{w}$ to a technology shock for two rules of thumb

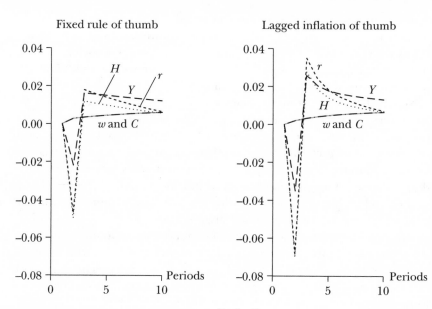

FIGURE 10.9 Short-term responses of $\tilde{Y}$, $\tilde{C}$, $\tilde{H}$, $\tilde{w}$, and $\tilde{r}$ to a technology shock for two rules of thumb

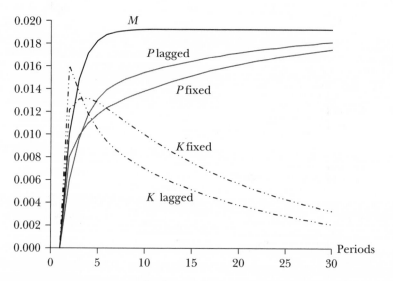

FIGURE 10.10 Responses of $\tilde{M}$, $\tilde{P}$, and $\tilde{K}$ to a money growth shock under two rules of thumb

to a .01 money growth shock for both rules of thumb. The initial response of prices in the economy with lagged inflation is less than under the fixed prices, but prices later adjust more rapidly to money growth. The response of capital is initially sharper but shows less persistence than in the fixed price model.

Figure 10.11 shows the responses of $\tilde{w}, \tilde{r}, \tilde{Y}, \tilde{C}$, and $\tilde{H}$ to the same .01 money growth shock for the two rules of thumb. The initial responses are positive (in response to a positive money shock) and larger for real variables in the economy with the lagged inflation rule of thumb. These larger initial responses occur, in part because the response of prices is less and the real variables need to adjust more to reach equilibrium. The larger initial responses are somewhat compensated by a larger negative response beginning in period 3. By period 10, the responses of economies with the two rules of thumb are very similar.

We can use the graph we developed for comparing responses as another way to see how the two rules of thumb, the fixed prices and the lagged inflation rules, differ in the way they respond to a monetary shock. Figure 10.12 shows this graph with the responses for the fixed price rule on the horizontal axis and the responses for the lagged inflation rule on the vertical axis. Since the immediate responses are above the 45 degree line, it should be clear that the short-term response of output, rentals, and hours is greater with the lagged inflation rate rule of thumb. The medium-term response is different for these

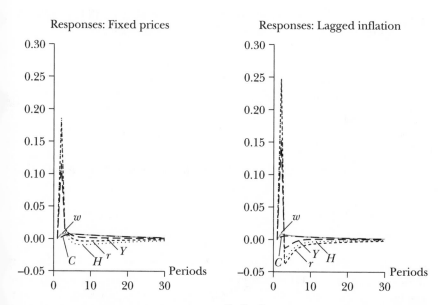

FIGURE 10.11 Short-term responses of $\tilde{Y}, \tilde{C}, \tilde{H}, \tilde{w}$, and $\tilde{r}$ to a money shock for two rules of thumb

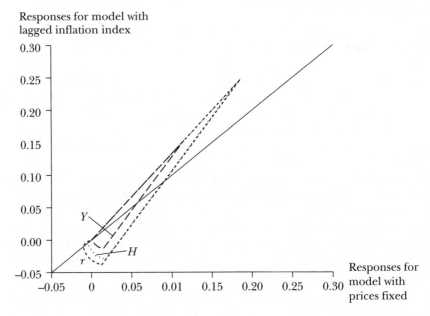

FIGURE 10.12   Comparing responses to monetary shock for two rules of thumb

variables as well. They all quickly go negative for the lagged inflation rule but remain positive for a number of periods with the fixed price rule.

> **EXERCISE 10.3**   Work out the dynamics for an economy idential to the one above but where the rule of thumb for nonoptimizing firms is
>
> $$P_t(k) = \frac{P_{t-2}}{P_{t-3}} P_{t-1}(k).$$
>
> This rule could be the case for an economy where aggregate price data is known with a lag.

10.6   REPRISE

The Calvo method of putting staggered prices into the model produces a model with a type of Phillips curve: in the short run, output responds to monetary shocks. The fewer the number of intermediate goods firms that can adjust their prices in each period, the larger the effects of a monetary shock on the real variables.

Two useful technologies for modeling real business cycles were introduced in this chapter: quasi differencing and additional lagged variables. Quasi differencing the log-linear version of the pricing equation allows one to simplify an infinite sequence of expected future values by operating on all parts of the equation with a polynomial in the lag operator (as leads). When this polynomial is chosen carefully, future elements of the infinite sequence cancel out. However, the variables of the equation that were not part of the infinite sequence were operated on as well, and the changes in how these variables enter the equation correct for the loss of the infinite sequence. In one sense, we convert an infinite sequence into a recursive format.

Additional lags entered the model when we apply a rule of thumb for the nonoptimizing firms that adjusts their prices by lagged inflation. Since lagged inflation is determined by periods $t-1$ and $t-2$ prices, we have an additional lag of prices in the model. This additional lag is put into the state variables. One also adds another equation (an identity) to the model that makes the value of the $t-1$ price in the time t state variable equal to the time $t-2$ price in the time $t+1$ state variable. Additional lags can enter our models by using, for example, a different rule of thumb or by adding habit persistence[2] to the utility function. Additional lags normally mean that the effects of shocks will persist longer in a model.

Models with staggered pricing are quite popular, especially with central banks, because they produce relatively large positive responses of real variables to positive monetary policy shocks. This result is consistent with much of what is observed in the data, particularly for OECD countries. Christiano, Eichenbaum, and Evans [30] discuss alternatives to staggered pricing as ways of getting models to capture the behavior observed in the data.

---

2. In models with habit persistence, utility is a function of the difference between current consumption and a function of past consumption or of an average of several periods of past consumption. A good paper on habit persistence is Boldrin, Christiano, and Fisher [15].

Staggered Wage Setting

In this chapter we apply to wages the same type of staggered price setting that we used in the previous chapter for intermediate goods prices. Here, households have differentiated labor and an independent and perfectly competitive firm[1] (or firms) bundles this differentiated labor into a single type of labor that is used by a second level of firms to produce goods. The way labor is bundled means that workers can exploit some monopoly power and set their wage rate, when they can set it, above the marginal rate of substitution of labor for consumption. As in the staggered pricing model, there is a Calvo type rule for wage setting, and each period a randomly chosen fraction $1 - \rho_w$ of the unit mass of workers get to fix their wages. There is evidence that wage rigidity of this type goes quite far in helping Real Business Cycle models capture correlations similar to those observed in the data of real economies, especially if it is used in conjunction with a staggered pricing rule.[2]

The Calvo rule for wage settings means that many households will continue to receive the wage that they received the previous period (which may be adjusted or not by some rule based on inflation). This means that past wages are important in determining the current equilibrium, and so wages, as were prices in the staggered price setting model, become a state variable in the dynamic system in this chapter.

---

1. Some authors refer to this labor bundling firm as an "employment agency."
2. See, for example, Christiano, Eichenbaum, and Evans [32].

11.1 THE LABOR BUNDLER

Define H_t as the time t effective labor that is supplied to the firms, with

$$H_t = \left[\int_0^1 \left(h_t^i \right)^{\frac{\psi_w - 1}{\psi_w}} di \right]^{\frac{\psi_w}{\psi_w - 1}},$$

where h_t^i is the amount of differentiated labor that is provided by the family or household i. Each type of labor, i, gets paid a nominal wage at time t of $W_t(i)$ and, since the bundling firm is perfectly competitive, the aggregate nominal wage rate at time t, W_t, is equal to

$$W_t = \left[\int_0^1 W_t(i)^{1 - \psi_w} di \right]^{\frac{1}{1 - \psi_w}}.$$

The demand by the bundling firm for each type of labor is

$$h_t^i = H_t \left(\frac{W_t}{W_t(i)} \right)^{\psi_w}.$$

As should be clear from the notation, the modeling of the staggered wage setting parallels the modeling of staggered pricing, with the households acting like the intermediate goods firms and the labor bundler acting like the final goods firm.

In each period, a randomly and independently chosen fraction, $1 - \rho_w$, of the families get to choose their wages optimally. The remaining ρ_w of the families follow a rule-of-thumb wage setting rule. In the simplest of economies, the rule of thumb is that they keep their nominal wages fixed, so that for this group,

$$W_t(i) = W_{t-1}(i).$$

Other possible rules for the nonoptimizing families include

$$W_t(i) = \bar{\pi} W_{t-1}(i),$$

where $\bar{\pi}$ is the stationary state inflation rate, or

$$W_t(i) = \frac{P_{t-1}}{P_{t-2}} W_{t-1}(i),$$

where P_{t-1}/P_{t-2} is the one-period lagged inflation rate. In the model that follows, we will use the rule of thumb that a household i that cannot optimally fix its wages keeps the nominal wage of the previous period, $W_t(i) = W_{t-1}(i)$.

As in the model with indivisible labor, we assume that there exists a labor insurance plan that ends up producing an equilibrium in which each family gets the same wage income and consumption during period t. To see why this assumption is important, assume it does not hold. Let $W_s^*(i)$ be the nominal wage that a family i chose in period s. Assume that in each period t, all families face the same future, have the same marginal utility of consumption, and have the same market power, so they would all choose the same optimal wage. The nominal wage fixing rule implies that in period t there is a fraction $1 - \rho_w$ of the population of families with their nominal wages equal to $W_t^*(i)$, a fraction $(1 - \rho_w)\rho_w$ of the families with nominal wages equal to $W_{t-1}^*(i)$, and fractions $(1 - \rho_w)\rho_w^n$ of the families with their nominal wages equal to $W_{t-n}^*(i)$. But this distribution of wages implies that, without any wage income insurance, there will be an infinite number of different wage incomes among the families. Given these different wage incomes, there will be different desired and realized savings and, because of that, different holdings of capital and different amounts of income from nonlabor sources. With different nonlabor incomes, families with the same wage income will have different consumptions and different marginal utility of consumption. Given different marginal utilities of consumption, families that can optimize in period t will *not* end up choosing the same wage. The assumption that all families will choose the same nominal wage is contradicted. In each period, an infinite distribution of wages will be chosen by the families that can optimize. The problem is clearly unworkable.

Introducing the appropriate kind of insurance market can help make the model workable. In each period, after aggregate uncertainties (the time t technology shock and money growth shock in this case) are realized and known to all the families and firms, but before the families know if they can set their wage this period or not, an insurance market opens where payments of premiums to a mutual insurance plan or of payouts from the mutual insurance plan depend on the outcome of the random process that selects which families can change their wages. Some families with relatively high nominal wages will have to make payments into the mutual insurance plan, while others will receive payments. This will depend on the history of the realizations of the shocks.

Since the contracts for insurance payments are signed before the realization of the uncertainty about which families get to choose their wages, at the moment of choosing wages, these payments are viewed by the family as lump sum (fixed) and do not enter into its wage setting calculations. Setting out the details for the operation of the insurance market is complicated and we do not develop them here. We simply use the result that in period t, goods consumption for all families ends up the same (see Christiano, Eichenbaum, and Evans [32] for details on how this market might work). Note that because the insurance plan is either mutual or perfectly competitive, when we sum across all families in the economy, the aggregate lump sum payments and transfers will be zero. In the aggregate version of the model, the insurance company disappears, but it has served the purpose of making the consumption and marginal utility of consumption in period t the same for all families.

With the assumption of the insurance plan and with the same initial capital stocks, all families who can optimize their wages in period t will choose the same nominal wage, $W_t^*(i) = W_t^*$. Since a fraction $(1 - \rho_w)$ of the families choose this nominal wage and the rest stay with the nominal wage they had the period before, aggregate nominal wages follow the rule

$$W_t = \left[(1 - \rho_w) \left(W_t^* \right)^{1 - \psi} + \rho_w \left(W_{t-1} \right)^{1 - \psi} \right]^{\frac{1}{1 - \psi}}.$$

We assume that, in period t, every family supplies all the labor of their type that is demanded given their period t wage. In period t, family i with nominal wage $W_t(i)$ will provide

$$h_t^i = H_t \left(\frac{W_t}{W_t(i)} \right)^{\psi_w}$$

units of labor to the market. In period t, a family i maximizes the expected discounted utility,

$$E_t \sum_{j=0}^{\infty} \beta^j \left[\ln c_{t+j}^i + A \ln(1 - h_{t+j}^i) \right],$$

subject to the budget constraints (we include a cash-in-advance constraint in this model)

$$P_t c_t^i = m_{t-1}^i + \left(g_t - 1 \right) M_{t-1}$$

and

$$k_{t+1}^i + \frac{m_t^i}{P_t} = \frac{W_t(i)}{P_t} h_t^i + r_t k_t^i + (1 - \delta) k_t^i + b_t^i,$$

where b_t^i is the wage insurance premium or payout and all other variables are as before. The insurance premium or payout is viewed by the family as a lump sum payment. For the $(1 - \rho_w)$ fraction of families who can set their wage in period t, they know that they face the probability $(\rho_w)^n$ that the wage they choose in this period, $W_t^*(i)$, will still be in effect n periods in the future. When family i gets to choose its wage $W_t^*(i)$, it maximizes

$$E_t \sum_{j=0}^{\infty} (\beta \rho_w)^j \left[\ln c_{t+j}^i + A \ln(1 - h_{t+j}^i) \right]$$

subject to the sequence of cash-in-advance constraints

$$P_{t+j} c_{t+j}^i = m_{t+j-1}^i + (g_{t+j} - 1) M_{t+j-1}$$

and budget constraints

$$k_{t+j+1}^i + \frac{m_{t+j}^i}{P_{t+j}} = \frac{W_t^*(i)}{P_{t+j}} h_{t+j}^i + r_{t+j} k_{t+j}^i + (1 - \delta) k_{t+j}^i + b_{t+j}^i,$$

where

$$h_{t+j}^i = H_{t+j} \left(\frac{W_{t+j}}{W_t^*(i)} \right)^{\psi_w},$$

is the demand function for family i's labor.

11.1.1   First-Order Conditions for Families

The first-order conditions for the family's maximization problem with respect to consumption, money, and period $t + 1$ capital are, respectively,

$$0 = \frac{1}{c_t^i} + \vartheta_t^1 P_t,$$

$$0 = -E_t \beta \vartheta_{t+1}^1 + \vartheta_t^2 \frac{1}{P_t},$$

and

$$0 = \vartheta_t^2 - \beta E_t \vartheta_{t+1}^2 \left(r_{t+1} + (1 - \delta) \right),$$

where ϑ_s^m is the Lagrangian multiplier on restriction $m = 1, 2$ in period s. These simplify to

$$\vartheta_t^1 = -\frac{1}{P_t c_t^i},$$

$$\vartheta_t^2 = -\beta E_t \frac{P_t}{P_{t+1} c_{t+1}^i},$$

and

$$E_t \frac{P_t}{P_{t+1} c^i_{t+1}} = \beta E_t \frac{P_{t+1}}{P_{t+2} c^i_{t+2}} \left(r_{t+1} + (1 - \delta) \right).$$

These first-order conditions give a relationship among period t's prices and expected prices in period $t + 1$ and $t + 2$. These equations have the effect of giving price formation an important forward-looking component. There are some minor technical difficulties in using our solution methods that come from the period $t + 2$ prices. Our solution technique normally requires variables dated periods $t - 1$, t, and $t + 1$.[3] We will deal with these problems when we do the log linearization. One cannot resolve the timing problem by simply using this first-order condition dated one period earlier, as

$$\frac{P_{t-1}}{P_t c^i_t} = \beta E_t \frac{P_t}{P_{t+1} c^i_{t+1}} \left(r_t + (1 - \delta) \right).$$

There are two reasons why this equation cannot be used. The original relationship is between two sets of expectations and not between realizations and expectations. Moving the relationship back one period also changes the dynamics in an important way. In the original formation, prices are forward looking, but in the altered formation, they are also backward looking, the time $t - 1$ price level would seem to be important in determining current prices. Mistakenly including this particular backward-looking price formation makes the model explosive.[4]

In addition to these first-order conditions, two other equations for the model come from this part of the family's optimization problem. These are the period t cash-in-advance constraint and real budget constraint. Because of staggered wage setting, the labor supply choice is more involved than before.

Following the same logic that we used in the staggered pricing chapter, a family that can set its wages in period t chooses a wage, $W_t^*(i)$, to maximize

---

3. In Chapter 10, we showed how to deal with addition lags, in that case, a variable where period $t - 2$ dated values entered the model.

4. With this backward formation, prices do not respond enough to shocks and, because of the cash-in-advance constraint, neither does consumption. A positive shock to capital ends up generating additional investment that makes capital accumulation grow without bound.

$$E_t \sum_{j=0}^{\infty} (\beta \rho_w)^j \left\{ \left[\ln c_{t+j}^i + A \ln \left(1 - H_{t+j} \left(\frac{W_{t+j}}{W_t^*(i)} \right)^{\psi_w} \right) \right] \right.$$

$$+ \vartheta_{t+j}^1 \left[P_{t+j} c_{t+j}^i - m_{t+j-1}^i - (g_{t+j} - 1) M_{t+j-1} \right]$$

$$+ \vartheta_{t+j}^2 \left[k_{t+j+1}^i + \frac{m_{t+j}^i}{P_{t+j}} - \frac{W_t^*(i)}{P_{t+j}} H_{t+j} \left(\frac{W_{t+j}}{W_t^*(i)} \right)^{\psi_w} \right.$$

$$\left. \left. - r_{t+j} k_{t+j}^i - (1 - \delta) k_{t+j}^i - b_{t+j}^i \right] \right\}.$$

The first-order condition for this problem is

$$0 = E_t \sum_{j=0}^{\infty} (\beta \rho_w)^j \left[A \frac{1}{1 - H_{t+j} \left(\frac{W_{t+j}}{W_t^*(i)} \right)^{\psi_w}} \left(\frac{W_{t+j}}{W_t^*(i)} \right)^{\psi_w} \frac{\psi_w H_{t+j}}{W_t^*(i)} \right.$$

$$\left. + \vartheta_{t+j}^2 \left[(\psi_w - 1) \frac{H_{t+j}}{P_{t+j}} \left(\frac{W_{t+j}}{W_t^*(i)} \right)^{\psi_w} \right] \right],$$

which becomes, after substituting in the results from above for the Lagrangian multipliers,

$$\frac{\psi_w A}{W_t^*(i)} E_t \sum_{j=0}^{\infty} (\beta \rho_w)^j \frac{1}{1 - H_{t+j} \left(\frac{W_{t+j}}{W_t^*(i)} \right)^{\psi_w}} H_{t+j} \left(\frac{W_{t+j}}{W_t^*(i)} \right)^{\psi_w}$$

$$= \beta (\psi_w - 1) E_t \sum_{j=0}^{\infty} (\beta \rho_w)^j \frac{1}{P_{t+1+j} c_{t+1+j}^i} H_{t+j} \left(\frac{W_{t+j}}{W_t^*(i)} \right)^{\psi_w},$$

or the wage setting rule,

$$W_t^*(i) = \frac{\psi_w}{(\psi_w - 1)} \frac{A}{\beta} \frac{E_t \sum_{j=0}^{\infty} (\beta \rho_w)^j \frac{1}{1 - h_{t+j}^i} h_{t+j}^i}{E_t \sum_{j=0}^{\infty} (\beta \rho_w)^j \frac{1}{P_{t+1+j} c_{t+1+j}^i} h_{t+j}^i}.$$

11.1.2 The Rest of the Model

The rest of the model is similar to the standard competitive, cash-in-advance model with nominal monetary transfers. Production is perfectly competitive, so with an aggregate production function of

$$Y_t = \lambda_t K_t^\theta H_t^{1-\theta},$$

the aggregate real wage is equal to

$$w_t = \frac{W_t}{P_t} = (1-\theta)\,\lambda_t K_t^\theta H_t^{-\theta} = (1-\theta)\,\frac{Y_t}{H_t},$$

and the real rental rate is

$$r_t = \theta \lambda_t K_t^{\theta-1} H_t^{1-\theta} = \theta \frac{Y_t}{K_t},$$

where, because of the labor bundler,

$$H_t = \left[\int_0^1 \left(h_t^i \right)^{\frac{\psi_w-1}{\psi_w}} di \right]^{\frac{\psi_w}{\psi_w-1}},$$

and, since capital is summed,

$$K_t = \int_0^1 k_t^i di.$$

11.1.3 Equilibrium Conditions

Since all families will end up identical in terms of income and preferences, in equilibrium the equation for capital aggregation becomes simply

$$K_t = k_t^i$$

and that for consumption is

$$C_t = c_t^i,$$

for all families i. Aggregating the real budget constraints for all families in period t gives

$$K_{t+1} + \frac{M_t}{P_t} = \int_0^1 \frac{W_t(i)}{P_t} h_t^i di + r_t K_t + (1-\delta)K_t,$$

where the insurance payments or premiums drop out. Given that the insurance companies act as if they are perfectly competitive, they make zero profits, so

$$\int_0^1 b_t^i di = 0$$

in every period. From the assumption that the labor bundling firms are also perfectly competitive, in equilibrium they make neither profits nor losses and in each period

$$W_t H_t = \int_0^1 W_t(i) h_t^i di.$$

Putting this into the aggregated family real budget constraint gives

$$K_{t+1} + \frac{M_t}{P_t} = \frac{W_t}{P_t} H_t + r_t K_t + (1 - \delta) K_t.$$

11.1.4 The Full Model

The full model with the variables $C_t, r_t, K_t, M_t, W_t, H_t, W_t^*, P_t, h_t^*, Y_t$ and the shocks λ_t and g_t contains the aggregate version of the first-order condition,

$$E_t \frac{P_t}{P_{t+1} C_{t+1}} = \beta E_t \frac{P_{t+1}}{P_{t+2} C_{t+2}} \left(r_{t+1} + (1 - \delta) \right),$$

the aggregate version of the budget constraint,

$$K_{t+1} + \frac{M_t}{P_t} = \frac{W_t}{P_t} H_t + r_t K_t + (1 - \delta) K_t,$$

the cash-in-advance constraint,

$$P_t C_t = g_t M_{t-1},$$

the money supply growth rule,

$$M_t = g_t M_{t-1},$$

the nominal wage setting equation,

$$W_t^*(i) = \frac{\psi_w}{(\psi_w - 1)} \frac{A}{\beta} \frac{E_t \sum_{j=0}^{\infty} (\beta \rho_w)^j \frac{1}{1 - h_{t+j}^i} h_{t+j}^i}{E_t \sum_{j=0}^{\infty} (\beta \rho_w)^j \frac{1}{P_{t+1+j} C_{t+1+j}} h_{t+j}^i},$$

the demand from the bundler for labor of the families that can fix their wages in period t,

$$h_t^* = H_t \left(\frac{W_t}{W_t^*(i)} \right)^{\psi_w},$$

the aggregate nominal wage equation from the labor bundler,

$$W_t^{1-\psi} = \left(1 - \rho_w\right) \left(W_t^*\right)^{1-\psi} + \rho_w \left(W_{t-1}\right)^{1-\psi},$$

the demand for bundled labor from the firms,

$$\frac{W_t}{P_t} = (1 - \theta) \frac{Y_t}{H_t},$$

the demand for capital by the firms,

$$r_t = \theta \frac{Y_t}{K_t},$$

and the production function,

$$Y_t = \lambda_t K_t^\theta H_t^{1-\theta}.$$

In addition, there are the two stochastic processes for technology and money growth,

$$\ln \lambda_t = \gamma \ln \lambda_{t-1} + \varepsilon_t^\lambda$$

and

$$\ln g_t = \pi \ln g_{t-1} + \varepsilon_t^g.$$

11.2 THE STATIONARY STATE

In the stationary state all the real variables are constants, both the technology and money growth shocks are equal to one, money and prices are at their initial values, and wages are constant. The aggregate wage equation gives the result that

$$\bar{W}^* = W,$$

which implies that

$$\bar{h}^* = \bar{H}.$$

The first-order condition gives, as usual,

$$\bar{r} = \frac{1}{\beta} - 1 + \delta.$$

The budget constraints give

$$\overline{M/P} = \overline{W/P}\,\bar{H} + (\bar{r} - \delta)\bar{K}$$

and

$$\overline{M/P} = \bar{C}.$$

The wage setting equation gives the real wage as

$$\overline{W/P} = \frac{\psi_w}{(\psi_w - 1)} \frac{A}{\beta} \frac{\bar{C}}{(1 - \bar{H})}.$$

Notice that the markup on wages is similar to that on prices. From the production side we have

$$\bar{Y} = \bar{K}^\theta \bar{H}^{1-\theta},$$

$$\overline{W/P} = (1 - \theta)\frac{\bar{Y}}{\bar{H}},$$

and

$$\bar{r} = \theta\frac{\bar{Y}}{\bar{K}}.$$

Using the standard values for the parameters of the system, $\beta = .99$, $\delta = .025$, $\theta = .36$, and $A = 1.72$, and taking from Christiano, Eichenbaum, and Evans [32] their baseline values of $\rho_w = .7$ and $\psi_w = 21$, the rental rate on capital is $\bar{r} = .00351$. From the conditions on the production side, we get

$$\overline{W/P} = (1 - \theta)\left[\frac{\theta}{\bar{r}}\right]^{\frac{\theta}{1-\theta}} = 2.3706.$$

From the wage setting equation, we use

$$\overline{W/P} = \frac{\psi_w}{(\psi_w - 1)} \frac{A}{\beta} \frac{\bar{C}}{(1 - \bar{H})}$$

or

$$\bar{C} = \overline{W/P}\frac{\beta\,(\psi_w - 1)}{A\psi_w}\,(1 - \bar{H}) = 1.2995\,(1 - \bar{H}),$$

and from the budget constraints and the production side, we get

$$\bar{C} = \overline{W/P}\bar{H} + (\bar{r} - \delta)\bar{K} = \overline{W/P}\left(1 + \frac{\theta(\bar{r} - \delta)}{(1 - \theta)\bar{r}}\right)\bar{H} = 2.7543\bar{H},$$

so

$$1.2995\,(1 - \bar{H}) = 2.7543\bar{H},$$

Table 11.1 Stationary state values for staggered wage economy

	$\bar{r}$	$\overline{W/P}$	$\bar{C} = \overline{M/P}$	$\bar{H}$	$\bar{K}$	$\bar{Y}$
Values	.0351	2.3706	0.8830	0.3206	12.1795	1.1875

or

$$\bar{H} = 0.3206$$

and

$$\bar{C} = 2.7543 * 0.3206 = 0.8830.$$

The other stationary state values are immediate from the conditions given above and the production function. The set of stationary state values for this economy is given in Table 11.1:

11.3 LOG LINEARIZATION

The one log linearization that is at all complicated is that for the wage equation. We begin with the wage setting equation

$$W_t^*(i) = \frac{\psi_w}{(\psi_w - 1)} \frac{A}{\beta} \frac{E_t \sum_{j=0}^{\infty} (\beta\rho_w)^j \frac{1}{1-h_{t+j}^i} h_{t+j}^i}{E_t \sum_{j=0}^{\infty} (\beta\rho_w)^j \frac{1}{P_{t+1+j} C_{t+1+j}} h_{t+j}^i}.$$

This can be written as

$$W_t^*(i) E_t \sum_{j=0}^{\infty} (\beta\rho_w)^j \frac{1}{P_{t+1+j} C_{t+1+j}} h_{t+j}^i$$

$$= \frac{\psi_w}{(\psi_w - 1)} \frac{A}{\beta} E_t \sum_{j=0}^{\infty} (\beta\rho_w)^j \frac{1}{1-h_{t+j}^i} h_{t+j}^i.$$

Log linearization of the left side gives

$$\overline{W/P} \frac{\bar{H}}{\bar{C}} E_t \sum_{j=0}^{\infty} (\beta\rho_w)^j \left(1 + \tilde{W}_t^*(i) + \tilde{h}_{t+j}^i - \tilde{P}_{t+1+j} - \tilde{C}_{t+1+j}\right)$$

and of the right side is

$$\frac{\psi_w}{(\psi_w - 1)} \frac{A}{\beta} \frac{\bar{H}}{1 - \bar{H}} E_t \sum_{j=0}^{\infty} (\beta\rho_w)^j \left(1 + \frac{1}{1 - \bar{H}} \tilde{h}_{t+j}^i\right).$$

Note, in doing the log linearization of the right side, one needs to take several approximations. First one finds that

$$\frac{h_t^i}{1-h_t^i} = \frac{\bar{H}e^{\tilde{h}_t^i}}{1-\bar{H}e^{\tilde{h}_t^i}} \approx \frac{\bar{H}\left(1+\tilde{h}_t^i\right)}{1-\bar{H}\left(1+\tilde{h}_t^i\right)} = \frac{\bar{H}}{1-\bar{H}}\frac{\left(1+\tilde{h}_t^i\right)}{\left(1-\frac{\bar{H}}{1-\bar{H}}\tilde{h}_t^i\right)}.$$

The last item in the denominator,

$$\left(1-\frac{\bar{H}}{1-\bar{H}}\tilde{h}_t^i\right),$$

is approximately equal to $e^{-\frac{\bar{H}}{1-\bar{H}}\tilde{h}_t^i}$. Substituting in, one gets

$$\frac{\bar{H}}{1-\bar{H}}\frac{\left(1+\tilde{h}_t^i\right)}{e^{-\frac{\bar{H}}{1-\bar{H}}\tilde{h}_t^i}} = \frac{\bar{H}}{1-\bar{H}}\left(1+\tilde{h}_t^i\right)e^{\frac{\bar{H}}{1-\bar{H}}\tilde{h}_t^i}$$

$$\approx \frac{\bar{H}}{1-\bar{H}}\left(1+\tilde{h}_t^i\right)\left(1+\frac{\bar{H}}{1-\bar{H}}\tilde{h}_t^i\right)$$

$$= \frac{\bar{H}}{1-\bar{H}}\left(1+\frac{1}{1-\bar{H}}\tilde{h}_{t+j}^i\right).$$

The stationary state of the above equation is

$$\overline{W/P}\frac{\bar{H}}{\bar{C}} = \frac{\psi_w}{(\psi_w-1)}\frac{A}{\beta}\frac{\bar{H}}{1-\bar{H}},$$

so

$$E_t\sum_{j=0}^{\infty}\left(\beta\rho_w\right)^j\left(\tilde{W}_t^*(i) - \frac{\bar{H}}{1-\bar{H}}\tilde{h}_{t+j}^i - \tilde{P}_{t+1+j} - \tilde{C}_{t+1+j}\right) = 0,$$

or the families that can set their wages choose

$$\tilde{W}_t^* = \left(1-\beta\rho_w\right)E_t\sum_{j=0}^{\infty}\left(\beta\rho_w\right)^j\left(\tilde{P}_{t+1+j} + \tilde{C}_{t+1+j} + \frac{\bar{H}}{1-\bar{H}}\tilde{h}_{t+j}^i\right).$$

Using the log-linear version of the wage evolution equation from the bundler,

$$\tilde{W}_t = (1-\rho_w)\tilde{W}_t^* + \rho_w\tilde{W}_{t-1},$$

gives

$$\tilde{W}_t - \rho_w \tilde{W}_{t-1}$$

$$= (1 - \rho_w) \left(1 - \beta \rho_w\right) E_t \sum_{j=0}^{\infty} (\beta \rho_w)^j \left(\tilde{P}_{t+1+j} + \tilde{C}_{t+1+j} + \frac{\bar{H}}{1 - \bar{H}} \tilde{h}^i_{t+j} \right).$$

Applying the quasi-differencing operator, $1 - \beta \rho_w L^{-1}$, to both sides gives for the left side

$$\left(1 + \beta \rho_w \rho_w\right) \tilde{W}_t - \rho_w \tilde{W}_{t-1} - \beta \rho_w E_t \tilde{W}_{t+1}$$

and for the right side

$$(1 - \rho_w) \left(1 - \beta \rho_w\right) E_t \sum_{j=0}^{\infty} (\beta \rho_w)^j \left(\tilde{P}_{t+1+j} + \tilde{C}_{t+1+j} + \frac{\bar{H}}{1 - \bar{H}} \tilde{h}^i_{t+j} \right)$$

$$- (1 - \rho_w) \left(1 - \beta \rho_w\right) E_t \sum_{j=0}^{\infty} (\beta \rho_w)^{j+1} \left(\tilde{P}_{t+2+j} + \tilde{C}_{t+2+j} + \frac{\bar{H}}{1 - \bar{H}} \tilde{h}^i_{t+j+1} \right)$$

$$= (1 - \rho_w) \left(1 - \beta \rho_w\right) E_t \left(\tilde{P}_{t+1} + \tilde{C}_{t+1} + \frac{\bar{H}}{1 - \bar{H}} \tilde{h}^i_t \right).$$

Therefore,

$$\left(1 + \beta \rho_w \rho_w\right) \tilde{W}_t - \rho_w \tilde{W}_{t-1} - \beta \rho_w E_t \tilde{W}_{t+1} \tag{11.1}$$

$$= (1 - \rho_w) \left(1 - \beta \rho_w\right) E_t \left(\tilde{P}_{t+1} + \tilde{C}_{t+1} + \frac{\bar{H}}{1 - \bar{H}} \tilde{h}^*_t \right),$$

where we put in $\tilde{h}^*_t$ for $\tilde{h}^i_t$ since all who can fix their wage will choose the same labor quantity. Finally, we want to remove the individual labor quantities from the equation, so we use the log-linear versions of the demand function for labor and the bundler's aggregate wage rule,

$$\tilde{h}^*_t = \tilde{H}_t + \psi_w \tilde{W}_t - \psi_w \tilde{W}^*_t,$$

$$\tilde{W}_t = \left(1 - \rho_w\right) \tilde{W}^*_t + \rho_w \tilde{W}_{t-1}.$$

These give the result that

$$\tilde{h}^*_t = \tilde{H}_t - \frac{\psi_w \rho_w \tilde{W}_t}{\left(1 - \rho_w\right)} + \frac{\psi_w \rho_w \tilde{W}_{t-1}}{\left(1 - \rho_w\right)}.$$

Putting this into equation 11.1 gives

$$\left[\left(1-\beta\rho_w\right)\frac{\psi_w\rho_w\bar{H}}{1-\bar{H}}+\left(1+\beta\rho_w\rho_w\right)\right]\tilde{W}_t$$

$$-\left[\left(1-\beta\rho_w\right)\frac{\psi_w\rho_w\bar{H}}{1-\bar{H}}+\rho_w\right]\tilde{W}_{t-1}-\beta\rho_w E_t\tilde{W}_{t+1}$$

$$=\left(1-\rho_w\right)\left(1-\beta\rho_w\right)E_t\left(\tilde{P}_{t+1}+\tilde{C}_{t+1}+\frac{\bar{H}}{1-\bar{H}}\tilde{H}_t\right).$$

The one other equation that requires some care is the nonwage first-order conditions from the family's optimization problem. That condition is

$$E_t\frac{P_t}{P_{t+1}c_{t+1}^i}=\beta E_t\frac{P_{t+1}}{P_{t+2}c_{t+2}^i}\left(r_{t+1}+(1-\delta)\right).$$

Given our solution method, there is an inherent difficulty in this equation in the period $t+2$ expected values for prices and consumption. Using the cash-in-advance constraint, we can replace $P_{t+2}c_{t+2}^i$ with $g_{t+2}m_{t+1}^i$ and write the first-order condition in aggregate form as

$$E_t\frac{P_t}{P_{t+1}C_{t+1}}=\beta E_t\frac{P_{t+1}}{g_{t+2}M_{t+1}}\left(r_{t+1}+(1-\delta)\right).$$

The log linearization of this equation yields, after some simplification,

$$E_t\left[\tilde{P}_t-\tilde{P}_{t+1}-\tilde{C}_{t+1}\right]=E_t\left[\tilde{P}_{t+1}-\tilde{g}_{t+2}-\tilde{M}_{t+1}+\beta\bar{r}\tilde{r}_{t+1}\right].\quad(11.2)$$

We now use the stochastic process for the growth rate of money,

$$\tilde{g}_t=\pi\tilde{g}_{t-1}+\varepsilon_t^g,$$

to find the expected value for $\tilde{g}_{t+2}$ in terms of $\tilde{g}_{t+1}$ and substitute that into equation 11.2 to get

$$E_t\left[\tilde{P}_t-\tilde{P}_{t+1}-\tilde{C}_{t+1}\right]=E_t\left[\tilde{P}_{t+1}-\pi\tilde{g}_{t+1}-\tilde{M}_{t+1}+\beta\bar{r}\tilde{r}_{t+1}\right].$$

The error term drops out because $E_t\tilde{\varepsilon}_{t+2}^g=0$. All variables are now from period t and $t+1$.

The log-linearized version of the model (the equations are in the order given in section 11.1.4,) is

$$0 = \tilde{P}_t - 2E_t\tilde{P}_{t+1} - E_t\tilde{C}_{t+1} + \pi E_t\tilde{g}_{t+1} + E_t\tilde{M}_{t+1} - \beta\bar{r}E_t\tilde{r}_{t+1}, \quad (11.3)$$

$$0 = \bar{K}\tilde{K}_{t+1} + \overline{M/P}\left[\tilde{M}_t - \tilde{P}_t\right] - \bar{Y}\tilde{Y}_t - (1-\delta)\,\bar{K}\tilde{K}_t,$$

$$0 = \tilde{P}_t + \tilde{C}_t - \tilde{g}_t - \tilde{M}_{t-1},$$

$$0 = \tilde{M}_t - \tilde{g}_t - \tilde{M}_{t-1}, \quad (11.4)$$

$$0 = \left[(1-\beta\rho_w)\frac{\psi_w\rho_w\bar{H}}{1-\bar{H}} + (1+\beta\rho_w\rho_w)\right]\tilde{W}_t \quad (11.5)$$

$$- \left[(1-\beta\rho_w)\frac{\psi_w\rho_w\bar{H}}{1-\bar{H}} + \rho_w\right]\tilde{W}_{t-1} - \beta\rho_w E_t\tilde{W}_{t+1}$$

$$- (1-\rho_w)(1-\beta\rho_w)\,E_t\left(\tilde{P}_{t+1} + \tilde{C}_{t+1} + \frac{\bar{H}}{1-\bar{H}}\tilde{H}_t\right),$$

$$0 = \tilde{W}_t - \tilde{P}_t - \tilde{Y}_t + \tilde{H}_t, \quad (11.6)$$

$$0 = \tilde{r}_t - \tilde{Y}_t + \tilde{K}_t,$$

$$0 = \tilde{Y}_t - \tilde{\lambda}_t - \theta\tilde{K}_t - (1-\theta)\,\tilde{H}_t,$$

plus the two stochastic equations,

$$0 = \tilde{\lambda}_t - \gamma\tilde{\lambda}_{t-1} - \varepsilon_t^\lambda$$

and

$$0 = \tilde{g}_t - \pi\tilde{g}_{t-1} - \varepsilon_t^g.$$

Here, $\tilde{X}_t = \ln X_t - \ln \bar{X}$, so all variables are measuring log differences from the stationary state.

11.4 SOLVING THE MODEL

As in earlier chapters, we solve this model by dividing the variables into state variables and "jump" endogenous variables and by dividing the system of equations into a group of expectational equations and a group of equations in which expectations do not appear. The state variables we choose are $x_t = [\tilde{K}_{t+1}, \tilde{M}_t, \tilde{P}_t, \tilde{W}_t]'$, the jump variables are $y_t = [\tilde{r}_t, \tilde{C}_t, \tilde{Y}_t, \tilde{H}_t]'$, and the stochastic shocks are $z_t = [\tilde{\lambda}_t, \tilde{g}_t]$. Wages, $\tilde{W}_t$, are included in the state variables since lagged wages are part of what determines the current equilibrium and because, from a technical point of view, we have past, current, and expected future wages appearing in equation 11.5 and our solution method needs to put variables occurring in three periods in the x_t vector. Recall that we have removed $\tilde{W}_t^*$ and $\tilde{h}_t^*$ from the system by substituting them out. The group of expectational equations that we choose are equations 11.3, 11.4, 11.5, and 11.6 from the equations in the log linearization list. As before, we write the system as

$$0 = Ax_t + Bx_{t-1} + Cy_t + Dz_t,$$

$$0 = E_t \left[Fx_{t+1} + Gx_t + Hx_{t-1} + Jy_{t+1} + Ky_t + Lz_{t+1} + Mz_t \right],$$

$$z_{t+1} = Nz_t + \varepsilon_{t+1},$$

where

$$A = \begin{bmatrix} \bar{K} & \bar{C} & -\bar{C} & 0 \\ 0 & 0 & 1 & 0 \\ 0 & 0 & 0 & 0 \\ 0 & 0 & 0 & 0 \end{bmatrix},$$

$$B = \begin{bmatrix} -(1-\delta)\bar{K} & 0 & 0 & 0 \\ 0 & -1 & 0 & 0 \\ 1 & 0 & 0 & 0 \\ -\theta & 0 & 0 & 0 \end{bmatrix},$$

$$C = \begin{bmatrix} 0 & 0 & -\bar{Y} & 0 \\ 0 & 1 & 0 & 0 \\ 1 & 0 & -1 & 0 \\ 0 & 0 & 1 & -(1-\theta) \end{bmatrix},$$

$$D = \begin{bmatrix} 0 & 0 \\ 0 & -1 \\ 0 & 0 \\ -1 & 0 \end{bmatrix},$$

$$F = \begin{bmatrix} 0 & 1 & -2 & 0 \\ 0 & 0 & 0 & 0 \\ 0 & 0 & -(1-\rho_w)(1-\beta\rho_w) & -\beta\rho_w \\ 0 & 0 & 0 & 0 \end{bmatrix},$$

$$G = \begin{bmatrix} 0 & 0 & 1 & 0 \\ 0 & 1 & 0 & 0 \\ 0 & 0 & 0 & 1 + \beta\rho_w^2 + \left(1 - \beta\rho_w\right)\frac{\psi_w\rho_w\bar{H}}{1-\bar{H}} \\ 0 & 0 & -1 & 1 \end{bmatrix},$$

$$H = \begin{bmatrix} 0 & 0 & 0 & 0 \\ 0 & -1 & 0 & 0 \\ 0 & 0 & 0 & -\rho_w - \left(1 - \beta\rho_w\right)\frac{\psi_w\rho_w\bar{H}}{1-\bar{H}} \\ 0 & 0 & 0 & 0 \end{bmatrix},$$

$$J = \begin{bmatrix} -\bar{r}\beta & -1 & 0 & 0 \\ 0 & 0 & 0 & 0 \\ 0 & -\left(1 - \rho_w\right)\left(1 - \beta\rho_w\right) & 0 & 0 \\ 0 & 0 & 0 & 0 \end{bmatrix},$$

$$K = \begin{bmatrix} 0 & 0 & 0 & 0 \\ 0 & 0 & 0 & 0 \\ 0 & 0 & 0 & -\left(1 - \rho_w\right)\left(1 - \beta\rho_w\right)\frac{\bar{H}}{1-\bar{H}} \\ 0 & 0 & -1 & 1 \end{bmatrix},$$

$$L = \begin{bmatrix} 0 & \pi \\ 0 & 0 \\ 0 & 0 \\ 0 & 0 \end{bmatrix},$$

and

$$M = \begin{bmatrix} 0 & 0 \\ 0 & -1 \\ 0 & 0 \\ 0 & 0 \end{bmatrix}.$$

As before

$$N = \begin{bmatrix} \gamma & 0 \\ 0 & \pi \end{bmatrix}.$$

A solution to this model is a pair of policy equations of the form

$$x_{t+1} = Px_t + Qz_t$$

and

$$y_t = Rx_t + Sz_t.$$

Using the techniques that we have described in previous chapters for finding a solution, our results for the standard economy, where $\rho_w = .7$ and $\psi_w = 21$, are

$$P = \begin{bmatrix} 0.9394 & 0.0988 & 0 & -0.0988 \\ 0 & 1 & 0 & 0 \\ -0.5479 & 0.7504 & 0 & 0.2496 \\ -0.0093 & 0.0758 & 0 & 0.9242 \end{bmatrix},$$

$$Q = \begin{bmatrix} 0.1583 & 0.1546 \\ 0 & 1 \\ -0.4385 & 1.0028 \\ 0.0274 & 0.1118 \end{bmatrix},$$

$$R = \begin{bmatrix} -0.9575 & 1.1993 & 0 & -1.1993 \\ 0.5479 & 0.2496 & 0 & -0.2496 \\ 0.0425 & 1.1993 & 0 & -1.1993 \\ -0.4960 & 1.8739 & 0 & -1.8739 \end{bmatrix},$$

and

$$S = \begin{bmatrix} 1.9494 & 1.5840 \\ 0.4385 & -0.0028 \\ 1.9494 & 1.5840 \\ 1.4835 & 2.4750 \end{bmatrix}.$$

These results illustrate one of our claims about the solution technique. They are telling us that we did not need to include prices as a state variable. Time $t - 1$ prices do not provide any information about the values of the time t variables (that is why the columns for prices in both the matrices P and R are all zeros). We could just as easily have made prices one of the jump variables. Our solution technique, in one sense, rejects state variables that are not really state variables by fixing all of their coefficients to zero in the P and R matrices. One could have solved the model by having declared all the variables as state variables and the solution technique would have set the columns for the other variables that are not really state variables to zero, just as it did for prices in this case.

Simulations were used to calculate the standard errors and correlations for the set of variables shown in Table 11.2. Notice that the standard error of the technology shock is the one we have been using in previous chapters, and the one for the money growth shock was chosen so that the relative standard error of output is equal to 1.76 percent. This money growth shock is larger than that in the staggered pricing model.

11.4.1 Impulse Response Functions

Figures 11.1 and 11.2 show the response of the standard staggered wage setting economy (with $\rho_w = .7$ and $\psi_w = 21$) to a .01 shock in technology and money growth, respectively.

The responses to a technology shock are very similar to those of the standard Cooley-Hansen model (see Figure 8.2 on page 210). Most of the variables

Table 11.2 Standard errors and correlations

$\sigma_\lambda = .00178$ $\sigma_g = .00333$	Relative standard error	Correlation with output
Output	1.76%	100.00%
Consumption	.97%	73.77%
Investment	5.09%	93.84%
Capital	1.32%	62.60%
Hours	2.20%	92.31%
Prices	2.04%	43.50%
Wages	2.02%	24.63%

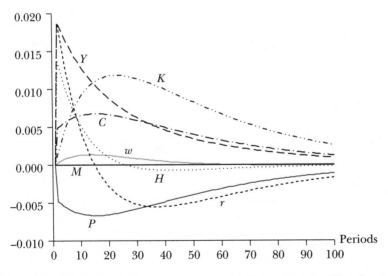

FIGURE 11.1 Response of staggered wage setting economy to a .01 technology shock

move pretty much the same way during the first ten or so periods, except for prices and consumption, which respond more in the Cooley-Hansen model. The staggered wage setting model tends to show more persistence, and, in general, the responses take more time to return to their stationary state values. Figure 11.3 shows the response of real wages (since the wages in Figure 11.1 are nominal wages) in the two models. The responses are very similar, but that of the staggered wage setting model is a bit larger initially and continue somewhat longer.

The responses of the staggered wage setting model to a money growth shock are very different from those of the Cooley-Hansen model. Not only are they much larger, but real variables respond strongly to the money growth shock. The responses of real variables are quite similar in form to those that result from a technology shock: the initial responses are large and there is substantial persistence. The responses of the nominal variables are also interesting. Prices initially respond much more than nominal wages so that, at first, real wages decline and the demand for labor jumps. Later, since nominal wages are closer to the money growth line than are prices, real wages move above the stationary state.

The responses of the staggered price setting economy to either a technology shock or a money growth shock do not exhibit the very strong, very short-term responses that occurred in the staggered pricing model. The ini-

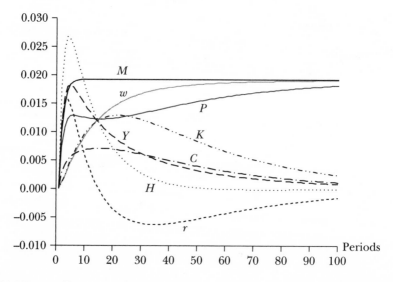

FIGURE 11.2   Response of staggered wage setting economy to a .01 money growth shock

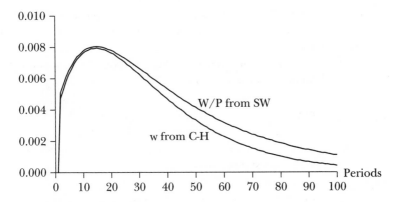

FIGURE 11.3 Responses of real wages in the Cooley-Hansen model and in the staggered wage setting model

tial reaction of the economy to a technology shock is more like that of other models. The big benefit of the staggered wage setting model is that money growth shocks generate responses, both immediate and medium term, that are in keeping with the data.

11.5 REPRISE

The staggered wage setting model provides an attractive alternative to staggered pricing as a way of generating a model where monetary policy can have real effects where these effects are in the direction that one tends to observe in the data. In practice, most models used by central banks or other practitioners include both staggered pricing and staggered wage setting, as do most models that go under the heading of New Keynesian models.

Solving models with staggered wage setting is very similar to solving those with staggered pricing. Both models use quasi differencing in exactly the same way. Both models permit a number of different rules of thumb, and an interesting exercise is to study how the choice of a rule of thumb predicates the results of the model.

An advantage of staggered wage models is that they do not display the rather strange large drop in output that occurs from a positive technology shock in a staggered pricing model. Without having this weakness, staggered wage models can add a persistence coming from monetary shocks that is similar to that found in staggered pricing models.

EXERCISE 11.1 How does this model change if the stationary state rate of growth of money is greater than zero? Write out the basic model and find the values for variables in the stationary state. What feasibility or boundary conditions for labor supply need to hold?

EXERCISE 11.2 Write out the basic model when the wages of those who cannot optimally fix their wages are adjusted by a one-period lagged inflation rate in an economy where the stationary state gross money supply growth, $\bar{g}$, is equal to one. Write out the log-linear version of this model and solve for the P, Q, R, and S matrices. Compare the impulse response functions to those without the inflation adjustment.

EXERCISE 11.3 Write out the model and solve the log-linear version for the above problem with wages for the nonoptimizer being indexed by one-period lagged inflation but for the case where the stationary state gross money growth rate, $\bar{g}$, is greater than one. Compare the impulse response functions for two different stationary state growth rates of money.

EXERCISE 11.4 Write out and solve a model with both staggered pricing and staggered wage setting. To keep things simple, let $\bar{g} = 1$, and have the rules of thumb be to keep the nonoptimizing prices and wages fixed.

Financial Markets and Monetary Policy

We have two objectives in this chapter. First we add a financial intermediary (a kind of bank) to the cash-in-advance model of Chapter 8. This financial sector takes deposits of money from the households and lends it to the firms as working capital to pay for the wage bill. If we allow monetary shocks to enter the economy via this financial sector, rather than via households, higher money growth results in higher output. This is good in the sense that many empirical studies[1] have shown that, at least in economies with relatively low inflation rates, output growth and money growth are correlated. The dynamics of the model also give positive correlations between money shocks and output. This is a very different result from tax that resulted from monetary shocks in the Cooley-Hansen model of Chapter 8.

Once we have a model that says that money can have positive effects for the economy, we can start thinking about what the optimal monetary policy is for a central bank (who normally operates the monetary policy of a country). We do this in the second half of this chapter by considering two quite famous monetary policy rules: the Taylor rule and the Friedman rule. A Taylor rule is a feedback rule for setting short-term interest rates based on how much output and inflation differ from desired levels. A Friedman rule is a constant money growth rule. Since we impose monetary policy rules, it is difficult to justify money shocks coming from the central bank (except, perhaps, through incompetence or faulty information). Therefore, in this section money shocks enter the economy as they did in the Cooley-Hansen model: through direct money transfers or taxes to the households.

---

1. See, for example, McCandless and Weber [62].

In the model here, firms need to pay for labor services before the goods are sold, so firms borrow to cover the wage bill. A simple, perfectly competitive mutual fund (or banking) sector takes in deposits of money from individuals and makes in-period loans to the firms. The loan is made at the beginning of a period and is paid back once the goods have been sold at the end of the same period. This kind of financial intermediary allows one to introduce a monetary policy where a central bank can make monetary transfers either to the public directly (as in the Cooley-Hansen model) or to the financial system. In this chapter we limit the transfers from the central bank to go directly to the financial system. Financial systems similar to this have been explored by Cooley and Quadrini [37], Fuerst [42], Carlstrom and Fuerst [22], and Christiano, Eichenbaum, and Evans [29], [31] and [32].

We continue to use the same cash-in-advance constraint that we used in Chapter 8. Writing the constraint in this way says that only money carried over from the previous period can be used for consumption expenditures or for deposits in the financial system. A number of models of this type allow money wages paid in the period to enter the cash-in-advance constraint.[2] The argument is that if the wages are paid at the beginning of the period, then it seems strange that these wages must be held until the next period to be used for purchasing consumption goods. It also means that wages paid at the beginning of the period can go to deposits in the financial system that are lent to finance wages in this period. The issue is really one of timing and of trying to force, in a logical way, a continuous process of earning income and making a flow of consumption expenditures into a discrete time model. Which assumption to use is related to how long one thinks a period is and how long the lags are between receiving income and spending it. We use the older cash-in-advance assumption that current income does not enter into the cash-in-advance constraint.

There is another good way of adding a financial system to a model via the agency costs method, where there is aggregate risk in borrowing and firm owners put up their wealth as collateral for the loans. These models require a number of additional complications to make them work and are not developed in this book. The interested reader can consult Bernanke and Gertler [9], Fuerst [43], and Carlstrom and Fuerst [23] for good examples of agency cost models.

---

2. For example, the models of Fuerst [42], Carlstrom and Fuerst [22], and Christiano, Eichenbaum, and Evans [30] all allow current money wage income to be used for consumption and for bank deposits in the period it is earned.

12.1 WORKING CAPITAL

Consider an economy where firms need to borrow working capital from a financial intermediary in order to pay the wage bill for the current period. The loans are made and paid back during the period. Since in-period uncertainty is revealed before the loans take place, this type of lending is not risky and the firms always pay back the loans. There is a cash-in-advance constraint on consumption purchases. At the beginning of each period, the households are holding money that they are carrying over from the previous period. They lend some of this money to a financial intermediary who lends it to the firms for working capital. The firms use this money to pay wages. The households use the rest of their money to purchase consumption. As mentioned above, the way we set up the model, money that is used for financing working capital in period t cannot be used to purchase consumption in period t. Some versions of working capital models permit period t wage income to be used by the households to purchase period t consumption. This one does not.

Monetary policy works through the financial intermediaries. In each period, they receive an injection of new money from or pay a lump sum monetary tax to the monetary authority. In the model we present in this first section, no money transfers go to the households (as in the Cooley-Hansen model of Chapter 8). The reader will want to compare the results of this model to that of Chapter 8. How money enters an economy matters a lot for its impact on output and utility.

12.1.1 Households

Households are the owners of physical capital and can invest in new capital outside of the cash-in-advance constraint. Period t wage income can be used to finance investment in new capital even though it can't be used for period t consumption. Firms rent capital and hire labor from the households in perfectly competitive markets.[3]

The economy has three types of agents: households, firms, and financial intermediaries. The households want to maximize a utility function of the form

$$E_t \sum_{t=0}^{\infty} \beta^t u(c_t^i, 1 - h_t^i),$$

---

3. Of course, these models can be done with staggered pricing and staggered wage setting, but we exclude these characteristics here to keep the model relatively simple and concentrate on the financial aspects.

subject to a cash-in-advance constraint,

$$P_t c_t^i \leq m_{t-1}^i - N_t^i,$$

and the budget constraint,

$$\frac{m_t^i}{P_t} + k_{t+1}^i = w_t h_t^i + r_t k_t^i + (1-\delta)k_t^i + \frac{r_t^n N_t^i}{P_t}, \tag{12.1}$$

where most variables are as before with the addition of N_t^i as family i's period t nominal lending to the financial intermediary and r_t^n as the gross nominal interest rate paid by the financial intermediary. Notice that in the cash-in-advance constraint, money is used both for paying for consumption goods and for deposits in the financial intermediary. The gross income from the deposits appears in the budget constraint because it can be used to finance the next period's capital or money holdings.

The interest rate r_t^n is simultaneously nominal and real. It is nominal in that it is paid in money based on the amount of money deposited in the financial intermediary. However, the deposit is made at the beginning of a period and interest is paid at the end of the same period. Prices change between periods, but not during them, so inflation is not included in r_t^n. The household budget constraint, equation 12.1, indicates that the earnings from this interest can go into a real good (capital) as well as into money holdings. Since these earnings can go immediately into a real good, they need not be affected by interperiod inflation.

In keeping with the Cooley-Hansen cash-in-advance model, we assume indivisible labor. The subutility function is

$$u(c_t^i, 1 - h_t^i) = \ln(c_t^i) + h_t^i B,$$

where $B = \ln(1 - h_0)/h_0$, and h_0 is the amount of indivisible labor that a household contracts to provide if it is one of the families that is randomly chosen to provide labor. The ratio h_t^i/h_0 is the probability that the family will be providing labor in period t. As before, there is an insurance market that all households join that makes wage income independent of the amount of labor each family ends up providing. As the household's optimization problem is written here, the decision to lend to the financial intermediary is made after the time t information is known. This information includes the period t technology and money growth shocks.

Alternative assumptions about the information that is available can change the dynamics of the model. In what are called *limited participation* models,[4] the decision on how much to lend to the financial intermediary is made before the monetary shock is known. One possible way to model this limited participation is to move forward the decision about how much to send to the financial intermediaries market and write the two constraints as

$$P_t c_t^i \leq m_{t-1}^i \tag{12.2}$$

and

$$\frac{N_t^i}{P_t} + \frac{m_t^i}{P_t} + k_{t+1}^i = w_t h_t^i + r_t k_t^i + (1 - \delta)k_t^i + \frac{r_t^n N_{t-1}^i}{P_t},$$

and require as an equilibrium condition that the sum of the end-of-period lending to the financial intermediaries and the end-of-period money holdings for consumption expenditures equal the end-of-period money supply,

$$M_t = \int_0^1 m_t^i di + \int_0^1 N_t^i di.$$

The division of money between holdings for consumption and lending to the financial intermediary are both made in the period before this money is used. N_t^i will be used to finance time $t + 1$ wages and m_t^i will finance time $t + 1$ consumption. As the problem is described in this paragraph, the decision of how much to lend to the intermediary is made before any of the period t monetary uncertainty is revealed. It should be noted that the cash-in-advance constraint (equation 12.2) in these models often includes wages earned in the period, and these are left out of the flow budget constraint.

12.1.2   Firms

A single representative firm that behaves as if it is perfectly competitive rents capital and hires labor so as to maximize profits in each period. As before, the production function is

$$Y_t = \lambda_t K_t^\theta H_t^{1-\theta},$$

and the representative firm maximizes profits subject to the budget constraint

$$Y_t = r_t^f w_t H_t + r_t K_t,$$

---

4. See, for example, Christiano [27], Christiano and Gust [33], Christiano, Eichenbaum, and Evans [30], Fuerst [42], and Lucas [57].

where r_t^f is the gross interest rate that the firm pays on the working capital that it borrows. This is one of the crucial innovations of this model; because working capital is needed to finance wages, changes in the interest rate, r_t^f, will change production decisions and have a direct effect on output.

12.1.3   Financial Intermediaries

The financial intermediary (or intermediaries) operates as if it were perfectly competitive and takes deposits from the households and makes riskless loans to the firms for financing their working capital. In addition, it is through the financial intermediaries that the "central bank" or monetary authority operates its monetary policy with stochastic injections or withdrawals of money. The budget constraint for the financial intermediary is

$$r_t^f \left(N_t + \left(g_t - 1 \right) M_{t-1} \right) = \int_0^1 r_t^n N_t^i di = r_t^n N_t,$$

where g_t is the gross growth rate of money in period t. This budget constraint is simply a zero profit condition. All that the financial intermediary earns on loans is paid out to the depositors. An equilibrium condition for the financial market is that

$$\left(N_t + \left(g_t - 1 \right) M_{t-1} \right) = P_t w_t H_t.$$

All of the funds that households have lent to the financial intermediary plus net financial injections or withdrawals from the monetary authority are lent by the financial intermediary to firms and are used to finance wage payments.

For simplicity, we have assumed that financial intermediaries have no costs of operation and take no risk. These characteristics can be added without very much effect on the results and may make the results of the model fit real economies better.

12.1.4   The Full Model

The model consists of the variables w_t, r_t, C_t, P_t, M_t, N_t, K_t, Y_t, H_t, r_t^n, r_t^f, and g_t. The first-order conditions for the households, taking aggregation into account, are

$$\frac{B}{w_t} = -\beta E_t \frac{P_t}{P_{t+1}C_{t+1}}, \tag{12.3}$$

$$\frac{1}{w_t} = \beta E_t \frac{r_{t+1} + 1 - \delta}{w_{t+1}}, \tag{12.4}$$

and

$$r_t^n = -\frac{w_t}{BC_t} = \frac{1}{E_t \frac{\beta P_t C_t}{P_{t+1}C_{t+1}}}. \tag{12.5}$$

In addition, the household side of the economy adds the two aggregated budget constraints, at equality, the cash-in-advance constraint for household consumption,

$$P_t C_t = M_{t-1} - N_t, \tag{12.6}$$

and the real flow budget constraint,

$$\frac{M_t}{P_t} + K_{t+1} = w_t H_t + r_t K_t + (1 - \delta)K_t + \frac{r_t^n N_t}{P_t}. \tag{12.7}$$

For the firms, given competitive factor markets and labor input financed by borrowing, the marginal product of labor needs to cover the real wage and the financing costs,

$$r_t^f w_t = (1 - \theta) \lambda_t K_t^\theta H_t^{-\theta}, \tag{12.8}$$

and the marginal product of capital is equal to the rental,

$$r_t = \theta \lambda_t K_t^{\theta-1} H_t^{1-\theta}. \tag{12.9}$$

The production function,

$$Y_t = \lambda_t K_t^\theta H_t^{1-\theta}, \tag{12.10}$$

gives output. The zero profit condition for the financial intermediary implies that the income they receive from lending to the firms what they get from the households, plus the money transfer or withdrawal, is equal to what they pay back to the households, or

$$r_t^f \left(N_t + (g_t - 1) M_{t-1} \right) = r_t^n N_t. \tag{12.11}$$

Clearing of the credit market implies that all lending by the financial intermediary goes to finance hiring labor,

$$\left(N_t + \left(g_t - 1\right) M_{t-1}\right) = P_t w_t H_t. \tag{12.12}$$

To close the model we need to add the growth rate of money, a very simple form of monetary policy,

$$M_t = g_t M_{t-1}. \tag{12.13}$$

We assume that the growth rate of money, g_t, follows the law of motion,

$$\ln g_t = \pi \ln g_{t-1} + \varepsilon_t^g,$$

where the expected value of the shock is $E_{t-1}\varepsilon_t^g = 0$.

12.1.5   The Stationary State

In a stationary state, all real variables have the same value throughout time. The nominal variables can grow or decline, but the real values of the nominal variables stay constant. We define the variables $\overline{M/P}$ as stationary state real balances of the households and $\overline{N/P}$ as stationary state real household lending to the financial intermediaries. The stationary state gross growth rate of money, $\bar{g}$, will need to be equal to the stationary state inflation rate, $\bar{\pi}$, so that M_t/P_t will be equal to $\overline{M/P}$ for all t. As we have seen many times before, equation 12.4 implies that in the stationary state, the real return on capital is

$$\bar{r} = \frac{1}{\beta} - 1 + \delta.$$

From equation 12.5, we get the stationary state nominal return on lending to the financial intermediary,

$$\bar{r}^n = \frac{\bar{\pi}}{\beta} = \frac{\bar{g}}{\beta}.$$

Notice that from equation 12.11, when $\bar{g} = 1$,

$$\bar{r}^f = \bar{r}^n = \frac{1}{\beta}.$$

These two interest rates are not equal for other stationary state growth rates of the money stock and, as we will see, the stationary state interest rate on household lending to the financial intermediary, $\bar{r}^n$, will go up as the stationary state growth rate of the money stock increases, while the stationary state interest rate paid by the firms, $\bar{r}^f$, will go down. Equation 12.5 also gives the equation

$$\bar{C} = -\frac{\bar{w}\beta}{\bar{g}B}.$$

Using equations 12.8 and 12.9, we get

$$\bar{r}^f \bar{w} = (1 - \theta) \left(\frac{\theta}{\bar{r}}\right)^{\frac{\theta}{1-\theta}}$$

and

$$\overline{K} = \overline{H} \left(\frac{\theta}{\bar{r}}\right)^{\frac{1}{1-\theta}}.$$

One can eliminate wages from the first of these equations and get

$$\bar{r}^f = -\frac{\beta (1 - \theta) \left(\frac{\theta}{\bar{r}}\right)^{\frac{\theta}{1-\theta}}}{\overline{C}\bar{g}B}. \tag{12.14}$$

Using the production function, equation 12.10, and the equation for capital, we get

$$\overline{Y} = \overline{H} \left(\frac{\theta}{\bar{r}}\right)^{\frac{\theta}{1-\theta}}.$$

The two equations on the financial market, equations 12.11 and 12.12, written in terms of stationary state real balances and lending, are

$$\left[\bar{r}^n - \bar{r}^f\right] \overline{N/P} = \bar{r}^f \left[1 - \frac{1}{\bar{g}}\right] \overline{M/P} \tag{12.15}$$

and

$$-\frac{\overline{C}\bar{g}B}{\beta} \overline{H} = \overline{N/P} + \left[1 - \frac{1}{\bar{g}}\right] \overline{M/P}, \tag{12.16}$$

where in the last equation, we have replaced wages by what it equals. In a stationary state, the cash-in-advance constraint is written as

$$\overline{C} = \frac{\overline{M/P}}{\bar{g}} - \overline{N/P}, \tag{12.17}$$

and the household flow budget constraint, after replacing wages and interest rates by what they equal in stationary states, is

$$\overline{M/P} = \frac{\bar{g}}{\beta} \overline{N/P} + \left[(\bar{r} - \delta) \left[\frac{\theta}{\bar{r}}\right]^{\frac{1}{1-\theta}} - \frac{\overline{C}\bar{g}B}{\beta}\right] \overline{H}. \tag{12.18}$$

Table 12.1   Stationary states for working capital model

Annual inflation	-4%	0	10%	100%	400%
$\bar{g}$	.99	1	1.024	1.19	1.41
$\bar{r}$	.035101	.035101	.035101	.035101	.035101
$\bar{r}^n$	1.0000	1.0101	1.0343	1.2020	1.4242
$\bar{r}^f$	1.0221	1.0101	0.9824	0.8259	0.6820
$\frac{M_l}{P_t} = \overline{M/P}$	1.6557	1.6675	1.6960	1.8896	2.1395
$\frac{N_l}{P_t} = \overline{N/P}$	.7736	.76715	0.7523	0.6626	0.5716
$\overline{C}$	.8988	.90038	0.9040	0.9253	0.9458
$\overline{Y}$	1.2087	1.2108	1.2158	1.2444	1.2720
$\overline{w}$	2.3193	2.3469	2.4130	2.8702	3.4762
$\overline{H}$	.3263	.32688	0.3282	0.3360	0.3434
$\overline{K}$	12.3967	12.418	12.4690	12.7627	13.0454
utility	-0.9488	-0.9485	-0.9479	-0.9445	-0.9418

The set of equations 12.14 through 12.18 is a system of five equations in five unknowns: $\overline{M/P}$, $\overline{N/P}$, $\bar{r}^f$, $\overline{C}$, and $\overline{H}$. Except for the case where $\bar{g} = 1$, this system is not easily worked out analytically. Therefore, we calculate the stationary state values for different growth rates of the money stock for an economy with our standard parameter values.[5]

The standard values for the model's parameters are $\beta = .99$, $\delta = .025$, $\theta = .36$, and $B = -2.5805$. Table 12.1 gives the stationary state values of the variables in this model for quarterly gross growth rates of the money stock of .99, 1, 1.024, 1.19, and 1.41. These quarterly rates of growth of the money stock correspond to the same annual inflation rates that we calculated in the basic cash-in-advance model.

The results for the stationary states shown in Table 12.1 are quite interesting. Notice that as the stationary state growth rate of money increases, output increases, consumption increases, hours worked and the capital stock increase, real money holdings increase, real lending to the intermediaries declines, and utility increases. The interest rate paid to the households for

---

5. We use the Matlab routine fsolve to find the zeros to the five equation systems described in equations 12.14 through 12.18.

their lending to the financial intermediaries goes up while that paid by the firms declines. Economies with higher inflation rates produce more, and their households have higher welfare than similar economies with lower inflation rates.

These results are dramatically different from those found by Cooley and Hansen in the standard cash-in-advance model that we developed in Chapter 8. There, increasing inflation reduces welfare, production, consumption, and hours worked. In the Cooley-Hansen model, economies with higher inflation rates are clearly worse off than similar economies with lower inflation rates.

One needs to consider what is so different about the model of this section when compared to that of Cooley and Hansen. Both models use cash-in-advance constraints and in both we use indivisible labor. In the Cooley-Hansen model, inflation occurs through lump sum transfers of money directly to consumers. These transfers reduce the return on money held over from the previous period and reduce incentives to use money. In addition, labor supplied by the families declines as they substitute leisure for consumption.

In the model of this section, new issues of money go directly to the financial intermediaries as a kind of lump sum addition to loanable funds on which the intermediaries do not need to pay interest. These transfers are what generate the wedge between the interest rate received by the families and that paid by the firms. New money issues reduce real borrowing costs of the firms and, therefore, reduce the cost of using labor. Demand for labor increases, real wages increase, more labor is provided by the households, and output increases. With additional labor, the marginal product of capital increases and the capital stock grows until the marginal product of capital again equals $1/\beta - 1 + \delta$. In economies with higher inflation rates, households hold relatively more money for consumption purchases and lend less to the financial intermediaries. However, even with a decline in household lending to the financial intermediaries, the higher transfers from the monetary authority to the financial intermediaries that come with higher inflation means that the real value of the total loanable funds of the financial intermediaries increases with inflation.

Our model with working capital generates a type of stationary state Phillips curve, or Fisher curve, as it probably should be called since Irving Fisher [39] first wrote about the statistical relationship between unemployment and price changes. With our assumption of indivisible labor, H/h_0, the average hours worked divided by the indivisible number of hours that a household works when it is employed is simply the fraction of families who are working. Therefore, $1 - H/h_0$ is the unemployment rate, the fraction of households that are unemployed. Figure 12.1 shows the relationship between this unemployment rate and the inflation rate in stationary states of our model.

12.1.6 Log Linear Version of the Model

To see how the working capital assumption affects the dynamic properties of the economy, we need to get a linear version of the model. Applying our log linearization techniques to the working capital model results in the set of equations

$$0 = \tilde{w}_t + \tilde{P}_t - E_t\tilde{P}_{t+1} - E_t\tilde{C}_{t+1},$$

$$0 = \tilde{w}_t - E_t\tilde{w}_{t+1} + \beta\bar{r}E_t\tilde{r}_{t+1},$$

$$0 = \tilde{r}_t^n - \tilde{w}_t + \tilde{C}_t,$$

$$0 = \overline{C}\left[\tilde{P}_t + \tilde{C}_t\right] - \frac{\overline{M/P}}{\bar{g}}\tilde{M}_{t-1} + \overline{N/P}\tilde{N}_t,$$

$$0 = \overline{M/P}\tilde{M}_t + \left[\bar{r}^n\overline{N/P} - \overline{M/P}\right]\tilde{P}_t + \overline{K}\tilde{K}_{t+1} - \tilde{w}\overline{H}(\tilde{w}_t + \tilde{H}_t)$$

$$\quad - \bar{r}\overline{K}\tilde{r}_t - (\bar{r} + 1 - \delta)\overline{K}\tilde{K}_t - \bar{r}^n\overline{N/P}\tilde{N}_t - \bar{r}^n\overline{N/P}\tilde{r}_t^n,$$

$$0 = \tilde{w}_t + \tilde{r}_t^f - \tilde{\lambda}_t - \theta\tilde{K}_t + \theta\tilde{H}_t,$$

$$0 = \tilde{r}_t - \tilde{\lambda}_t - (\theta - 1)\tilde{K}_t - (1 - \theta)\tilde{H}_t,$$

$$0 = \tilde{Y}_t - \tilde{\lambda}_t - \theta\tilde{K}_t - (1 - \theta)\tilde{H}_t,$$

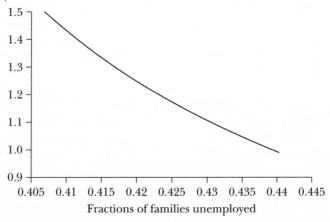

Gross growth rate of
money = inflation rate

FIGURE 12.1   Stationary state Phillips curve

$$0 = \bar{r}^f \left[\overline{N/P} + \overline{M/P} \left(1 - \frac{1}{\bar{g}} \right) \right] \tilde{r}_t^f + \left(\bar{r}^f - \bar{r}^n \right) \overline{N/P} \tilde{N}_t$$

$$- \left[\left(\bar{r}^f - \bar{r}^n \right) \overline{N/P} + \bar{r}^f \overline{M/P} \left(1 - \frac{1}{\bar{g}} \right) \right] \tilde{P}_t$$

$$+ \bar{r}^f \overline{M/P} \tilde{g}_t + \bar{r}^f \overline{M/P} \left(1 - \frac{1}{\bar{g}} \right) \tilde{M}_{t-1} - \bar{r}^n \overline{N/P} \tilde{r}_t^n,$$

$$0 = \overline{N/P} \tilde{N}_t + \overline{M/P} \left(1 - \frac{1}{\bar{g}} \right) \tilde{M}_{t-1} - \left[\overline{N/P} + \overline{M/P} \left(1 - \frac{1}{\bar{g}} \right) \right] \tilde{P}_t$$

$$+ \overline{M/P} \tilde{g}_t - \bar{w} \overline{H} \tilde{w}_t - \bar{w} \overline{H} \tilde{H}_t,$$

$$0 = \tilde{M}_t - \tilde{g}_t - \tilde{M}_{t-1}.$$

In addition, we have the two equations for the stochastic processes of $\tilde{\lambda}_t$ and $\tilde{g}_t$:

$$\tilde{\lambda}_t = \gamma \tilde{\lambda}_{t-1} + \varepsilon_t^\lambda$$

and

$$\tilde{g}_t = \pi \tilde{g}_{t-1} + \varepsilon_t^g.$$

Defining the state variables as $x_t = [\tilde{K}_{t+1}, \tilde{M}_t, \tilde{P}_t]'$, the jump variables as $y_t = [\tilde{r}_t, \tilde{w}_t, \tilde{Y}_t, \tilde{C}_t, \tilde{H}_t, \tilde{N}_t, \tilde{r}_t^n, \tilde{r}_t^f]'$, and the stochastic variables as $z_t = [\tilde{\lambda}_t, \tilde{g}_t]'$, the system can be written as

$$0 = Ax_t + Bx_{t-1} + Cy_t + Dz_t,$$

$$0 = E_t \left[Fx_{t+1} + Gx_t + Hx_{t-1} + Jy_{t+1} + Ky_t + Lz_{t+1} + Mz_t \right],$$

$$z_{t+1} = Nz_t + \varepsilon_{t+1},$$

where

$$A = \begin{bmatrix} 0 & 0 & 0 \\ 0 & 0 & \overline{C} \\ \overline{K} & \overline{M/P} & \bar{r}^n \overline{N/P} - \overline{M/P} \\ 0 & 0 & 0 \\ 0 & 0 & 0 \\ 0 & 0 & 0 \\ 0 & 0 & -\left[\left(\bar{r}^f - \bar{r}^n \right) \overline{N/P} + \bar{r}^f \overline{M/P} \left(1 - \frac{1}{\bar{g}} \right) \right] \\ 0 & 0 & -\left[\overline{N/P} + \overline{M/P} \left(1 - \frac{1}{\bar{g}} \right) \right] \end{bmatrix},$$

$$B = \begin{bmatrix} 0 & 0 & 0 \\ 0 & -\frac{\overline{M/P}}{g} & 0 \\ -(r+1-\delta)K & 0 & 0 \\ -\theta & 0 & 0 \\ -(\theta-1) & 0 & 0 \\ -\theta & 0 & 0 \\ 0 & \bar{r}^f\overline{M/P}(1-\frac{1}{g}) & 0 \\ 0 & \overline{M/P}(1-\frac{1}{g}) & 0 \end{bmatrix},$$

$$C = \begin{bmatrix} 0 & 1 & 0 & -1 & 0 & 0 & -1 & 0 \\ 0 & 0 & 0 & \overline{C} & 0 & \overline{N/P} & 0 & 0 \\ -\bar{r}\overline{K} & -\bar{w}\overline{H} & 0 & 0 & -\bar{w}\overline{H} & -\bar{r}^n\overline{N/P} & -\bar{r}^n\overline{N/P} & 0 \\ 0 & 1 & 0 & 0 & \theta & 0 & 0 & 1 \\ 1 & 0 & 0 & 0 & -(1-\theta) & 0 & 0 & 0 \\ 0 & 0 & 1 & 0 & -(1-\theta) & 0 & 0 & 0 \\ 0 & 0 & 0 & 0 & 0 & (\bar{r}^f-\bar{r}^n)\overline{N/P} & -\bar{r}^n\overline{N/P} & \bar{r}^f\left(\frac{\overline{N}}{P}+\frac{\overline{M}}{P}(1-\frac{1}{g})\right) \\ 0 & -wH & 0 & 0 & -wH & \overline{N/P} & 0 & 0 \end{bmatrix}$$

$$D = \begin{bmatrix} 0 & 0 \\ 0 & 0 \\ 0 & 0 \\ -1 & 0 \\ -1 & 0 \\ -1 & 0 \\ 0 & \bar{r}^f\overline{M/P} \\ 0 & \overline{M/P} \end{bmatrix},$$

$$F = \begin{bmatrix} 0 & 0 & -1 \\ 0 & 0 & 0 \\ 0 & 0 & 0 \end{bmatrix},$$

$$G = \begin{bmatrix} 0 & 0 & 1 \\ 0 & 0 & 0 \\ 0 & 1 & 0 \end{bmatrix},$$

$$H = \begin{bmatrix} 0 & 0 & 0 \\ 0 & 0 & 0 \\ 0 & -1 & 0 \end{bmatrix},$$

$$J = \begin{bmatrix} 0 & 0 & 0 & -1 & 0 & 0 & 0 & 0 \\ \beta\bar{r} & -1 & 0 & 0 & 0 & 0 & 0 & 0 \\ 0 & 0 & 0 & 0 & 0 & 0 & 0 & 0 \end{bmatrix},$$

$$K = \begin{bmatrix} 0 & 1 & 0 & 0 & 0 & 0 & 0 & 0 \\ 0 & 1 & 0 & 0 & 0 & 0 & 0 & 0 \\ 0 & 0 & 0 & 0 & 0 & 0 & 0 & 0 \end{bmatrix},$$

$$L = \begin{bmatrix} 0 & 0 \\ 0 & 0 \\ 0 & 0 \end{bmatrix},$$

$$M = \begin{bmatrix} 0 & 0 \\ 0 & 0 \\ 0 & -1 \end{bmatrix},$$

and

$$N = \begin{bmatrix} \gamma & 0 \\ 0 & \pi \end{bmatrix}.$$

We look for policy matrices that can be expressed in the form

$$x_{t+1} = Px_t + Qz_t$$

and

$$y_t = Rx_t + Sz_t,$$

using the solution techniques described in previous chapters. For the case where $\bar{g} = 1$, the matrices of interest are

$$P = \begin{bmatrix} 0.9430 & 0 & 0 \\ 0 & 1 & 0 \\ -0.3340 & 1 & 0 \end{bmatrix},$$

$$Q = \begin{bmatrix} 0.1490 & 0.2020 \\ 0 & 1 \\ -1.0337 & 0.6287 \end{bmatrix},$$

$$
R = \begin{bmatrix} -0.9236 & 0 & 0 \\ 0.5315 & 0 & 0 \\ 0.0764 & 0 & 0 \\ 0.5434 & 0 & 0 \\ -0.4432 & 0 & 0 \\ -0.2457 & 1 & 0 \\ -0.0119 & 0 & 0 \\ -0.0119 & 0 & 0 \end{bmatrix},
$$

and

$$
S = \begin{bmatrix} 1.8309 & 1.2411 \\ 0.4701 & 0.1791 \\ 1.8309 & 1.2411 \\ 0.4077 & -1.1172 \\ 1.2982 & 1.9392 \\ 0.7347 & 0.5734 \\ 0.0625 & 1.2964 \\ 0.0625 & -0.8772 \end{bmatrix}.
$$

The average relative standard errors and correlations from 50 simulations of 115 periods each are given in Table 12.2. The choices of the standard errors for the technology and money supply shocks need to be explained. The standard errors for the exogenous shocks that were used in the basic (Cooley-

Table 12.2   Standard errors and correlations for working capital model

$\bar{g} = 1$	Standard errors $\sigma^\lambda = .00268$ $\sigma^g = .009$	Correlation with output	Standard errors $\sigma^\lambda = .00178$ $\sigma^g = .01134$	Correlation with output
Output	0.0176	1.0000	0.0176	1.0000
Consumption	0.0133	−0.3161	0.0150	−0.6762
Investment	0.0874	0.9111	0.1027	0.9510
Capital	0.0117	0.5063	0.0111	0.4481
Prices	0.0678	−0.0220	0.0841	0.0432
Rentals	0.0171	0.7882	0.0183	0.8169
Wages	0.0083	0.6896	0.0073	0.6050
Hours	0.0206	0.8697	0.0246	0.9287

Hansen) cash-in-advance model are $\sigma^\lambda = .00178$ and $\sigma^g = .009$. Using these standard errors in this model gives a relative standard error for output of only 1.48 percent. To get a relative standard error for output of 1.76 percent with the standard error for technology shock kept to $\sigma^\lambda = .00178$, one needs a standard error for the money supply shock of $\sigma^g = .01134$. If one wishes to maintain the standard error of the money supply shock at $\sigma^g = .009$, one needs a standard error for the technology shock of $\sigma^\lambda = .00268$ to get a relative standard error for output of 1.76 percent. Simulations using each of these two sets of standard errors are reported.

The combination of a larger money supply shock and a smaller technology shock results in larger standard errors for all variables except real wages. This combination results in correlations with output that are more positively correlated for investment, prices, rentals, and hours. Prices were negatively correlated with output in the case where the technology shock is larger. In both cases here, consumption is negatively correlated with output. If one allows the technology shock to become larger (and the money supply shock smaller), one can find cases where the correlation of consumption with output is positive. With smaller money supply shocks, the correlation of prices with output can be very negative (-43 percent for simulations where $\sigma^g = .003$).

12.1.7 Impulse Response Functions

Impulse response functions for the variables in the model responding to technology and money supply shocks are shown in Figures 12.2 through 12.5.

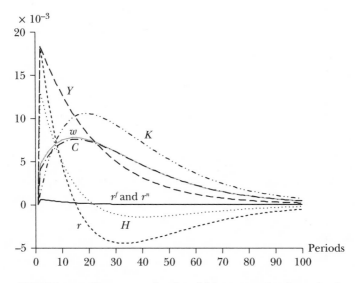

FIGURE 12.2 Response of real variables to a technology shock

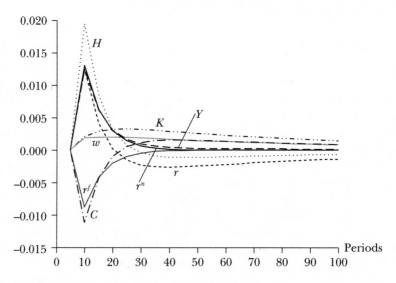

FIGURE 12.3   Response of real variables to a money growth shock

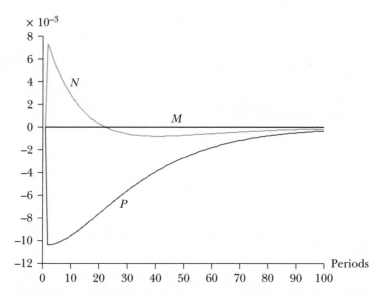

FIGURE 12.4   Response of nominal variables to a technology shock

Notice that most of the impact of the shocks dies out relatively quickly. The longer effect of technology shock is largely due to the stochastic process for technology, $\tilde{\lambda}_t$, where the coefficient on the first lag is .95. In all cases, the response is to a single positive shock of .01 that occurs in period 2. Notice that the response of the real variables to the technology shock is very similar to that of the Hansen model with indivisible labor (compare Figure 12.2 with Figure 6.6). For the nominal variables, prices decline and deposits in the financial intermediaries initially rise in response to a positive technology shock.

The initial impact of a monetary growth shock is large for many real variables; this can be seen in the spikes at time $t = 2$. Working through the financial intermediary, the responses to money growth shocks are much larger than in the Cooley-Hansen model. In addition, a number of important variables respond in a direction opposite to that in the original Cooley-Hansen model. These variables include the labor supply and rental on capital. Since we have nomalized the nominal variables in this model by dividing them by the price level, the nominal log differences have a unit root and are cointegrated. The money supply, price level, and nominal deposits all converge toward the same new level, with the money supply moving faster than the other two variables.

12.1.8   Economy with Annual Inflation of 100 Percent

For an economy with a stationary state quarterly gross money growth rate of $\bar{g} = 1.19$, which corresponds to an annual rate of 100 percent, the solution to

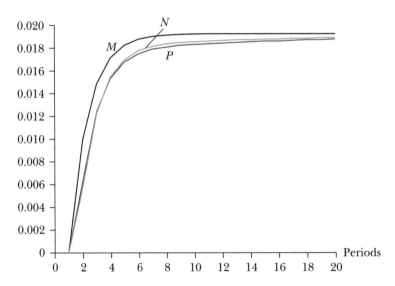

FIGURE 12.5   Response of nominal variables to a money growth shock

the model changes. Here the matrix policy functions are

$$P = \begin{bmatrix} 0.9498 & 0 & 0 \\ 0 & 1 & 0 \\ -0.3969 & 1 & 0 \end{bmatrix},$$

$$Q = \begin{bmatrix} 0.1256 & 0.1602 \\ 0 & 1 \\ -0.8588 & 0.7299 \end{bmatrix},$$

$$R = \begin{bmatrix} -0.8409 & 0 & 0 \\ 0.5531 & 0 & 0 \\ 0.1591 & 0 & 0 \\ 0.5613 & 0 & 0 \\ -0.3139 & 0 & 0 \\ -0.2296 & 1 & 0 \\ -0.0082 & 0 & 0 \\ -0.0801 & 0 & 0 \end{bmatrix},$$

and

$$S = \begin{bmatrix} 1.5712 & 0.8758 \\ 0.4252 & 0.1513 \\ 1.5712 & 0.8758 \\ 0.3807 & -1.0322 \\ 0.8924 & 1.3685 \\ 0.6678 & 0.4222 \\ 0.0446 & 1.1835 \\ 0.2535 & -0.6440 \end{bmatrix}.$$

Simulation of this economy gives the results shown in Table 12.3. In the simulation shown, the standard error for the technology shock was fixed at $\sigma^\lambda = .00178$ and that for the money supply shock was adjusted until the standard error of output was 1.76 percent. The standard error for the money shock that gave this result is $\sigma^g = .0164$, somewhat more than in the economy with no inflation. The major differences in this set of results are the generally higher standard errors of the other variables reported, especially investment and prices, and that prices are slightly more positively correlated and consumption slightly more negatively correlated with output.

12.1.9 Comparative Impulse Response Functions

The comparative impulse response functions for the economy with a stationary state annual inflation rate of 0 percent and of 100 percent are shown in Figures 12.6 through 12.9. In these graphs, the responses of the economy with 0 percent inflation are being measured on the horizontal axis and the responses of the economy with 100 percent inflation are being measured on the vertical axis. In general, real variables respond less to the same size technology or money growth shock when there is a higher stationary state money growth rate. This can be seen from the fact that the comparative lines are generally below the 45 degree line in the graphs. Some variables stand out. The labor supply, $\tilde{H}$, responds much stronger to a real shock when inflation is lower. The interest rate paid by firms to the financial intermediary, $\tilde{r}^f$, responds positively in both economies but the response is greater in the economy with higher inflation.

In response to a money growth shock, $\tilde{H}$, $\tilde{r}$, and $\tilde{Y}$ respond relatively more than other variables in the 0 percent inflation economy than in the 100 percent inflation economy. The lending interest rate, $\tilde{r}^f$, responds more. Prices and deposits respond slower than money in both models but prices react faster in the higher inflation economy and deposits react slower than in the lower inflation economy.

Table 12.3 Standard errors and correlations with output for economy with stationary state inflation

$\bar{g} = 1.19$	Standard errors $\sigma^\lambda = .00178$ $\sigma^g = .0164$	Correlation with output
Output	0.0176	1.0000
Consumption	0.0195	−0.7414
Investment	0.1166	0.9465
Capital	0.0124	0.4645
Prices	0.1215	0.1149
Rentals	0.0187	0.7766
Wages	0.0081	0.6199
Hours	0.0248	0.9247

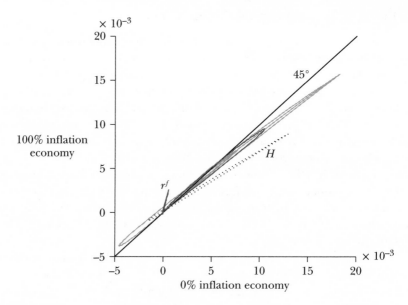

FIGURE 12.6 Comparative responses of real variables to technology shock with 0 and 100% inflation in stationary state

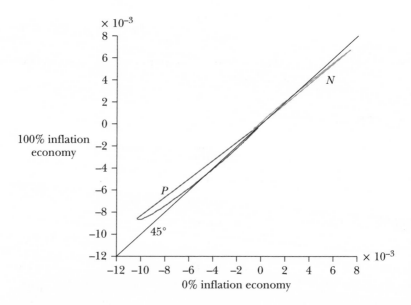

FIGURE 12.7 Comparative responses of nominal variables to technology shock with 0 and 100 percent inflation in stationary state

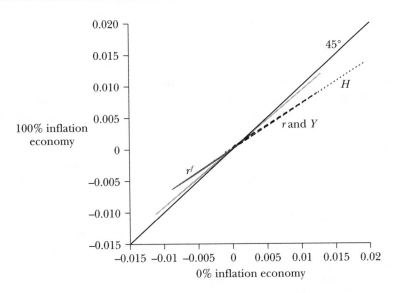

FIGURE 12.8 Comparative responses of real variables to money growth shock with 0 and 100 percent inflation in stationary state

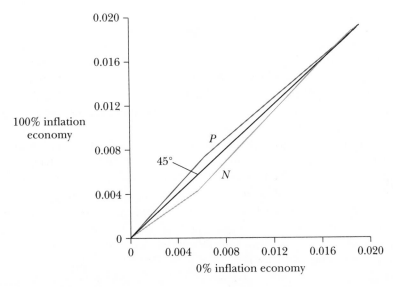

FIGURE 12.9 Comparative responses of nominal variables to money growth shock with 0 and 100 percent inflation in stationary state

12.2 CENTRAL BANKING AND MONETARY POLICY RULES

Monetary policy in the model with financial intermediaries is somewhat strange and unrealistic; it is simply a stochastic process for money growth. Perhaps a money growth shock can be interpreted as a surprise change in policy, but this is not what is normally meant by a policy. In this section, we consider a central bank (or other government office that issues money to the financial system) that can credibly commit itself to follow a policy rule. The credibility aspect is important and there is a long literature, beginning at least with Kydland and Prescott [51] and Calvo [18], about a government's ability to make a creditable commitment to a policy rule. We ignore those problems here and consider only a central bank that can commit itself to a policy rule.

Probably the two most famous rules for monetary policy are those of Friedman [40] and Taylor [85]. Friedman's rule is a simple constant money supply growth rule. At least part of Friedman's logic for offering this rule is the argument that a constant money supply growth is less likely to create additional sources of cycles in the economy and therefore make the economy more predictable for its participants.

Taylor [85] recommended that central banks follow a monetary policy rule by which they set an appropriate short-term interest rate, r_t^f, following the feedback rule

$$r_t^f = a \left(Y_t - \overline{Y} \right) + b \left(\pi_t - \bar{\pi} \right) + \bar{r}^f,$$

where Y_t is output and π_t is the inflation rate. Variables with bars over them are the stationary state values (or the desired values, in Taylor's terminology). When r_t^f is a nominal interest rate, Taylor suggested that $a = .5$ and $b = 1.5$ would be representative values that "captures the spirit of recent research and is quite straightforward."[6]

Most central banks today follow some kind of Taylor rule, at least for their models if not for actual policy making. In practice, one finds a Taylor rule is simply added to a small reduced-form macroeconomic model that includes an IS curve equation, a Phillips curve equation (which is justified by a Calvo price setting model like that of Chapter 10), and, in open economies, an equation for determining the exchange rate.[7] There is usually nothing in the model that tells one exactly how the central bank manages to set the interest rate determined from the Taylor rule.

In this section, we add a Taylor rule to the financial intermediary model of the previous section. The central bank controls the injections of money into the financial section and by injecting or removing money it can set the

---

6. Taylor [85], page 202.
7. See, as an almost randomly chosen example, Clarida, Galí, and Gertler [34], page 169.

interest rate that the firms pay for borrowing funds for their wage bill. Since the central bank follows this rule, the monetary shocks that occurred in the financial intermediation model no longer exist: the central bank follows an explicit rule and does so exactly. We need another source for monetary shocks and to find one we go back to the Cooley-Hansen cash-in-advance model of Chapter 8. We assume that some other part of the government (the fiscal authorities, perhaps) makes stochastic, lump sum transfers of money to or withdrawals of money from the households in the economy.

12.2.1   The Model with a Taylor Rule

We begin with the Taylor rule, which is a bit more complicated than the Friedman rule. The basic model is the same for both rules.

HOUSEHOLDS

A unit mass of identical households each maximizes the expected utility function,

$$E_t \sum_{i=0}^{\infty} \beta^i \left(\ln \left(c_{t+i}^j \right) + B h_{t+i}^j \right),$$

subject to the sequence of budget constraints,

$$c_s^j + k_{s+1}^j + \frac{m_s^j}{P_s} = w_s h_s^j + r_s k_s^j + (1 - \delta) k_s^j$$

$$+ \left(r_s^n - 1 \right) \frac{N_s^j}{P_s} + \frac{m_{s-1}^j}{P_s} + \left(g_t^f - 1 \right) M_{s-1},$$

and the sequence of cash-in-advance constraints,

$$P_s c_s^j \leq m_{s-1}^j + \left(g_t^f - 1 \right) M_{s-1} - N_s^j,$$

where c_s^j is time s consumption of family j, h_s^j is the labor it supplies, k_s^j its beginning of period capital, m_s^j its beginning of period money holdings, N_s^j its deposits in the financial system, β its discount rate, and δ the depreciation rate on capital. The fiscal part of the government makes a lump sum transfer of money to each household equal to $(g_t^f - 1) M_{s-1}$. This transfer is of the nature of the transfers in the Cooley-Hansen model of Chapter 8 and can be positive or negative. The growth rate of money from a fiscal transfer follows the law of motion,

$$\ln g_t^f = \pi^f \ln g_{t-1}^f + \varepsilon_t^f.$$

The household takes as given time s prices, P_s, wages, w_s, rental, r_s, the lump sum money transfer, $(g_t^f - 1)M_{s-1}$, and the gross interest rate on deposits in a financial intermediary, r_s^n.

This utility maximization problem (along with the aggregation conditions that $X_s = \int_0^1 x_s^j dj$) results in the aggregate version of the first-order condition as

$$\frac{B}{w_t} = -\beta E_t \frac{P_t}{P_{t+1}C_{t+1}},$$

$$\frac{1}{w_t} = \beta E_t \frac{r_{t+1} + 1 - \delta}{w_{t+1}},$$

$$r_t^n = -\frac{w_t}{BC_t} = \frac{1}{E_t \frac{\beta P_t C_t}{P_{t+1}C_{t+1}}},$$

an aggregate cash-in-advance constraint for household consumption,

$$P_t C_t = g_t^f M_{t-1} - N_t,$$

and an aggregate real flow budget constraint,

$$\frac{M_t}{P_t} + K_{t+1} = w_t H_t + r_t K_t + (1 - \delta)K_t + \frac{r_t^n N_t}{P_t}.$$

In addition, there is the law of motion for the growth rate of money from the fiscal transfer policy,

$$\ln g_t^f = \pi^f \ln g_{t-1}^f + \varepsilon_t^f.$$

We assume that ε_t^f has a mean of zero, so that the stationary state value of $\bar{g}^f = 1$.

FIRMS

Firms are competitive and face competitive factor markets. The Cobb-Douglas production function (in aggregate terms) in period t is

$$Y_t = \lambda_t K_t^\theta H_t^{1-\theta},$$

where the stochastic process for technology, λ_t, follows

$$\ln \lambda_t = \gamma \ln \lambda_{t-1} + \varepsilon_t^\lambda.$$

The budget constraint for firms is

$$Y_t \geq r_t^f w_t H_t + r_t K_t,$$

where r_t^f is the gross interest rate paid on the working capital borrowed from the financial institutions to finance the wage bill. The assumption of competitive factor markets means that

$$r_t^f w_t = (1 - \theta)\, \lambda_t K_t^\theta H_t^{-\theta}$$

and

$$r_t = \theta \lambda_t K_t^{\theta-1} H_t^{1-\theta}.$$

Firms borrow from the financial intermediary at the beginning of the period and pay off the loan at the end of the period when they have sold the goods that they produced. This means that there is no uncertainty related with the loans because the time t value of the technology shock is known before the borrowing takes place.

FINANCIAL INTERMEDIARIES AND THE TAYLOR RULE

The financial intermediaries are competitive and make zero profits. They face a budget constraint of

$$N_t + \left(g_t^M - 1\right) M_{t-1} = P_t w_t H_t$$

and a zero profit condition of

$$r_t^n N_t = r_t^f P_t w_t H_t,$$

where $\left(g_t^M - 1\right) M_{t-1}$ is the money transfer to or tax on the financial system coming from the central bank's monetary policy. For the central bank to obtain the desired borrowing interest rate, r_t^f, the growth rate of money in period t must be

$$g_t^M = \frac{\left(r_t^n - r_t^f\right)}{r_t^f} \frac{N_t}{M_{t-1}} + 1.$$

The central bank's choice for its growth rate of money is determined by the model and the choice of r_t^f that comes from the Taylor rule,

$$r_t^f = a\left(Y_t - \overline{Y}\right) + b\left(\pi_t - \bar{\pi}\right) + \bar{r}^f.$$

The parameter pair of the Taylor rule, (a, b), are the policy parameters determined by the central bank. The stock of money that the households carry over to the next period is equal to the sum of the two growth rates,

$$M_t = \left(g_t^f + g_t^M - 1 \right) M_{t-1}.$$

The sum may seem a bit odd, but both growth rates are gross growth rates and the sum $g_t^f + g_t^M = \widehat{g}_t^f + 1 + \widehat{g}_t^M + 1 = \widehat{g}_t^f + \widehat{g}_t^M + 2$ when $\widehat{g}_t^i$ is a net growth rate.

In this model, the interest rate, r_t^f, that the central bank is setting is really a real interest rate and not a nominal interest rate. The loans are taken out at the beginning of the period and paid back at the end of the period. The model has discrete periods and during a period prices do not change; they change only between periods.[8] Taylor recommended that central banks used (.5, 1.5) for the parameter pair (a, b), but in the model given here, the values (.5, .5) capture the spirit of his recommendation.

12.2.2   Stationary States

Stationary states for this economy are found the same way as for a standard model with financial intermediaries with $\bar{g} = \bar{\pi}$. In a stationary state, the Taylor rule is simply

$$\bar{r}^f = a \left(\bar{Y} - \bar{Y} \right) + b \left(\bar{\pi} - \bar{\pi} \right) + \bar{r}^f$$

$$= \bar{r}^f.$$

In this model the stationary state interest rate is a function of the target inflation rate. For a standard (U.S.) economy that we have been using, the

----

8. The argument is straightforward. The Taylor rule in nominal terms is

$$r_t^f = a \left(Y_t - \bar{Y} \right) + b \left(\pi_t - \bar{\pi} \right) + \bar{r}^f.$$

The Fisher equation is

$$r_t^f = i_t^f + \pi_t$$

and in terms of the stationary state interest rate,

$$\bar{r}^f = \bar{i}^f + \bar{\pi}.$$

Putting the two Fisher equations into the Taylor rule gives

$$i_t^f + \pi_t = a \left(Y_t - \bar{Y} \right) + b \left(\pi_t - \bar{\pi} \right) + \bar{i}^f + \bar{\pi},$$

or

$$i_t^f = a \left(Y_t - \bar{Y} \right) + (b - 1) \left(\pi_t - \bar{\pi} \right) + \bar{i}^f.$$

relationship between the target inflation rate ($\bar{\pi}$) and the corresponding interest rate rule ($\bar{r}^r$) is shown in Figure 12.10.

For a quarterly version of the standard Hansen [48] type economy of the United States, the parameters frequently used are $\beta = .99$, $\delta = .025$, $\theta = .36$, and $B = -2.5805$. Here we choose $\bar{g} = 1.03$ so that the target inflation rate is 3 percent. The rest of the stationary state values of the variables for this economy are given in Table 12.4.

12.2.3 Log-Linear Version and Its Solution

The log-linear version of the model is comprised of the set of 12 variables $\{\tilde{K}_{t+1}, \tilde{M}_t, \tilde{P}_t, \tilde{r}_t, \tilde{w}_t, \tilde{Y}_t, \tilde{C}_t, \tilde{H}_t, \tilde{N}_t, \tilde{r}_t^n, \tilde{r}_t^f, \tilde{g}_t^M\}$ and the 12 equations

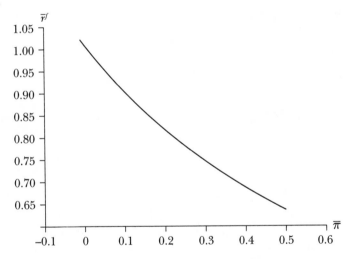

FIGURE 12.10   Stationary state target $\bar{\pi}$ and associated $\bar{r}^r$

Table 12.4   Values in stationary state for g=1.03

Variable	$\overline{K}$	$\overline{Y}$	$\overline{C}$	$\overline{H}$	$\overline{M/P}$
Stationary state value	12.481	1.217	.905	.328	1.703
Variable	$\overline{N/P}$	$\bar{r}$	$\bar{w}$	$\bar{r}^n$	$\bar{r}^f$
Stationary state value	.749	0.0351	2.439	1.0404	.9757

$$0 = \tilde{w}_t + \tilde{P}_t - E_t \tilde{P}_{t+1} - E_t \tilde{C}_{t+1},$$

$$0 = \tilde{w}_t - E_t \tilde{w}_{t+1} + \beta \bar{r} E_t \tilde{r}_{t+1},$$

$$0 = \tilde{r}_t^n - \tilde{w}_t + \tilde{C}_t,$$

$$0 = \overline{C} \tilde{C}_t - \frac{\overline{M/P}}{\bar{g}^M} \tilde{g}_t^f - \frac{\overline{M/P}}{\bar{g}^M} \tilde{M}_{t-1} + \overline{N/P} \tilde{N}_t + \overline{C} \tilde{P}_t,$$

$$0 = \overline{M/P} \tilde{M}_t + \left[\bar{r}^n \overline{N/P} - \overline{M/P} \right] \tilde{P}_t + \overline{K} \tilde{K}_{t+1} - \bar{w} \overline{H} (\tilde{w}_t + \tilde{H}_t)$$

$$- \bar{r} \overline{K} \tilde{r}_t - (\bar{r} + 1 - \delta) \overline{K} \tilde{K}_t - \bar{r}^n \overline{N/P} \tilde{N}_t - \bar{r}^n \overline{N/P} \tilde{r}_t^n,$$

$$0 = \tilde{w}_t + \tilde{r}_t^f - \tilde{\lambda}_t - \theta \tilde{K}_t + \theta \tilde{H}_t,$$

$$0 = \tilde{r}_t - \tilde{\lambda}_t - (\theta - 1) \tilde{K}_t - (1 - \theta) \tilde{H}_t,$$

$$0 = \tilde{Y}_t - \tilde{\lambda}_t - \theta \tilde{K}_t - (1 - \theta) \tilde{H}_t,$$

$$0 = \tilde{r}_t^n + \tilde{N}_t - \tilde{P}_t - \tilde{r}_t^f - \tilde{w}_t - \tilde{H}_t,$$

$$0 = \overline{N/P} \tilde{N}_t + \overline{M/P} \left(1 - \frac{1}{\bar{g}^M} \right) \tilde{M}_{t-1} - \bar{w} \overline{H} \tilde{P}_t$$

$$+ \overline{M/P} \tilde{g}_t^M - \bar{w} \overline{H} \tilde{w}_t - \bar{w} \overline{H} \tilde{H}_t$$

$$0 = \tilde{M}_t - \frac{1}{\bar{g}^M} \tilde{g}_t^f - \tilde{g}_t^M - \tilde{M}_{t-1}$$

$$0 = a \overline{Y} \tilde{Y}_t + b \bar{g}^M \tilde{P}_t - b \bar{g}^M \tilde{P}_{t-1} - \bar{r}^f \tilde{r}_t^f \qquad (12.19)$$

In addition, the two stochastic technology variables, $\tilde{\lambda}_t$ and $\tilde{g}_t^f$, are determined by the equations

$$\tilde{\lambda}_t = \gamma \tilde{\lambda}_{t-1} + \varepsilon_t^\lambda$$

and

$$\tilde{g}_t^f = \pi^f \tilde{g}_{t-1}^f + \varepsilon_t^\lambda.$$

Defining the set of state variables as $x_t = [\tilde{K}_{t+1}, \tilde{M}_t, \tilde{P}_t]'$, the set of jump variables as $y_t = [\tilde{r}_t, \tilde{w}_t, \tilde{Y}_t, \tilde{C}_t, \tilde{H}_t, \tilde{N}_t, \tilde{r}_t^n, \tilde{r}_t^f, \tilde{g}_t^M]'$, and the stochastic variable as $z_t = [\tilde{\lambda}_t, \tilde{g}_t^f]$, the system can be written as

$$0 = Ax_t + Bx_{t-1} + Cy_t + Dz_t,$$

$$0 = E_t\left[Fx_{t+1} + Gx_t + Hx_{t-1} + Jy_{t+1} + Ky_t + Lz_{t+1} + Mz_t\right],$$

$$z_{t+1} = Nz_t + \varepsilon_{t+1},$$

where

$$
A = \begin{bmatrix}
0 & 0 & 0 \\
0 & 0 & \overline{C} \\
\overline{K} & \overline{M/P} & \bar{r}^n\overline{N/P} - \overline{M/P} \\
0 & 0 & 0 \\
0 & 0 & 0 \\
0 & 0 & 0 \\
0 & 0 & -1 \\
0 & 0 & -\bar{w}\bar{H} \\
0 & 0 & b\bar{g}^M
\end{bmatrix},
$$

$$
B = \begin{bmatrix}
0 & 0 & 0 \\
0 & -\dfrac{\overline{M/P}}{\bar{g}^M} & 0 \\
-(r+1-\delta)\overline{K} & 0 & 0 \\
-\theta & 0 & 0 \\
-(\theta-1) & 0 & 0 \\
-\theta & 0 & 0 \\
0 & 0 & 0 \\
0 & \overline{M/P}\left(1-\dfrac{1}{\bar{g}^M}\right) & 0 \\
0 & 0 & -b\bar{g}^M
\end{bmatrix},
$$

$$
C = \begin{bmatrix}
0 & 1 & 0 & -1 & 0 & 0 & -1 & 0 & 0 \\
0 & 0 & 0 & \overline{C} & 0 & \overline{N/P} & 0 & 0 & 0 \\
-\bar{r}\overline{K} & -\bar{w}\overline{H} & 0 & 0 & -\bar{w}\overline{H} & -\bar{r}^n\overline{N/P} & -\bar{r}^n\overline{N/P} & 0 & 0 \\
0 & 1 & 0 & 0 & \theta & 0 & 0 & 1 & 0 \\
1 & 0 & 0 & 0 & -(1-\theta) & 0 & 0 & 0 & 0 \\
0 & 0 & 1 & 0 & -(1-\theta) & 0 & 0 & 0 & 0 \\
0 & -1 & 0 & 0 & -1 & 1 & 1 & -1 & 0 \\
0 & -\bar{w}\overline{H} & 0 & 0 & -\bar{w}\overline{H} & \overline{N/P} & 0 & 0 & \overline{M/P} \\
0 & 0 & a\overline{Y} & 0 & 0 & 0 & 0 & -\bar{r}^f & 0
\end{bmatrix},
$$

$$D = \begin{bmatrix} 0 & 0 \\ 0 & -\dfrac{M/P}{\bar{g}^M} \\ 0 & 0 \\ -1 & 0 \\ -1 & 0 \\ -1 & 0 \\ 0 & 0 \\ 0 & 0 \\ 0 & 0 \end{bmatrix},$$

$$F = \begin{bmatrix} 0 & 0 & -1 \\ 0 & 0 & 0 \\ 0 & 0 & 0 \end{bmatrix},$$

$$G = \begin{bmatrix} 0 & 0 & 1 \\ 0 & 0 & 0 \\ 0 & 1 & 0 \end{bmatrix},$$

$$H = \begin{bmatrix} 0 & 0 & 0 \\ 0 & 0 & 0 \\ 0 & -1 & 0 \end{bmatrix},$$

$$J = \begin{bmatrix} 0 & 0 & 0 & -1 & 0 & 0 & 0 & 0 & 0 \\ \beta\bar{r} & -1 & 0 & 0 & 0 & 0 & 0 & 0 & 0 \\ 0 & 0 & 0 & 0 & 0 & 0 & 0 & 0 & 0 \end{bmatrix},$$

$$K = \begin{bmatrix} 0 & 1 & 0 & 0 & 0 & 0 & 0 & 0 & 0 \\ 0 & 1 & 0 & 0 & 0 & 0 & 0 & 0 & 0 \\ 0 & 0 & 0 & 0 & 0 & 0 & 0 & 0 & -1 \end{bmatrix},$$

$$L = \begin{bmatrix} 0 & 0 \\ 0 & 0 \\ 0 & 0 \end{bmatrix},$$

$$M = \begin{bmatrix} 0 & 0 \\ 0 & 0 \\ 0 & -\dfrac{1}{\bar{g}^M} \end{bmatrix},$$

and

$$N = \begin{bmatrix} \gamma & 0 \\ 0 & \pi^f \end{bmatrix}.$$

We look for policy matrices that can be expressed in the form

$$x_{t+1} = P x_t + Q z_t$$

and

$$y_t = R x_t + S z_t,$$

using the solution techniques of Chapter 6. Using the values suggested above of $a = .5$ and $b = .5$, the four matrices of the policy functions are

$$P = \begin{bmatrix} 0.9588 & -0.0576 & 0.0576 \\ 0.0560 & 0.7025 & 0.2975 \\ -0.2667 & 0.7219 & 0.2781 \end{bmatrix},$$

$$Q = \begin{bmatrix} 0.1367 & -0.0501 \\ -0.2800 & 0.8878 \\ -0.9570 & 1.4391 \end{bmatrix},$$

$$R = \begin{bmatrix} -0.8450 & -0.2949 & 0.2949 \\ 0.5194 & -0.0312 & 0.0312 \\ 0.1550 & -0.2949 & 0.2949 \\ 0.4317 & 0.3975 & -0.3975 \\ -0.3203 & -0.4608 & 0.4608 \\ -0.1995 & 0.8557 & 0.1443 \\ 0.0877 & -0.4287 & 0.4287 \\ -0.0441 & 0.1971 & -0.1971 \\ 0.0560 & -0.2975 & 0.2975 \end{bmatrix},$$

and

$$S = \begin{bmatrix} 1.6184 & -0.6316 \\ 0.1480 & -0.0104 \\ 1.6184 & -0.6316 \\ 0.2913 & -0.1579 \\ 0.9663 & -0.9869 \\ 0.8047 & 0.6601 \\ -0.1433 & 0.1475 \\ 0.5041 & 0.3657 \\ -0.2800 & -0.0831 \end{bmatrix}.$$

12.2.4   Comparing a Taylor Rule to a Friedman Rule

We want to compare the results of the Taylor rule to alternative policy rules. One such policy rule is the constant money growth rule mentioned at the beginning of this section. As was noted, Milton Friedman pretty much built the monetary policy part of his career recommending a constant money growth policy, known as a Friedman rule, so such a policy has a venerable heritage. In the version of this rule that we use here, the central bank declares a constant money growth target, $\bar{g}^M$, and adjusts the money growth each period so that this rate is obtained. Since the only other source of money growth in these models is from the fiscal money shocks, g_t^f, the money growth rule for the central bank under this kind of policy is

$$g_t^M - \bar{g}^M = -\left(g_t^f - 1\right).$$

The central bank issues or withdraws money from the financial intermediaries so that the growth rate of the money supply stays constant. Note that these two money shocks have different effects on the economy: a positive fiscal shock works as a tax while a positive shock from the central bank, working through the financial system, is a subsidy.

The only technical change necessary in the model is to replace the Taylor rule with a Friedman rule: replacing the interest rate rule with the money growth rule given above. The households, firms, and financial intermediaries behave exactly as they did in the model with the Taylor rule. In a stationary state, $\bar{g}^f = 1$, money grows at the rate $\bar{g}^M$, and the stationary state for this model is the same as that in the model with the Taylor rule.

The log-linear version of the above Friedman rule is simply

$$0 = \bar{g}^M \tilde{g}_t^M + \tilde{g}_t^f,$$

and this rule replaces the Taylor rule (equation 12.19) as the only change in the log-linear version of the model.

Define the set of policy variables as $x_t = [\tilde{K}_{t+1}, \tilde{M}_t, \tilde{P}_t]'$, the set of jump variables as $y_t = [\tilde{r}_t, \tilde{w}_t, \tilde{Y}_t, \tilde{C}_t, \tilde{H}_t, \tilde{N}_t, \tilde{r}_t^n, \tilde{r}_t^f, \tilde{g}_t^M]'$, and the stochastic variable as $z_t = [\tilde{\lambda}_t, \tilde{g}_t^f]$. We find policy matrices of the form

$$x_{t+1} = Px_t + Qz_t$$

and

$$y_t = Rx_t + Sz_t,$$

where

$$P = \begin{bmatrix} 0.9445 & 0 & 0 \\ 0 & 1 & 0 \\ -0.3468 & 1 & 0 \end{bmatrix},$$

$$Q = \begin{bmatrix} 0.1439 & -0.2216 \\ 0 & 0 \\ -0.9973 & 0.9560 \end{bmatrix},$$

$$R = \begin{bmatrix} -0.9061 & 0 & 0 \\ 0.5358 & 0 & 0 \\ 0.0939 & 0 & 0 \\ 0.5469 & 0 & 0 \\ -0.4158 & 0 & 0 \\ -0.2419 & 1 & 0 \\ -0.0111 & 0 & 0 \\ -0.0261 & 0 & 0 \\ 0 & 0 & 0 \end{bmatrix},$$

and

$$S = \begin{bmatrix} 1.7750 & -1.7226 \\ 0.4608 & -0.1865 \\ 1.7750 & -1.7226 \\ 0.4023 & 0.7395 \\ 1.2109 & -2.6916 \\ 0.7192 & 0.1593 \\ 0.0585 & -0.9260 \\ 0.1032 & 1.1555 \\ 0 & -0.9709 \end{bmatrix}.$$

The constant money supply growth rule means that prices do not feed back into the economy (the zeros in the third column of matrices P and R mean that they are not really a state variable) and that the only long run effect of a change in the money stock is in money, prices, and bank deposits, all nominal variables. The results of technology and money shocks are best seen in the impulse response functions.

IMPULSE RESPONSE FUNCTIONS

The responses of the two models to a .01 shock in technology are given in Figure 12.11. The responses of the two economies to the technology shock

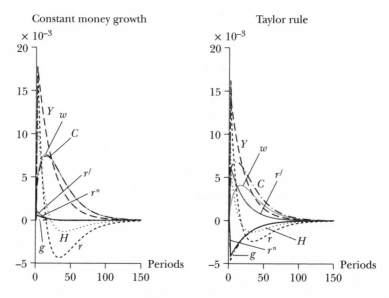

FIGURE 12.11   Responses of the real variables to a technology shock

are quite similar. The Taylor rule shows a smaller response for output, wages, and the rental on capital. The responses of consumption and labor supply are similar in both economies. The big differences are in the responses of money growth (rather obviously given the rules), the deposit interest rate, r^n, and the borrowing rate, r^f.

The responses of the nominal variables are very different, since the Taylor rule produces a persistent response in money growth (variable g in Figure 12.11) to meet the interest rate rule. This means that the money supply will not return to the original value but converges to a new, lower level. In the Taylor rule economy, prices and deposits all converge to the same long run level— they are cointegrated—so real balances and the real value of deposits return to the stationary state amounts. Since the money supply does not change (around its trend) in the economy with the constant money supply growth rate, neither prices nor deposits adjust as much. Figure 12.12 shows the response of the nominal variables to a technology shock.

The really important differences between the constant money supply growth rule and the Taylor rule are in the responses to a "fiscal" monetary shock. Figure 12.13 shows the responses of the real variables. It is clear how much the Taylor rule reduces the reaction of the real variables to the monetary shock when compared to the responses with a constant money supply

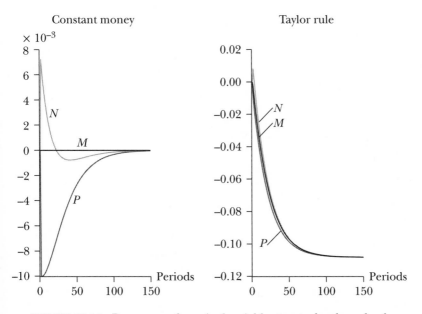

FIGURE 12.12 Responses of nominal variables to a technology shock

rule. For the economy with a constant money supply rule, the positive monetary shock acts as a tax on consumers, and the policy response of reducing the money supply through the financial system acts as a tax on production. Given its parameters, the Taylor rule generates a smaller response in r^f, and this results in smaller declines in the other real variables.

Figure 12.14 shows the responses of the nominal variables and, as before, the Taylor rule takes the nominal variables to a new level. The fact that the nominal variables go to a new level makes it difficult to compare the effects of the two rules on inflation. Figure 12.15 shows the response of inflation to the monetary shock in the two models. The magnitude of the variance of inflation is about the same in the two models, the one associated with the constant money supply growth rule having smaller initial inflation and then some deflation and the one associated with the Taylor rule having a larger initial inflation and then gradually returning to the stationary state rate. An economy with a constant money supply growth rule needs deflation after inflation to get back to the stationary state.

The specific Taylor rule that we use here (with $a = .5$, $b = .5$, and with the current values of output and inflation as variables) is only one of many variations on this rule. A number of important questions are not addressed in this chapter. What are the optimal values of a and b and what loss function are we going to use to find this optimum? Are there multiple equilibria and

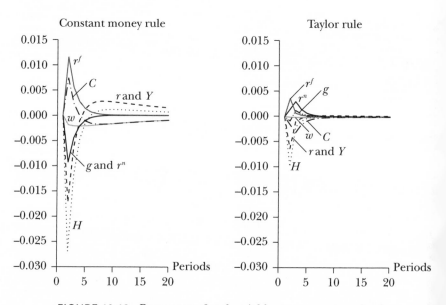

FIGURE 12.13 Responses of real variables to a monetary shock

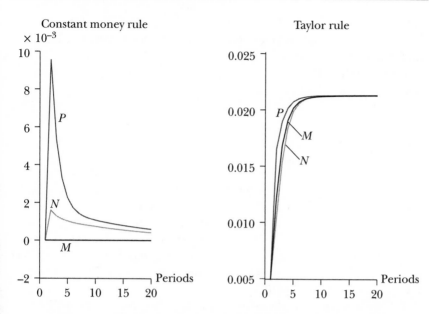

FIGURE 12.14   Responses of the nominal variables to a monetary shock

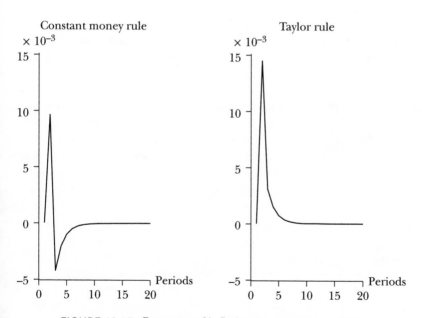

FIGURE 12.15   Response of inflation to a monetary shock

do these depend on the choices for a and b and for the timing of output and inflation used in the rule? Carlstrom and Fuerst [24], Clarida, Galí, and Gertler [34], and Schmitt-Grohe and Uribe [73] have provided a useful discussion on the stability of Taylor rules and the potential importance of the choice of the variables to use in that rule.

12.3   REPRISE

Adding a financial sector can be done fairly simply via working capital. The assumption that the entire wage bill needs to be financed with working capital may be somewhat restrictive and could be forcing some of the results. However, it is not really more severe than a cash-in-advance constraint since it works as a kind of cash-in-advance constraint on production. Firms need to acquire sufficient cash to cover their wage bill. With a government that can inject money directly into the financial system, this model can produce a stationary state Phillips curve, and money growth is positively correlated with output. While central banks normally do not make direct injections of money into the financial system, traditional monetary policy through operations involving the short-term interest rates can be thought of as a subsidy on lending working capital to firms. Lowering the interest rates lowers the costs that financial intermediaries have to pay for funds.

The working capital model also adds some interesting dynamics. The effects of money growth shocks is increased and is positively correlated with important real variables. Although Lucas has warned us to beware of economists bearing free parameters, adding working capital and money shocks to an economy can help make a model better fit the time series of real economies.

Cooley and Quadrini [37] produced an interesting model with open market monetary policy and a search theory type of unemployment that gave rise to a Phillips curve type relationship from monetary shocks. Although it is quite a challenge to introduce a search theory unemployment decision process into a general equilibrium model and the authors rightly make much of this, it is not the search theory that is generating the Phillips curve relationship. The model has a banking system that holds all government debt and also lends to the productive sector. Open market operations performed by the central bank exchange some of government debt for money. The banks can only lend this extra money to the productive sector, resulting in a reduction in interest rates paid by the firms and an increase in output (and therefore in the demand for labor). The process for the Phillips curve that is hidden in their model operates under exactly the same principles as the much simpler one of this chapter. In their model, open market operations work as a subsidy to the productive sector just as they do in our working capital model.

Once one has a model where monetary policy can have positive effects on real variables, one needs to start thinking about what the best policy is for a central bank to follow. We have looked at two famous rules: a Taylor rule and the older Friedman rule. In doing this we have assumed that governments can commit themselves to following an announced policy rule and will not deviate from that rule. We observe that the Taylor rule used here responds less aggressively to "fiscal" monetary shocks and is better able to dampen the effects of these shocks. The responses of the two rules to technology shocks are quite similar.

EXERCISE 12.1 Construct a model with financial intermediaries that finance working capital for the wage bill in an economy with Calvo type sticky wages (as in Chapter 11). How does adding sticky wages change the responses of the economy to technology and money growth shocks?

EXERCISE 12.2 Construct a model with financial intermediaries that finance working capital for the wage bill. Allow government some of the money injections to go to households and some to financial intermediaries, where a stochastic variable, $\chi_t \in [0, 1]$, measures the fraction of the money injection that goes to the households. Be careful in defining the stochastic process for χ_t so that it stays within its bounds. How does adding this additional stochastic variable change the dynamic properties of the model? How do the variables of the model respond to an impulse in this variable?

EXERCISE 12.3 Compare the response functions of the Taylor rule with $(a, b) = (1, .1)$ and with $(a, b) = (.1, 1)$ to the response functions of the $(.5, .5)$ Taylor rule studied in the chapter. Which of these rules does a better job of minimizing the sum of the variances of output and inflation?

13

Small Open Economy Models

Open economy models usually include an international asset, frequently a risk-free, one-period bond, that the citizens of a small country can hold in any amount without influencing the interest rate or price of the asset. This is frequently the definition of a small country, that whatever it does has no effect on international prices. While including such an asset seems normal and useful, it is not done without adding some difficulties.

The problems are based on the fact that arbitrage implies that one has two assets that give the same expected return. In a linear model, only the expected returns matter, so it is only expected returns that determine which assets one holds. Since both give the same return, if there are no restrictions or costs, the amount of each that individuals wish to hold is undetermined. In the first section of this chapter, we set up one such model and show where the problem arises.

One can partially resolve this problem by adding adjustment costs to capital. Schmitt-Grohé and Uribe [74] show that, under certain conditions that include adjustment costs, adding an international asset can produce a multiple of stationary state equilibria. First, in deterministic versions of the model, the initial amount of international assets or debts of a country may determine the characteristics of its stationary state. With large initial debt, for example, a stationary state will require that the country has a current account surplus sufficient to cover the interest rate payments for that debt. If the country is initially a net international creditor, this results in a different stationary state.

In stochastic models, arbitrage opportunities imply that the expected international interest rate will equal the expected domestic interest rate,[1] and technology shocks do not end up changing domestic interest rates but rather generate additional savings or borrowings in the international market. As a result of technology shocks, for example, net international assets of a country can follow a random walk. Since different levels of international assets imply a different nonstochastic stationary state, these models do not have a fixed stationary state around which we can take a linear approximation.

This problem is important because the approximate log-linear dynamic models we build are only valid in a neighborhood of a particular stationary state. If the stationary state is not well defined, then neither is the dynamic model, and our linear approximation methods are not valid for open economy models.

In this chapter we use an open economy version of the simple Hansen indivisible labor model to first show the problem of indeterminacy between the international asset and capital. In the second section we add capital adjustment costs to determine capital accumulation and international savings. In the third section, we allow international interest rates to be a function of a country's net foreign debt or savings, and this causes the economy to have a single, determined stationary state around which one can study the dynamics. Alternative methods for solving these indeterminacy problems can be found in Mendoza [63] and Uribe [87]. Finally, we add domestic cash-in-advance money and an exchange rate to the model and allow for domestic monetary shocks and shocks to foreign prices in addition to the standard domestic technology shock.

13.1 THE PRELIMINARY MODEL

In this section we build the basic model and show how the indeterminacy problem arises when, because of arbitrage possibilities, there are two assets with the same rate of return. The economy used here does not have money, so there are no exchange rate issues.

13.1.1 The Household

We first build a simple, small, open economy, Hansen type model without money. Since the model will have only one good and does not include money, it does not have exchange rates. What it does have, and what makes it different

---

1. This is always true in the linearized versions of our models. In models where risk aversion can be important, domestic and international interest rates can be different if they are subject to different stochastic processes.

from the generic Hansen model, is an international market for risk-free bonds that, in each period, give a real net return equal to $r^f = 1/\beta - 1$, where β is the time discount factor of the families.

As with the Hansen model, with indivisible labor, each of a unit mass of families chooses the sequence of values for $\{c_t, h_t, k_{t+1}, b_t\}_{t=0}^{\infty}$ to maximize

$$\max_{\{c_t, h_t, k_{t+1}, b_t\}} E_t \sum_{t=0}^{\infty} \beta^t \left[\ln c_t + B h_t\right],$$

where c_t is time t consumption and h_t is the average time t labor, and

$$B = \frac{A \ln(1 - h_0)}{h_0},$$

with $A > 0$, where $0 < h_0 < 1$ is the amount of labor that a family must supply to the production process if it is one of the randomly chosen families that are to supply labor. The fraction h_t/h_0 is the probability that a particular family will be chosen to supply labor in period t. Given that in the Hansen model with indivisible labor there is an insurance scheme for all families to receive the same labor income whether or not they are chosen to work, the budget constraint for a family is

$$b_t + k_{t+1} + c_t = w_t h_t + r_t k_t + (1 - \delta)k_t + (1 + r^f)b_{t-1} + \xi_t,$$

where k_t is the capital that the family brings into period t, r_t is the real rental rate on capital, δ is the rate of depreciation, w_t is the real wage, ξ_t is the lump sum transfer from the wage insurance program, and b_t is the amount of international bonds (or international debt if it is negative) that the family is holding at the end of period t. Since the international interest rate is a constant and there are no apparent restrictions on the amount that a family might want to borrow, there is the possibility that a family might try to borrow an ever-growing amount from the international market. As usual, we need an additional restriction to prevent this type of "Ponzi" game. We limit how fast debt can grow by assuming the transversality (limit) condition

$$\lim_{t \to \infty} \frac{b_t}{(1 + r^f)^t} = \lim_{t \to \infty} \beta^t b_t = 0.$$

The holding of international bonds or debt cannot grow faster, in the limit, than $1/\beta$. The second equality holds because we have assumed that the international interest rate is $r^f = 1/\beta - 1$. If the international interest rate were different from $1/\beta - 1$, the economy would not have stationary states in the sense that consumption could be constant through time. This will be seen presently in the first-order conditions that come from the household's maximization problem.

The Lagrangian problem is written as

$$\mathcal{L} = E_t \sum_{t=0}^{\infty} \beta^t \left\{ \ln c_t + Bh_t \right.$$

$$\left. + \lambda_t \left[w_t h_t + r_t k_t + (1-\delta)k_t + (1+r^f)b_{t-1} + \xi_t - b_t - k_{t+1} - c_t \right] \right\}.$$

The first-order conditions are

$$\frac{\partial \mathcal{L}}{\partial c_t} = \frac{1}{c_t} - \lambda_t = 0,$$

$$\frac{\partial \mathcal{L}}{\partial h_t} = B + \lambda_t w_t = 0,$$

$$\frac{\partial \mathcal{L}}{\partial k_{t+1}} = -\lambda_t + \beta E_t \lambda_{t+1} \left[r_{t+1} + (1-\delta) \right] = 0,$$

$$\frac{\partial \mathcal{L}}{\partial b_t} = -\lambda_t + \beta E_t \lambda_{t+1}(1+r^f) = 0$$

and

$$\lim_{t \to \infty} \frac{b_t}{(1+r^f)^t} = 0.$$

These first-order conditions and the budget constraint give the set of equations that come from the family's decision process,

$$B = -\frac{w_t}{c_t},$$

$$\frac{1}{\beta c_t} = E_t \frac{1}{c_{t+1}} \left(1 + r^f\right),$$ (13.1)

$$\frac{1}{\beta} = E_t \frac{c_t}{c_{t+1}} \left[r_{t+1} + (1-\delta) \right],$$

$$b_t + k_{t+1} + c_t = w_t h_t + r_t k_t + (1-\delta)k_t + (1+r^f)b_{t-1} + \xi_t,$$

and

$$\lim_{t \to \infty} \frac{b_t}{(1+r^f)^t} = 0.$$

13.1.2 The Firm

The production function is given by

$$f(\lambda_t, k_t, h_t) = \lambda_t k_t^\theta h_t^{1-\theta},$$

where λ_t is a random technology variable that follows the process

$$\lambda_{t+1} = \gamma \lambda_t + \varepsilon_{t+1},$$

with $0 < \gamma < 1$, $\varepsilon_{t+1} > 0$, and $E_t \varepsilon_{t+1} = 1 - \gamma$. These assumptions imply that the unconditional expectation of technology is one or $E\lambda_t = 1$. Assuming that the factor markets are competitive, we get conditions for real wages and rentals of

$$r_t = \theta \lambda_t k_t^{\theta-1} h_t^{1-\theta}$$

and

$$w_t = (1 - \theta) \lambda_t k_t^\theta h_t^{-\theta}.$$

13.1.3 Equilibrium Conditions

Since all of the unit mass of families are identical, we have as equilibrium conditions that

$$C_t = c_t,$$
$$K_t = k_t,$$
$$H_t = h_t,$$

and

$$B_t = b_t.$$

13.1.4 Stationary State

In a stationary state, the technology shock is constant and equal to one and the real variables do not change over time. We set each aggregate real variable $X_s = \bar{X}$ for every s and get the system of equations

$$B = -\frac{\bar{w}}{\bar{C}}, \tag{13.2}$$

$$\frac{1}{\beta} = 1 + r^f \tag{13.3}$$

$$\frac{1}{\beta} = \bar{r} + (1 - \delta), \tag{13.4}$$

$$\bar{C} = \bar{w}\bar{H} + (\bar{r} - \delta)\,\bar{K} + r^f\bar{B}, \tag{13.5}$$

$$\bar{r} = \theta\bar{K}^{\theta-1}\bar{H}^{1-\theta}, \tag{13.6}$$

$$\bar{w} = (1-\theta)\,\bar{K}^\theta\bar{H}^{-\theta}. \tag{13.7}$$

Equation 13.3 is a stationary state condition that comes from the first-order condition of equation 13.1. If this condition did not hold, then we could not get the stationary state condition on consumption that $C_t = C_{t+1}$, and no stationary state would exist. Note that B is a coefficient while $\bar{B}$ is the stationary state quantity of foreign bonds or debt, and that r^f is the international interest rate while $\bar{r}$ is the real rental rate on capital. This system has six unknowns, $\bar{C}$, $\bar{K}$, $\bar{H}$, $\bar{w}$, $\bar{r}$, and $\bar{B}$, and six equations. The choice of a constant value of $\bar{B}$ is a condition for a stationary state: each choice of $\bar{B}$ implies a different stationary state with different values for some of the other variables.

As before, from equation 13.4, we find that

$$\bar{r} = \frac{1}{\beta} - (1-\delta),$$

from equations 13.6 and 13.7 that

$$\bar{w} = (1-\theta)\left(\frac{\theta}{\bar{r}}\right)^{\frac{\theta}{1-\theta}},$$

and from equation 13.2 that

$$\bar{C} = -\frac{\bar{w}}{B}.$$

Since from the two equations on the factor markets, equations 13.6 and 13.7,

$$\bar{H} = \frac{(1-\theta)}{\theta}\frac{\bar{r}}{\bar{w}}\bar{K},$$

we can use the aggregate form of the budget constraint, equation 13.5, and get

$$\left[\frac{\bar{r}}{\theta} - \delta\right]\bar{K} = \bar{C} - r^f\bar{B}.$$

The interesting part of this last equation is that the capital stock is determined, in part, by the holding of international assets. The capital stock, hours worked, and output (from the production function) in the stationary state are all functions of the country's holdings of international assets or debt. Since utility is a function of consumption (which is not a function of international assets) and average hours worked, since hours worked decline as $\bar{B}$ falls, utility in the stationary state is also an increasing function of the holdings of international assets, $\bar{B}$.

We have just demonstrated the first of the claims made in the introduction to this chapter: that there are an infinite number of possible stationary state equilibria. Since international asset holdings can have any real value, we have an infinite number of potential stationary state equilibria, values for $\bar{K}$, $\bar{H}$, and $\bar{Y}$, one for each potential $\bar{B}$. It is interesting that the stationary state values for $\bar{C}$, $\bar{r}$, and $\bar{w}$ do not depend on the initial holdings of the international asset.

One final point about stationary states: in this model there is a natural limit to the amount of international debt that citizens of a country can accumulate. Since labor is indivisible and each family that works supplies h_0 units of labor, the maximum labor available in the economy with a unit mass of families is $\bar{H} = h_0$. Rewriting equation 13.5 by substituting out capital, using

$$\bar{K} = \frac{\theta}{(1-\theta)} \frac{\bar{w}}{\bar{r}} \bar{H},$$

gives

$$\bar{C} = \bar{w} \left[1 + \frac{(\bar{r} - \delta)\,\theta}{(1 - \theta)\,\bar{r}} \right] \bar{H} + r^f \bar{B}.$$

The maximum foreign debt possible (a negative number) in a stationary state is

$$\bar{B} = \frac{\bar{C} - \bar{w} \left[1 + \frac{(\bar{r} - \delta)\theta}{(1-\theta)\bar{r}} \right] h_0}{r^f},$$

where $\bar{C}$, $\bar{w}$, and $\bar{r}$ have their constant stationary state values. For our standard economy, the maximum debt possible (minimum $\bar{B}$) is

$$\bar{B} = -1.6609,$$

13.1.5   The Dynamic (Log-Linear) Model

The equations for the dynamic version of the model, written in terms of the aggregate variables, are

$$B = -\frac{w_t}{C_t},$$

$$\frac{1}{C_t} = E_t \frac{1}{C_{t+1}},$$

$$\frac{1}{\beta} = E_t \frac{C_t}{C_{t+1}} \left[r_{t+1} + (1 - \delta) \right],$$

$$B_t + K_{t+1} + C_t = w_t H_t + r_t K_t + (1 - \delta) K_t + (1 + r^f) B_{t-1},$$

$$r_t = \theta \lambda_t K_t^{\theta-1} H_t^{1-\theta},$$

$$w_t = (1 - \theta) \lambda_t K_t^{\theta} H_t^{-\theta},$$

and

$$\lim_{t \to \infty} \frac{B_t}{\left(1 + r^f\right)^t} = 0,$$

and the process for the stochastic technology shock is

$$\lambda_{t+1} = \gamma \lambda_t + \varepsilon_{t+1}.$$

In the second equation, we used the fact that $1/\beta = 1 + r^f$ to simplify.

The log-linear version of the model, written in terms of $\tilde{X}_t = \ln X_t - \ln \bar{X}$, for each variable $X_t = \{C_t, H_t, K_t, r_t, w_t, B_t, \lambda_t\}$, is

$$0 = \tilde{C}_t - \tilde{w}_t,$$

$$0 = \tilde{C}_t - E_t \tilde{C}_{t+1},$$

$$0 = \tilde{C}_t - E_t \tilde{C}_{t+1} + \beta \bar{r} E_t \tilde{r}_{t+1},$$

$$0 = \bar{B} \tilde{B}_t + \bar{K} \tilde{K}_{t+1} + \bar{C} \tilde{C}_t - \bar{w} \bar{H} \tilde{w}_t - \bar{w} \bar{H} \tilde{H}_t$$

$$- \bar{r} \bar{K} \tilde{r}_t - [\bar{r} + (1 - \delta)] \bar{K} \tilde{K}_t - (1 + r^f) \bar{B} \tilde{B}_{t-1},$$

$$0 = \tilde{\lambda}_t + (\theta - 1) \tilde{K}_t + (1 - \theta) \tilde{H}_t - \tilde{r}_t,$$

$$0 = \tilde{\lambda}_t + \theta \tilde{K}_t - \theta \tilde{H}_t - \tilde{w}_t,$$

and the stochastic equation is

$$\tilde{\lambda}_{t+1} = \gamma \tilde{\lambda}_t + \mu_{t+1},$$

where $\mu_{t+1} = \varepsilon_{t+1} - (1 - \gamma)$.

One would like to do as in previous chapters and solve this linear system for a pair of linear policy functions determining $\tilde{K}_{t+1}$ and $\tilde{B}_t$ and the jump variables. However, the household decision problem does not separate these two variables. The log-linear version of this model cannot be solved for distinct values of $\tilde{B}_t$ and $\tilde{K}_{t+1}$. These two variables offer the same expected returns, and there is nothing in this version of the model to determine how much of period t wealth goes to the bonds and how much goes to capital. This can be shown more specifically by simplifying the log-linear version of the model.

First, we remove consumption, $\tilde{C}_t$, from the model. That gives the five-equation system

$$0 = \tilde{w}_t - E_t \tilde{w}_{t+1},$$

$$0 = \beta \bar{r} E_t \tilde{r}_{t+1},$$

$$0 = \bar{B} \tilde{B}_t + \bar{K} \tilde{K}_{t+1} + \bar{C} \tilde{w}_t - \bar{w} \bar{H} \tilde{w}_t - \bar{w} \bar{H} \tilde{H}_t$$
$$- \bar{r} \bar{K} \tilde{r}_t - [\bar{r} + (1-\delta)] \bar{K} \tilde{K}_t - (1+r^f) \bar{B} \tilde{B}_{t-1},$$

$$0 = \tilde{\lambda}_t + (\theta - 1) \tilde{K}_t + (1-\theta) \tilde{H}_t - \tilde{r}_t,$$

$$0 = \tilde{\lambda}_t + \theta \tilde{K}_t - \theta \tilde{H}_t - \tilde{w}_t.$$

Combining the last two equations gives the results

$$0 = \tilde{\lambda}_t - \theta \tilde{r}_t + (\theta - 1) \tilde{w}_t$$

and

$$\tilde{H}_t = \tilde{K}_t + \tilde{r}_t - \tilde{w}_t, \tag{13.8}$$

so we can eliminate $\tilde{H}_t$ from the system and have a system in four equations,

$$0 = \tilde{w}_t - E_t \tilde{w}_{t+1},$$

$$0 = \beta \bar{r} E_t \tilde{r}_{t+1},$$

$$0 = \bar{B} \tilde{B}_t + \bar{K} \tilde{K}_{t+1} + \bar{C} \tilde{w}_t - [\bar{w} \bar{H} + \bar{r} \bar{K}] \tilde{r}_t$$
$$- [[\bar{r} + (1-\delta)] \bar{K} + \bar{w} \bar{H}] \tilde{K}_t - (1+r^f) \bar{B} \tilde{B}_{t-1},$$

$$0 = \tilde{\lambda}_t - \theta \tilde{r}_t + (\theta - 1) \tilde{w}_t.$$

The last line must hold in each period, so we can write it in terms of period $t+1$ and take the expectations in period t. This gives

$$0 = E_t \tilde{\lambda}_{t+1} - \theta E_t \tilde{r}_{t+1} + (\theta - 1) E_t \tilde{w}_{t+1},$$

which, using the second line of the model and the equation for the $\tilde{\lambda}_{t+1}$ process, is

$$E_t \tilde{w}_{t+1} = \frac{\gamma}{(1-\theta)} \tilde{\lambda}_t.$$

Therefore, the first equation of the four-equation model gives

$$\tilde{w}_t = \frac{\gamma}{(1-\theta)} \tilde{\lambda}_t,$$

and using the last equation, one gets

$$0 = \tilde{\lambda}_t - \theta \tilde{r}_t + (\theta - 1) \frac{\gamma}{(1-\theta)} \tilde{\lambda}_t,$$

or

$$\tilde{r}_t = \frac{(1-\gamma)}{\theta} \tilde{\lambda}_t.$$

Note that wages, rentals, and consumption (because consumption is determined by wages) depend only on the current technology shock and not on capital or bonds. Equation 13.8 gives

$$\tilde{H}_t = \tilde{K}_t + \left[\frac{(1-\gamma)}{\theta} - \frac{\gamma}{(1-\theta)} \right] \tilde{\lambda}_t,$$

so labor depends on capital (with a coefficient of one) and on the technology shock. Only the third equation of the model remains and, after substituting in the above results, is

$$\bar{B} \tilde{B}_t + \bar{K} \tilde{K}_{t+1} = \left[[\bar{r} + (1-\delta)] \bar{K} + \bar{w} \bar{H} \right] \tilde{K}_t + (1+r^f) \bar{B} \tilde{B}_{t-1} \quad (13.9)$$

$$- \left[\frac{\gamma \bar{C}}{(1-\theta)} - \frac{(1-\gamma) \left[\bar{w} \bar{H} + \bar{r} \bar{K} \right]}{\theta} \right] \tilde{\lambda}_t.$$

The weighed sum of bonds and capital for the next period is determined, but there is nothing in the model that tells us how much of each we should have. Recall that bonds and capital have the same expected returns (this because the model implies that $E_t \tilde{r}_{t+1} = 0$). As it is formulated, the linear version of the model cannot be solved. Equation 13.9 is a single policy function (notice that all the variables on the right-hand side are state variables) for the combination of the two control variables, $\tilde{K}_{t+1}$ and $\tilde{B}_t$.

13.2   MODEL WITH CAPITAL ADJUSTMENT COSTS

One fairly common way to attempt to resolve the indeterminacy in the above model is to make it costly to change capital. Adding a capital adjustment cost changes the rates of return between capital and bonds and will give us another condition that will permit separating bonds and capital in the log-linear version of the model. There remain other problems, as we shall see, but first we study why open economy models with both capital and foreign bonds usually include capital adjustment costs.

For each family, changing their capital holdings involves an adjustment cost of

$$\frac{\kappa}{2}\left(k_{t+1} - k_t\right)^2,$$

so that faster adjustments in the capital stock are more expensive. The costs are symmetric, so that reducing capital is as expensive as expanding it. The way adjustment costs are written here, replacing depreciated capital does not generate adjustment costs. With these adjustment costs, each family's flow budget constraint is

$$b_t + k_{t+1} + \frac{\kappa}{2}\left(k_{t+1} - k_t\right)^2 + c_t = w_t h_t + r_t k_t + (1 - \delta)k_t + (1 + r^f)b_{t-1}.$$

The Lagrangian problem is written as

$$\mathcal{L} = E_t \sum_{t=0}^{\infty} \beta^t \left\{ \ln c_t + B h_t \right.$$

$$\left. + \lambda_t \left[w_t h_t + r_t k_t + (1 - \delta)k_t + (1 + r^f)b_{t-1} - b_t - k_{t+1} - \frac{\kappa}{2}\left(k_{t+1} - k_t\right)^2 - c_t \right] \right\}.$$

The derivatives of the Lagrangian are

$$\frac{\partial \mathcal{L}}{\partial c_t} = \frac{1}{c_t} - \lambda_t = 0,$$

$$\frac{\partial \mathcal{L}}{\partial h_t} = B + \lambda_t w_t = 0,$$

$$\frac{\partial \mathcal{L}}{\partial k_{t+1}} = -\lambda_t \left(1 + \kappa \left(k_{t+1} - k_t\right)\right) + \beta E_t \lambda_{t+1} \left[r_{t+1} + (1 - \delta) + \kappa \left(k_{t+2} - k_{t+1}\right)\right] = 0$$

$$\frac{\partial \mathcal{L}}{\partial b_t} = -\lambda_t + \beta E_t \lambda_{t+1}(1 + r^f) = 0.$$

The first-order conditions for the family (including the budget constraint) are

$$B = -\frac{w_t}{c_t},$$

$$\frac{1}{c_t} = E_t \frac{1}{c_{t+1}},$$

$$\frac{1}{\beta} \left(1 + \kappa \left(k_{t+1} - k_t\right)\right) = E_t \frac{c_t}{c_{t+1}} \left[r_{t+1} + (1 - \delta) + \kappa \left(k_{t+2} - k_{t+1}\right)\right],$$

$$b_t + k_{t+1} + \frac{\kappa}{2} \left(k_{t+1} - k_t\right)^2 + c_t = w_t h_t + r_t k_t + (1 - \delta)k_t + (1 + r^f)b_{t-1}.$$

The full model uses these four equations plus the factor market equations that determine rentals on capital and wages from the marginal products of capital and labor, respectively:

$$w_t = (1 - \theta) \lambda_t K_t^\theta H_t^{-\theta},$$

$$r_t = \theta \lambda_t K_t^{\theta-1} H_t^{1-\theta}.$$

The stationary state for this version of the model is exactly the same as that for the first model since in a stationary state $k_{t+1} = k_t$ and the adjustment costs are zero. The capital adjustment cost components drop out, and the stationary state version of the model is the same as in the first section of this chapter.

The log-linear version of the third equation, after aggregation, is

$$0 = \tilde{C}_t - E_t \tilde{C}_{t+1} + \beta \bar{r} E_t \tilde{r}_{t+1} + \beta \kappa \bar{K} E_t \tilde{K}_{t+2} - (1 + \beta) \kappa \bar{K} \tilde{K}_{t+1} + \kappa \bar{K} \tilde{K}_t.$$

The full log-linear model is

$$0 = \tilde{C}_t - \tilde{w}_t,$$

$$0 = \tilde{C}_t - E_t \tilde{C}_{t+1},$$

$$0 = \tilde{C}_t - E_t \tilde{C}_{t+1} + \beta \bar{r} E_t \tilde{r}_{t+1} + \beta \kappa \bar{K} E_t \tilde{K}_{t+2} - (1 + \beta) \kappa \bar{K} \tilde{K}_{t+1} + \kappa \bar{K} \tilde{K}_t,$$

$$0 = \bar{B} \tilde{B}_t + \bar{K} \tilde{K}_{t+1} + \bar{C} \tilde{C}_t - \bar{w} \bar{H} \tilde{w}_t - \bar{w} \bar{H} \tilde{H}_t - \bar{r} \bar{K} \tilde{r}_t$$

$$- [\bar{r} + (1 - \delta)] \bar{K} \tilde{K}_t - (1 + r^f) \bar{B} \tilde{B}_{t-1},$$

$$0 = \tilde{\lambda}_t + (\theta - 1) \tilde{K}_t + (1 - \theta) \tilde{H}_t - \tilde{r}_t,$$

$$0 = \tilde{\lambda}_t + \theta \tilde{K}_t - \theta \tilde{H}_t - \tilde{w}_t.$$

Notice that since the adjustment costs are purely quadratic in the fourth equation of the system (the flow budget constraint), they do not appear in the log linearization of that equation since there is no linear component of the adjustment costs and the Taylor approximation that we are using ignores second-order or larger components.

First, we can remove consumption, $\tilde{C}_t$, from the model and get

$$0 = \tilde{w}_t - E_t \tilde{w}_{t+1},$$

$$0 = \beta \bar{r} E_t \tilde{r}_{t+1} + \beta \kappa \bar{K} E_t \tilde{K}_{t+2} - (1+\beta) \kappa \bar{K} \tilde{K}_{t+1} + \kappa \bar{K} \tilde{K}_t,$$

$$0 = \bar{B} \tilde{B}_t + \bar{K} \tilde{K}_{t+1} + \bar{C} \tilde{w}_t - \bar{w} \bar{H} \tilde{w}_t - \bar{w} \bar{H} \tilde{H}_t - \bar{r} \bar{K} \tilde{r}_t$$

$$\quad - [\bar{r} + (1-\delta)] \bar{K} \tilde{K}_t - (1+r^f) \bar{B} \tilde{B}_{t-1},$$

$$0 = \tilde{\lambda}_t + (\theta - 1) \tilde{K}_t + (1-\theta) \tilde{H}_t - \tilde{r}_t,$$

$$0 = \tilde{\lambda}_t + \theta \tilde{K}_t - \theta \tilde{H}_t - \tilde{w}_t.$$

The last two equations can be reduced to

$$0 = \tilde{\lambda}_t - \theta \tilde{r}_t + (\theta - 1) \tilde{w}_t$$

and

$$\tilde{H}_t = \tilde{K}_t + \tilde{r}_t - \tilde{w}_t.$$

Using the first of these as one of the equations of the model and using the second to remove $\tilde{H}_t$ from the system, the set of equations of the model simplifies to

$$0 = \tilde{w}_t - E_t \tilde{w}_{t+1},$$

$$0 = \beta \bar{r} E_t \tilde{r}_{t+1} + \beta \kappa \bar{K} E_t \tilde{K}_{t+2} - (1+\beta) \kappa \bar{K} \tilde{K}_{t+1} + \kappa \bar{K} \tilde{K}_t,$$

$$0 = \bar{B} \tilde{B}_t + \bar{K} \tilde{K}_{t+1} + \bar{C} \tilde{w}_t - \bar{w} \bar{H} \tilde{K}_t - [\bar{w} \bar{H} + \bar{r} \bar{K}] \tilde{r}_t$$

$$\quad - [\bar{r} + (1-\delta)] \bar{K} \tilde{K}_t - (1+r^f) \bar{B} \tilde{B}_{t-1},$$

$$0 = \tilde{\lambda}_t - \theta \tilde{r}_t + (\theta - 1) \tilde{w}_t.$$

The last equation written as expectations in period $t+1$ is

$$0 = E_t \tilde{\lambda}_{t+1} - \theta E_t \tilde{r}_{t+1} + (\theta - 1) E_t \tilde{w}_{t+1}$$

$$= \gamma \tilde{\lambda}_t - \theta E_t \tilde{r}_{t+1} + (\theta - 1) E_t \tilde{w}_{t+1}$$

$$= \gamma \tilde{\lambda}_t - \theta E_t \tilde{r}_{t+1} + (\theta - 1) \tilde{w}_t,$$

so

$$E_t \tilde{r}_{t+1} = \frac{\gamma}{\theta} \tilde{\lambda}_t + \frac{(\theta - 1)}{\theta} \tilde{w}_t.$$

Removing $\tilde{r}_t$ and $E_t \tilde{r}_{t+1}$, the system can be written as

$$0 = \tilde{w}_t - E_t \tilde{w}_{t+1},$$

$$0 = \beta \bar{r} \frac{\gamma}{\theta} \tilde{\lambda}_t + \beta \bar{r} \frac{(\theta - 1)}{\theta} \tilde{w}_t + \beta \kappa \bar{K} E_t \tilde{K}_{t+2} - (1 + \beta) \kappa \bar{K} \tilde{K}_{t+1} + \kappa \bar{K} \tilde{K}_t,$$

$$0 = \bar{B} \tilde{B}_t + \bar{K} \tilde{K}_{t+1} - \bar{w} \bar{H} \tilde{K}_t - \frac{[\bar{w}\bar{H} + \bar{r}\bar{K}]}{\theta} \tilde{\lambda}_t + \left[\bar{C} + \frac{(1 - \theta)}{\theta} [\bar{w}\bar{H} + \bar{r}\bar{K}] \right] \tilde{w}_t$$

$$- [\bar{r} + (1 - \delta)] \bar{K} \tilde{K}_t - (1 + r^f) \bar{B} \tilde{B}_{t-1}.$$

We now remove wages from the system. Defining

$$\xi \equiv \frac{\theta \kappa \bar{K}}{\beta \bar{r} (1 - \theta)},$$

the second equation can be written as

$$\tilde{w}_t = \frac{\gamma}{(1 - \theta)} \tilde{\lambda}_t + \beta \xi E_t \tilde{K}_{t+2} - \xi (1 + \beta) \tilde{K}_{t+1} + \xi \tilde{K}_t,$$

and using this twice, once in expectations, the first equation of the system can be written as

$$0 = \frac{\gamma (1 - \gamma)}{(1 - \theta)} \tilde{\lambda}_t - \xi \left[\beta E_t \tilde{K}_{t+3} - (1 + 2\beta) E_t \tilde{K}_{t+2} + (2 + \beta) \tilde{K}_{t+1} - \tilde{K}_t \right],$$

$$(13.10)$$

and the last equation is

$$0 = \bar{B} \tilde{B}_t - \left(\frac{(1 - \gamma)}{\theta} [\bar{w}\bar{H} + \bar{r}\bar{K}] - \frac{\gamma \bar{C}}{(1 - \theta)} \right) \tilde{\lambda}_t \qquad (13.11)$$

$$- \left(\left[\bar{C} + \frac{(1 - \theta)}{\theta} [\bar{w}\bar{H} + \bar{r}\bar{K}] \right] \xi (1 + \beta) - \bar{K} \right) \tilde{K}_{t+1}$$

$$+ \left(\left[\bar{C} + \frac{(1 - \theta)}{\theta} [\bar{w}\bar{H} + \bar{r}\bar{K}] \right] \xi - [\bar{r} + (1 - \delta)] \bar{K} - \bar{w}\bar{H} \right) \tilde{K}_t$$

$$+ \xi \beta \left[\bar{C} + \frac{(1 - \theta)}{\theta} [\bar{w}\bar{H} + \bar{r}\bar{K}] \right] E_t \tilde{K}_{t+2} - (1 + r^f) \bar{B} \tilde{B}_{t-1}.$$

Since the first equation only contains K_s's, this two-equation system is recursive, and we can first find a rule for $\tilde{K}_{t+1}$ and then use this $\tilde{K}_{t+1}$ rule to solve for $\tilde{B}_t$.

Following the usual procedure, we look for a pair of policy rules of the form

$$\tilde{K}_{t+1} = P_{11}\tilde{K}_t + Q_1\tilde{\lambda}_t$$

and

$$\tilde{B}_t = P_{21}\tilde{K}_t + P_{22}\tilde{B}_{t-1} + Q_2\tilde{\lambda}_t.$$

We know that the first equation can be solved for $\tilde{K}_{t+1}$ without knowing $\tilde{B}_{t-1}$, so it must be that $P_{12} = 0$. Assuming that policy rules like these exist, we can write the expectations, $E_t\tilde{K}_{t+2}$, as

$$E_t\tilde{K}_{t+2} = P_{11}\tilde{K}_{t+1} + Q_1 E_t\tilde{\lambda}_{t+1}$$

$$= P_{11}\left[P_{11}\tilde{K}_t + Q_1\tilde{\lambda}_t\right] + Q_1\gamma\tilde{\lambda}_t$$

$$= \left(P_{11}\right)^2\tilde{K}_t + Q_1\left(P_{11} + \gamma\right)\tilde{\lambda}_t.$$

In a similar manner we can write

$$E_t\tilde{K}_{t+3} = P_{11}E_t\tilde{K}_{t+2} + Q_1 E_t\tilde{\lambda}_{t+2}$$

$$= P_{11}\left[P_{11}\tilde{K}_{t+1} + Q_1 E_t\tilde{\lambda}_{t+1}\right] + Q_1\gamma E_t\tilde{\lambda}_{t+1}$$

$$= P_{11}\left[P_{11}\left[P_{11}\tilde{K}_t + Q_1\tilde{\lambda}_t\right] + Q_1\gamma\tilde{\lambda}_t\right] + Q_1\gamma^2\tilde{\lambda}_t$$

$$= \left(P_{11}\right)^3\tilde{K}_t + Q_1\left(\left(P_{11}\right)^2 + \gamma P_{11} + \gamma^2\right)\tilde{\lambda}_t.$$

Substituting these equations for $\tilde{K}_{t+1}$, $E_t\tilde{K}_{t+2}$, and $E_t\tilde{K}_{t+3}$ into equation 13.10, we get

$$0 = \frac{\gamma\left(1-\gamma\right)}{1-\theta}\tilde{\lambda}_t - \xi\left[\beta P_{11}^3 - (1+2\beta)P_{11}^2 + (2+\beta)P_{11} - 1\right]\tilde{K}_t$$

$$- \xi Q_1\left[\beta\left(P_{11}^2 + \gamma P_{11} + \gamma^2\right) - (1+2\beta)(P_{11} + \gamma) + (2+\beta)\right]\tilde{\lambda}_t.$$

For this rule to hold for all values of $\tilde{K}_t$ and $\tilde{\lambda}_t$, the coefficient on $\tilde{K}_t$ must be zero. We can find P_{11} using

$$\beta P_{11}^3 - (1+2\beta)P_{11}^2 + (2+\beta)P_{11} - 1 = 0. \tag{13.12}$$

The coefficient on $\tilde{\lambda}_t$ on the right-hand side of the equation must equal that on the left, so

$$\frac{\gamma\,(1-\gamma)}{\xi\,(1-\theta)} = Q_1\left[\beta\left(P_{11}^2 + \gamma P_{11} + \gamma^2\right) - (1+2\beta)\left(P_{11}+\gamma\right) + (2+\beta)\right].$$

$$(13.13)$$

Values of P_{11} that solve equation 13.12 are

$$P_{11} = 1 \text{ or } = \frac{1}{\beta},$$

and equation 13.13 (using the respective values for P_{11}) when

$$Q_1 = -\frac{\gamma}{\xi\,(1-\theta)\,(1-\beta\gamma)}, \text{ or } = -\frac{\gamma}{\xi\,(1-\theta)\,\beta\,(1-\gamma)}.$$

When $P_{11} = 1/\beta$, the capital stock is explosive, so we reject that solution. Using the random walk of $P_{11} = 1$ and the corresponding Q_1 in equation 13.11, one finds

$$P_{21} = \frac{[\bar{r} - \delta)]\,\bar{K} + \bar{w}\bar{H}}{\bar{B}}$$

and

$$P_{22} = 1 + r^f.$$

One can also solve for Q_2, but the result is rather complicated and not very enlightening and is not reported here. Recall that for reasons of stability, we set the international interest rate to give $1 + r^f = 1/\beta$, so $P_{22} = 1/\beta$.

Unfortunately, as one can see from the above solution, in the components of the policy matrix P_{21} (and, while not shown, also in Q_2), the dynamics of the system depend on the initial holdings of foreign bonds. More important, the component of the policy matrix for capital, P_{11}, follows a random walk and that for foreign bonds, P_{22}, is explosive. Therefore, the economy can move far from the initial stationary state around which the log-linear version of the dynamic model is found. Since our linear versions of the dynamic model are only valid in a neighborhood of some "stationary" state, the model does not do a good job of describing the dynamics of the system when it drifts away from the initial stationary state.

Adding adjustment costs for capital allows us to find policy functions for the economy, but the log-linear approximations that we make are not valid since the economy will drift away from the initial stationary state around which the approximation was found. One needs additional assumptions to allow one to "close" the open economy model and to force it to have a unique stationary state. Then one can study the dynamic properties of the model around that stationary state.

13.3 CLOSING THE OPEN ECONOMY

One way to close this model is to change the way that the rest of the world deals with citizens of the small country. Closing the model[2] means finding a single stationary state equilibrium and then being able to find a log-linear approximation of the dynamic model around this stationary state.

13.3.1 Interest Rates and Country Risk

Suppose that there is a concept of country risk (loosely specified here) so that the interest rate a citizen of a country pays on international borrowing is an increasing function of the country's total international debt (and the interest rate its citizens get for international savings declines as a function of total savings). We hypothesis a simple, linear function of the form

$$r_t^f = r^* - aB_t,$$

where r_t^f is the international (foreign) real interest rate at time t and a is a positive constant. The minus sign says that as a country accumulates foreign debt, the international interest rate it must pay rises. The constant r^* is added so that international savings can occur at a positive interest rate. Since the rate is a function of the country's total borrowing or savings, and not that of a single family, the first-order conditions for the families are not changed. When we write out the aggregate version of the model, this equation shows up as one of the equilibrium conditions, and we replace r^f in the initial economy with $r_t^f = r^* - aB_t$.

The first-order conditions for the family are the same as in the previous model, except the equation

$$\frac{\partial \mathcal{L}}{\partial b_t} = -\lambda_t + \beta E_t \lambda_{t+1}(1 + r_t^f) = 0$$

is now

$$\frac{\partial \mathcal{L}}{\partial b_t} = -\lambda_t + \beta E_t \lambda_{t+1}(1 + r^* - aB_t) = 0.$$

The full set of equations for the family (written in aggregate form) that come from the first-order conditions is now

---

2. This phrase comes from Schmitt-Grohé and Uribe [74] who use it to describe the assumptions necessary to generate a unique equilbrium for an open macroeconomy.

$$B = -\frac{w_t}{C_t},$$

$$\frac{1}{C_t} = \beta E_t \frac{1}{C_{t+1}}(1 + r^* - aB_t),$$

$$\frac{1}{\beta}\left(1 + \kappa\left(K_{t+1} - K_t\right)\right) = E_t \frac{C_t}{C_{t+1}}\left[r_{t+1} + (1 - \delta) + \kappa\left(K_{t+2} - K_{t+1}\right)\right],$$

$$B_t + K_{t+1} + C_t = w_t H_t + r_t K_t + (1 - \delta)K_t - \frac{\kappa}{2}\left(K_{t+1} - K_t\right)^2$$

$$+ (1 + r^* - aB_{t-1})B_{t-1}.$$

In a stationary state, $\bar{C} = C_t = C_{t+1}$, so the second equation is

$$\frac{1}{\bar{C}} = \beta\frac{1}{\bar{C}}(1 + r^* - a\bar{B}),$$

or

$$\bar{B} = \frac{r^* + 1 - \frac{1}{\beta}}{a}.$$

In the stationary state, the holding of foreign bonds or debt is exactly that which makes the real interest rate that the country pays (or receives) for foreign borrowing (or lending) equal to $1/\beta$. For an economy with the standard values for the other parameters and with $a = .01$ and $r^* = .03$, the stationary state is as shown in Table 13.1. In this example, the economy has net international savings (net holdings of foreign bonds). The base international interest rate, r^*, is high enough so that there are positive net holdings of foreign bonds. Positive holdings of foreign assets bring down the interest rate on foreign assets so that it is equal, in equilibrium, to the net return on domestic capital.

For the same economy but where $r^* = 0$, the stationary state is given in Table 3.2. In this case, the economy has net international borrowings. The base international interest rate, r^*, is sufficiently low so that the country has net international borrowings, in equilibrium, to raise the international interest rate to be equal to the net return on domestic capital.

Table 13.1 Stationary state with $a = .01$ and $r^* = .03$

$\bar{K}$	$\bar{B}$	$\bar{C}$	$\bar{r}$	$\bar{w}$	$\bar{H}$	$\bar{Y}$
12.3934	1.9899	.9187	.0351	2.3706	.3262	1.2084

Table 13.2   Stationary state values with $a = .01$ and $r^* = 0$

$\bar{K}$	$\bar{B}$	$\bar{C}$	$\bar{r}$	$\bar{w}$	$\bar{H}$	$\bar{Y}$
12.8114	−1.0101	.9187	.0351	2.3706	.3372	1.2491

13.3.2   The Dynamic Version

The full model with country risk for international lending is

$$B = -\frac{w_t}{C_t},$$

$$\frac{1}{\beta} = E_t \frac{C_t}{C_{t+1}} (1 + r^* - a B_t), \tag{13.14}$$

$$\frac{1}{\beta} \left(1 + \kappa \left(K_{t+1} - K_t \right) \right) = E_t \frac{C_t}{C_{t+1}} \left[r_{t+1} + (1 - \delta) + \kappa \left(K_{t+2} - K_{t+1} \right) \right],$$

$$B_t + K_{t+1} + C_t = w_t H_t + r_t K_t + (1 - \delta) K_t$$

$$- \frac{\kappa}{2} \left(K_{t+1} - K_t \right)^2 + \left(1 + r^* \right) B_{t-1} - a B_{t-1}^2, \tag{13.15}$$

$$r_t = \theta \lambda_t K_t^{\theta-1} H_t^{1-\theta},$$

$$w_t = (1 - \theta) \lambda_t K_t^{\theta} H_t^{-\theta}.$$

The log-linear model is the same as that with adjustment costs, except for the log-linear versions of equations 13.14 and 13.15. These equations are now

$$0 = \tilde{C}_t - E_t \tilde{C}_{t+1} - \beta a \bar{B} \tilde{B}_t$$

and

$$0 = \bar{B} \tilde{B}_t + \bar{K} \tilde{K}_{t+1} + \bar{C} \tilde{C}_t - \bar{w} \bar{H} \left(\tilde{w}_t + \tilde{H}_t \right)$$

$$- \bar{r} \bar{K} \tilde{r}_t - \frac{\bar{K}}{\beta} \tilde{K}_t - \left(\left(1 + r^* \right) \bar{B} - 2a \bar{B}^2 \right) \tilde{B}_{t-1}.$$

Recall that the capital adjustment costs do not appear in the log-linear version of the flow budget constraint because they are purely quadratic, and quadratic components fall out during the linearization.

The full log-linear version of the model has six variables, $\tilde{K}_{t+1}$, $\tilde{B}_t$, $\tilde{C}_t$, $\tilde{r}_t$, $\tilde{w}_t$, and $\tilde{H}_t$, the stochastic variable, $\tilde{\lambda}_t$, and the equations

$$0 = \tilde{C}_t - \tilde{w}_t,$$

$$0 = \tilde{C}_t - E_t \tilde{C}_{t+1} - \beta a \bar{B} \tilde{B}_t,$$

$$0 = \beta \bar{r} E_t \tilde{r}_{t+1} + \tilde{C}_t - E_t \tilde{C}_{t+1} + \beta \kappa \bar{K} E_t \tilde{K}_{t+2} - (1+\beta) \kappa \bar{K} \tilde{K}_{t+1} + \kappa \bar{K} \tilde{K}_t,$$

$$0 = \bar{B} \tilde{B}_t + \bar{K} \tilde{K}_{t+1} + \bar{C} \tilde{C}_t - \bar{w} \bar{H} \left(\tilde{w}_t + \tilde{H}_t \right) - \bar{r} \bar{K} \tilde{r}_t - \frac{\bar{K}}{\beta} \tilde{K}_t$$

$$- \left((1+r^*) \bar{B} - 2a\bar{B}^2 \right) \tilde{B}_{t-1},$$

$$0 = \tilde{\lambda}_t + (\theta - 1) \tilde{K}_t + (1 - \theta) \tilde{H}_t - \tilde{r}_t,$$

$$0 = \tilde{\lambda}_t + \theta \tilde{K}_t - \theta \tilde{H}_t - \tilde{w}_t.$$

Let $x_t = [\tilde{K}_{t+1}, \tilde{B}_t]'$ be the vector of state variables, $y_t = [\tilde{C}_t, \tilde{r}_t, \tilde{w}_t, \tilde{H}_t]'$ be the vector of jump variables, and $z_t = [\tilde{\lambda}_t]'$ be the one stochastic variable. We can write the system as

$$0 = Ax_t + Bx_{t-1} + Cy_t + Dz_t,$$

$$0 = E_t \left[Fx_{t+1} + Gx_t + Hx_{t-1} + Jy_{t+1} + Ky_t + Lz_{t+1} + Mz_t \right],$$

$$z_{t+1} = Nz_t + \varepsilon_{t+1}.$$

Only the second and third equations of the system contain variables in expectations, and these two equations go into the second block of the system.

We solve the log-linear version of this model with the standard coefficients and with $a = .01$ and $r^* = .03$, so the country is, in the stationary state, a net international saver. This gives linear policy functions of the form

$$x_{t+1} = Px_t + Qz_t,$$

where

$$P = \begin{bmatrix} 0.9572 & 0.0072 \\ 0.1419 & 0.8019 \end{bmatrix}$$

and

$$Q = \begin{bmatrix} 0.0797 \\ 0.0606 \end{bmatrix}.$$

The jump functions are

$$y_t = Rx_t + Sz_t,$$

where

$$R = \begin{bmatrix} 0.3741 & 0.0933 \\ -0.6650 & -0.1658 \\ 0.3741 & 0.0933 \\ -0.0391 & -0.2591 \end{bmatrix}$$

and

$$S = \begin{bmatrix} 0.7331 \\ 1.4745 \\ 0.7331 \\ 0.7414 \end{bmatrix}.$$

The impulse response functions for an impulse of .01 in technology are shown in Figure 13.1.

When the parameter $r^* = 0$, the country is, in the stationary state, a net borrower of international funds, and the matrices P and Q of the policy functions are

$$P = \begin{bmatrix} 0.9567 & -0.0036 \\ -0.2718 & 0.8146 \end{bmatrix}$$

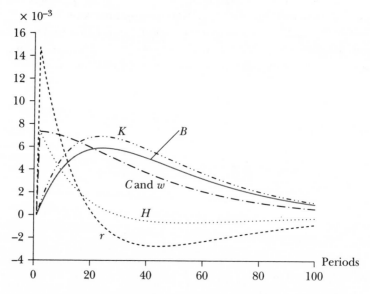

FIGURE 13.1 Impulse response functions to technology shock, $r^* = .03$

and

$$Q = \begin{bmatrix} 0.0759 \\ -0.1357 \end{bmatrix}.$$

The matrices R and S of the jump functions are

$$R = \begin{bmatrix} 0.3853 & -0.0514 \\ -0.6849 & 0.0914 \\ 0.3853 & -0.0514 \\ -0.0702 & 0.1429 \end{bmatrix}$$

and

$$S = \begin{bmatrix} 0.7518 \\ 1.4413 \\ 0.7518 \\ 0.6895 \end{bmatrix}.$$

The impulse response functions for a technology shock of .01 are shown in Figure 13.2.

The main difference between the impulse response functions of Figure 13.1 and those of Figure 13.2 is the response of international savings or debt, $\tilde{B}_t$, to a technology shock. For the economy shown in Figure 13.1, international

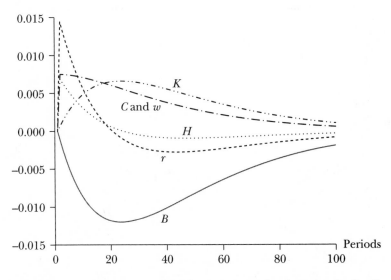

FIGURE 13.2 Impulse response functions to technology shock, $r^* = 0$

savings is positive in the stationary state, and a positive technology shock causes these savings to increase temporarily. The increased productivity goes into increasing both capital and international savings. For the economy of Figure 13.2, international savings is negative in the stationary state (the country is a net borrower), and the impulse response function marked B_t declines as a result of the positive technology shock. Recall that

$$\tilde{B}_t = \log\left(\frac{B_t}{\bar{B}}\right)$$

and that both $\bar{B}$ and B_t are negative (for small shocks to technology). The decline in $\tilde{B}_t$ says that the ratio, $B_t/\bar{B}$, declines. Since $\bar{B}$ is a constant, negative number, that means that B_t becomes a smaller negative number or that foreign debt declines. When the country is a borrower in the stationary state, a positive technology shock causes international savings to increase, and this is manifested in the decline in international borrowing. Whether a country is a net borrower or lender in the stationary state, a positive technology shock increases capital and increases international savings.

One can usefully compare the impulse response functions of the open economy to those of an otherwise identical closed economy. This closed economy is simply the Hansen indivisible labor economy we studied in Chapter 6. Figure 13.3 shows the response functions of the two economies side by side;

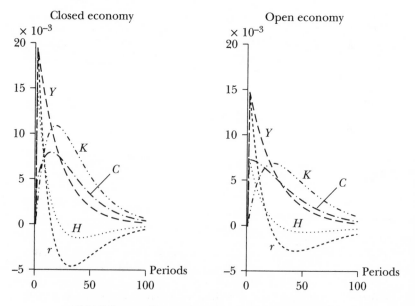

FIGURE 13.3 Responses to a .01 technology shock

the one on the left is the Hansen closed economy model (Figure 6.6), and the one on the right is the same model but with international savings and $r^* = .03$ (Figure 13.1 with output added). Both economies received the same .01 technology shock in period 2. As Figure 13.3 shows, the closed economy experiences larger responses to the technology variable than the open economy. The open economy uses the international asset to smooth out the effects of the shock in most variables. Although consumption increases more in the short term in the open economy, the peak is higher in the closed economy. The return to the stationary state is slower for all variables in the open economy. The responses to a negative shock are completely symmetric, so the existence of holding of international assets reduces the effects of negative technology shocks. In this model, international assets function as a kind of shock absorber, slowing up and shrinking domestic technology shocks. The graphs do not change if the country is a net foreign borrower.

> **EXERCISE 13.1** Find the policy and jump functions for a "closed" open economy where the foreign interest rate is stochastic:
>
> $$r_t^f = r_t^* - a B_t,$$
>
> where
>
> $$r_t^* = \left(1 - \gamma^r\right) r^* + \gamma^r r_{t-1}^* + \varepsilon_t^r.$$
>
> Find the impulse response functions for this economy showing how it responds to a foreign interest rate shock. In particular, does it matter if the country is a net foreign debtor or a net foreign saver?

13.4 THE "CLOSED" OPEN ECONOMY WITH MONEY

The above model adds an international asset to the economy and permits studying how international assets or debt can affect the dynamics. In addition, although we did not do it above, it is possible to make the foreign interest rate rule stochastic by simply adding some random noise to the international interest rate rule. Since there is neither money nor an exchange rate, one cannot use these models to study how monetary shocks affect an open economy and the exchange rate. In this section, we add domestic and foreign money to the open economy. This implies that there is an exchange rate, although only a simple purchasing power parity one, and that foreign price shocks and domestic monetary shocks can have dynamic effects.

Adding money to the open economy means that a number of additional variables and constraints need to be taken into account. If we have a domestic money, we need to assume a foreign money as well and an exchange rate between these two monies. We require conditions that will equalize the balance of payments and a rule to determine the exchange rate in each period. Since this is a "closed" open economy, we need to choose some restriction that will make foreign bond holdings defined in a stationary state. Note that in this model, we will only have monetary shocks that enter through transfers directly to households and that directly affect the household's cash-in-advance constraint.

13.4.1   The Open Economy Conditions

Now we add money to the open economy with capital adjustment costs and an interest rate on foreign debt and bonds that depends on the country's foreign indebtedness or wealth. Domestic money is added using a domestic cash-in-advance constraint for consumption purchases and for purchasing foreign money to use for paying foreign debt or buying foreign goods. The foreign bond is denominated in the foreign currency and pays interest (or if the bond is negative, the interest on the debt is paid) in the foreign currency. The period t exchange rate, measured in terms of units of domestic money per unit of foreign money, is e_t. There is a foreign market that in each period has a clearing condition of

$$B_t - (1 + r^f_{t-1})B_{t-1} = P^*_t X_t,$$

where X_t is total net exports of the single good, B_t is the nominal quantity of foreign bonds, measured in the foreign currency, held at the end of period t, and P^*_t is the foreign price of the one good. The foreign interest rate is a function of the real (foreign) value of the stock of nominal foreign bonds (debt) held by the home country,

$$r^f_t = r^* - a\frac{B_t}{P^*_t}.$$

To keep things from being too simple-minded, we assume that the foreign price level follows a stochastic process of

$$P^*_t = 1 - \gamma^* + \gamma^* P^*_{t-1} + \varepsilon^*_t,$$

where $E_{t-1}\varepsilon^*_t = 0$ and ε^*_t is bounded below by $-(1-\gamma^*)$ and bounded above. We assume purchasing power parity, so the exchange rate, e_t, is defined in terms of units of the local currency per unit of the foreign currency as

$$e_t = \frac{P_t}{P_t^*}.$$

13.4.2 The Household

In an economy with indivisible labor and a cash-in-advance constraint, the household maximizes

$$E_t \sum_{j=0}^{\infty} \beta^j \left[\ln c_{t+j}^i + B h_{t+j}^i \right]$$

subject to its budget constraints. The cash-in-advance condition for domestic household i in period t is

$$P_t c_t^i = m_{t-1}^i + (g_t - 1) M_{t-1}.$$

Households can receive lump sum money transfers or pay lump sum money taxes. The flow budget constraint for household i in period t is

$$c_t^i + \frac{m_t^i}{P_t} + \frac{e_t b_t^i}{P_t} + k_{t+1}^i = w_t h_t^i + r_t k_t^i + (1 - \delta) k_t^i - \frac{\kappa}{2} \left(k_{t+1}^i - k_t^i \right)^2$$

$$+ \frac{e_t (1 + r_{t-1}^f) b_{t-1}^i}{P_t} + \frac{m_{t-1}^i + (g_t - 1) M_{t-1}}{P_t},$$

which, after removing the elements from the cash-in-advance constraint, simplifies to

$$\frac{m_t^i}{P_t} + \frac{e_t b_t^i}{P_t} + k_{t+1}^i + \frac{\kappa}{2} \left(k_{t+1}^i - k_t^i \right)^2 = w_t h_t^i + r_t k_t^i + (1 - \delta) k_t^i$$

$$+ \frac{e_t (1 + r_{t-1}^f) b_{t-1}^i}{P_t}.$$

The term $\kappa/2 \left(k_{t+1} - k_t \right)^2$ is the capital adjustment costs the family must pay for changing the level of capital holdings. At the end of each period, the household's holdings of wealth are comprised of domestic money, foreign bonds, and physical capital.

In each period t, the household chooses $c_t^i, k_{t+1}^i, b_t^i, m_t^i$, and h_j^i to maximize its utility function subject to the budget constraints. The first-order conditions that come from this maximization are

$$0 = E_t \frac{e_t}{P_{t+1}c_{t+1}^i} - \beta E_t \frac{e_{t+1}(1 + r_t^f)}{P_{t+2}c_{t+2}^i},$$

$$0 = E_t \frac{P_t}{P_{t+1}c_{t+1}^i} \left[1 + \kappa \left(k_{t+1}^i - k_t^i \right) \right]$$

$$- \beta E_t \frac{P_{t+1}}{P_{t+2}c_{t+2}^i} \left(r_{t+1} + (1 - \delta) + \kappa \left(k_{t+2}^i - k_{t+1}^i \right) \right),$$

$$0 = \frac{B}{w_t} + \beta E_t \frac{P_t}{P_{t+1}c_{t+1}^i},$$

and the budget constraints are

$$0 = P_t c_t^i - m_{t-1}^i - (g_t - 1) M_{t-1},$$

and

$$0 = \frac{m_t^i}{P_t} + \frac{e_t b_t^i}{P_t} + k_{t+1}^i + \frac{\kappa}{2} \left(k_{t+1}^i - k_t^i \right)^2$$

$$- w_t h_t^i - r_t k_t^i - (1 - \delta) k_t^i - \frac{e_t(1 + r_{t-1}^f)b_{t-1}^i}{P_t}.$$

13.4.3   Firms

Domestic firms are completely competitive and have the standard Cobb-Douglas production function

$$Y_t = \lambda_t K_t^\theta H_t^{1-\theta}.$$

The equilibrium condition for the labor market is

$$w_t = (1 - \theta) \lambda_t K_t^\theta H_t^{-\theta}$$

and for the capital market is

$$r_t = \theta \lambda_t K_t^{\theta-1} H_t^{1-\theta}.$$

13.4.4   Equilibrium Conditions

The aggregate resource constraint for the domestic economy is

$$\lambda_t K_t^\theta H_t^{1-\theta} = C_t + K_{t+1} - (1 - \delta) K_t + X_t.$$

Domestic output can be used as consumption, domestic net capital accumulation (investment), or net exports. This is not an additional restriction since it is already incorporated in the aggregated form of the budget constraint of the household, the cash-in-advance constraint, and the balance of payments. Since the unit mass of households are identical, we have the aggregation conditions

$$C_t = c_t^i,$$

$$M_t = m_t^i,$$

$$B_t = b_t^i,$$

$$H_t = h_t^i,$$

and

$$K_{t+1} = k_{t+1}^i.$$

In addition, the money supply follows the rule

$$M_t = g_t M_{t-1}.$$

13.4.5   The Full Model

The full model is in the 11 variables, C_t, K_{t+1}, H_t, M_t, B_t, P_t, e_t, r_t, w_t, r_t^f, and X_t, and the stochastic processes, P_t^*, λ_t, and g_t. The full set of 11 equations of the model, written in aggregate terms, is

$$0 = E_t \frac{e_t}{P_{t+1}C_{t+1}} - \beta E_t \frac{e_{t+1}(1+r_t^f)}{P_{t+2}C_{t+2}},$$

$$0 = E_t \frac{P_t}{P_{t+1}C_{t+1}} \left[1 + \kappa \left(K_{t+1} - K_t\right)\right]$$

$$- \beta E_t \frac{P_{t+1}}{P_{t+2}C_{t+2}} \left(r_{t+1} + (1-\delta) + \kappa \left(K_{t+2} - K_{t+1}\right)\right),$$

$$0 = \frac{B}{w_t} + \beta E_t \frac{P_t}{P_{t+1}C_{t+1}},$$

$$0 = P_t C_t - M_t,$$

$$0 = \frac{M_t}{P_t} + \frac{e_t B_t}{P_t} + K_{t+1} + \frac{\kappa}{2} \left(K_{t+1} - K_t \right)^2$$

$$- w_t H_t - r_t K_t - (1 - \delta) K_t - \frac{e_t (1 + r_{t-1}^f) B_{t-1}}{P_t},$$

$$0 = w_t - (1 - \theta) \lambda_t K_t^\theta H_t^{-\theta},$$

$$0 = r_t - \theta \lambda_t K_t^{\theta-1} H_t^{1-\theta},$$

$$0 = B_t - (1 + r_{t-1}^f) B_{t-1} - P_t^* X_t,$$

$$0 = r_t^f - r^* + a \frac{B_t}{P_t^*},$$

$$0 = e_t - \frac{P_t}{P_t^*},$$

$$0 = M_t - g_t M_{t-1}.$$

In addition, there are the three equations that define the stochastic processes for P_t^*, λ_t, and g_t.

13.4.6   The Stationary State

Define $\pi = P_{t+1+j}/P_{t+j}$ as the stationary state rate of inflation. As usual, we assume a constant growth rate of money, $\bar{g}$, and look for a stationary state where the real variables of the economy are constant and ratios of nominal variables are constant. The foreign price level follows a stochastic process,

$$P_t^* = 1 - \gamma^* + \gamma^* P_{t-1}^* + \varepsilon_t^*,$$

so, in a stationary state, the foreign price level is $\bar{P}^* = 1$. Using the full model, some conditions for the stationary state are

$$\pi = \beta (1 + \bar{r}^f) \frac{e_{t+1}}{e_t}, \tag{13.16}$$

$$\frac{1}{\beta} = (\bar{r} + (1 - \delta)),$$

$$-B\pi\bar{C} = \beta\bar{w}, \tag{13.17}$$

$$\bar{C} = \overline{M/P},$$

$$\overline{M/P} + \frac{e_t \bar{B}}{P_t} = \bar{w}\bar{H} + (\bar{r} - \delta)\,\bar{K} + \frac{e_t(1 + \bar{r}^f)\bar{B}}{P_t}, \qquad (13.18)$$

$$\bar{w} = (1 - \theta)\,\bar{K}^\theta \bar{H}^{-\theta}, \qquad (13.19)$$

$$\bar{r} = \theta \bar{K}^{\theta-1} \bar{H}^{1-\theta}, \qquad (13.20)$$

$$-\bar{r}^f \bar{B} = \bar{X}, \qquad (13.21)$$

$$\bar{r}^f = r^* - a\bar{B}, \qquad (13.22)$$

$$\frac{e_t}{P_t} = 1, \qquad (13.23)$$

$$M_t = \bar{g}M_{t-1}. \qquad (13.24)$$

These conditions can be further simplified to find stationary state values of all the variables of the model as functions of the model's parameters. Notice that since we are dealing with stationary states, the capital adjustment costs, which are based on the changes in capital, do not appear in the above equations.

Using equation 13.23, equation 13.16 becomes

$$\pi = \beta(1 + \bar{r}^f)\frac{P_{t+1}}{P_t} = \beta(1 + r^f)\pi,$$

so

$$\bar{r}^f = \frac{1}{\beta} - 1.$$

Equation 13.22 then determines the stationary state foreign bond (debt) holdings as

$$\bar{B} = \frac{r^* + 1 - \frac{1}{\beta}}{a},$$

and $\bar{X}$ can be found from equation 13.21 as

$$\bar{X} = -\bar{r}^f \bar{B} = \frac{(1 - \beta)^2 - (1 - \beta)\,\beta r^*}{a\beta^2}.$$

As with earlier stationary states, since $\bar{r}$ is given, the conditions for competitive factor markets (equations 13.19 and 13.20) imply that

$$\bar{w} = (1 - \theta)\left(\frac{\theta}{\bar{r}}\right)^{\frac{\theta}{1-\theta}},$$

and equation 13.17 gives us stationary state consumption as

$$\bar{C} = \frac{\beta \bar{w}}{-B\pi},$$

where the condition for the stationary state gross inflation rate, $\pi = \bar{g}$, is found using equation 13.24 and the argument

$$M_t = \bar{g} M_{t-1},$$

$$\frac{M_t}{P_t} = \bar{g} \frac{M_{t-1}}{P_t} \frac{P_{t-1}}{P_{t-1}} = \bar{g} \frac{M_{t-1}}{P_{t-1}} \frac{P_{t-1}}{P_t},$$

so

$$\overline{M/P} = \frac{\bar{g}\overline{M/P}}{\pi}.$$

To find $\bar{K}$, we use equation 13.18, to get

$$\overline{M/P} = \bar{w}\bar{H} + (\bar{r} - \delta)\,\bar{K} + \bar{r}^f \bar{B},$$

and substituting in the usual result (from the factor market conditions) that

$$\bar{H} = \frac{\bar{r}\,(1-\theta)}{\bar{w}\theta} \bar{K},$$

we get

$$\bar{K} = \frac{\theta\left(\overline{M/P} - \bar{r}^f \bar{B}\right)}{\bar{r} - \theta\delta}.$$

For the standard economy, the stationary state values are $\bar{r} = .0351$, $\bar{w} = 2.3706$, and $\bar{r}^f = .0101$ in all cases. The values for the other variables are shown in Table 13.3.

Notice that, as in the basic model with cash-in-advance money with transfers to the household, stationary states with higher money growth have lower stationary state consumption and production. Net foreign debt or savings does not change consumption in the stationary state but does change capital holding and the fraction of the population that is working in each period. Countries with foreign debt need to have higher production, capital, and employment to be able to meet interest rate payments and maintain consumption.

13.4.7 Log-Linear Version of Full Model

We use the now familiar method of Uhlig to find the log-linear version of the model around the stationary state found in the section above. We define the log difference variable $\tilde{Z}_t = \ln Z_t - \ln \bar{Z}$. The variables of the model are $\tilde{K}_{t+1}$, $\tilde{M}_t$, $\tilde{P}_t$, $\tilde{B}_t$, $\tilde{r}_t^f$, $\tilde{C}_t$, $\tilde{r}_t$, $\tilde{w}_t$, $\tilde{H}_t$, $\tilde{e}_t$, and $\tilde{X}_t$. The variables $\tilde{\lambda}_t$, $\tilde{g}_t$, and $\tilde{P}_t^*$ follow independent stochastic processes. The log-linear version of the full model is

$$0 = \tilde{e}_t - E_t\tilde{e}_{t+1} - E_t\tilde{P}_{t+1} + E_t\tilde{P}_{t+2} - E_t\tilde{C}_{t+1} + E_t\tilde{C}_{t+2} - \beta\bar{r}^f\tilde{r}_t^f, \quad (13.25)$$

$$0 = \tilde{P}_t - 2E_t\tilde{P}_{t+1} + E_t\tilde{P}_{t+2} - E_t\tilde{C}_{t+1} + E_t\tilde{C}_{t+2} \quad (13.26)$$

$$- \kappa\bar{K}\tilde{K}_t + (1+\beta)\kappa\bar{K}\tilde{K}_{t+1} - \beta E_t\kappa\bar{K}\tilde{K}_{t+2} - \beta E_t\bar{r}\tilde{r}_{t+1},$$

$$0 = \tilde{w}_t + \tilde{P}_t - E_t\tilde{P}_{t+1} - E_t\tilde{C}_{t+1},$$

$$0 = \tilde{P}_t + \tilde{C}_t - \tilde{M}_t, \quad (13.27)$$

$$0 = \overline{M/P}\tilde{M}_t - \left[\overline{M/P} - \bar{B}\bar{r}^f\right]\tilde{P}_t + \bar{B}\tilde{B}_t + \bar{K}\tilde{K}_{t+1} - \bar{w}\bar{H}\tilde{w}_t - \bar{w}\bar{H}\tilde{H}_t$$

$$- \bar{r}\bar{K}\tilde{r}_t - [\bar{r} + (1-\delta)]\bar{K}\tilde{K}_t - \bar{B}\bar{r}^f\tilde{e}_t - \bar{B}\bar{r}^f\tilde{r}_{t-1}^f - \bar{B}\left(1+\bar{r}^f\right)\tilde{B}_{t-1},$$

$$0 = \tilde{w}_t - \tilde{\lambda}_t - \theta\tilde{K}_t + \theta\tilde{H}_t,$$

$$0 = \tilde{r}_t - \tilde{\lambda}_t + (1-\theta)\tilde{K}_t - (1-\theta)\tilde{H}_t,$$

$$0 = \bar{B}\tilde{B}_t - \left(1+\bar{r}^f\right)\bar{B}\tilde{B}_{t-1} - \bar{r}^f\bar{B}\tilde{r}_{t-1}^f - \bar{X}\tilde{P}_t^* - \bar{X}\tilde{X}_t,$$

$$0 = \bar{r}^f\tilde{r}_t^f + a\bar{B}\tilde{B}_t - a\bar{B}\tilde{P}_t^*,$$

$$0 = \tilde{e}_t - \tilde{P}_t + \tilde{P}_t^*,$$

$$0 = \tilde{M}_t - \tilde{g}_t - \tilde{M}_{t-1}. \quad (13.28)$$

The log-linear versions of the three stochastic processes are

Table 13.3 Stationary state values for the open economy with money

	$\bar{C}$	$\bar{K}$	$\bar{B}$	$\bar{H}$	$\bar{Y}$	$\bar{X}$
$r^* = .03$ $\bar{g} = 1$	.9095	12.2667	1.9899	.3229	1.1960	−.0201
$r^* = .03$ $\bar{g} = 1.19$	.7643	10.2639	1.9899	.2702	1.0008	−.0201
$r^* = .00$ $\bar{g} = 1$	.9095	12.6847	−1.0101	.3339	1.2368	.0102
$r^* = .00$ $\bar{g} = 1.19$	.7643	10.6819	−1.0101	.2812	1.0415	.0102

$$\tilde{\lambda}_t = \gamma^\lambda \tilde{\lambda}_{t-1} + \varepsilon_t^\lambda,$$

$$\tilde{g}_t = \gamma^g \tilde{g}_{t-1} + \varepsilon_t^g,$$

and

$$\tilde{P}_t^* = \gamma^* \tilde{P}_{t-1}^* + \varepsilon_t^*.$$

The first two equations (equations 13.25 and 13.26) present a problem for our solution technique. The method we use only allows one-period leads on variables, and these equations include the variables $E_t \tilde{P}_{t+2}$ and $E_t \tilde{C}_{t+2}$, although they always appear as a sum: $E_t \tilde{P}_{t+2} + E_t \tilde{C}_{t+2}$. Using equations 13.27 and 13.28, that sum can be written as

$$E_t \tilde{P}_{t+2} + E_t \tilde{C}_{t+2} = E_t \tilde{M}_{t+2} = E_t \tilde{g}_{t+2} + E_t \tilde{M}_{t+1}$$

$$= \gamma^g E_t \tilde{g}_{t+1} + E_t \tilde{M}_{t+1}.$$

Substituting in this result, equations 13.25 and 13.26 can be written as

$$0 = \tilde{e}_t - E_t \tilde{e}_{t+1} - E_t \tilde{P}_{t+1} - E_t \tilde{C}_{t+1} - \beta \bar{r}^f \tilde{r}_t^f \tag{13.29}$$

$$+ \gamma^g E_t \tilde{g}_{t+1} + E_t \tilde{M}_{t+1},$$

$$0 = \tilde{P}_t - 2 E_t \tilde{P}_{t+1} - E_t \tilde{C}_{t+1} + \gamma^g E_t \tilde{g}_{t+1} + E_t \tilde{M}_{t+1} \tag{13.30}$$

$$- \kappa \bar{K} \tilde{K}_t + (1 + \beta) \kappa \bar{K} \tilde{K}_{t+1} - \beta E_t \kappa \bar{K} \tilde{K}_{t+2} - \beta E_t \bar{r} \tilde{r}_{t+1}.$$

In this form, the model is now written entirely in terms of variables at dates $t - 1$, t, and $t + 1$, and our standard solution technique is applicable.

Let $x_t = [\tilde{K}_{t+1}, \tilde{M}_t, \tilde{P}_t, \tilde{B}_t, \tilde{r}_t^f]'$ be the vector of the five state variables, $y_t = [\tilde{C}_t, \tilde{r}_t, \tilde{w}_t, \tilde{H}_t, \tilde{e}_t, \tilde{X}_t]'$ be the vector of the six jump variables, and $z_t = [\tilde{\lambda}_t, \tilde{g}_t, \tilde{P}_t^*]'$ be the three stochastic variables. We can write the system as

$$0 = A x_t + B x_{t-1} + C y_t + D z_t,$$

$$0 = E_t \left[F x_{t+1} + G x_t + H x_{t-1} + J y_{t+1} + K y_t + L z_{t+1} + M z_t \right],$$

$$z_{t+1} = N z_t + \varepsilon_{t+1},$$

where

$$
A = \begin{bmatrix}
0 & -1 & 1 & 0 & 0 \\
\bar{K} & \overline{M/P} & -\overline{M/P} + \bar{B}\bar{r}^f & \bar{B} & 0 \\
0 & 0 & 0 & 0 & 0 \\
0 & 0 & 0 & 0 & 0 \\
0 & 0 & 0 & \bar{B} & 0 \\
0 & 0 & -1 & 0 & 0
\end{bmatrix},
$$

$$
B = \begin{bmatrix}
0 & 0 & 0 & 0 & 0 \\
-[\bar{r} + 1 - \delta]\bar{K} & 0 & 0 & -(1+\bar{r}^f)\bar{B} & -\bar{B}\bar{r}^f \\
-\theta & 0 & 0 & 0 & 0 \\
1 - \theta & 0 & 0 & 0 & 0 \\
0 & 0 & 0 & -(1+\bar{r}^f)\bar{B} & -\bar{B}\bar{r}^f \\
0 & 0 & 0 & 0 & 0
\end{bmatrix},
$$

$$
C = \begin{bmatrix}
1 & 0 & 0 & 0 & 0 & 0 \\
0 & -\bar{r}\bar{K} & -\bar{w}\bar{H} & -\bar{w}\bar{H} & -\bar{B}\bar{r}^f & 0 \\
0 & 0 & 1 & \theta & 0 & 0 \\
0 & 1 & 0 & -(1-\theta) & 0 & 0 \\
0 & 0 & 0 & 0 & 0 & -\bar{X} \\
0 & 0 & 0 & 0 & 1 & 0
\end{bmatrix},
$$

$$
D = \begin{bmatrix}
0 & 0 & 0 \\
0 & 0 & 0 \\
-1 & 0 & 0 \\
-1 & 0 & 0 \\
0 & 0 & -\bar{X} \\
0 & 0 & 1
\end{bmatrix},
$$

$$
F = \begin{bmatrix}
0 & 1 & -1 & 0 & 0 \\
-\beta\kappa\bar{K} & 1 & -2 & 0 & 0 \\
0 & 0 & -1 & 0 & 0 \\
0 & 0 & 0 & 0 & 0 \\
0 & 0 & 0 & 0 & 0
\end{bmatrix},
$$

$$G = \begin{bmatrix} 0 & 0 & 0 & 0 & -\beta \bar{r}^f \\ (1+\beta)\,\kappa\bar{K} & 0 & 1 & 0 & 0 \\ 0 & 0 & 1 & 0 & 0 \\ 0 & 0 & 0 & a\bar{B} & \bar{r}^f \\ 0 & 1 & 0 & 0 & 0 \end{bmatrix},$$

$$H = \begin{bmatrix} 0 & 0 & 0 & 0 & 0 \\ -\kappa\bar{K} & 0 & 0 & 0 & 0 \\ 0 & 0 & 0 & 0 & 0 \\ 0 & 0 & 0 & 0 & 0 \\ 0 & -1 & 0 & 0 & 0 \end{bmatrix},$$

$$J = \begin{bmatrix} -1 & 0 & 0 & 0 & -1 & 0 \\ -1 & -\beta\bar{r} & 0 & 0 & 0 & 0 \\ -1 & 0 & 0 & 0 & 0 & 0 \\ 0 & 0 & 0 & 0 & 0 & 0 \\ 0 & 0 & 0 & 0 & 0 & 0 \end{bmatrix},$$

$$K = \begin{bmatrix} 0 & 0 & 0 & 0 & 1 & 0 \\ 0 & 0 & 0 & 0 & 0 & 0 \\ 0 & 0 & 1 & 0 & 0 & 0 \\ 0 & 0 & 0 & 0 & 0 & 0 \\ 0 & 0 & 0 & 0 & 0 & 0 \end{bmatrix},$$

$$L = \begin{bmatrix} 0 & \gamma^g & 0 \\ 0 & \gamma^g & 0 \\ 0 & 0 & 0 \\ 0 & 0 & 0 \\ 0 & 0 & 0 \end{bmatrix},$$

$$M = \begin{bmatrix} 0 & 0 & 0 \\ 0 & 0 & 0 \\ 0 & 0 & 0 \\ 0 & 0 & -a\bar{B} \\ 0 & -1 & 0 \end{bmatrix},$$

and

$$N = \begin{bmatrix} \gamma^\lambda & 0 & 0 \\ 0 & \gamma^g & 0 \\ 0 & 0 & \gamma^* \end{bmatrix}.$$

The policy and jump functions are of the form

$$x_{t+1} = Px_t + Qz_t$$

and

$$y_t = Rx_t + Sz_t.$$

For the economy with $\bar{g} = 1$ and $r^* = .03$, the matrices of the policy and jump functions are

$$P = \begin{bmatrix} 0.9852 & 0 & 0 & 0.0102 & 0.0001 \\ 0 & 1 & 0 & 0 & 0 \\ -0.3241 & 1 & 0 & -0.0919 & -0.0009 \\ 0.0436 & 0 & 0 & 0.8068 & 0.0081 \\ -0.0859 & 0 & 0 & -1.5894 & -0.0159 \end{bmatrix},$$

$$Q = \begin{bmatrix} 0.0586 & 0.0031 & -0.0735 \\ 0 & 1 & 0 \\ -0.7477 & 1.4201 & 0.4768 \\ 0.1674 & 0.1408 & 1.1701 \\ -0.3299 & -0.2774 & -2.3052 \end{bmatrix},$$

$$R = \begin{bmatrix} 0.3241 & 0 & 0 & 0.0919 & 0.0009 \\ -0.5761 & 0 & 0 & -0.1634 & -0.0016 \\ 0.3241 & 0 & 0 & 0.0919 & 0.0009 \\ 0.0998 & 0 & 0 & -0.2552 & -0.0026 \\ -0.3241 & 1 & 0 & -0.0919 & -0.0009 \\ -4.3162 & 0 & 0 & 20.1257 & 0.2013 \end{bmatrix},$$

and

$$S = \begin{bmatrix} 0.7477 & -0.4201 & -0.4768 \\ 1.4485 & -0.0532 & 0.8476 \\ 0.7477 & -0.4201 & -0.4768 \\ 0.7009 & -0.0832 & 1.3244 \\ -0.7477 & 1.4201 & -0.5232 \\ -16.5774 & -13.9391 & -116.8437 \end{bmatrix}.$$

The zeros in the columns for prices in P and R indicate that prices are not really a state variable. Money only affects itself, domestic prices, and the exchange rate. The coefficients on net exports (the last row of R and S) are quite large and come from the relatively small stationary state values for net exports when compared to foreign savings or borrowing. Relatively small adjustments in foreign asset holdings can create relatively large changes in the log differences of net exports.

The policy and jump functions for the same economy with stationary state money growth and inflation of $\bar{g} = 1.19$ are very similar to those shown above, except for the coefficient S_{32}—the coefficient in the S matrix for the effect of a monetary shock on wages. That coefficient becomes 0.0279, implying that a monetary shock will have a small but positive effect on real wages.

The response functions to a technology impulse of .01 for the economy with $\bar{g} = 1$ and $r^* = .03$ are shown in Figure 13.4. Compare these to the response functions in Figure 13.1 of the same model without money. Most interestingly, the response of capital is slower and smoother and that of foreign bond holdings is faster. The rest are similar.

Figure 13.5 shows the response functions to the technology impulse for an economy where $r^* = .00$. This figure is quite similar to Figure 13.4, except that the response function for foreign bonds is now identical to that for the foreign interest rate. These responses are identical only in the particular case

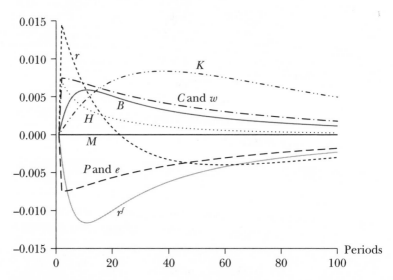

FIGURE 13.4 Response functions to a technology shock, $\bar{g} = 1, r^* = .03$

where $r^* = .00$. The response functions for similar economies with higher stationary state inflation rates are not shown since they are quite similar to these.

The impulse response functions for a monetary shock are shown in Figure 13.6, for an economy that is a net foreign saver, and in Figure 13.7, for an economy that is a net foreign debtor. The money, price, and exchange rate impulses have been left out of the figures. These shocks all converge to the same positive value, with prices and the exchange converging faster than money. The response functions for economies with stationary state inflation rates of $\bar{g} = 1.19$ are very similar. The shocks decay faster, so only the first 50 periods after the shock are shown.

The final shock is the foreign price level. Figure 13.8 shows the responses of an economy that is a net foreign saver and Figure 13.9 shows them for an economy that is a net foreign debtor. The response functions for the same economies with stationary state money growth are not shown since they are very similar to these. The shocks decay rapidly and many of the response functions are close together, so for clarity only the first 25 periods are shown.

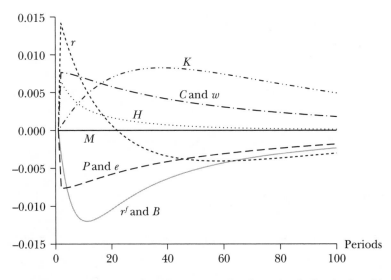

FIGURE 13.5 Response functions to a technology shock, $\bar{g} = 1, r^* = .00$

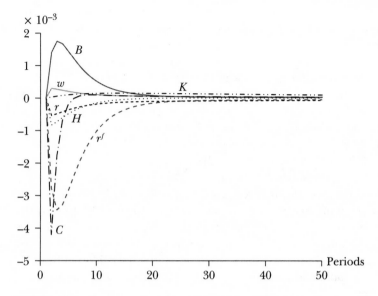

FIGURE 13.6   Response functions to monetary shock, $\bar{g} = 1, r^* = .03$

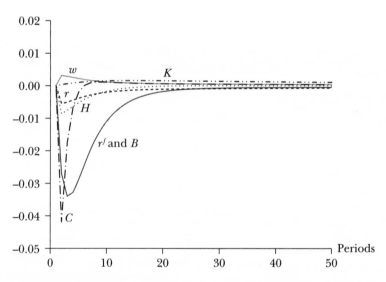

FIGURE 13.7   Response functions to monetary shock, $\bar{g} = 1, r^* = .00$

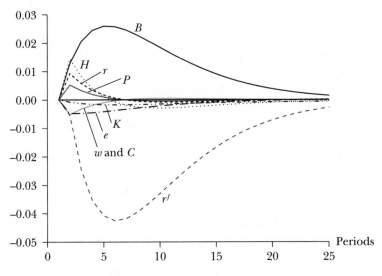

FIGURE 13.8   Response functions to foreign price shock, $\bar{g} = 1, r^* = .03$

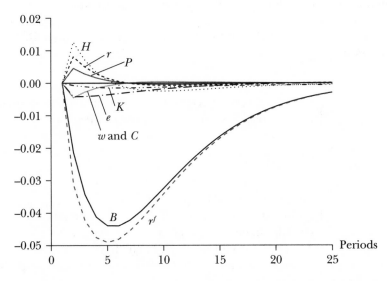

FIGURE 13.9   Response functions to foreign price shock, $\bar{g} = 1, r^* = .00$

13.5   REPRISE

Models of small open economies can suffer from indeterminacies since households have available two assets that offer the same rates of return. The indeterminacy was solved here by adding adjustment costs to capital formation and making the foreign interest rate that the country gets a function of net foreign asset (debt) holdings. This was necessary, in part, because the model has been made linear and the usual portfolio conditions that come from decisions with risky assets cannot be applied. One might expect that in an economy with very large technology shocks, for instance, portfolio diversification would lead the households to want to hold a lot of less risky foreign assets, especially if domestic and foreign shocks are uncorrelated. Models that do this are not yet well developed. Uribe [87] gives a number of other ways of closing the open economy models that the reader might find preferable to the one given here.

An open economy, with or without money, provides households with a way of better smoothing out their consumption in response to domestic shocks. The model here captures some of this effect. However, small open economies sometimes seem to suffer from the impacts that they receive from international price shocks and changes in international capital flows. The phenomenon of "sudden stops," as the rapid change in international capital flows into a country is called, now has a large literature. Some examples are Arellano and Mendoza [3], Calvo [20], Chari, Kehoe and McGratten [26], and Mendoza [64].

> **EXERCISE 13.2**   Construct a small open economy without money where foreign citizens own a fraction of the domestic capital stock. Foreign capital in the country follows the law of motion
>
> $$K_{t+1}^{f} - (1-\delta)\, K_t^{f} = \varepsilon_t^{fk},$$
>
> where total capital is equal to $K_{t+1} = K_{t+1}^{d} + K_{t+1}^{f}$, and K_{t+1}^{d} is domestic capital that is accumulated domestically and has adjustment costs. The rent on foreign owned capital is exported each period. Domestic households can invest in domestic capital or in foreign bonds. Find the response functions to an impulse in ε_t^{fk}.

References

[1]   Amato, Jeffery D., and Thomas Laubach (2004) "Implications of Habit Formation for Optimal Monetary Policy," *Journal of Monetary Economics*, 51, March, pp. 305–325.

[2]   Anderson, Evan, Lars P. Hansen, Ellen R. McGrattan, Thomas J. Sargent (1996) "Mechanics of Forming and Estimating Dynamic Linear Economies," in *Handbook of Computational Economics*, H. M. Amman, D. A. Kendrick, and J. Rust, eds., North-Holland, Amsterdam, pp. 171–252.

[3]   Arellano, Cristina, and Enrique Mendoza (2003) "Credit Frictions and 'Sudden Stops' in Small Open Economies: An Equilibrium Business Cycle Framework for Emerging Markets Crises," in *Dynamic Macroeconomic Analysis: Theory and Policy in General Equilibrium*, S. Altug, J. Chadha, and C. Nolan, eds., Cambridge University Press.

[4]   Azariadis, Costas (1993) *Intertemporal Macroeconomics*, Blackwell Publishers, Oxford.

[5]   Bailey, Martin (1956) "The Welfare Cost of Inflationary Finance," *Journal of Political Economy*, 64(2), p. 93–110.

[6]   Barro, Robert, and Xavier Sala-i-Martin (2003) *Growth Theory*, 2nd edition, MIT Press, Cambridge, Mass.

[7]   Bellman, R. (1957) *Dynamic Programming*, Princeton University Press, Princeton.

[8]   Benveniste, L., and Jose Scheinkman (1979) "On the Differentiability of the Value Function in Dynamic Models of Economics," *Econometrica*, 47, pp. 727–732.

[9]   Bernanke, Ben, and Mark Gertler (1989) "Agency Costs, Net Worth, and Business Fluctuations," *American Economic Review*, 79, pp. 14–31.

[10] Bertsekas, Dimitri (2000) *Dynamic Programming and Optimal Control*, 2nd edition, Athena Scientific, Belmont, Mass.

[11] Bewley, Truman (1983) "A difficulty with the Optimum Quantity of Money," *Econometrica*, 51(5), Sept., pp. 1485–1504.

[12] Blake, Andrew, and Emilio Fernandez-Corugedo (2006) *Solving Rational Expectations Models: A Practical Approach Using Scilab*, CCBS, Handbooks in Central Banking, Bank of England.

[13] Blanchard, Olivier, and Stanley Fischer (1989) *Lectures on Macroeconomics*, MIT Press, Cambridge, Mass.

[14] Blanchard, Olivier, and Charles Kahn (1980) "The Solution of Linear Difference Models under Rational Expectations," *Econometrica*, 48(5), pp. 1305–1311.

[15] Boldrin, Michele, Lawrence J. Christiano, and Jonas D. M. Fisher (2001) "Habit Persistence, Asset Returns, and the Business Cycle," *American Economic Review*, 91(1), March, pp. 149–166.

[16] Breiman, Leo (1968) *Probability*, Addison-Wesley, Reading, Mass.

[17] Brock, William (1974) "Money and Growth: The Case of Long Run Perfect Foresight," *International Economic Review*, 15(3), Oct., pp. 750–777.

[18] Calvo, Guillermo (1978) "On the Time Consistency of Optimal Policy in a Monetary Economy", *Econometrica*, 46, pp. 1411–28.

[19] Calvo, Guillermo (1983) "Staggered Prices in a Utility-Maximizing Framework," *Journal of Monetary Economics*, 12, pp. 383–398.

[20] Calvo, Guillermo (2003) "Explaining Sudden Stops, Growth Collapse and BOP Crises: The Case of Distortionary Output Taxes," NBER working paper 9864.

[21] Canova, Fabio (2007) *Methods for Applied Macroeconomic Research*, Princeton University Press, Princeton.

[22] Carlstrom, Charles T. and Fuerst, Timothy S. (1995) "Interest Rate Rules vs. Money Growth Rules: A Welfare Comparison in a Cash-in-Advance Economy," *Journal of Monetary Economics*, 36, pp. 247–267.

[23] Carlstrom, Charles T. and Fuerst, Timothy S. (2001) "Monetary Shocks, Agency Costs, and Business Cycles," *Carnegie-Rochester Conference Series on Public Policy*, Elsevier, 54(1), June, pp. 1–27.

[24] Carlstrom, Charles T. and Fuerst, Timothy S. (2001) "Timing and Real Indeterminacy in Monetary Models," *Journal of Monetary Economics*, 47, pp. 285–298.

[25] Champ, Bruce, and Scott Freeman (1994) *Modeling Monetary Economies*, John Wiley & Sons, Inc., New York.

[26] Chari, V. V., Patrick J. Kehoe, and Ellen R. McGrattan (2005) "Sudden Stops and Output Drops," *American Economic Review Papers and Proceedings*, 95(2), pp. 381–387.

[27] Christiano, Lawrence J. (1991) "Modeling the Liquidity Effect of a Money Shock," *Federal Reserve Bank of Minneapolis Quarterly Review*, Winter, 15, pp. 3–34.

[28] Christiano, Lawrence (2002) "Solving Dynamic Equilibrium Models by a Method of Undetermined Coefficients," *Computational Economics*, 20 pp. 21–55.

[29] Christiano, Lawrence J., Martin Eichenbaum, and Charles L. Evans (1996) "Technical Appendix for Modeling Money," working paper, Northwestern University.

[30] Christiano, Lawrence J., Martin Eichenbaum, and Charles L. Evans (1997) "Sticky Price and Limited Participation Models of Money: A Comparison," *European Economic Review*, 41(6), June, p. 1201–1249.

[31] Christiano, Lawrence J., Martin Eichenbaum, and Charles L. Evans (1998) "Modeling Money," NBER working paper No. W6371, January.

[32] Christiano, Lawrence, Martin Eichenbaum, and Charles Evans (2005) "Nominal Rigidities and the Dynamic Effects of a Shock to Monetary Policy," *Journal of Political Economy*, 113(1), February, pp. 1–45.

[33] Christiano, Lawrence, and Christopher L. Gust (1999) "Taylor Rules in a Limited Participation Model," NBER Working Papers, 7017.

[34] Clarida, Richard, Jordi Galí, and Mark Gertler (2000) "Monetary Policy Rules and Macroeconomic Stability: Evidence and Some Theory," *The Quarterly Journal of Economics*, 115(1), Feb., pp. 147–180.

[35] Clower, Robert (1967) "A Reconsideration of the Microfoundations of Monetary Theory," *Western Economic Journal*, 6(1), December, pp. 1–9.

[36] Cooley, Thomas, and Gary Hansen (1989) "The Inflation Tax in a Real Business Cycle Model," *The American Economic Review*, 79(4), September, pp. 733–748.

[37] Cooley, T., and V. Quadrini (1999) "A Neoclassical Model of the Phillips Curve Relation," *Journal of Monetary Economics*, 44, 2, October, pp. 165–193.

[38] Diamond, Peter A. (1965) "National Debt in a Neoclassical Growth Model," *American Economic Review*, 55, December, pp. 1126–1150.

[39] Fisher, Irving (1973) "I Discovered the Phillips Curve: 'A Statistical Relation between Unemployment and Price Changes,'" *Journal of Political Economy*, 81(2) Part 1, March–April, pp. 496–502.

[40] Friedman, Milton (1960) *A Program for Monetary Stability*, Fordham University Press, New York.

[41] Friedman, Milton (1969) "The Optimum Quantity of Money," *The Optimum Quantity of Money and Other Essays*, Aldine Publishing Co, Chicago, pp. 1–50.

[42] Fuerst, Timothy S. (1992) "Liquidity, Loanable Funds, and Real Activity," *Journal of Monetary Economics*, 29, pp. 3–24.

[43] Fuerst, Timothy S. (1995) "Monetary and Financial Interactions in the Business Cycle," *Journal of Money, Credit and Banking*, 27(4) Part 2, November, pp. 1321–1338.

[44] Galí, J. (2003) "New Perspectives on Monetary Policy, Inflation, and the business Cycle," in *Advances in Economic Theory, Vol. III*, M. Dewatripont, L. Hansen, and S. Turnovsky, eds., Cambridge University Press, Cambridge, pp. 151–197.

[45] Galí, J., M. Gertler, and D. López-Salido (2001) "European Inflation Dynamics," *European Economic Review*, 45(7), pp. 1237–70.

[46] Hadley, G. and Murray C. Kemp (1971) *Variational Methods in Economics*, North-Holland, Amsterdam.

[47] Hamilton, James (1994) *Time Series Analysis*, Princeton University Press, Princeton.

[48] Hansen, Gary (1985) "Indivisible Labor and the Business Cycle," *Journal of Monetary Economics*, 16, pp. 309–328.

[49] Karaken, John, and Neil Wallace (1980) "Introduction," *Models of Monetary Economies*, Federal Reserve Bank of Minneapolis, pp. 1–9.

[50] Kim, Jinill, Sunghyun Kim, Ernst Schaumburg, and Christopher A. Sims (2005) "Calculating and Using Second Order Accurate Solutions of Discrete Time Dynamic Equilibrium Models," working paper, February 3, Princeton University.

[51] Kydland, Finn, and Edward C. Prescott (1977) "Rules Rather Than Discretion: The Inconsistency of Optimal Plans," *Journal of Political Economy*, 85, pp. 473–92.

[52] Kydland, Finn, and Edward C. Prescott (1982) "Time to Build and Aggregate Fluctuations," *Econometrica*, 50, pp. 1345–1371.

[53] Lagos, Ricardo, and Randall Wright (2005) "Unified Framework for Monetary Theory and Policy Analysis," *Journal of Political Economy*, 113, pp. 463–84.

[54] Ljungqvist, Lars, and Thomas Sargent (2000) *Recursive Macroeconomic Theory*, MIT Press, Cambridge, Mass.

[55] Lucas, Robert E. (1976) "Econometric Policy Evaluation: A Critique," *Carnegie-Rochester Conference Series on Public Policy*, 1, pp. 19–46.

[56] Lucas, Robert E. (1988) "On the Mechanics of Economic Development," *Journal of Monetary Economics*, 22(1), pp. 3–42.

[57] Lucas, Robert E. (1990) "Liquidity and Interest Rates," *Journal of Economic Theory*, 50, pp. 237–264.

[58] Lucas, Robert E., and Nancy Stokey (1987) "Money and Interest in a Cash-in-Advance Economy," *Econometrica*, 55, pp. 491–513.

[59] Mas-Colell, Andreu, Michael Whinston, and Jerry R. Green (1995) *Microeconomic Theory*, Oxford University Press, New York.

[60] McCallum, Bennet (1983) "On Non-uniqueness in Rational Expectations Models: An Attempt at Perspective," *Journal of Monetary Economics*, 11, March, pp. 139–68.

[61] McCandless, George T., and Neil Wallace (1991) *Introduction to Dynamic Macroeconomic Theory: An Overlapping Generations Approach*, Harvard University Press, Cambridge, Mass.

[62] McCandless, George T., and Warren Weber (1995) "Some Monetary Facts," *Federal Reserve Bank of Minneapolis Quarterly Review*, 3, pp. 2–11.

[63] Mendoza, Enrique (1991) "Real Business Cycles in a Small-Open Economy," *American Economic Review*, 81, pp. 797–818.

[64] Mendoza, Enrique (2002) "Credit, Prices and Crashes: Business Cycles with a Sudden Stop," in *Preventing Currency Crises in Emerging Markets*, ed. S. Edwards and J. Frankel, NBER, University of Chicago Press, Chicago.

[65] Milgrom, Paul, and Ilya Segal (2002) "Envelope Theorems for Arbitrary Choice Sets," *Econometrica*, 70(2), March, pp. 583–601.

[66] Nicolini, Juan Pablo (1998) "Tax Evasion and the Optimal Inflation Tax," *Journal of Development Economics*, 55, pp. 215–232.

[67] Parente, Stephen L., and Edward C. Prescott (1993) "Changes in the Wealth of Nations," *Quarterly Review*, Federal Reserve Bank of Minneapolis, Spring, pp. 3–16.

[68] Phelps, Edmund (1961) "The Golden Rule of Accumulation: A Fable for Growthmen," *American Economic Review*, 51(4) Sept., pp. 638–643.

[69] Romer, Paul M. (1986) "Increasing Returns and Long-Run Growth," *Journal of Political Economy*, 94(5), pp. 1002–1037.

[70] Samuelson, Paul A. (1958) "An Exact Consumption-Loan Model of Interest with or without the Social Contrivance of Money," *Journal of Political Economy*, 66, December, pp. 467–482.

[71] Sargent, Thomas J. (1979) *Macroeconomic Theory*, Academic Press, New York.

[72] Sargent, Thomas J. (1987) *Dynamic Macroeconomic Theory*, Harvard University Press, Cambridge, Mass.

[73] Schmitt-Grohé, Stephanie, and Martín Uribe (2000) "Price Level Determinacy and Monetary Policy under a Balanced Budget Requirement," *Journal of Monetary Economics*, 45(1), pp. 211–246.

[74] Schmitt-Grohé, Stephanie, and Martín Uribe (2003) "Closing Small Open Economy Models," *Journal of International Economics*, 61, October, pp. 163–185.

[75] Schmitt-Grohé, Stephanie, and Martín Uribe (2004) "Solving Dynamic General Equilibrium Models Using a Second-Order Approximation to the Policy Function," *Journal of Economic Dynamics & Control*, 28, pp. 755–775.

[76] Sidrauski, M. (1967) "Rational Choice and Patterns of Growth in a Monetary Economy," *American Economic Association Papers and Proceedings*, 57, pp. 534–544.

[77] Sims, Christopher A. (1989) "Models and Their Uses" in *Proceedings: Policy Analysis with Time-Series Econometric Models, American Journal of Agricultural Economics*, 71(2), May, pp. 489–494.

[78] Sims, Christopher A. (2001) "Solving Linear Rational Expectations Models," *Computational Economics*, 20, pp. 1–20.

[79] Smets, Frank, and Rafael Wouters (2004) "Forecasting with a Bayesian DSGE Model: An Application to the Euro Area," ECB working paper No. 389, September.

[80] Solow, Robert M. (1956) "A Contribution to the Theory of Economic Growth," *Quarterly Journal of Economics*, 70, pp. 65–94.

[81] Solow, Robert M. (1957) "Technical Change and the Aggregate Production Function," *Review of Economics and Statistics*, 39, August, pp. 312–320.

[82] Solow, Robert M. (1970) *Growth Theory: an Exposition*, Oxford University Press, New York.

[83] Stokey, Nancy, Robert Lucas, and Edward Prescott (1989) *Recursive Methods in Economic Dynamics*, Harvard University Press, Cambridge, Mass.

[84] Taylor, John B. (1980) "Aggregate Dynamics and Staggered Contracts," *Journal of Political Economy*, 88, No. 1, pp. 1–16.

[85] Taylor, John B. (1993) "Discretion versus Policy Rules in Practice," *Carnegie-Rochester Conference Series on Public Policy*, 39, North-Holland, pp. 195–214.

[86] Uhlig, Harald (1999) "A Toolkit for Analysing Nonlinear Dynamic Stochastic Models Easily," in Ramon Marimon and Andrew Scott, eds., *Computational Methods for the Study of Dynamic Economies*, Oxford University Press, Oxford, pp. 30–61.

[87] Uribe, Martín (2005), *Lectures in Open Economy Macroeconomics*, draft, Duke University.

[88] Vaughan, D.R. (1970) "A Nonrecursive Algorithm Solution for the Discrete Ricatti Equation," *IEEE Transactions on Automatic Control*, 15, pp. 597–599.

[89] Walsh, Carl (2003) *Monetary Theory and Policy*, 2nd edition, MIT Press, Cambridge, Mass.

[90] Woodford, Michael (2003) *Interest and Prices*, Princeton University Press, Princeton.

[91] Zhu, Tao, and Neil Wallace (2007) "Pairwise Trade and Coexistence of Money and Higher Return Assets," *Journal of Economic Theory*, 133(1), pp. 524–535.

Index